THE WORKS OF HENRY VAUGHAN

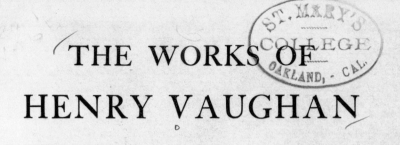
EDITED BY

LEONARD CYRIL MARTIN

M.A., B.Litt. (Oxon.)

LECTURER IN ENGLISH IN THE UNIVERSITY OF LUND, SWEDEN

VOLUME I

OXFORD

AT THE CLARENDON PRESS

1914

OXFORD UNIVERSITY PRESS
LONDON   EDINBURGH   GLASGOW   NEW YORK
TORONTO   MELBOURNE   BOMBAY
HUMPHREY MILFORD, M.A.
PUBLISHER TO THE UNIVERSITY

PREFACE.

THESE volumes are intended to supply the need for an accurate text of Henry Vaughan's works, preserving the essential features of the original editions. Long 'ſ' and such purely typographical devices as 'ũ' for 'um', 'VV' for 'W', have been discarded; errors of spacing, wrong founts, and turned letters have been silently corrected; otherwise all departures from the original texts are recorded in the foot-notes.

Different copies of each of the early issues have been collated with one another, and the early texts with modern editions. I have made no attempt, however, to record all the modern variants, which have often arisen from disregard of seventeenth-century usage, or sometimes even from insufficient scrutiny of the original texts. But the more important readings and conjectures of Vaughan's editors have been noted. Differences of punctuation, but not of spelling, in the small portions of Vaughan's works that were printed twice during the seventeenth century are also recorded.

I have altered the punctuation in a few places, where it seemed to me that inconvenience would have been given to a contemporary reader; but I have altered it with a respect for seventeenth-century conventions, and as seldom as possible. Thus, I have purposely left untouched the numerous instances in the poems (and particularly in *Silex Scintillans*) where, at the end of a line, the comma or semicolon demanded by the sense seems to have been thought unnecessary.

The main object of the notes at the end of Volume II is to throw some fresh light on Vaughan's literary affinities, particularly with earlier and contemporary authors. It has seemed unnecessary to point out once more his obvious anticipations of later poets. Explanatory notes, too, have been kept within the smallest possible compass. I have tried, not, I regret, with complete success, to find a source for all the quotations in Vaughan's original work, except those from the Bible, which are so numerous, and sometimes so involved, that to annotate them would only obscure matter of more real interest. His quotations from patristic and other Latin writers do not always imply a first-hand acquaintance with them and, wherever possible, I have given the actual rather than the original source of his knowledge. Further, I have attempted to distinguish between what is original in Vaughan's work and what is directly borrowed or translated. It has long been known that in *Silex Scintillans* he was indebted to George Herbert for a large number of thoughts and phrases; and in the citation of correspondences with *The Temple* I have added little to the labours of earlier editors and critics. But Vaughan's appropriations of the work of certain other writers are sometimes even more remarkable, and as most of these seem not to have been noticed before I have devoted considerable space to their illustration. Again, it has been taken for granted that his translations followed their originals closely, and that where he mentions no source his work is not immediately derivative. But the facts are less simple. It will be seen, for example, that the translations from Nieremberg in *Flores Solitudinis* are frequently interrupted by insertions which must be of importance in any estimation of Vaughan's distinctive qualities; and that the *Life of Paulinus* at the end of that volume is almost entirely a translation from a work that he did not find it necessary to mention. The notes, it must be added, do not claim completeness in this respect, but only record his longer or more characteristic departures from his originals.

I wish to thank all those who have assisted me during the preparation of this edition ; and particularly to acknowledge my indebtedness to Mr. D. Nichol Smith for the encouragement and advice which he has always generously imparted. Other valuable help has been afforded by Professor G. S. Gordon and Mr. Percy Simpson, who have read different parts of my proofs and made important suggestions ; by Professor E. Bensly, who has found sources for several obscure Latin quotations ; and by Sir James Murray, who has kindly allowed me access to the unpublished material of the *Oxford English Dictionary*. I am also indebted to Mr. John Ballinger, of the National Library of Wales, who, from time to time, has verified on separate points my collation of the Aberystwyth copies; and to the members of the Clarendon Press staff for the care with which they have checked and improved my work.

It remains to point out that a list of errata will be found on page 708.

L. C. MARTIN.

Epping, *June 1914.*

CONTENTS.

VOL. I.

Contents.

Contents.

LIST OF ORIGINAL EDITIONS,

WITH BIBLIOGRAPHICAL NOTES.

(The original title-pages are reproduced literatim in the present
edition, without correction of the misprints.)

1. *Poems, with the tenth Satyre of Iuvenal*, 8°, 1646. Text from
British Museum copy (12304. a. 24). Collated with the other two
British Museum copies.

   MS. alterations in an early hand are found in the British
Museum copy (12304. a. 24), and are given in the foot-notes
below.

2. *Silex Scintillans*, 8°, 1650. Text from British Museum copy
(238. b. 8).

   See note on No. 6.

3. *Olor Iscanus*, 8°, 1651. Text from Bodleian copy (Art. 8° M. 5. BS.).
Collated with those in the British Museum; Dyce Collection,
South Kensington; National Library of Wales, Aberystwyth, and
with the copies of 1679 mentioned below.

   A list of errata is usually to be found at the end of this volume.
One of the mistakes ('faith' for 'fate' page 76, l. 5 below) is
silently corrected in the text of the Dyce copy, which contains the
list of errata, and the British Museum copy, which omits it.

4. *The Mount of Olives*, 12°, 1652. Text from Bodleian copy (I. g.
124). Collated with that in the British Museum.

5. *Flores Solitudinis*, 12°, 1654. Text from Bodleian copy (Th. 8°
F. 2. BS.). Collated with those in the British Museum; National
Library of Wales, Aberystwyth; Christ Church Library, Oxford;
New York Public Library.

   In different copies there is variance as to the relative order of
the Epistle Dedicatory, the Address to the Reader, the poem
(page 218 below) and the second title-page (p. 219 below). Of
some half-dozen copies which I have seen, no two are alike in this
respect.

6. *Silex Scintillans*, 8°, 1655. Text from British Museum copy (11626. b. 52). Collated with that in the National Library of Wales, Aberystwyth, and with the copies of 1650 there and in the British Museum.

In this reissue of the edition of 1650 with new introductory matter and a second part (beginning on page 481 below) only pages 19, 20, 21, and 22 of the first part were set up afresh. In those four pages (represented by page 407, 75–page 410, 22 in the present edition), besides changes of spelling and punctuation there are alterations of sense and phrase. The edition of 1655 has been used as a basis for the present text; but the four pages in question having been reprinted somewhat carelessly the readings of 1650 have been preferred in a few places. Apart from those four pages '1655' in the foot-notes indicates the readings of both editions.[1] The two parts are printed together in the present edition.

7. *Hermetical Physick*, 12°, 1655. Text from British Museum copy (E. 1714. (1)). Collated with that in the National Library of Wales, Aberystwyth.

8. *Thalia Rediviva*, 8°, 1678. Text from Bodleian copy (Antiq. f. E. 4). Collated with that in the British Museum.

The 'Remains' of Thomas Vaughan, mentioned on the first title-page, follow Henry Vaughan's poems with a separate title-page. Two or three MS. alterations in an early hand are found in the Bodleian copy, and are given in the foot-notes below.

9. *Olor Iscanus*, 1679. A reissue (not a reprint) of the edition of 1651. The two copies that I have seen (*The National Library of Wales, Aberystwyth*, and *Cardiff Public Library*) contain all the original misprints as well as the list of errata. The new title-page is reproduced.

---

[1] The apparent reading of the British Museum copy of 1655 'fee' for 'fee' (*The Retreate*, l. 4) may be a press correction; also its 'infufed' (?) for 'infufed' (*Repentance*, l. 4).

OLOR ISCANVS.

A COLLECTION
Of ſome SELECT
POEMS,

Together with theſe Tranſlations following, *viz.*

1. Of the benefit wee may get by our *Enemies,*
2. Of the diſeaſes of the mind, and of the body. Both
written in *Greek*, by that great *Philoſopher Plutarch.*
3. Of the diſeaſes of the mind, and of the body, and
which of them is moſt pernicious, written in *Greek* by
Maximus Tyrius.
4. Of the praiſe and happineſs of a Country Life;
written in *Spaniſh* by *Antonio de Guevara*: Biſhop of
Carthagena.

All Engliſhed by *H. Vaughan, Siluriſt.*

LONDON:

Printed, and are to be ſold by *Peter Parker,*
at the *Leg* and *Star* in *Cornhil,* againſt the
Royal Exchange, 1679.

MODERN REPRINTS COLLATED WITH THE ORIGINAL EDITIONS.

1. *The Sacred Poems and Private Ejaculations of Henry Vaughan with a Memoir by the Rev. H. F. Lyte* (William Pickering, 1847).

   This was the first edition of a complete work of Henry Vaughan to be published since the seventeenth century. It was reprinted in 1856 (Boston, U.S.A.), 1858, and 1883 (the last is the Aldine Edition), and contains *Silex Scintillans* with the Pious Thoughts and Ejaculations from *Thalia Rediviva*. The text of the 1847 edition presents an appearance, not wholly delusive, of fidelity to the original editions, but it embodies several unacknowledged attempts to improve Vaughan's work, and in the subsequent 'corrected' versions these were not all removed.

2. *The Works in Verse and Prose Complete of Henry Vaughan, Silurist, for the first time collected and edited: ... by the Rev. Alexander B. Grosart, ... In four volumes. Printed for Private Circulation.* 1871. [The Fuller Worthies Library.] This is in no sense a trustworthy edition. A number of unnecessary emendations are contained in it, and inadvertent mistakes, including the omission of several lines, are still more common. The spelling and punctuation are altered here and there in accordance with modern conventions and the use of italics is discarded.

3. *The Poems of Henry Vaughan, Silurist, edited by E. K. Chambers, with an introduction by H. C. Beeching ... London Lawrence & Bullen, ... 1896* &c. [Two volumes.]

   The text is based on the original editions, but modernized. It contains several unintentional departures from what Vaughan wrote, notably in *Olor Iscanus*, where the list of errata was not used.

4. *The Mount of Olives and Primitive Holiness set forth in the Life of Paulinus Bishop of Nola. By Henry Vaughan, Silurist Edited by L. I. Guiney London Henry Frowde ... 1902.*

   Many of the mistakes in Dr. Grosart's text were corrected in this modernized edition.

5. *Silex Scintillans by Henry Vaughan Silurist. With an introduction by W. A. Lewis Bettany. Blackie and Son Ld. London 1905.*

   The text of other small editions and books of extracts is often based on or influenced by one or other of the above-mentioned reprints.

LIST OF SIGLA USED IN THE FOOT-NOTES.

The original editions are referred to by their dates of issue; the above-mentioned reprints by the letters *L*, *G*, *Gu*, *C*, *B*, respectively. *M* indicates the present editor. Other sigla, in the separate volumes, are as follows :

In *Poems* (1646), *MS* = the alterations mentioned in the bibliographical note above.

,, *Olor Iscanus, Er* = the list of errata. (See bibliographical note above.)

,, *Olor Iscanus, Ct* = *The Plays and Poems of William Cartwright*, 1651. (See note to page 55 below.)

,, *Olor Iscanus, El Opt* = *Elementa Opticæ* by Thomas Powell. (See note to page 93 below.)

,, *Flores Solitudinis, Vita* = *Vita Divi Paulini*. (See note to page 337 below.)

,, *Silex Scintillans, WR* = *Wit's Recreations*. (See note to page 434 below.)

,, *Thalia Rediviva, KP* = *The Poems of Katherine Philips*. (See note to page 597 below.)

POEMS,

WITH
The tenth SATYRE of

IUVENAL

ENGLISHED.

By *Henry Vaughan*, Gent.

—— *Tam nil, nullâ tibi vendo*
Illiade ———

LONDON,
Printed for *G. Badger*, and are to be fold at his
fhop under Saint *Dunftans* Church in
Fleet-ftreet. 1646.

To all Ingenious Lovers
OF
POESIE.

Gentlemen,

    To you alone, whose more refined Spirits *out-wing these dull Times, and soare above the drudgerie of durty* Intelligence, *have I made sacred these* Fancies : *I know the yeares, and what course entertainment they affoord* Poetry. *If any shall question that* Courage *that durst send me abroad so late, and revell it thus in the* Dregs *of an Age, they have my silence: only,*

        Languescente seculo, liceat ægrotari ;

My more calme Ambition, *amidst the common noise, hath thus exposed me to the World : You have here a* Flame, *bright only in its* 10 *owne* Innocence, *that kindles nothing but a generous* Thought ; *which though it may warme the* Bloud, *the fire at highest is but* Platonick, *and the* Commotion, *within these limits, excludes* Danger : *For the* Satyre, *it was of purpose borrowed, to feather some slower Houres ; And what you see here, is but the* Interest : *It is one of his, whose* Roman *Pen had as much true* Passion, *for the infirmities of that state, as we should have* Pitty, *to the distractions of our owne : Honest (I am sure) it is, and offensive cannot be, except it meet with such* Spirits *that will quarrell with* Antiquitie, *or purposely* Arraigne *themselves ; These indeed may thinke, that they have slept out so* 20 *many* Centuries *in this* Satyre, *and are now awaked ; which, had it been still* Latine, *perhaps their Nap had been Everlasting : But enough of these,—It is for you only that I have adventured thus far, and invaded the Presse with* Verse ; *to whose more noble* Indulgence, *I shall now leave it ; and so am gone.*——

                                    H. V.

To my Ingenuous
Friend, *R. W.*

When we are dead, and now, no more
Our harmles mirth, our wit, and score
Distracts the Towne; when all is spent
That the base niggard world hath lent
Thy purse, or mine; when the loath'd noise
Of Drawers, Prentises, and boyes
Hath left us, and the clam'rous barre
Items no pints i'th' Moone, or Starre;
When no calme whisp'rers wait the doores,
To fright us with forgotten scores;   10
And such aged, long bils carry,
As might start an Antiquary;
When the sad tumults of the Maze,
Arrests, suites, and the dreadfull face
Of Seargeants are not seene, and wee
No Lawyers Ruffes, or Gownes must fee:
When all these Mulcts are paid, and I
From thee, deare wit, must part, and dye;
Wee'le beg the world would be so kinde,
To give's one grave, as wee'de one minde;   20
There (as the wiser few suspect,
That spirits after death affect)
Our soules shall meet, and thence will they
(Freed from the tyranny of clay)
With equall wings, and ancient love
Into the Elysian fields remove,
Where in those blessed walkes they'le find,
More of thy Genius, and my mind:
   First, in the shade of his owne bayes,
Great *B E N* they'le see, whose sacred Layes,   30
The learned Ghosts admire, and throng,
To catch the subject of his Song.
Then *Randolph* in those holy Meades,
His Lovers, and *Amyntas* reads,

34 Lovers] Looers *1646*

B 2

Whilst his Nightingall close by,
Sings his, and her owne Elegie ;
From thence dismiss'd by subtill roades,
Through airie paths, and sad aboads ;
They'le come into the drowsie fields
Of Lethe, which such vertue yeelds,   40
That (if what Poets sing be true)
The streames all sorrow can subdue.
Here on a silent, shady greene,
The soules of Lovers oft are seene,
Who in their lifes unhappy space,
Were murther'd by some perjur'd face.
All these th' inchanted streames frequent,
To drowne their Cares, and discontent,
That th' inconstant, cruell sex
Might not in death their spirits vex :   50
    And here our soules bigge with delight
Of their new state will cease their flight :
And now the last thoughts will appeare,
They'le have of us, or any here ;
But on those flowry banks will stay,
And drinke all sense, and cares away.
    So they that did of these discusse,
    Shall find their fables true in us.

Les Amours.

Tyrant farewell : This heart, the prize
And triumph of thy scornfull eyes,
I sacrifice to Heaven, and give
To quit my sinnes, that durst believe
A Womans easie faith, and place
True joyes in a changing face.
    Yet e're I goe ; by all those teares,
And sighs I spent 'twixt hopes, and feares ;
By thy owne glories, and that houre
Which first inslav'd me to thy power ;   10
I beg, faire One, by this last breath,
This tribute from thee after death.
If when I'm gone, you chance to see
That cold bed where I lodged bee :

43 greene, *GC* : greene ; *1646*

.Let not your hate in death appeare,
But blesse my ashes with a teare :
This influxe from that quickning eye,
By secret pow'r, which none can spie,
The cold dust shall informe, and make
Those flames (though dead) new life partake.   20
Whose warmth help'd by your tears shall bring,
O're all the tombe a sudden spring
Of Crimson flowers, whose drooping heads
Shall curtaine o're their mournfull beds :
And on each leafe by Heavens command,
These Emblemes to the life shall stand :
 Two Hearts, the first a shaft withstood ;
The second, shot, and washt in bloud ;
And on this heart a dew shall stay,
Which no heate can court away ;   30
But fixt for ever witnesse beares,
That hearty sorrow feeds on teares.
 Thus Heaven can make it knowne, and true,
 That you kill'd me, 'cause I lov'd you.

To Amoret.
The Sigh.

Nimble Sigh on thy warme wings,
 Take this Message, and depart,
Tell *Amoret*, that smiles, and sings,
At what thy airie voyage brings,
 That thou cam'st lately from my heart.

Tell my lovely foe, that I
Have no more such spies to send,
 But one or two that I intend
Some few minutes ere I dye,
 To her white bosome to commend.   10

Then whisper by that holy Spring
 Where for her sake I would have dyed,

22-4 *The reading of C. 1646 has*
 O're all the tombe a sudden spring :
 If Crimson flowers, whose drooping heads
 Shall curtaine o're their mournfull heads :
3 sings, *GC* : sings. *1646*   5 thou] thon *1646*

Whilst those water Nymphs did bring
    Flowers to cure what she had tryed;
And of my faith, and love did sing.

That if my *Amoret*, if she
    In after-times would have it read,
How her beauty murther'd mee,
With all my heart I will agree,
    If shee'le but love me, being dead.   20

To his Friend
Being in Love.

Aske Lover, ere thou dyest; let one poor breath
Steale from thy lips, to tell her of thy Death;
Doating Idolater! can silence bring
Thy Saint propitious? or will *Cupid* fling
One arrow for thy palenes? leave to trye
This silent Courtship of a sickly eye;
Witty to tyranny: She too well knowes
This but the incense of thy private vowes,
That breaks forth at thine eyes, and doth betray
The sacrifice thy wounded heart would pay;   10
Aske her, foole, aske her, if words cannot move,
The language of thy teares may make her love:
    Flow nimbly from me then; and when you fall
On her breasts warmer snow, O may you all,
By some strange Fate fixt there, distinctly lye
The much lov'd Volume of my Tragedy.
    Where if you win her not, may this be read,
The cold that freez'd you so, did strike me dead.

Song.

Amyntas *goe, thou art undone,*
    Thy faithfull heart is crost by fate;
That Love is better not begunne,
    Where Love is come to love too late;
Had she professed hidden fires,
    Or shew'd one knot that tyed her heart:
I could have quench'd my first desires,
    And we had only met to part;

4 *Where Love is come to love*] Whose pure offering comes *MS.*
5 *professed*] profess'd her *MS.*   6 *one*] y^t *MS.*

But Tyrant, thus to murther men,
And shed a Lovers harmles bloud,   10
And burne him in those flames agen,
   Which he at first might have withstood :
Yet, who that saw faire Chloris *weep*
   Such sacred dew, with such pure grace ;
Durst thinke them fained teares, or seeke
   For Treason in an Angels face :
This is her Art, though this be true,
   Mens joyes are kil'd with griefes and feares ;
Yet she like flowers opprest with dew,
   Doth thrive and flourish in her teares :   20
This Cruell thou hast done, and thus,
   That Face hath many servants slaine.
Though th' end be not to ruine us,
   But to seeke glory by our paine.

To Amoret,
Walking in a Starry Evening.

If *Amoret,* that glorious Eye,
   In the first birth of light,
   And death of Night,
Had with those elder fires you spye
   Scatter'd so high
   Received forme, and sight ;

We might suspect in the vast Ring,
   Amidst these golden glories,
   And fierie stories ;
Whether the Sunne had been the King,   10
   And guide of Day,
   Or your brighter eye should sway ;

But, *Amoret,* such is my fate,
   That if thy face a Starre
   Had shin'd from farre,
I am perswaded in that state
   'Twixt thee, and me,
   Of some predestin'd sympathie.

14 *such pure*] such a *MS.*   18 *kil'd with*] kill'd by *MS.*   23 *Though th' end be not*] Your aim is sure *MS.*   24 *But to seeke glory*] seeking your glory *MS.*   7 might] may *MS.*   8 Amidst these golden glories] w^h rolls those fiς'ry Spheres *MS.*   9. And fierie stories] Thro' years & years *MS.*   18 Of some predestin'd] There w^d be perfect *MS.*

For sure such two conspiring minds,
 Which no accident, or sight,
  Did thus unite ;
Whom no distance can confine,
  Start, or decline,
One, for another, were design'd.

To Amoret gone from him.

Fancy, and I, last Evening walkt,
And, *Amoret*, of thee we talkt ;
The West just then had stolne the Sun,
And his last blushes were begun :
We sate, and markt how every thing
Did mourne his absence ; How the Spring
That smil'd, and curl'd about his beames,
Whilst he was here, now check'd her streames :
The wanton Eddies of her face
Were taught lesse noise, and smoother grace ; 10
And in a slow, sad channell went,
Whisp'ring the banks their discontent :
The carelesse ranks of flowers that spread
Their perfum'd bosomes to his head,
And with an open, free Embrace,
Did entertaine his beamy face ;
Like absent friends point to the West,
And on that weake reflection feast.
If Creatures then that have no sence,
But the loose tye of influence, 20
(Though fate, and time each day remove
Those things that element their love)
At such vast distance can agree,
 Why, *Amoret*, why should not wee.

A Song to *Amoret.*

If I were dead, and in my place,
 Some fresher youth design'd,
To warme thee with new fires, and grace
 Those Armes I left behind ;

Were he as faithfull as the Sunne,
    That's wedded to the Sphere;
His bloud as chaste, and temp'rate runne,
    As Aprils mildest teare;

Or were he rich, and with his heapes,
    And spacious share of Earth,   10
Could make divine affection cheape,
    And court his golden birth:

For all these Arts I'de not believe,
    (No though he should be thine)
The mighty Amorist could give
    So rich a heart as mine.

Fortune and beauty thou mightst finde,
    And greater men then I:
But my true resolved minde,
    They never shall come nigh.   20

For I not for an houre did love,
    Or for a day desire,
But with my soule had from above,
    This endles holy fire.

An Elegy.

'Tis true, I am undone; Yet e're I dye,
I'le leave these sighes, and teares a legacye
To after-Lovers; that remembring me,
Those sickly flames which now benighted be,
Fann'd by their warmer sighs may love; and prove
In them the Metempsuchosis of Love.
'Twas I (when others scorn'd) vow'd you were fair,
And sware that breath enrich'd the courser aire,
Lent Roses to your cheekes, made *Flora* bring
Her Nymphs with all the glories of the Spring   10
To waite upon thy face, and gave my heart
A pledge to *Cupid* for a quicker dart,
To arme those eyes against my selfe; to me
Thou owest that tongues bewitching harmonye:
I courted Angels from those upper joyes,
And made them leave their spheres to heare thy voice:

19 But my true resolved] But with my true steadfast *MS.*   20 They never
shall come nigh.] None can pretend to vie. *MS.*

I made the Indian curse the houres he spent
To seeke his pearles, and wisely to repent
His former folly, and confesse a sinne
Charm'd by the brighter lustre of thy skinne.   20
I borrow'd from the winds, the gentler wing
Of *Zephirus*, and soft soules of the Spring:
And made (to ayre those cheeks wth fresher grace)
The warme Inspirers dwell upon thy face.

      Oh! jam satis ————

A Rhapsodis.

Occasionally written upon a meeting with some of his
    friends at the Globe Taverne, in a Chamber painted
    over head with a Cloudy Skie, and some few dispersed
    Starres, and on the sides with Land-scapes, Hills,
    Shepheards, and Sheep.

Darknes, & Stars i' th' mid day! they invite
Our active fancies to beleeve it night:
For Tavernes need no Sunne, but for a Signe,
Where rich Tobacco, and quick tapers shine;
And royall, witty Sacke, the Poets soule,
With brighter Suns then he doth guild the bowl;
As though the Pot, and Poet did agree,
Sack should to both Illuminator be.
That artificiall Cloud with it's curl'd brow,
Tels us 'tis late; and that blew space below   10
Is fir'd with many Stars; Marke, how they breake
In silent glaunces o're the hills, and speake
The Evening to the Plaines; where shot from far,
They meet in dumbe salutes, as one great Star.
   The roome (me thinks) growes darker; & the aire
Contracts a sadder colour, and lesse faire:
Or is't the Drawers skill, hath he no Arts
To blind us so, we cann't know pints from quarts?
No, no, 'tis night; looke where the jolly Clowne
Musters his bleating heard, and quits the Downe.   20
Harke! how his rude pipe frets the quiet aire,
Whilst ev'ry Hill proclaimes *Lycoris* faire.
Rich, happy man! that canst thus watch, and sleep,
Free from all cares; but thy wench, pipe & sheep.

But see the Moone is up ; view where she stands
Centinell o're the doore, drawn by the hands
Of some base Painter, that for gaine hath made
Her face the Landmarke to the tipling trade.
This Cup to her, that to *Endymion* give ;
'Twas wit at first, and wine that made them live : 30
Choake may the Painter ! and his Boxe disclose
No other Colours then his fiery Nose ;
And may we no more of his pencill see,
Then two Churchwardens, and Mortalitie.
Should we goe now a wandring, we should meet
With Catchpoles, whores, & Carts in ev'ry street :
Now when each narrow lane, each nooke & Cave,
Signe-posts, & shop-doors, pimp for ev'ry knave,
When riotous sinfull plush, and tell-tale spurs
Walk Fleet street, & the Strand, when the soft stirs 40
Of bawdy, ruffled Silks, turne night to day ;
And the lowd whip, and Coach scolds all the way ;
When lust of all sorts, and each itchie bloud
From the Tower-wharfe to Cymbelyne, and Lud,
Hunts for a Mate, and the tyr'd footman reeles
'Twixt chaire-men, torches, & the hackny wheels :
Come, take the other dish ; it is to him
That made his horse a Senatour : Each brim
Looke big as mine ; The gallant, jolly Beast
Of all the Herd (you'le say) was not the least. 50
Now crown the second bowle, rich as his worth,
I'le drinke it to ; he ! that like fire broke forth
Into the Senates face, crost Rubicon,
And the States pillars, with their Lawes thereon :
And made the dull gray beards, & furr'd gowns fly
Into *Brundusium* to consult, and lye :
This to brave *Sylla* ! why should it be sed,
We drinke more to the living, then the dead ?
Flatt'rers, and fooles doe use it : Let us laugh
At our owne honest mirth ; for they that quaffe 60
To honour others, doe like those that sent
Their gold and plate to strangers to be spent :
Drink deep ; this Cup be pregnant ; & the wine
Spirit of wit, to make us all divine,

52 to ; he ! *M* : to he ! *1646* : to ; he, *C*

That big with Sack, and mirth we may retyre
Possessours of more soules, and nobler fire ;
And by the influxe of this painted Skie,
And labour'd formes, to higher matters flye ;
So, if a Nap shall take us, we shall all,
    After full Cups have dreames Poeticall.   70

Lets laugh now, and the prest grape drinke,
Till the drowsie Day-Starre winke ;
And in our merry, mad mirth run
Faster, and further then the Sun ;
And let none his Cup forsake,
Till that Starre againe doth wake ;
So we men below shall move
    Equally with the gods above.

To Amoret, *of the difference 'twixt him, and other Lovers,*
and what true Love is.

Marke, when the Evenings cooler wings
    Fanne the afflicted ayre, how the faint Sunne,
        Leaving undone,
        What he begunne,
Those spurious flames suckt up from slime, and earth
        To their first, low birth,
        Resignes, and brings.

They shoot their tinsill beames, and vanities,
    Thredding with those false fires their way ;
        But as you stay   10
        And see them stray,
You loose the flaming track, and subt'ly they
        Languish away,
        And cheate your Eyes.

Just so base, Sublunarie Lovers hearts
    Fed on loose prophane desires,
        May for an Eye,
        Or face comply :
But those removed, they will as soone depart,
        And shew their Art,
        And painted fires.   20

Whil'st I by pow'rfull Love, so much refin'd,
   That my absent soule the same is,
      Carelesse to misse,
      A glaunce, or kisse,
Can with those Elements of lust and sence,
      Freely dispence,
      And court the mind.

Thus to the North the Loadstones move,
   And thus to them th' enamour'd steel aspires :   30
      Thus, *Amoret,*
      I doe affect ;
And thus by winged beames, and mutuall fire,
      Spirits and Stars conspire,
      And this is L O V E.

To Amoret Weeping.

Leave, *Amoret,* melt not away so fast
Thy Eyes faire treasure, Fortunes wealthiest Cast
Deserves not one such pearle ; for these well spent,
Can purchase Starres, and buy a Tenement
For us in Heaven ; though here the pious streames
Availe us not ; who from that Clue of Sun-beams
Could ever steale one thread ? or with a kinde
Perswasive Accent charme the wild, lowd winde ?
   Fate cuts us all in Marble, and the Booke
Forestalls our glasse of minutes ; we may looke,   10
But seldome meet a change ; thinke you a teare
Can blot the flinty Volume ? shall our feare,
Or griefe adde to their triumphes ? and must wee
Give an advantage to adversitie ?
Deare, idle Prodigall ! is it not just
We beare our Stars ?   What though I had not dust
Enough to cabinett a worme ? nor stand
Enslav'd unto a little durt, or sand ?
I boast a better purchase, and can shew
The glories of a soule that's simply true.   20
   But grant some richer Planet at my birth
Had spyed me out, and measur'd so much earth
Or gold unto my share ; I should have been
Slave to these lower Elements, and seen

My high borne soul flagge with their drosse, & lye
A pris'ner to base mud, and Alchymie ;
I should perhaps eate Orphans, and sucke up
A dozen distrest widowes in one Cup ;
Nay further, I should by that lawfull stealth,
(Damn'd Usurie) undoe the Common-wealth ;   30
Or Patent it in Soape, and Coales, and so
Have the Smiths curse me, and my Laundres too ;
Geld wine, or his friend Tobacco ; and so bring
The incens'd subject Rebell to his King ;
And after all (as those first sinners fell)
Sinke lower then my gold ; and lye in Hell.

    Thanks then for this deliv'rance ! blessed pow'rs,
You that dispence mans fortune, and his houres,
How am I to you all engag'd ! that thus
By such strange means, almost miraculous,   40
You should preserve me ; you have gone the way
To make me rich by taking all away.
For I (had I been rich) as sure as fate,
Would have bin medling with the King, or State,
Or something to undoe me ; and 'tis fit
(We know) that who hath wealth, should have no wit.
But above all, thanks to that providence,
That arm'd me with a gallant soule, and sence
'Gainst all misfortunes ; that hath breath'd so much
Of Heav'n into me, that I scorne the touch   50
Of these low things ; and can with courage dare
What ever fate, or malice can prepare :
I envy no mans purse, or mines ; I know,
That loosing them, I've lost their curses too ;
And, *Amoret,* (although our share in these
Is not contemptible, nor doth much please)
Yet whilst Content, and Love we joyntly vye,
    We have a blessing which no gold can buye.

UPON THE PRIORIE GROVE,

His usuall Retyrement.

Haile sacred shades ! coole, leavie House !
Chaste Treasurer of all my vowes,
And wealth ! on whose soft bosome layd
My loves faire steps I first betrayd :
   Henceforth no melancholy flight,
No sad wing, or hoarse bird of Night,
Disturbe this Aire, no fatall throate
Of Raven, or Owle, awake the Note
Of our laid Eccho, no voice dwell
Within these leaves, but *Philomel.*   10
The poisonous Ivie here no more
His false twists on the Oke shall score,
Only the Woodbine here may twine,
As th' Embleme of her Love, and mine ;
The Amorous Sunne shall here convey
His best beames, in thy shades to play ;
The active ayre, the gentlest show'rs,
Shall from his wings raine on thy flowers ;
And the Moone from her dewie lockes
Shall decke thee with her brightest drops :   20
What ever can a fancie move,
Or feed the eye ; Be on this Grove ;
   And when at last the Winds, and Teares
Of Heaven, with the consuming yeares,
Shall these greene curles bring to decay,
And cloathe thee in an aged Gray :
(If ought a Lover can foresee ;
Or if we Poets, Prophets be)
From hence transplanted, thou shalt stand
A fresh Grove in th' Elysian Land ;   30

Where (most blest paire !) as here on Earth
Thou first didst eye our growth, and birth ;
So there againe, thou 'lt see us move
In our first Innocence, and Love :
And in thy shades, as now, so then,
Wee'le kisse, and smile, and walke agen.

FINIS.

IVVENALS
TENTH
SATYRE
TRANSLATED.

Nèc verbum verbo curabit reddere fidus
Interpres —————

LONDON,
Printed for *G. B.* and are to be sold at his Shop
under Saint *Dunstans* Church. 1646.

JVVENALS tenth Satyre
TRANSLATED.

In all the parts of Earth, from farthest West,
And the Atlanticke Isles, unto the East
And famous Ganges ; Few there be that know
What's truly good, and what is good in show
Without mistake : For what is't we desire,
Or feare discreetly ? to what e're aspire,
So throughly blest ; but ever as we speed,
Repentance seales the very Act, and deed.
The easie gods mov'd by no other Fate,
Then our owne pray'rs whole Kingdomes ruinate,　　　　10
And undoe Families, thus strife, and warre
Are the swords prize, and a litigious barre
The Gownes prime wish ; vain confidence to share
In empty honours, and a bloudy care,
To be the first in mischiefe, makes him dye
Fool'd 'twixt ambition, and credulitie ;
An oilie tongue with fatall, cunning sence,
And that sad vertue ever, Eloquence,
Are th' others ruine ; but the common curse,
And each dayes ill waits on the rich mans purse :　　　　20
He, whose large acres, and imprison'd gold
So far exceeds his Fathers store of old,
As Brittish Whales the Dolphins doe surpasse.
　　In sadder times therefore, and when the Lawes
Of *Nero's fiat* raign'd ; an armed band
Ceas'd on *Longinus*, and the spacious Land
Of wealthy *Seneca*, besieg'd the gates
Of *Lateranus*, and his faire estate
Divided as a spoile ; In such sad Feasts,
Souldiers (though not invited) are the guests.　　　　30
　　Though thou small peeces of the blessed Mine
Hast lodg'd about thee ; travelling in the shine
Of a pale Moone, if but a Reed doth shake,
Mov'd by the wind, the shadow makes thee quake.
Wealth hath its cares, and want hath this reliefe,
It neither feares the Souldier, nor the Thiefe ;

2 unto] unro *1646*

Thy first choyce vowes, and to the Gods best knowne,
Are for thy stores encrease, that in all towne
Thy stocke be greatest, but no poyson lyes
I'th' poore mans dish, he tasts of no such spice :   40
Be that thy care, when with a Kingly gust,
Thou suck'st whole Bowles clad in the guilded dust
Of some rich minerall ; whilst the false Wine
Sparkles aloft, and makes the draught Divine.
  Blam'st thou the Sages then ? because the one
Would still be laughing, when he would be gone
From his owne doore, the other cryed to see
His times addicted to such vanity ?
Smiles are an easie purchase, but to weep
Is a hard act, for teares are fetch'd more deep ;   50
Democritus his nimble Lungs would tyre
With constant laughter, and yet keep entire
His stocke of mirth, for ev'ry object was
Addition to his store ; though then (Alas !)
Sedans, and Litters, and our Senat Gownes,
With Robes of honour, fasces, and the frownes
Of unbrib'd Tribunes were not seene ; but had
He lived to see our *Roman Prætor* clad
In *Ioves* owne mantle, seated on his high
Embroyder'd Chariot 'midst the dust and Crie   60
Of the large Theatre, loaden with a Crowne
Which scarse he could support, (for it would downe,
But that his servant props it) and close by
His page a witnes to his vanitie :
To these his Scepter, and his Eagle adde
His Trumpets, Officers, and servants clad
In white, and purple ; with the rest that day,
He hir'd to triumph for his bread, and pay ;
Had he these studied, sumptuous follies seene,
'Tis thought his wanton, and effusive spleene   70
Had kill'd the Abderite, though in that age
(When pride & greatnes had not swell'd the stage
So high as ours) his harmles, and just mirth
From ev'ry object had a suddaine birth ;
Nor wast alone their avarice, or pride,
Their triumphs, or their cares he did deride ;

62 (for *GC* : for *1646*

C 2

Their vaine contentions, or ridiculous feares;
But even their very poverty, and teares.
He would at fortunes threats as freely smile
As others mourne; nor was it to beguile   80
His crafty passions; but this habit he
By nature had, and grave Philosophie.
He knew their idle and superfluous vowes,
And sacrifice, which such wrong zeale bestowes,
Were meere Incendiaries; and that the gods
Not pleas'd therewith, would ever be at ods;
Yet to no other aire, nor better place
Ow'd he his birth, then the cold, homely *Thrace*;
Which shewes a man may be both wise, & good,
Without the brags of fortune, or his bloud.   90

   But envy ruines all: What mighty names
Of fortune, spirit, action, bloud, and fame,
Hath this destroy'd? yea, for no other cause
Then being such; their honour, worth, and place,
Was crime enough; their statues, arms & crowns;
Their ornaments of Triumph, Chariots, Gowns,
And what the Herauld with a learned care,
Had long preserv'd, this madnes will not spare.

   So once *Sejanus* Statue Rome allow'd
Her Demi-god, and ev'ry Roman bow'd   100
To pay his safeties vowes; but when that face
Had lost *Tyberius* once, it's former grace
Was soone eclips'd; no diff'rence made (Alas!)
Betwixt his Statue then, and common Brasse;
They melt alike, and in the Workmans hand
For equall, servile use, like others stand.

   Goe now fetch home fresh Bayes, and pay new vowes
To thy dumbe Capitoll gods! thy life, thy house,
And state are now secur'd; *Sejanus* lyes
I'th' Lictors hands; ye gods! what hearts, & eyes   110
Can one dayes fortune change? the solemne crye
Of all the world is, Let *Sejanus* dye:
They never lov'd the man they sweare, they know
Nothing of all the matter; when, or how,
By what accuser, for what cause, or why,
By whose command, or sentence he must dye.
But what needs this? the least pretence will hit,
When Princes feare, or hate a Favourite.

A large Epistle stuff'd with idle feare,
Vaine dreames, and jealousies, directed here   120
From *Caprea* does it ; And thus ever dye
Subjects, when once they grow prodigious high.

   'Tis well, I seeke no more ; but tell me how
This tooke his friends ? no private murmurs now ?
No teares ? no solemne mourner seene ? must all
His Glory perish in one funerall ?
O still true Romans !   State-wit bids them praise
The Moone by night ; but court the warmer rayes
O' th' Sun by day ; they follow fortune still,
And hate, or love discreetly, as their will   130
And the time leades them ; This tumultuous fate
Puts all their painted favours out of date :

   And yet this people that now spurne, & tread
This mighty Favourites once honour'd head,
Had but the Tuscaine goddesse, or his Stars
Destin'd him for an Empire, or had wars,
Treason, or policie, or some higher pow'r
Opprest secure *Tyberius* ; that same houre
That he receiv'd the sad Gemonian doome,
Had crown'd him Emp'ror of the world, & Rome.   140

   But Rome is now growne wise, & since that she
Her Suffrages, and ancient Libertie,
Lost in a Monarchs name ; she takes no care
For Favourite, or Prince ; nor will she share
Their fickle glories, though in *Cato's* dayes
She rul'd whole States, & Armies with her voice,
Of all the honours now within her walls,
She only doats on Playes, and Festivalls :
Nor is it strange ; for when these Meteors fall,
They draw an ample ruine with them ; All   150
Share in the storm ; each beame sets with the Sun,
And equall hazard friends, and flatt'rers run.
This makes, that circled with distractive feare
The livelesse, pale Sejanus limbes they teare,
And least the action might a witnesse need,
They bring their servants to confirme the deed,
Nor is it done for any other end,
Then to avoid the title of his friend.
So fals ambitious man, and such are still
All floating States built on the peoples will :   160

Hearken all you ! whom this bewitching lust
Of an houres glory, and a little dust
Swels to such deare repentance ! you that can
Measure whole kingdoms with a thought or span
Would you be as *Sejanus*? would you have
So you might sway as he did, such a grave?
Would you be rich as he? command, dispose,
All Acts, and Offices? All friends, and foes?
Be Generalls of Armies, and Colleague
Unto an Emperour? breake, or make a league?   170
No doubt you would ; for both the good, and bad,
An equall itch of honour ever had :
But O what State can be so great, or good,
As to be bought with so much shame, and bloud !
Alas ! *Sejanus* will too late confesse
'Twas only pride, and greatnes made him lesse :
For he that moveth with the lofty wind
Of Fortune, and ambition, unconfin'd
In act, or thought ; doth but increase his height,
That he may loose it with more force, & weight ;   180
Scorning a base, low ruine, as if he
Would of misfortune, make a Prodigie.
    Tell mighty *Pompey, Crassus,* and O thou
That mad'st Rome kneele to thy victorious brow,
What but the weight of honours, and large fame
After your worthy Acts, and height of name,
Destroy'd you in the end? the envious Fates
Easie to further your aspiring States,
Us'd them to quell you too ; pride, and excesse
In ev'ry Act did make you thrive the lesse :   190
Few Kings are guiltie of gray haires, or dye
Without a stab, a draught, or trecherie :
And yet to see him, that but yesterday
Saw letters first, how he will scrape, and pray ;
And all her Feast-time tyre *Minervaes* eares
For Fame, for Eloquence, and store of yeares
To thrive and live in ; and then lest he doates,
His boy assists him with his boxe, and notes ;
Foole that thou art ! not to discerne the ill
These vows include ; what, did Rom's Consull kill   200
Her *Cicero*? what, him whose very dust
Greece celebrates as yet ; whose cause though just,

172 equall] eqnall *1646*

Scarse banishment could end ; nor poyson save
His free borne person from a forraigne grave :
All this from Eloquence ! both head, and hand,
The tongue doth forfeit ; pettie wits may stand
Secure from danger, but the nobler veine,
With losse of bloud the barre doth often staine.

    *   *   *   *   *   } *Carmen*
O fortunatam natam me Consule Romam. } *Ciceroni-*
    *   *   *   *   *   } *anum.*

Had all been thus, thou might'st have scorn'd the sword   210
Of fierce *Antonius,* here is not one word
Doth pinch, I like such stuffe ; 'tis safer far
Then thy Philippicks, or Pharsalia's war :
What sadder end then his, whom Athens saw
At once her Patriot, Oracle, and Law ?
Unhappy then is he, and curs'd in Stars,
Whom his poore Father, blind with soot, & scars
Sends from the Anviles harmles chime, to weare
The factious gowne, and tyre his Clients eare,
And purse with endles noise ; Trophies of war   220
Old rusty armour, with an honour'd scar ;
And wheeles of captiv'd Chariots, with a peece
Of some torne Brittish Galley, and to these
The Ensigne too, and last of all the traine
The pensive pris'ner loaden with his Chaine,
Are thought true Roman honors ; these the Greek
And rude Barbarians equally doe seeke.
Thus aire, and empty fame, are held a prize
Beyond faire vertue ; for all vertue dyes
Without reward ; And yet by this fierce lust   230
Of Fame, and titles to ovtlive our dust,
And Monuments ; (though all these things must dye
And perish like our selves) whole Kingdomes lye
Ruin'd, and spoil'd : Put *Hannibal* i'th' scale,
What weight affords the mighty Generall ?
This is the man, whom Africks spacious Land
Bounded by th' Indian Sea, and Niles hot sand,
Could not containe ; (Ye gods ! that give to men
Such boundles appetites, why state you them
So short a time ? either the one deny,   240
Or give their acts, and them Eternitie)

    218 chime *M*: chine *1646*   227 seeke. *GC* : seeke *1646*

All Æthiopia, to the utmost bound
Of *Titans* course, (then which no Land is found
Lesse distant from the Sun) with him that ploughs
That fertile soile where fam'd Iberus flowes,
Are not enough to conquer; past now o're
The Pyrene hills, The Alps with all its store
Of Ice, and Rocks clad in eternall snow
(As if that Nature meant to give the blow)
Denyes him passage; straight on ev'ry side   250
He wounds the Hill, and by strong hand divides
The monstrous pile, nought can ambition stay,
The world, and nature yeeld to give him way:
And now past o're the Alps, that mighty bar
'Twixt France, and Rome, feare of the future war
Strikes Italy; successe, and hope doth fire
His lofty spirits with a fresh desire.
All is undone as yet (saith he) unlesse
Our Pænish forces we advance, and presse
Upon Rome's selfe; break downe her gates, & wall,   260
And plant our Colours in *Suburra's* Vale.
O the rare sight! if this great souldier wee
Arm'd on his Getick Elephant might see!
But what's the event? O glory! how the itch
Of thy short wonders doth mankinde bewitch!
He that but now all Italy, and Spaine,
Had conquer'd o're, is beaten out againe;
And in the heart of Africk, and the sight
Of his owne Carthage, forc'd to open flight.
Banish'd from thence, a fugitive he posts   270
To Syria first, then to Bythinia's Coasts;
Both places by his sword secur'd; though he
In this distresse must not acknowledg'd be;
Where once a Generall he triumphed, now
To shew what Fortune can, he begs as low.
    And thus that soule, which through all nations hurl'd
Conquest, and warre, and did amaze the world;
Of all those glories rob'd at his last breath,
Fortune would not vouchsafe a souldiers death,
For all that bloud the field of Cannæ boasts,   280
And sad Apulia fill'd with Roman ghoasts:

No other end (freed from the pile, and sword)
Then a poore Ring would Fortune him afford.
   Goe now ambitious man ! new plots designe,
March o're the snowie Alps, and Apennine ;
That after all, at best thou mayst but be
A pleasing story to posteritie !
   The *Macedon* one world could not containe,
We heare him of the narrow Earth complaine,
And sweat for roome, as if Seryphus Ile,   290
Or Gyara had held him in Exile :
But Babylon this madnes can allay,
And give the great man but his length of clay ;
The highest thoughts, and actions under Heaven,
Death only with the lowest dust layes even.
It is believed (if what Greece writes be true)
That *Xerxes* with his Persian Fleet did hewe
Their waies throgh mountains, that their sails full blowne,
Like clouds hung over Athos, and did drowne
The spacious Continent, and by plaine force   300
Betwixt the Mount, and it made a divorce ;
That Seas exhausted were, and made firme land,
And Sestos joyned unto Abidos Strand ;
That on their march, his Meades but passing by,
Dranke thee Scamander, and Melenus dry ;
With what soe're incredible designe
Sostratus sings inspired with pregnant Wine :
But what's the end ? He that the other day
Divided Hellespont, and forc'd his way
Through all her angry billowes ; that assigned   310
New punishments unto the waves, and wind :
No sooner saw the Salaminian Seas,
But he was driven out by *Themistocles,*
And of that Fleet (suppos'd to be so great,
That all mankinde shar'd in the sad defeate)
Not one Sayle sav'd, in a poore Fishers boat,
Chas'd o're the working surge, was glad to float,
Cutting his desp'rate course through the tyr'd floud,
And fought againe with Carkasses, and bloud.
O foolish mad ambition ! these are still   320
The famous dangers that attend thy will.

    305 thee Scamander,] the Scamander! *G*: thee, Scamander, *C*
    316 sav'd, *C* : sav'd *1646*

Give store of dayes, good *Iove*, give length of yeares,
Are the next vowes ; these with religious feares,
And Constancie we pay ; but what's so bad,
As a long, sinfull age ? what crosse more sad
Then misery of yeares ? how great an Ill
Is that, which doth but nurse more sorrow still ?
It blacks the face, corrupts, and duls the bloud,
Benights the quickest eye, distasts the food,
And such deep furrowes cuts i'th' Checker'd skin   330
As in th'old Okes of Tabraca are seene.
    Youth varies in most things ; strength, beauty, wit,
Are severall graces ; but where age doth hit,
It makes no diff'rence ; the same weake voice,
And trembling ague in each member lyes :
A generall, hatefull baldnes, with a curst
Perpetuall pettishnes ; and which is worst,
A foule, strong fluxe of humors, and more paine
To feed, then if he were to nurse again.
So tedious to himselfe,-his wife, and friends,   340
That his owne sonnes, and servants, wish his end,
His tast, and feeling dyes ; and of that fire
The am'rous Lover burnes in, no desire :
Or if there were, what pleasure could it be,
Where lust doth raigne without abilitie ?
Nor is this all, what matters it, where he
Sits in the spacious Stage ? who can nor see,
Nor heare what's acted, whom the stiller voice
Of spirited, wanton ayres, or the loud noise
Of Trumpets cannot pierce ; whom thunder can   350
But scarse informe who enters, or what man
He personates, what 'tis they act, or say ?
How many Scænes are done ? what time of day ?
Besides that little bloud, his carkasse holds,
Hath lost its native warmth, & fraught wth colds,
Catarrhs, and rheumes, to thick, black jelly turns,
And never but in fits, and feavers burns ;
Such vast infirmities, so huge a stock
Of sicknes, and diseases to him flock,
That *Hyppia* ne're so many Lovers knew,   360
Nor wanton *Maura* ; Phisick never slew

334 diff'rence] difference *C*   355 lost *GC*: low *1646*

So many Patients, nor rich Lawyers spoile
More Wards, and Widowes; it were lesser toile
To number out what Mannors, and Demaines,
Licinius razer purchas'd : One complaines
Of weaknes in the back, another pants
For lack of breath, the third his eyesight wants;
Nay some so feeble are, and full of paine,
That Infant like they must be fed againe.
These faint too at their meales; their wine they spill,　370
And like young birds, that wait the Mothers Bill
They gape for meat; but sadder far then this
Their senslesse ignorance, and dotage is;
For neither they, their friends, nor servants know,
Nay those themselves begot, and bred up too
No longer now they'le owne; for madly they
Proscribe them all, and what on the last day,
The Misers cannot carry to the Grave
For their past sinnes, their prostitutes must have.
　　But grant age lack'd these plagues; yet must they see　380
As great, as many : Fraile Mortalitie
In such a length of yeares, hath many falls,
And deads a life with frequent funerals.
The nimblest houre in all the span, can steale
A friend, or brother from's; there's no Repeale
In death, or time; this day a wife we mourne,
To morrowes teares a sonne, and the next Urne
A Sister fills; Long-livers have assign'd
These curses still : That with a restles mind,
An age of fresh renewing cares they buye,　390
And in a tide of teares grow old and dye.
　　Nestor, (if we great *Homer* may believe)
In his full strength three hundred yeares did live :
Happy (thou'lt say) that for so long a time
Enjoy'd free nature, with the grape, and Wine
Of many Autumnes; but I prethee, heare
What *Nestor* sayes himselfe, when he his deare
Antilochus had lost, how he complaines
Of life's too large Extent, and copious paines?
Of all he meets, he askes what is the cause　400
He lived thus long; for what breach of their Laws

The gods thus punish'd him? what sinne had he
Done worthy of a long lifes miserie?
Thus *Peleus* his *Achilles* mourned, and he
Thus wept that his *Vlysses* lost at Sea.
Had *Priam* dyed, before *Phereclus* Fleet
Was built, or *Paris* stole the fatall Greeke,
Troy had yet stood, and he perhaps had gone
In peace unto the lower shades; His sonne
Saved with his plenteous offspring, and the rest   410
In solemne pompe bearing his fun'rall Chest;
But long life hinder'd this: Unhappy he,
Kept for a publick ruine; lived to see
All Asia lost, and e're he could expire,
In his owne house saw both the sword, and fire;
All white with age, and cares, his feeble arme
Had now forgot the warre; but this Allarme
Gathers his dying spirits; and as wee
An aged Oxe worne out with labour, see,
By his ungratefull Master, after all   420
His yeares of toyle, a thankles victime fall:
So he by *Ioves* owne Altar; which shewes, wee
Are no where safe from Heaven, and destinie:
Yet dyed a man; but his surviving Queene,
Freed from the Greekish sword was barking seen.

I haste to Rome, and Pontus King let passe,
With Lydian *Cræsus*, whom in vaine (Alas!)
Just *Solons* grave advice bad to attend,
That happines came not before the end.

What man more blest in any age to come   430
Or past, could Nature shew the world, or Rome,
Then *Marius* was? if 'midst the pompe of war,
And triumphs fetch'd with Roman bloud from far
His soule had fled; Exile, and fetters then,
He ne're had seen, nor known *Mynturna's* fenne;
Nor had it, after Carthage got, been sed,
A Roman Generall had beg'd his bread.

Thus *Pompey* th' envious gods, & Romes ill stars
(Freed from *Campania's* feavers, and the Wars)
Doom'd to *Achilles* sword: Our publick vowes   440
Made *Cæsar* guiltles; but sent him to loose
His head at Nile; This curse *Cethegus* mist;
This *Lentulus*, and this made him resist

That mangled by no Lictors axe, fell dead
Entirely *Catiline*, and saved his head.
   The anxious Matrons, with their foolish zeale,
Are the last Votaries, and their Appeale
Is all for beauty; with soft speech, and slow,
They pray for sons, but with a louder vow
Commend a female feature: All that can   450
Make woman pleasing now they shift, and scan:
And why reprov'd they say, *Latona's* paire
The Mother never thinks can be too faire.
   But sad *Lucretia* warnes to wish no face
Like hers; *Virginia* would bequeath her grace
To Crooke-backe *Rutila* in exchange; for still
The fairest children do their Parents fill
With greatest cares; so seldome Chastitie
Is found with beauty; though some few there be
That with a strict, religious care contend   460
Th' old, modest, Sabine Customes to defend:
Besides, wise nature to some faces grants
An easie blush, and where shee freely plants,
A lesse Instruction serves; but both these joyn'd,
At *Rome* would both be forc'd or else purloyn'd.
   So steel'd a forehead vice hath, that dares win,
And bribe the Father to the Childrens sin;
But whom have gifts defiled not? what good face
Did ever want these tempters? pleasing grace
Betraies it selfe; what time did *Nero* mind   470
A course, maim'd shape? what blemish'd youth confin'd
His goatish Pathick? whence then flow these joies
Of a faire issue? whom these sad annoies
Waite, and grow up with; whom perhaps thou'lt see
Publick Adulterers, and must be
Subject to all the Curses, Plagues, and awe
Of jealous mad men, and the *Iulian* Law;
Nor canst thou hope they'le find a milder Starre,
Or more escapes then did the God of Warre;
But worse then all, a jealous braine confines   480
His furie to no Law; what rage assignes,
Is present justice: Thus the rash Sword spils
This Lechers bloud, the scourge another kils.

452 why] when GC

But thy spruce boy must touch no other face
Then a *Patrician*? Is of any race
So they be rich; *Servilia* is as good
With wealth, as shee that boasts *Iulus* blood:
To please a servant all is cheape; what thing
In all their stocke to the last suite, and Ring
But lust exacts? the poorest whore in this,   490
As generous as the *Patrician* is.

But thou wilt say what hurt's a beauteous skin
With a chaste soule? aske *Theseus* sonne, and him
That *Stenobœa* murther'd; for both these
Can tell how fatall 'twas in them to please;
A womans spleene then carries most of fate,
When shame and sorrow aggravate her hate:
Resolve me now, had *Silius* been thy sonne,
In such a hazzard what should he have done?
Of all *Romes* youth, this was the only best,   500
In whom alone beauty, and worth did rest:
This *Messalina* saw, and needs he must
Be ruin'd by the Emp'rour, or her lust,
All in the face of *Rome*, and the worlds eye,
Though *Cesars* wife, a publicke Bigamie
Shee dares attempt; and that the act might beare
More prodigie, the notaries appeare,
And Augures to't; and to compleat the sin
In solemne forme, a dowrie is brought in;
All this (thou'lt say) in private might have past,   510
But shee'le not have it so; what course at last?
What should he doe? If *Messaline* be crost
Without redresse thy *Silius* will be lost;
If not, some two daies length is all he can
Keep from the grave; just so much as will span
This newes to *Hostia*, to whose fate he owes
That *Claudius* last his owne dishonour knowes.

But he obeyes, and for a few houres lust,
Forfeits that glory should outlive his dust,
Nor was it much a fault; for, whether he   520
Obey'd, or not; 'twas equall destinie:
So fatall beauty is, and full of wast,
That neither wanton can be safe, nor chast.

489 Ring *M*: King *1646*   503 lust,] lust; *G*: lust. *C*

What then should man pray for? what is't that he
Can beg of Heaven, without Impiety?
Take my advice: first to the Gods commit
All cares; for they things competent, and fit
For us foresee; besides man is more deare
To them, then to himselfe: we blindly here
Led by the world, and lust, in vaine assay   530
To get us portions, wives, and sonnes; but they
Already know all that we can intend,
And of our Childrens Children see the end.
   Yet that thou may'st have something to commend
With thankes unto the Gods for what they send;
Pray for a wise, and knowing soule; a sad
Discreet, true valour, that will scorne to adde
A needlesse horrour to thy death; that knowes
'Tis but a debt which man to nature owes;
That starts not at misfortunes, that can sway,   540
And keep all passions under locke and key;
That couets nothing, wrongs none, and preferres
An honest want before rich injurers;
All this thou hast within thy selfe, and may
Be made thy owne, if thou wilt take the way;
What boots the worlds wild, loose applause? what can
Fraile, perillous honours adde unto a man?
What length of years, wealth, or a rich faire wife?
Vertue alone can make a happy life.
To a wise man nought comes amisse: but we   550
Fortune adore, and make our Deity.

546 what can GC: what 1646

FINIS

Ad Posteros.

Diminuat ne sera dies præsentis honorem,
  Quis, qualisq; fui, percipe Posteritas.
CAMBRIA me genuit, patulis ubi vallibus errans
  Subjacet aeriis montibus ISCA pater.
Inde sinu placido suscepit maximus arte
  HERBERTUS, Latiæ gloria prima Scholæ,
Bis ternos, illo me Conducente, per annos
  Profeci, & geminam Contulit unus opem,
Ars & amor, mens atɋ manus certare solebant,
  Nec lassata Illi mensve, manusve fuit.   10
Hinc qualem cernis crevisse: Sed ut mea Certus
  Tempora Cognoscas, dura fuere, scias.
Vixi, divisos cum fregerat hæresis Anglos
  Intèr Tysiphonas presbyteri & populi.
His primùm miseris per amæna furentibus arva
  Prostravit sanctam vilis avena rosam,
Turbârunt fontes, & fusis pax perit undis,
  Mæstaɋ Cœlestes obruit umbra dies.
Duret ut Integritas tamen, & pia gloria, partem
  Me nullam in tantâ strage fuisse, scias;   20
Credidimus nempè insonti vocem esse Cruori,
  Et vires quæ post funera flere docent.
Hinc Castæ, fidæq; pati me more parentis
  Commonui, & Lachrymis fata levare meis;
Hinc nusquàm horrendis violavi Sacra procellis,
  Nec mihi mens unquàm, nec manus atra fuit.
Si pius es, ne plura petas; Satur Ille recedat
  Qui sapit, & nos non Scripsimus Insipidis.

OLOR ISCANUS.

A COLLECTION

OF SOME SELECT

POEMS,

AND

TRANSLATIONS,

Formerly written by

Mr. Henry Vaughan *Siluriſt.*

Publiſhed by a Friend.

Virg. Georg.
Flumina amo, Sylvaſ̌q̌ Inglorius——

LONDON,
Printed by *T.W.* for *Humphrey Moſeley,*
and are to be ſold at his ſhop, at the
Signe of the Prince's Arms in St. *Pauls*
Church-yard, 1651.

D

The truly Noble, and most
Excellently accomplish'd, the
Lord KILDARE DIGBY.

MY LORD,

It is a Position *anciently* known, and *modern Experience* hath allowed it for a *sad truth*, that *Absence* and *time*, (like *Cold weather*, and an *unnaturall dormition*) will *blast* and *wear* out of memorie the most *Endearing obligations*; And hence it was that some *Politicians* in *Love* have lookt upon the *former* of these *two* as a main remedy against the *fondness* of that *Passion*. But for my own part (my Lord) I shall deny this *Aphorisme* of the *people*, and beg leave to assure your *Lordship*, that, though these *reputed obstacles* have lain long in my way, yet neither of them could *work* 10 upon me : for I am now (without adulation) as *warm* and *sensible* of those *numerous* favours, and *kind Influences* receiv'd sometimes from your Lordship, as I really was at the *Instant* of *fruition*. I have no *plott* by *preambling* thus, to set any *rate* upon this present *address*, as if I should presume to value a *Return* of this nature equall with your Lordships *Deserts*, but the *designe* is, to let you see that this *habit* I have got of being *troublesome* flowes from two *excusable principles*, Gratitude, and Love. These inward *Counsellours* (I know not how discreetly) perswaded me to this *Attempt* and *Intrusion* upon your *name*, which if your Lordship 20 will vouchsafe to own as the *Genius* to these *papers*, you will *perfect* my *hopes*, and place me at my full *height*. This was the *Ayme*, my Lord, and is the *End* of this work, which though but a *Pazzarello* to the *voluminosè Insani*, yet as *Jezamin* and the *Violet* find room in the *bank* as well as *Roses* and *Lillies*, so happily may this, and (if *shin'd* upon by your *Lordship*) please as much. To whose *Protection*, Sacred as your *Name*, and those eminent *Honours* which have alwayes attended upon't through so many *generations*, I humbly offer it, and remain in all *numbers* of *gratitude*,

30

Newton by Usk
this 17. of *De-
cemb.* 1647.

My honour'd Lord,

Your most affectionate,
humblest Servant

VAUGHAN.

D 2

The Publisher to the Reader.

It was the glorious Maro, *that referr'd his* Legacies *to the* Fire, *and though* Princes *are seldome* Executors, *yet there came a* Cæsar *to his* Testament, *as if the* Act *of a* Poet *could not be* repeal'd *but by a* King. *I am not Reader* Augustus vindex: *Here is no* Royall Rescue, *but here is a* Muse *that* deserves *it. The* Author *had long agoe condemn'd these* Poems *to* Obscuritie, *and the* Consumption *of that* Further Fate, *which* attends *it. This* Censure *gave them a* Gust *of* Death, *and they have* partly *known that* Oblivion, *which our* Best Labours *must* come to *at* Last. *I present thee then not onely with a* Book, *but with a* Prey, *and in* 10 *this* kind *the first* Recoveries *from* Corruption. *Here is a* Flame *hath been sometimes* extinguished : *Thoughts that have been* lost *and* forgot, *but now they* break out *again like the* Platonic Reminiscencie. *I have not the* Author's Approbation *to the* Fact, *but I have* Law *on my* Side, *though never a* Sword : *I hold it no man's* Prærogative *to* fire *his* own House. *Thou seest how* Saucie *I am* grown, *and if thou doest expect I should* Commend *what is* published, *I must tell thee,* I crie no Sivill Oranges. *I will not say, Here is* Fine *or* Cheap: *that were an* Injurie *to the* Verse *it selfe, and to the* Effects *it can* produce. *Read on, and thou wilt find thy* Spirit 20 ingag'd : *not by the* Deserts *of what wee call* Tolerable, *but by the* Commands *of a* Pen, *that is* Above it.

Vpon the most Ingenious
pair of Twins, *Eugenius Philalethes,* and the *Authour* of these *Poems.*

What *Planet* rul'd your *birth*? what *wittie star*?
That you so like in *Souls* as *Bodies* are !
So like in *both*, that you seem *born* to free
The *starrie art* from *vulgar* Calumnie.
My *doubts* are solv'd, from hence my *faith* begins,
Not only your *faces*, but your *wits* are *Twins.*

When this bright *Gemini* shall from earth ascend,
They will *new light* to dull-ey'd mankind lend,
Teach the *Star-gazers*, and delight their *Eyes*,
Being fixt a *Constellation* in the Skyes. 10

T. Powell Oxoniensis.

37

To my friend the Authour
upon these his *Poems*.

I call'd it once my *sloth*: In such an age
So many *Volumes deep*, I not a *page*?
But I recant, and vow 'twas thriftie Care
That kept my *Pen* from spending on *slight ware*,
And breath'd it for a *Prize*, whose pow'rfull *shine*
Doth both *reward* the striver, and *refine*;
Such are thy *Poems*, friend: for since th'hast writ,
I cann't reply to any *name*, but *wit*;
And lest amidst the *throng* that make us *grone*,
Mine prove a groundless *Heresie* alone,   10
Thus I dispute, Hath there not rev'rence bin
Pay'd to the *Beard* at doore, for *Lord* within?
Who notes the *spindle-leg*, or *hollow eye*
Of the *thinne Usher*, the *faire Lady* by?
Thus I *sinne* freely, *neighbour* to a *hand*
Which while I aime to *strengthen*, gives *Command*
For my *protection*, and thou art to me
At once my *Subject* and *Securitie*.
                                    I. Rowlandson Oxoniensis.

Vpon the following
Poems.

I write not here, as if thy *last* in store
Of learned *friends*, 'tis known that thou hast *more*;
Who, were they told of this, would find a way
To rise a guard of *Poets* without *pay*,
And bring as many *hands* to thy *Edition*,
As th'*City* should unto their *May'rs* Petition,
But thou wouldst none of this, lest it should be
Thy *Muster* rather, than our *Courtesie*,
Thou wouldst not beg as *Knights* do, and appeare
Poet by *Voice*, and *suffrage* of the *Shire*,   10
That were enough to make thy *Muse* advance
Amongst the *Crutches*, nay it might enhance
Our *Charity*, and we should think it fit
The *State* should build an *Hospital* for wit.

11 thy *Er*: my *1651*

But here needs no *reliefe* : Thy richer *Verse*
Creates all *Poets,* that can but *reherse,*
And they, like *Tenants* better'd by their *land,*
Should pay thee *Rent* for what they understand,
Thou art not of that *lamentable Nation,*
Who make a blessed *Alms* of *approbation,*   20
Whose *fardel-notes* are *Briefes* in ev'ry thing,
But, that they are not licens'd *By the King.*
Without such *scrape-requests* thou dost come forth
Arm'd (though I speak it) with thy *proper worth,*
And needest not this *noise* of friends, for wee
Write out of *love,* not thy *necessitie ;*
And though this *sullen age* possessed be
With some strange *Desamour* to Poetrie,
Yet I suspect (thy fancy so delights)
The *Puritans* will turn thy *Proselytes,*   30
And that thy *flame* when once abroad it *shines,*
Will bring thee as many *friends,* as thou hast *lines.*

E U G E N I U S   P H I L A L E T H E S   *Oxoniensis.*

Olor Iscanus.

To the River *Isca.*

When *Daphne*'s Lover here first wore the *Bayes*,
Eurotas secret streams heard all his *Layes.*
And holy *Orpheus*, Natures *busie* Child
By headlong *Hebrus* his deep *Hymns* Compil'd.
Soft *Petrarch* (thaw'd by *Laura*'s flames) did weep
On *Tybers* banks, when she (*proud fair !*) cou'd sleep ;
Mosella boasts *Ausonius*, and the *Thames*
Doth murmure *SIDNEYS Stella* to her *streams*,
While *Severn* swoln with *Joy* and *sorrow*, wears
Castara's smiles mixt with fair *Sabrin*'s tears.   10
Thus *Poets* (like the *Nymphs*, their *pleasing themes*)
Haunted the *bubling Springs* and *gliding streams*,
And *happy banks* ! whence such *fair flowres* have sprung,
But happier those where they have *sate* and *sung* !
Poets (like *Angels*) where they once appear
Hallow the *place*, and each succeeding year
Adds *rev'rence* to't, such as at length doth give
This aged faith, *That there their Genii live.*
Hence th'*Auncients* say, That, from this *sickly aire*
They passe to *Regions* more *refin'd* and *faire*,   20
To *Meadows* strow'd with *Lillies* and the *Rose*,
And *shades* whose *youthfull green* no *old age* knowes,
Where all in *white* they walk, discourse, and Sing
Like Bees *soft murmurs*, or a *Chiding Spring.*
   But *Isca*, whensoe'r those *shades* I see,
And thy *lov'd Arbours* must no more *know* me,
When I am layd to *rest* hard by thy *streams*,
And my *Sun sets*, where first it *sprang* in beams,
I'le leave behind me such a *large, kind light*,
As shall *redeem* thee from *oblivious night*,   30
And in these *vowes* which (living yet) I pay
Shed such a *Previous* and *Enduring Ray,*
As shall from age to age thy *fair name* lead
'Till *Rivers* leave to *run*, and *men* to *read.*

   6 *proud C : prou'd 1651*   9 *swoln Er : sworn 1651*

First, may all *Bards* born after me
(When I am *ashes*) sing of thee !
May thy *green banks* and *streams* (or none)
Be both their *Hill* and *Helicon* ;
May *Vocall Groves* grow there, and all
The *shades* in them *Propheticall*, 40
Where (laid) men shall more *faire truths* see
Than *fictions* were of *Thessalie.*
May thy gentle *Swains* (like *flowres*)
Sweetly spend their *Youthfull houres,*
And thy *beauteous Nymphs* (like *Doves*)
Be *kind* and *faithfull* to their *Loves* ;
Garlands, and *Songs,* and *Roundelayes,*
Mild, dewie *nights,* and Sun-shine *dayes,*
The *Turtles voyce, Joy* without *fear,*
Dwell on thy *bosome* all the year ! 50
May the *Evet* and the *Tode*
Within thy Banks have no abode,
Nor the *wilie, winding Snake*
Her *voyage* through thy *waters* make.
In all thy *Journey* to the *Main*
No *nitrous Clay,* nor *Brimstone-vein*
Mixe with thy *streams,* but may they passe
Fresh as the *aire,* and cleer as *Glasse,*
And where the *wandring Chrystal* treads
Roses shall *kisse,* and *Couple* heads. 60
The *factour-wind* from far shall bring
The *Odours* of the *Scatter'd* Spring,
And *loaden* with the rich *Arreare,*
Spend it in *Spicie whispers* there.
No *sullen heats,* nor *flames* that are
Offensive, and *Canicular,*
Shine on thy *Sands,* nor *pry* to see
Thy *Scalie, shading familie,*
But *Noones* as mild as *Hesper's* rayes,
Or the first *blushes* of fair dayes. 70
What *gifts* more *Heav'n* or *Earth* can adde
With all those *blessings* be thou *Clad !*

    Honour, Beautie,
    Faith and *Dutie,*
    Delight and *Truth,*
    With *Love,* and *Youth*

Crown all about thee! And what ever *Fate*
Impose else-where, whether the graver state,
Or some toye else, may those *lowd, anxious Cares*
For *dead* and *dying things* (the Common *Wares*   80
And *showes* of time) ne'r break thy *Peace*, nor make
Thy *repos'd Armes* to a new warre *awake*!
  But *Freedome, safety, Joy and blisse*
  United in one loving *kisse*
  Surround thee quite, and *stile* thy borders
  The Land redeem'd from all disorders!

The Charnel-house.

Blesse me! what damps are here? how stiffe an aire?
Kelder of mists, a second *Fiats* care,
Frontspeece o'th' grave and darkness, a Display
Of ruin'd man, and the disease of day;
Leane, bloudless shamble, where I can descrie
Fragments of men, Rags of Anatomie;
Corruptions ward-robe, the transplantive bed
Of mankind, and th'Exchequer of the dead.
How thou arrests my sense? how with the sight
My *Winter'd* bloud growes stiffe to all delight?   10
Torpedo to the Eye! whose least glance can
Freeze our wild lusts, and rescue head-long man;
Eloquent silence! able to Immure
An *Atheists* thoughts, and blast an *Epicure*.
Were I a *Lucian*, Nature in this dresse
Would make me wish a Saviour, and Confesse.
 Where are you shoreless thoughts, vast tenter'd hope,
Ambitious dreams, *Aymes* of an Endless scope,
Whose stretch'd Excesse runs on a string too high
And on the rack of self-extension dye?   20
Chameleons of state, Aire-monging band,
Whose breath (like Gun-powder) blowes up a land,
Come see your dissolution, and weigh
What a loath'd nothing you shall be one day,
As th' Elements by Circulation passe
From one to th'other, and that which first was
Is so again, so 'tis with you; The grave
And Nature but Complott, what the one gave,

   83 *safety*] *fafety 1651*

The other takes ; Think then, that in this bed
There sleep the Reliques of as proud a head   30
As stern and subtill as your own, that hath
Perform'd, or forc'd as much, whose tempest-wrath
Hath levell'd Kings with slaves, and wisely then
Calme these high furies, and descend to men ;
Thus *Cyrus* tam'd the *Macedon*, a tombe
Checkt him, who thought the world too straight a Room.

   Have I obey'd the *Powers* of a face,
A beauty able to undoe the Race
Of easie man? I look but here, and strait
I am Inform'd, the lovely Counterfeit   40
Was but a smoother Clay.   That famish'd slave
Begger'd by wealth, who starves that he may save,
Brings hither but his sheet ; Nay, th'*Ostrich-man*
That feeds on *steele* and *bullet*, he that can
Outswear his *Lordship*, and reply as tough
To a kind word, as if his tongue were *Buffe*,
Is *Chap*-faln here, wormes without wit, or fear
Defie him now, death hath disarm'd the *Bear*.
Thus could I run o'r all the pitteous score
Of erring men, and having done meet more,   50
Their shuffled *Wills*, abortive, vain *Intents*,
Phantastick *humours*, perillous *Ascents*,
False, empty *honours*, traiterous *delights*,
And whatsoe'r a blind Conceit Invites ;
But these and more which the weak vermins swell,
Are Couch'd in this Accumulative Cell
Which I could scatter ; But the grudging Sun
Calls home his beams, and warns me to be gone,
Day leaves me in a double night, and I
Must bid farewell to my sad library.   60
Yet with these notes.   Henceforth with thought of thee
I'le season all succeeding Jollitie,
Yet damn not mirth, nor think too much is fit,
Excesse hath no *Religion*, nor *Wit*,
But should wild bloud swell to a lawless strain
One Check from thee shall *Channel* it again.

37 of a face *Er* : of face *1651*   52 Phantastick] Phautastick *1651*
66 One *Er* : On *1651*

Olor Iscanus. 43

In Amicum fœneratorem.

Thanks mighty *Silver*! I rejoyce to see
How I have spoyl'd his thrift, by spending thee.
Now thou art gone, he courts my wants with more,
His *Decoy* gold, and bribes me to restore.
As lesser lode-stones with the *North* consent
Naturally moving to their Element,
As bodyes swarm to th' Center, and that fire
Man stole from heaven, to heav'n doth still aspire,
So this vast crying summe drawes in a lesse,
And hence this bag more Northward layd I guesse,   10
For 'tis of *Pole-star* force, and in this sphere
Though th'least of many rules the master-bear.
Prerogative of debts! how he doth dresse
His messages in *Chink*? not an Expresse
Without a fee for reading, and 'tis fit,
For gold's the best restorative of wit,
O how he gilds them o'r! with what delight
I read those lines, where Angels doe Indite?
    But wilt have money *Og*? must I dispurse?
Will nothing serve thee but a *Poets* curse?   20
Wilt rob an Altar thus? and sweep at once
What *Orpheus*-like I forc'd from stocks and stones?
'Twill never swell thy *Bag*, nor ring one peale
In thy dark *Chest*. Talk not of *Shreeves*, or gaole,
I fear them not. I have no land to glutt
Thy durty appetite, and make thee strutt
Nimrod of acres; I'le no Speech prepare
To court the *Hopefull Cormorant*, thine heire.
Yet there's a Kingdome, at thy beck, if thou
But kick this drosse, *Parnassus* flowrie brow   30
I'le give thee with my *Tempe*, and to boot
That horse which struck a fountain with his foot.
A Bed of Roses I'le provide for thee,
And Chrystal Springs shall drop thee melodie;
The breathing shades wee'l haunt, where ev'ry leafe
Shall *Whisper* us asleep, though thou art deafe;
Those waggish *Nymphs* too which none ever yet
Durst make love to, wee'l teach the Loving fit,

18 where] which *GC*   21 thus] thu *1651*

Wee'l suck the *Corall* of their lips, and feed
Upon their spicie breath, a meale at need,   40
Rove in their *Amber-tresses*, and unfold
That glist'ring grove, the Curled wood of gold,
Then peep for babies, a new Puppet-play,
And riddle what their *pratling Eyes* would say.
But here thou must remember to dispurse,
For without money all this is a Curse,
Thou must for more bags call, and so restore
This Iron-age to gold, as once before ;
This thou must doe, and yet this is not all,
For thus the Poet would be still in thrall,   50
Thou must then (if live thus) my neast of honey,
Cancell old bonds, and beg to lend more money.

To his friend——.

I wonder, *James*, through the whole Historie
Of ages, such *Entailes* of povertie
Are layd on Poets ; Lawyers (they say) have found
A trick to cut them, would they were but bound
To practise on us, though for this thing wee
Should pay (if possible) their bribes and fee.
Search (as thou canst) the old and moderne store
Of *Rome* and ours, in all the wittie score
Thou shalt not find a rich one ; Take each Clime
And run o'r all the pilgrimage of time   10
Thou'lt meet them poor, and ev'ry where descrie
A thredbare, goldless genealogie.
Nature (it seems) when she meant us for Earth
Spent so much of her treasure in the birth
As ever after niggards her, and Shee,
Thus stor'd within, beggers us outwardly.
Wofull profusion ! at how dear a rate
Are wee made up? all hope of thrift and state
Lost for a verse : When I by thoughts look back
Into the wombe of time, and see the Rack   20
Stand useless there, untill we are produc'd
Unto the torture, and our soules infus'd
To learn afflictions, I begin to doubt
That as some tyrants use from their chain'd rout
Of slaves to pick out one whom for their sport
They keep afflicted by some lingring art,

So wee are meerly thrown upon the stage
The mirth of fooles, and Legend of the age.
When I see in the ruines of a sute
Some nobler brest, and his tongue sadly mute   30
Feed on the *Vocall silence* of his Eye,
And knowing cannot reach the remedie,
When soules of baser stamp shine in their store,
And he of all the throng is only poore,
When *French* apes for forraign fashions pay,
And *English* legs are drest th'outlandish way,
So fine too, that they their own shadows wooe,
While he walks in the *sad* and *Pilgrim-shooe,*
I'm mad at Fate, and angry ev'n to sinne,
To see deserts and learning clad so thinne :   40
To think how th'earthly Usurer can brood
Upon his bags, and weigh the pretious food
With palsied hands, as if his soul did feare
The Scales could rob him of what he layd there ;
Like Divels that on hid Treasures sit, or those
Whose jealous Eyes trust not beyond their nose
They guard the durt, and the bright Idol hold
Close, and Commit adultery with gold.
A Curse upon their drosse ! how have we sued
For a few scatter'd *Chips*? how oft pursu'd   50
Petitions with a blush, in hope to squeeze
For their souls health, more than our wants a peece?
Their steel-rib'd Chests and Purse (rust eat them both !)
Have cost us with much paper many an oath,
And Protestations of such solemn sense,
As if our soules were sureties for the Pence.
Should we a full nights learned cares present,
They'l scarce return us one short houres Content,
'Las ! they're but quibbles, things we Poets feign,
The short-liv'd Squibs and Crackers of the brain.   60
  But wee'l be wiser, knowing 'tis not they
That must redeem the hardship of our way,
Whether a Higher Power, or that starre
Which neerest heav'n, is from the earth most far
Oppresse us thus, or angel'd from that Sphere
By our strict Guardians are kept luckless here,
It matters not, wee shall one day obtain
Our native and Celestiall scope again.

To his retired friend, an Invitation
to *Brecknock.*

Since last wee met, thou and thy horse (my dear,)
Have not so much as drunk, or litter'd here,
I wonder, though thy self be thus deceast,
Thou hast the spite to Coffin up thy beast;
Or is the *Palfrey* sick, and his rough hide
With the penance of *One Spur* mortifide?
Or taught by thee (like *Pythagoras's Oxe*)
Is then his master grown more *Orthodox*?
What ever 'tis, a sober cause't must be
That thus long bars us of thy Companie.   10
The Town believes thee lost, and didst thou see
But half her suffrings, now distrest for thee,
Thou'ldst swear (like *Rome*) her foule, polluted walls
Were sackt by *Brennus*, and the salvage *Gaules*.
Abominable face of things! here's noise
Of bang'd Mortars, blew Aprons, and Boyes,
Pigs, Dogs, and Drums, with the hoarse hellish notes
Of politickly-deafe Usurers throats,
With new fine *Worships*, and the old cast *teame*
Of Justices vext with the *Cough*, and *flegme*.   20
Midst these the *Crosse* looks sad, and in the *Shire-*
-Hall furs of an old *Saxon Fox* appear,
With brotherly Ruffs and Beards, and a strange sight
Of high Monumentall Hats ta'ne at the fight
Of *Eighty eight*; while ev'ry *Burgesse* foots
The mortall *Pavement* in eternall boots.
 Hadst thou been batc'lour, I had soon divin'd
Thy Close retirements, and Monastick mind,
Perhaps some Nymph had been to visit, or
The beauteous Churle was to be waited for,   30
And like the *Greek*, e'r you the sport would misse
You stai'd, and stroak'd the *Distaffe* for a kisse.
But in this age, when thy coole, settled bloud
Is ty'd t'one flesh, and thou almost grown good,
I know not how to reach the strange device,
Except (*Domitian* like) thou murther'st flyes;
Or is't thy pietie? for who can tell
But thou may'st prove devout, and love a Cell,

And (like a Badger) with attentive looks
In the dark hole sit rooting up of books.   40
Quick Hermit! what a peacefull Change hadst thou
Without the noise of *haire-cloth*, *Whip*, or *Vow*?
But is there no redemption? must there be
No other penance but of liberty?
Why two months hence, if thou continue thus
Thy memory will scarce remain with us,
The Drawers have forgot thee, and exclaim
They have not seen thee here since *Charles* his raign,
Or if they mention thee, like some old man
That at each word inserts—Sir, *as I can*   50
Remember—So the *Cyph'rers* puzzle mee
With a dark, cloudie character of thee.
That (certs!) I fear thou wilt be lost, and wee
Must ask the *Fathers* e'r 't be long for thee.
    Come! leave this sullen state, and let not Wine
And precious Witt lye dead for want of thine,
Shall the dull *Market-land-lord* with his *Rout*
Of sneaking Tenants durtily swill out
This harmlesse liquor? shall they knock and beat
For Sack, only to talk of *Rye*, and *Wheat*?   60
O let not such prepost'rous tipling be
In our *Metropolis*, may I ne'r see
Such *Tavern-sacrilege*, nor lend a line
To weep the *Rapes* and *Tragedy* of wine!
Here lives that *Chimick*, quick fire which betrayes
Fresh Spirits to the bloud, and warms our layes,
I have reserv'd 'gainst thy approach a Cup
That were thy Muse stark dead, shall raise her up,
And teach her yet more Charming words and skill
Than ever *Cœlia*, *Chloris*, *Astrophil*,   70
Or any of the Thredbare names Inspir'd
Poore riming lovers with a *Mistris* fir'd.
Come then! and while the slow Isicle hangs
At the stiffe thatch, and Winters frosty pangs
Benumme the year, blith (as of old) let us
'Midst noise and War, of Peace, and mirth discusse.
This portion thou wert born for: why should wee
Vex at the times ridiculous miserie?
An age that thus hath fool'd it selfe, and will
(Spite of thy teeth and mine) persist so still.   80

Let's sit then at this *fire*, and while wee steal
A Revell in the Town, let others seal,
Purchase or Cheat, and who can, let them pay,
Till those black deeds bring on the darksome day ;
Innocent spenders wee ! a better use
Shall wear out our short Lease, and leave th'obtuse
Rout to their *husks* ; They and their bags at best
Have cares in *earnest*, wee care for a *Jest*.

Monsieur Gombauld.

I 'ave read thy Souls fair night-peece, and have seen
Th'*Amours* and Courtship of the *silent Queen*,
Her stoln descents to Earth, and what did move her
To Juggle first with *Heav'n*, then with a *Lover*,
With *Latmos* lowder rescue, and (alas !)
To find her out a *Hue and Crie* in Brasse,
Thy Journall of deep Mysteries, and sad
Nocturnall Pilgrimage, with thy dreams clad
In fancies darker than thy *Cave*, Thy *Glasse*
Of sleepie draughts, and as thy soul did passe   10
In her calm voyage what discourse she heard
Of Spirits, what dark Groves and ill-shap'd guard
Ismena lead thee through, with thy proud flight
O'r *Periardes*, and deep, musing night
Neere fair *Eurotas* banks, what solemn *green*
The neighbour shades weare, and what forms are seen
In their large Bowers, with that sad path and seat
Which none but light-heeld *Nymphs* and *Fairies* beat ;
Their solitary life, and how exempt
From Common frailtie, the severe contempt   20
They have of Man, their priviledge to live
A *Tree*, or *Fountain*, and in that *Reprieve*
What ages they consume, with the sad *Vale*
Of *Diophania*, and the mournfull tale,
Of th' bleeding vocall *Myrtle* ; These and more
Thy richer thoughts we are upon the score
To thy rare fancy for, nor doest thou fall
From thy first Majesty, or ought at all
Betray Consumption, thy full vig'rous *Bayes*
Wear the same *green*, and scorn the lene decayes   30

18 beat *GC* : heat *1651*

Of *stile*, or *matter*; Just so have I known
Some *Chrystal* spring, that from the neighbour down
Deriv'd her birth, in gentle murmurs steal
To their next Vale, and proudly there reveal
Her streams in lowder accents, adding still
More noise and waters to her Channell, till
At last swoln with Increase she glides along
The Lawnes and Meadows in a wanton throng
Of frothy billows, and in one great name
Swallows the tributary brooks drown'd fame. 40
   Nor are they meere Inventions, for we
In th' same peece find scatter'd *Philosophie*
And hidden, disperst truths that folded lye
In the dark shades of deep *Allegorie,*
So neatly weav'd, like *Arras,* they descrie
Fables with *Truth, Fancy* with *Historie.*
So that thou hast in this thy curious mould
Cast that commended mixture wish'd of old,
Which shall these Contemplations render far
Lesse mutable, and lasting as their star, 50
And while there is a *People,* or a *Sunne,*
Endymions storie with the *Moon* shall runne.

An Elegie on the death of Mr. *R. W.* slain in the late unfortunate differences at *Routon* Heath, neer *Chester,* 1645.

I am Confirm'd, and so much wing is given
To my wild thoughts, that they dare strike at heav'n.
A full years griefe I struggled with, and stood
Still on my sandy hopes uncertain good,
So loth was I to yeeld, to all those fears
I still oppos'd thee, and denyed my tears.
But thou art gone ! and the untimely losse
Like that one day, hath made all others Crosse.
Have you seen on some Rivers flowrie brow
A well-built *Elme,* or stately *Cedar* grow, 10
Whose Curled tops gilt with the Morning-ray
Becken'd the Sun, and whisperd to the day,
When unexpected from the angry *North*
A fatall sullen whirle-wind sallies forth,
And with a full-mouth'd blast rends from the ground
The *Shady twins,* which rushing scatter round

Their sighing leafes, whilst overborn with strength,
Their trembling heads bow to a prostrate length;
So forc'd fell he; So Immaturely Death
Stifled his able heart and active breath.   20
The world scarce knew him yet, his early Soule
Had but new-broke her day, and rather stole
A sight, than gave one; as if subt'ly she
Would learn our stock, but hide his treasurie.
His years (should time lay both his *Wings* and *glasse*
Unto his charge) could not be summ'd (alas!)
To a full *score*; Though in so short a span
His riper thoughts had purchas'd more of man
Than all those worthless livers, which yet quick,
Have quite outgone their own *Arithmetick.*   30
He seiz'd perfections, and without a dull
And mossie *gray* possess'd a solid skull,
No Crooked knowledge neither, nor did he
Wear the friends name for Ends and policie,
And then lay't by; As those *lost Youths* of th'stage
Who only flourish'd for the *Play's* short age
And then retir'd, like *Jewels* in each part
He wore his friends, but chiefly at his heart.
       Nor was it only in this he did excell,
His equall valour could as much, as well.   40
He knew no *fear* but of his *God*; yet durst
No injurie, nor (as some have) e'r purs't
The sweat and tears of others, yet would be
More forward in a royall gallantrie
Than all those vast pretenders, which of late
Swell'd in the ruines of their King and State.
He weav'd not *Self-ends*, and the *Publick* good
Into one piece, nor with the peoples bloud
Fill'd his own veins; In all the doubtfull way
Conscience and *Honour* rul'd him.   O that day   50
When like the *Fathers* in the *Fire* and *Cloud*
I mist thy face! I might in ev'ry *Crowd*
See Armes like thine, and men advance, but none
So neer to lightning mov'd, nor so fell on.
Have you observ'd how soon the nimble *Eye*
Brings th' *Object* to *Conceit*, and doth so vie
Performance with the *Soul*, that you would swear
The *Act* and *apprehension* both lodg'd there,

42 purs't *M*: pur'st *1651*

Just so mov'd he : like *shott* his active hand
Drew bloud, e'r well the foe could understand.   60
But here I lost him.   Whether the last turn
Of thy few sands call'd on thy hastie urn,
Or some fierce rapid fate (hid from the Eye)
Hath hurl'd thee Pris'ner to some distant skye
I cannot tell, but that I doe believe
Thy Courage such as scorn'd a base Reprieve.
What ever 'twas, whether that day thy breath
Suffer'd a *Civill* or the *Common* death,
Which I doe most suspect, and that I have
Fail'd in the *glories* of so known a grave,   70
Though thy lov'd ashes misse me, and mine Eyes
Had no acquaintance with thy Exequies,
Nor at the last farewell, torn from thy sight
On the *Cold sheet* have fix'd a *sad delight*,
Yet what e'r pious hand (in stead of mine)
Hath done this office to that dust of thine,
And till thou rise again from thy low bed
Lent a Cheap pillow to thy quiet head,
Though but a private *turffe*, it can do more
To keep thy name and memory in store   80
Than all those *Lordly fooles* which lock their bones
In the dumb piles of Chested brasse, and stones.
Th'art rich in thy own fame, and needest not
These *Marble-frailties*, nor the *gilded blot*
Of posthume honours ; There is not one sand
Sleeps o'r thy grave, but can outbid that hand
And pencill too, so that of force wee must
Confesse their *heaps* shew lesser than thy *dust*.
    And (blessed soule !) though this my sorrow can
Adde nought to thy perfections, yet as man   90
Subject to Envy, and the common fate
It may redeem thee to a fairer date ;
As some blind Dial, when the day is done,
Can tell us at mid-night, *There was a Sun*,
So these perhaps, though much beneath thy fame,
May keep some weak remembrance of thy name,
And to the faith of better times Commend
Thy loyall upright life, and gallant End.

    Nomen & arma locum servant, te, amice, nequivi
    Conspicere,——   100

Upon a Cloke lent him by Mr. *J. Ridsley.*

Here, take again thy *Sack-cloth*! and thank heav'n
Thy Courtship hath not kill'd me; Is't not Even
Whether wee dye by peecemeale, or at once
Since both but ruine, why then for the nonce
Didst husband my afflictions, and cast o're
Me this forc'd *Hurdle* to inflame the score?
Had I neer *London* in this *Rug* been seen
Without doubt I had executed been
For some bold *Irish* spy, and crosse a sledge
Had layn mess'd up for their *foure gates* and *bridge.*   10
When first I bore it, my oppressed feet
Would needs perswade me, 'twas some *Leaden sheet*;
Such deep Impressions, and such dangerous holes
Were made, that I began to doubt my soals,
And ev'ry step (so neer necessity)
Devoutly wish'd some honest Cobler by,
Besides it was so short, the *Jewish* rag
Seem'd Circumcis'd, but had a *Gentile* shag.
Hadst thou been with me on that day, when wee
Left craggie *Biston,* and the fatall *Dee,*   20
When beaten with fresh storms, and late mishap
It shar'd the office of a *Cloke,* and *Cap,*
To see how 'bout my clouded head it stood
Like a thick *Turband,* or some Lawyers *Hood,*
While the stiffe, hollow pletes on ev'ry side
Like *Conduit-pipes* rain'd from the *Bearded hide,*
I know thou wouldst in spite of that day's fate
Let loose thy mirth at my new shape and state,
And with a shallow smile or two professe
Some *Sarazin* had lost the *Clowted Dresse.*   30
Didst ever see the *good wife* (as they say)
March in her short cloke on the *Christning* day,
With what soft motions she salutes the Church,
And leaves the Bedrid Mother in the lurch;
Just so Jogg'd I, while my dull horse did trudge
Like a Circuit-beast plagu'd with a goutie Judge.
    But this was Civill.   I have since known more
And worser pranks: One night (as heretofore
Th' hast known) for want of change (a thing which I
And *Bias* us'd before me) I did lye   40

Pure *Adamite*, and simply for that end
Resolv'd, and made this for my bosome-*friend*.
O that thou hadst been there next morn, that I
Might teach thee new *Micro-cosmo-graphie*!
Thou wouldst have ta'ne me, as I naked stood,
For one of th' *seven pillars* before the floud,
Such *Characters* and *Hierogliphicks* were
In one night worn, that thou mightst justly swear
I'd slept in *Cere-cloth*, or at *Bedlam* where
The mad men lodge in straw, I'le not forbear   50
To tell thee all, his wild *Impress* and *tricks*
Like *Speeds* old *Britans* made me look, or *Picts*;
His villanous, biting, *Wire-embraces*
Had seal'd in me more strange formes and faces
Than *Children* see in dreams, or thou hast read
In *Arras, Puppet-playes*, and *Ginger-bread*,
With *angled Schemes*, and *Crosses* that bred fear
Of being handled by some *Conjurer*,
And neerer thou wouldst think (such *strokes* were drawn)
I'd been some rough statue of *Fetter-lane*,   60
Nay, I believe, had I that instant been
By *Surgeons* or *Apothecaries* seen,
They had Condemned my raz'd skin to be
Some walking *Herball*, or *Anatomie*.
   But (thanks to th'day!) 'tis off.   I'd now advise
Thee friend to put this peece to Merchandize;
The *Pedlars* of our age have business yet,
And gladly would against the *Fayr-day* fit
Themselves with such a *Roofe*, that can secure
Their *Wares* from *Dogs and Cats* rain'd in showre,   70
It shall performe; or if this will not doe
'Twill take the *Ale-wives* sure; 'Twill make them *two*
Fine *Roomes* of *One*, and spread upon a stick
Is a partition without Lime or Brick.
Horn'd obstinacie! how my heart doth fret
To think what *Mouthes* and *Elbowes* it would set
In a wet day? have you for two pence e're
Seen King *Harryes* Chappell at *Westminster*,
Where in their dustie gowns of *Brasse* and *Stone*
The Judges lye, and markt you how each one   80

70 rain'd] rained *C*

In sturdie Marble-plets about the knee
Bears up to shew his legs and symmetrie?
Just so would this; That I think't weav'd upon
Some stiffneckt *Brownists* exercising loome.
O that thou hadst it when this Jugling fate
Of Souldierie first seiz'd me! at what rate
Would I have bought it then, what was there but
I would have giv'n for the *Compendious hutt*?
I doe not doubt but (if the weight could please,)
'Twould guard me better than a *Lapland-lease*,   90
Or a *German* shirt with Inchanted lint
Stuff'd through, and th'devils *beard* and *face* weav'd in't.
　　But I have done.　And think not, friend, that I
This freedome took to Jeere thy Courtesie,
I thank thee for't, and I believe my Muse
So known to thee, thou'lt not suspect abuse;
She did this, 'cause (perhaps) thy *love* paid thus
Might with my *thanks* out-live thy *Cloke*, and *Us*.

Upon Mr. *Fletchers* Playes, published, 1647.

I knew thee not, nor durst *attendance* strive
Labell to *wit*, *Verser remonstrative*,
And in some *Suburb-page* (scandal to thine)
Like *Lent* before a *Christmasse* scatter mine.
This speaks thee not, since at the utmost rate
Such *remnants* from thy *peece* Intreat their date;
Nor can I *dub* the *Coppy*, or afford
Titles to *swell* the *reare* of *Verse* with Lord,
Nor politickly big to *Inch* low fame
Stretch in the *glories* of a strangers name,   10
And Clip those *Bayes* I Court, weak *striver* I,
But a faint *Echo* unto *Poetrie*.
I have not *Clothes* t'adopt me, nor must sit
For *Plush* and *Velvets* sake *Esquire* of wit,
Yet *Modestie* these *Crosses* would improve,
And *Rags* neer thee, some *Reverence* may move.
　　I did believe (great *Beaumont* being dead,)
Thy *Widow'd Muse* slept on his *flowrie bed*;
But I am *richly* Cosen'd, and can see
Wit *transmigrates*, his *Spirit* stayd with thee,   20
Which *doubly* advantag'd by thy *single* pen
In *life* and *death* now treads the *Stage* agen;

And thus are wee freed from that *dearth* of wit
Which *starv'd* the Land since into *Schismes* split,
Wherein th'hast done so much, wee must needs guesse
Wits last *Edition* is now i'th' *Presse*,
For thou hast *drain'd* Invention, and he
That writes hereafter, doth but *pillage* thee.
But thou hast *plotts*; and will not the *Kirk* strain
At the *Designes* of such a *Tragick brain*?   30
Will they themselves think safe, when they shall see
Thy most *abominable policie*?
Will not the *Eares* assemble, and think't fit
Their *Synod fast*, and *pray*, against thy wit?
But they'le not *tyre* in such an *idle Quest*,
Thou doest but *kill*, and *Circumvent* in *Jest*,
And when thy anger'd Muse *swells* to a blow
'Tis but for *Field*'s, or *Swansteed*'s overthrow.
Yet shall these *Conquests* of thy *Bayes* outlive
Their *Scotish zeale*, and *Compacts* made to grieve   40
The *Peace* of *Spirits*, and when such deeds fayle
Of their foule Ends, a *faire name* is thy *Bayle*.
  But (happy thou!) ne'r saw'st these *stormes*, our *aire*
Teem'd with even in thy time, though *seeming faire*;
Thy gentle *Soule* meant for the *shade*, and *ease*
Withdrew betimes into the *Land* of *Peace*;
So *neasted* in some Hospitable shore
The *Hermit-angler*, when the *mid-Seas* roare
Packs up his *lines*, and (ere the tempest *raves*,)
Retyres, and leaves his *station* to the *waves*.   50
Thus thou diedst almost with our *peace*, and wee
This *breathing time* thy last fair *Issue* see,
Which I think such (if *needless Ink* not soyle
So *Choice a Muse*,) others are but thy *foile*;
This, or that *age* may write, but never see
A *Wit* that dares run *Paralell* with thee.
True, *B E N* must live! but bate *him*, and thou hast
Undone all *future wits*, and match'd the *past*.

Upon the *Poems* and *Playes* of the ever memorable Mr. *William Cartwright.*

I did but *see* thee! and how *vain* it is
To *vex* thee for it with *Remonstrances*,
Though *things* in fashion, let those *Judge*, who sit

49 raves,) *GC*: raves, *1651*   2 *Remonstrances*,] Remonstrances *Ct*

Their *twelve-pence* out, to *clap* their *hands* at *wit*;
I fear to *Sinne* thus *neer* thee; for (*great Saint!*)
'Tis known, *true beauty* hath no need of *paint*.

   Yet, since a *Labell* fixt to thy fair *Hearse*
Is all the *Mode*, and *tears* put into *Verse*
Can teach *Posterity* our present *griefe*
And their own *losse*, but never give *reliefe*;   10
I'le tell them (and a *truth* which needs no *passe*,)
That *wit* in *Cartwright* at her *Zenith* was,
Arts, *Fancy*, *Language*, all *Conven'd* in thee,
With those *grand Miracles* which *deifie*
The old worlds *Writings*, kept yet from the *fire*,
Because they *force* these worst times to *admire*.
Thy matchless *Genius*, in all thou didst write,
Like the *Sun*, wrought with such *stayd heat*, and *light*,
That not a *line* (to the most *Critick* he)
Offends with *flashes*, or *obscuritie*.   20

   When thou the *wild* of *humours* trackst, thy *pen*
So Imitates that *Motley stock* in men,
As if thou hadst in all their *bosomes* been,
And seen those *Leopards* that lurk within.
The am'rous *Youth* steals from thy *Courtly page*
His *vow'd Addresse*, the *Souldier* his *brave rage*;
And those *soft beauteous Readers* whose *looks* can
Make some men *Poets*, and make any man
A *Lover*, when thy *Slave* but *seems* to dye,
Turn all his *Mourners*, and melt at the *Eye*.   30
Thus, thou thy *thoughts* hast *drest* in such a *strain*
As doth not only *speak*, but *rule* and *raign*,
Nor are those *bodyes* they assum'd, *dark Clouds*,
Or a *thick bark*, but *clear*, *transparent shrouds*,
Which who *lookes* on, the *Rayes* so strongly beat
They'l *brushe* and *warm* him with a *quickning heat*,
So *Souls* shine at the *Eyes*, and *Pearls* display
Through the *loose-Chrystal-streams* a *glaunce of day*.
But what's all this unto a *Royall Test*?
Thou art the *Man*, whom great *Charles* so exprest!   40
Then let the *Crowd* refrain their *needless humme*,
When *Thunder* speaks, then *Squibs* and *Winds* are *dumb*.

     9 *griefe*] grief, *Ct*   12 *was*,] *was*. *Ct*   32 *raign*,] raign; *Ct*

To the best, and most accomplish'd
Couple——

Blessings as rich and fragrant crown your heads
    As the mild heav'n on *Roses* sheds,
      When at their Cheeks (like Pearls) they weare
      The Clouds that court them in a teare,
    And may they be fed from above
    By him which first ordain'd your love!

Fresh as the *houres* may all your pleasures be,
    And healthfull as *Eternitie*!
      Sweet as the flowres *first breath*, and Close
      As th'*unseen spreadings* of the Rose,   10
    When he unfolds his Curtain'd head,
    And makes his bosome the *Suns bed*.

Soft as *your selves* run your whole lifes, and cleare
    As your own *glasse*, or *what shines* there ;
      Smooth as heav'ns *face*, and bright as he
      When without *Mask*, or *Tiffanie*,
    In all your time not one *Jarre* meet
    But peace as silent as his *feet*.

Like the dayes *Warmth* may all your Comforts be,
    Untoil'd for, and *Serene* as he,   20
      Yet free and full as is that *sheafe*
      Of Sun-beams gilding ev'ry leafe,
    When now the *tyrant-heat* expires
    And his Cool'd locks breath milder fires.

And as those *parcell'd glories* he doth shed
    Are the *faire Issues* of his head,
      Which ne'r so distant are soon known
      By th' *heat* and *lustre* for his own,
    So may each branch of yours wee see
    Your *Coppyes*, and our *Wonders* be!   30

And when no more on Earth you must remain
    Invited hence to heav'n again,
      Then may your vertuous, virgin-flames
      Shine in those *Heires* of your fair names,
    And teach the world that mysterie
    Your selves in your Posteritie!

So you to both worlds shall *rich presents* bring,
And *gather'd* up to heav'n, leave here a *Spring*.

An Elegie on the death of Mr. *R. Hall,* slain at *Pontefract,* 1648.

I knew it would be thus! and my Just fears
Of thy great spirit are Improv'd to tears.
Yet flow these not from any base distrust
Of a fair name, or that thy honour must
Confin'd to those cold reliques sadly sit
In the same Cell an obscure Anchorite.
Such low distempers *Murther,* they that must
Abuse thee so, *weep* not, but *wound* thy dust.
    But I past such dimme Mourners can descrie
Thy fame above all Clouds of obloquie,   10
And like the Sun with his victorious rayes
Charge through that darkness to the last of dayes.
'Tis true, fair *Manhood* hath a *female* Eye,
And tears are beauteous in a Victorie,
Nor are wee so high-proofe, but griefe will find
Through all our guards a way to wound the mind;
But in thy fall what addes the brackish summe
More than a blott unto thy *Martyrdome,*
Which scorns such wretched suffrages, and stands
More by thy single worth, than our whole bands.   20
Yet could the puling tribute rescue ought
In this sad losse, or wert thou to be brought
Back here by tears, I would in any wise
Pay down the summe, or quite Consume my Eyes.
Thou fell'st our double ruine, and this rent
Forc'd in thy life shak'd both the *Church and tent,*
Learning in others steales them from the *Van,*
And basely wise *Emasculates* the man,
But lodged in thy brave soul the *bookish feat*
Serve'd only as the light unto thy *heat*;   30
Thus when some quitted action, to their shame,
And only got a *discreet Cowards* name,
Thou with thy bloud mad'st purchase of renown,
And diedst the glory of the *Sword* and *Gown,*
Thy bloud hath hallow'd *Pomfret,* and this blow
(Prophan'd before) hath Church'd the Castle now.

34 *Gown, M: Gown 1651*: gown: *G*: gown. C

Nor is't a Common valour we deplore,
But such as with *fifteen* a *hundred* bore,
And lightning like (not coopt within a wall)
In stormes of *fire* and *steele* fell on them all.   40
Thou wert no *Wool-sack* souldier, nor of those
Whose Courage lies in *winking* at their foes,
That live at *loop-holes*, and consume their breath
On *Match* or *Pipes*, and sometimes *peepe* at death;
No, it were sinne to number these with thee,
But that (thus poiz'd) our losse wee better see.
The fair and open valour was thy *shield*,
And thy known station, the *defying field*.
   Yet these in thee I would not *Vertues* call,
But that this age must know, that thou hadst all.   50
Those richer graces that adorn'd thy mind
Like stars of the *first magnitude*, so shin'd,
That if oppos'd unto these lesser lights
All we can say, is this, *They were fair nights*.
Thy *Piety* and *Learning* did unite,
And though with *Sev'rall beames* made up *one light*,
And such thy Judgement was, that I dare swear
Whole *Counsels* might as soon, and *Synods* erre.
   But all these now are out! and as some *Star*
Hurl'd in Diurnall motions from far,   60
And seen to droop at night, is vainly sed
To fall, and find an *Occidentall bed*,
Though in that other world what wee Judge *West*
Proves *Elevation*, and a new, fresh *East*.
So though our weaker sense denies us sight
And bodies cannot trace the *Spirits* flight,
Wee know those graces to be still in thee,
But wing'd above us to eternitie.
Since then (thus flown) thou art so much refin'd,
That we can only reach thee with the mind,   70
   will not in this *dark* and *narrow glasse*
Let thy scant *shadow* for *Perfections* passe,
But leave thee to be read more high, more queint,
In thy own bloud a *Souldier* and a *Saint*.

   —— *Salve æternum mihi maxime Palla!*
   Æternum�q̃ vale!——

To my learned friend, Mr. *T. Powell,* upon
His Translation of *Malvezzi's*
Christian Politician.

Wee thank you, worthy Sir, that now we see
Malvezzi languag'd like our Infancie,
And can without suspition entertain
This forraign States-man to our brest or brain,
You have enlarg'd his praise, and from your store
By this Edition made his worth the more.
Thus by your learned hand (amidst the *Coile*)
Outlandish plants thrive in our thankless soile,
And wise men after death, by a strange fate,
Lye *Leiguer* here, and beg to serve our *State*.   10
Italy now, though *Mistris* of the *Bayes*,
Waits on this *Wreath*, proud of a forraign praise,
For, wise *Malvezzi*, thou didst lye before
Confin'd within the language of one shore,
And like those *Stars* which neer the *Poles* doe steer
Wer't but in one part of the *Globe* seen cleer,
Provence and *Naples* were the best and most
Thou couldst shine in, fixt to that single Coast,
Perhaps some *Cardinal* to be thought wise
And honest too, would ask, *what was thy price?*   20
Then thou must pack to *Rome*, where thou mightst lye
E'r thou shouldst have new cloathes eternally,
For though so neer the *seav'n hills*, ne'rthelesse
Thou cam'st to *Antwerp* for thy *Roman* dresse ;
But now thou art come hither, thou mayst run
Through any Clime as well known as the *Sun*,
And in thy *sev'rall dresses* like the *year*
Challenge acquaintance with each peopled Sphere.
   Come then rare Politicians of the time,
Brains of some standing, Elders in our Clime,   30
See here the method : A wise, solid state
Is quick in acting, friendly in debate,
Ioynt in advice, in resolutions just,
Mild in successe, true to the Common trust.
It cements ruptures, and by gentle hand
Allayes the heat and burnings of a land,
Religion guides it, and in all the Tract
Designes so twist, that heav'n confirms the act ;

If from these lists you wander as you steere,
Look back, and *Catechise* your actions here,   40
These are the *Marks* to which true States-men tend,
And *greatness* here with *goodness* hath one End.

To my worthy friend Master *T. Lewes.*

Sees not my friend, what a deep snow
Candies our Countries wooddy brow?
The yeelding branch his load scarse bears
Opprest with snow, and *frozen tears*,
While the *dumb* rivers slowly float,
All bound up in an *Icie Coat.*
   Let us meet then! and while this world
In wild *Excentricks* now is hurld,
Keep wee, like nature, the same *Key*,
And walk in our forefathers way;   10
Why any more cast wee an Eye
On what *may come*, not what is *nigh?*
Why vex our selves with *feare*, or *hope*
And cares beyond our *Horoscope?*
Who into future times would peere
Looks oft beyond his terme set here,
And cannot goe into those grounds
Bnt through a *Church-yard* which them bounds;
Sorrows and sighes and searches spend
And draw our bottome to an end,   20
But discreet Joyes lengthen the lease
Without which life were a disease,
And who this age a Mourner goes,
Doth with his tears but feed his foes.

To the most Excellently accomplish'd,
Mrs. *K. Philips.*

Say wittie fair one, from what Sphere
Flow these rich numbers you shed here?
For sure such *Incantations* come
From thence, which strike your Readers dumbe.
A strain, whose measures gently meet
Like *Virgin-lovers*, or times *feet*,

Where language *Smiles*, and accents rise
As quick, and pleasing as your *Eyes*,
The *Poem* smooth, and in each line
Soft as *your selfe*, yet *Masculine* ;   10
Where no Coorse trifles blot the page
With matter borrow'd from the age,
But thoughts as Innocent, and high
As *Angels* have, or *Saints* that dye.
  These Raptures when I first did see
New miracles in Poetrie,
And by a hand, their God would misse
His *Bayes* and *Fountaines* but to kisse,
My weaker *Genius* (crosse to fashion)
Slept in a silent admiration,   20
A Rescue, by whose grave disguise
Pretenders oft have past for wise,
And yet as *Pilgrims* humbly touch
Those *Shrines* to which they bow so much,
And Clouds in Courtship flock, and run
To be the Mask unto the Sun,
So I concluded, It was true
I might at distance worship you
A *Persian* Votarie, and say
It was your light shew'd me the way.   30
So *Lodestones* guide the duller *Steele*,
And high perfections are the *Wheele*
Which moves the lesse, for gifts divine
Are strung upon a *Vital line*
Which touch'd by you, Excites in all
Affections *Epidemicall.*
And this made me (a truth most fit)
Adde my weak *Eccho* to your wit,
Which pardon, Lady, for Assayes
Obscure as these might blast your Bayes,   40
As Common hands soyle *Flowres*, and make
That dew they wear, *weepe* the mistake.
But I'le wash off the *staine*, and vow
No *Lawrel* growes, but for your *Brow*.

11 no *Er*: not *1651*   17 God *Er*: good *1651*

An Epitaph upon the Lady *Elizabeth*, Second Daughter to his late Majestie.

Youth, Beauty, Vertue, Innocence
Heav'ns royall, and select Expence,
With Virgin-tears, and sighs divine,
Sit here the *Genii* of this shrine,
Where now (thy fair soule wing'd away,)
They guard the *Casket* where she lay.
   Thou hadst, e'r thou the light couldst see,
Sorrowes layd up, and stor'd for thee,
Thou suck'dst in woes, and the *brests* lent
Their *Milk* to thee, but to lament;   10
Thy portion here was *griefe*, thy years
Distilld no other rain, but tears,
Tears without noise, but (understood)
As lowd, and shrill as any bloud;
Thou seem'st a *Rose-bud* born in *Snow*,
A flowre of purpose sprung to bow
To headless tempests, and the rage
Of an Incensed, stormie Age.
Others, e're their afflictions grow,
Are tim'd, and season'd for the blow,   20
But thine, as *Rhumes* the tend'rest part,
Fell on a *young* and *harmless* heart.
And yet as *Balm-trees* gently spend
Their tears for those, that doe them rend,
So mild and pious thou wert seen,
Though full of *Suffrings*, free from *spleen*,
Thou didst nor murmure, nor revile,
But drank'st thy *Wormwood* with a *smile.*
   As envious Eyes blast, and Infect
And cause misfortunes by aspect,   30
So thy sad stars dispens'd to thee
No Influxe, but Calamitie,
They view'd thee with *Ecclypsed* rayes,
And but the *back-side* of bright dayes.
         *   *   *
These were the Comforts she had here,
As by an unseen hand 'tis cleer,
Which now she reads, and smiling wears
A Crown with him, who wipes off tears.

To Sir *William D'avenant,* upon
his *Gondibert.*

Well, wee are rescued! and by thy rare Pen
Poets shall live, when *Princes* dye like men.
Th'hast cleer'd the prospect to our harmless *Hill,*
Of late years clouded with imputed Ill,
And the *Soft, youthfull Couples* there may move
As chast as *Stars* converse and smile above.
Th'hast taught their *Language,* and their *love* to flow
Calme as *Rose-leafes,* and coole as *Virgin-snow,*
Which doubly feasts us, being so refin'd
They both *delight,* and *dignifie* the mind,   10
Like to the watrie Musick of some Spring,
Whose pleasant flowings at once *wash* and *sing.*
    And where before *Heroick Poems* were
Made up of *Spirits, Prodigies,* and *fear,*
And shew'd (through all the *Melancholy flight,*)
Like some dark Region overcast with night,
As if the Poet had been quite dismay'd,
While only *Giants* and *Inchantments* sway'd,
Thou like the *Sun,* whose Eye brooks no disguise
Hast Chas'd them hence, and with Discoveries   20
So rare and learned fill'd the place, that wee
Those fam'd *Grandeza's* find out-done by thee,
And under-foot see all those *Vizards* hurl'd,
Which bred the wonder of the former world.
'Twas dull to sit, as our fore-fathers did,
At *Crums* and *Voyders,* and because unbid
Refrain wise appetite.   This made thy *fire*
Break through the *ashes* of thy aged *Sire*
To lend the world such a Convincing light
As shewes his *fancy* darker than his sight.   30
Nor was't alone the *bars* and *length* of dayes
(Though those gave *strength* and *stature* to his *bayes,*)
Encounter'd thee, but what's an old Complaint
And kills the fancy, a *forlorn Restraint;*
How couldst thou mur'd in solitarie stones
Dresse *BIRTHA'S* smiles, though well thou might'st her *grones?*
And, strangely Eloquent, thy self divide
'Twixt *Sad misfortunes,* and a *Bloomie Bride?*

36 *smiles GC*: *similes 1651*

Through all the tenour of thy ample Song
Spun from thy own rich store, and shar'd among 40
Those fair *Adventurers*, we plainly see
Th' *Imputed* gifts, *Inherent* are in thee.
Then live for ever (and by high desert)
In thy own *mirrour*, matchless *Gondibert*,
And in *bright Birtha* leave thy *love* Inshrin'd
Fresh as her *Emrauld*, and *fair* as her *mind*,
While all Confesse thee (as they ought to doe)
The Prince of *Poets*, and of *Lovers* too.

Tristium Lib. 5°. *Eleg.* 3ª.
To his fellow-Poets at *Rome*, upon the birth-day of *Bacchus*.

This is the day (blith god of *Sack*) which wee
If I mistake not, Consecrate to thee,
When the soft *Rose* wee marry to the *Bayes*,
And warm'd with thy own wine reherse thy praise,
'Mongst whom (while to thy *Poet* fate gave way)
I have been held no small part of the day,
But now, dull'd with the Cold *Bears* frozen seat,
Sarmatia holds me, and the warlike *Gete*.
My former life, unlike to this my last,
With *Romes* best wits of thy full Cup did tast, 10
Who since have seen the savage *Pontick* band,
And all the *Choler* of the Sea and Land:
Whether sad Chance, or heav'n hath this design'd,
And at my birth some fatall Planet shin'd,
Of right thou shouldst the *Sisters* knots undoe,
And free thy *Votarie* and *Poet* too.
Or are you Gods (like us) in such a state
As cannot alter the decrees of fate?
I know with much adoe thou didst obtain
Thy *Jovial godhead*, and on earth thy pain 20
Was no whit lesse, for wandring thou didst run
To the *Getes* too, and Snow-weeping *Strymon*,
With *Persia*, *Ganges*, and what ever streams
The thirsty *Moore* drinks in the mid-day beames.
But thou wert twice-born, and the Fates to thee
(To make all sure) doubled thy miserie,

43 desert] defert *1651*

My suffrings too are many: if it be
Held safe for me to boast adversitie,
Nor was't a Common blow, but from above
Like his, that died for Imitating *Jove*,   30
Which when thou heardst, a ruine so divine
And *Mother*-like, should make thee pitty mine.
And on this day, which *Poets* unto thee
Crown with full bowles, ask, *What's become of me?*
  Help bucksome God then! so may thy lov'd *Vine*
Swarm with the num'rous grape, and *big* with Wine
Load the kind *Elm*, and so thy *Orgyes* be
With priests lowd showtes, and *Satyrs* kept to thee!
So may in death *Lycurgus* ne'r be blest,
Nor *Pentheus* wandring ghost find any rest!   40
And so for ever bright (thy Chiefe desires,)
May thy *Wifes Crown* outshine the lesser fires!
If but now, mindfull of my love to thee,
Thou wilt, in what thou canst, my helper be.
You *Gods* have Commerce with your selves, try then
If *Cæsar* will restore me *Rome* agen.
  And you my trusty friends (the Jollie Crew
Of careless *Poets*!) when, without me, you
Perform this dayes glad Myst'ries, let it be
Your first Appeal unto his Deitie,   50
And let one of you (touch'd with my sad name)
Mixing his wine with tears, lay down the same,
And (sighing) to the rest this thought Commend,
O! Where is Ovid *now our banish'd friend?*
This doe, if in your brests I e'r deserv'd
So large a share, nor spitefully reserv'd,
Nor basely sold applause, or with a brow
Condemning others, did my selfe allow.
And may your happier wits grow lowd with fame
As you (my best of friends!) preserve my name.   60

De Ponto, Lib. 3°.

To his friends (after his many sollicitations) refusing to petition *Cæsar* for his releasement.

You have Consum'd my language, and my pen
Incens'd with begging scorns to write agen.
You grant, you knew my sute: My Muse, and I
Had taught it you in frequent Elegie,

That I believe (yet seal'd) you have divin'd
Our *Repetitions*, and *forestal'd* my mind,
So that my thronging Elegies, and I
Have made you (more then *Poets*) prophesie.
    But I am now awak'd ; forgive my dream
Which made me Crosse the *Proverb* and the *Stream*,   10
And pardon, friends, that I so long have had
Such good thoughts of you, I am not so mad
As to continue them.   You shall no more
Complain of troublesome *Verse*, or write o're
How I endanger you, and vex my *Wife*
With the sad legends of a banish'd life.
I'le bear these plagues my selfe : for I have past
Through greater ones, and can as well at last
These pettie Crosses.   'Tis for some young beast
To kick his bands, or wish his neck release   20
From the sad Yoke.   Know then, That as for me
Whom Fate hath us'd to such calamitie,
I scorn her spite and yours, and freely dare
The highest ills your malice can prepare.
    'Twas Fortune threw me hither, where I now
Rude *Getes* and *Thrace* see, with the snowie brow
Of Cloudie *Æmus*, and if she decree
Her sportive pilgrims *last bed* here must be
I am content ; nay more, she cannot doe
That Act which I would not consent unto.   30
I can delight in vain hopes, and desire
That state more then her *Change* and *Smiles*, then high'r
I hugge a strong *despaire*, and think it brave
To *baffle* faith, and give those hopes a *grave*.
Have you not seen cur'd wounds enlarg'd, and he
That with the first wave sinks, yielding to th'free
Waters, without th'Expence of armes or breath
Hath still the easiest, and the quickest death.
Why nurse I sorrows then ? why these desires
Of Changing *Scythia* for the *Sun* and *fires*   40
Of some calm kinder aire ? what did bewitch
My frantick hopes to flye so vain a pitch,
And thus out-run my self ? Mad-man ! could I
Suspect fate had for me a Courtesie ?
These errours grieve : And now I must forget
Those pleas'd *Idæa's* I did frame and set

Unto my selfe, with many fancyed *Springs*
And *Groves*, whose only losse new sorrow brings.
And yet I would the worst of fate endure,
E're you should be repuls'd, or lesse secure,   50
But (base, low soules!) you left me not for this,
But 'cause you durst not.   *Cæsar* could not misse
Of such a trifle, for I know that he
Scorns the *Cheap triumphs* of my miserie.
    Then since (degen'rate friends) not he, but you
Cancell my hopes, and make afflictions new,
You shall Confesse, and fame shall tell you, I
At *Ister* dare as well as *Tyber* dye.

De Ponto, lib. 4°. *Eleg.* 3ª.
**To his Inconstant friend, translated for
the use of all the *Judases* of this
touch-stone-Age.**

Shall I complain, or not? Or shall I mask
Thy hatefull name, and in this bitter task
Master my just Impatience, and write down
Thy crime alone, and leave the rest unknown?
Or wilt thou the succeeding years should see
And teach thy person to posteritie?
No, hope it not; for know, most wretched man,
'Tis not thy base and weak detraction can
Buy thee a *Poem*, nor move me to give
Thy name the honour in my Verse to live.   10
    Whilst yet my *Ship* did with no stormes dispute
And temp'rate winds *fed* with a calme salute
My prosp'rous sailes, thou wert the only man
That with me then an equall fortune ran,
But now since angry heav'n with Clouds and night
Stifled those *Sun*-beams, thou hast ta'ne thy flight,
Thou know'st I want thee, and art meerly gone
To shun that rescue, I rely'd upon;
Nay, thou dissemblest too, and doest disclame
Not only my *Acquaintance*, but my name;   20
Yet know (though deafe to this) that I am he
Whose *years* and *love* had the same *Infancie*
With thine, Thy *deep familiar*, that did share
Soules with thee, and partake thy *Joyes* or *Care*,

Whom the same *Roofe* lodg'd, and my *Muse* those nights
So solemnly endear'd to her delights;
But now, perfidious traitour, I am grown
The *Abject* of thy brest, not to be known
In that *false Closet* more; Nay, thou wilt not
So much as let me know, I am forgot.   30
If thou wilt say, thou didst not love me, then
Thou didst dissemble: or, if love agen,
Why now Inconstant? came the Crime from me
That wrought this Change? Sure, if no Justice be
Of my side, thine must have it. Why dost hide
Thy reasons then? for me, I did so guide
My selfe and actions, that I cannot see
What could offend thee, but my miserie.
'Las! if thou wouldst not from thy store allow
Some rescue to my wants, at least I know   40
Thou couldst have writ, and with a line or two
Reliev'd my *famish'd Eye*, and eas'd me so.
I know not what to think! and yet I hear,
Not pleas'd with this, th'art *Witty*, and dost Jeare;
Bad man! thou hast in this those tears kept back
I could have shed for thee, shouldst thou but lack.
Know'st not that *Fortune* on a *Globe* doth stand,
Whose *upper* slipprie part without command
Turns *lowest* still? the sportive leafes and wind
Are but dull *Emblems* of her fickle mind,   50
In the whole world there's nothing I can see
Will throughly parallel her wayes, but thee.
All that we hold, hangs on a slender twine
And our best states by sudden chance decline;
Who hath not heard of *Cræsus* proverb'd gold
Yet knowes his foe did him a pris'ner hold?
He that once aw'd *Sicilia*'s proud Extent
By a poor art could famine scarce prevent;
And mighty *Pompey* e'r he made an end
Was glad to beg his slave to be his friend;   60
Nay, he that had so oft *Romes* Consull bin,
And forc'd *Jugurtha*, and the *Cimbrians* in,
Great *Marius*! with much want, and more disgrace
In a foul Marsh was glad to hide his face.
A divine hand swayes all mankind, and wee
Of one short houre have not the certaintie;

Hadst thou one day told me, the time should be
When the *Getes* bowes, and th'*Euxine* I should see,
I should have check'd thy madness, and have thought
Th' hadst need of all *Anticira* in a draught;   70
And yet 'tis come to passe! nor though I might
Some things foresee, could I procure a sight
Of my whole destinie, and free my state
From those eternall, higher *tyes* of fate.
Leave then thy pride, and though now *brave* and *high*,
Think thou mayst be as *poore* and *low* as *I.*

Tristium Lib. 3°. *Eleg.* 3ª.
To his Wife at *Rome*, when he was sick.

Dearest! if you those fair Eyes (wondring) stick
On this strange Character, know, *I am sick.*
Sick in the *skirts* of the lost world, where I
Breath hopeless of all Comforts, but to dye.
What heart (think'st thou?) have I in this sad seat
Tormented 'twixt the *Sauromate* and *Gete*?
Nor *aire* nor *water* please; their very *skie*
Looks strange and unaccustom'd to my Eye,
I scarse dare breath it, and I know not how
The Earth that bears me shewes unpleasant now.   10
Nor *Diet* here's, nor *lodging* for my Ease,
Nor any one that *studies* a disease;
No friend to comfort me, none to defray
With smooth discourse the Charges of the day.
All tir'd alone I lye, and (thus) what e're
Is absent, and at *Rome* I fancy here,
But when thou com'st, I blot the *Airie Scrowle,*
And give thee full possession of my soule,
Thee (absent) I embrace, thee only *voice,*
And night and day *bely* a Husbands Joyes;   20
Nay, of thy name so oft I mention make
That I am thought distracted for thy sake;
When my tir'd Spirits faile, and my sick heart
Drawes in that *fire* which actuates each part,
If any say, th'art come! I force my pain,
And hope to see thee, gives me life again.
Thus I for thee, whilst thou (perhaps) more blest
Careless of me doest breath all peace and rest,

Which yet I think not, for (*Deare Soule!*) too well
Know I thy griefe, since my first woes befell.   30
But if strict heav'n my stock of dayes hath spun
And with my life my errour wilbe gone,
How easie then (*O Cæsar!*) wer't for thee
To pardon one, that now doth cease to be?
That I might yeeld my native aire this breath,
And banish not my ashes after death;
Would thou hadst either spar'd me untill dead,
Or with my bloud redeem'd my absent head,
Thou shouldst have had both freely, but O! thou
Wouldst have me live to dye an *Exile* now.   40
And must I then from *Rome* so far meet death,
And double by the place my losse of breath?
Nor in my last of houres on my own bed
(In the sad Conflict) rest my dying head?
Nor my soules *Whispers* (the last pledge of life,)
Mix with the tears and kisses of a wife?
My last words none must treasure, none will rise
And (with a teare) seal up my vanquish'd Eyes,
Without these *Rites* I dye, distrest in all
The *splendid sorrowes* of a Funerall,   50
Unpittied, and unmourn'd for, my sad head
In a strange Land goes friendless to the dead.
When thou hear'st this, O how thy faithfull soule
Will sink, whilst griefe doth ev'ry part controule!
How often wilt thou look this way, and Crie,
O where is't yonder that my love doth lye!
Yet spare these tears, and mourn not now for me,
Long since (*dear heart!*) have I been dead to thee,
Think then I dyed, when *Thee* and *Rome* I lost
That death to me more griefe then this hath Cost;   60
Now, if thou canst (but thou canst not) *best wife*
Rejoyce, my Cares are ended with my life,
At least, yeeld not to sorrowes, frequent use
Should make these miseries to thee no newes.
And here I wish my Soul died with my breath
And that no part of me were free from death,
For, if it be Immortall, and outlives
The body, as *Pythagoras* believes,
Betwixt these *Sarmates ghosts*, a *Roman* I
Shall wander, vext to all Eternitie.   70

But thou (for after death I shall be free,)
Fetch home these bones, and what is left of me,
A few *Flowres* give them, with some *Balme*, and lay
Them in some *Suburb-grave* hard by the way,
And to Informe posterity, who's there,
This sad Inscription let my marble weare,
   „ *Here lyes the soft-soul'd Lecturer of Love,*
   „ *Whose envy'd wit did his own ruine prove.*
But thou, (who e'r thou beest, that passing by
Lendst to this *sudden stone* a *hastie* Eye,)   80
If e'r thou knew'st of *Love* the sweet disease,
Grudge not to say, *May* Ovid *rest in peace !*
This for my tombe : but in my books they'l see
More strong and lasting Monuments of mee,
Which I believe (though fatall) will afford
An Endless name unto their ruin'd Lord.
   And now thus gone, It rests for love of me
Thou shewst some sorrow to my memory ;
Thy Funerall offrings to my ashes beare
With Wreathes of *Cypresse* bath'd in many a teare,   90
Though nothing there but dust of me remain,
Yet shall that *Dust* perceive thy pious pain.
But I have done, and my tyr'd sickly head
Though I would fain write more, desires the bed ;
Take then this word (perhaps my last to tell)
Which though I want, I wish it thee, *Fare-well.*

Ausonii Cupido, Edyl. 6.

In those blest fields of *Everlasting aire*
(Where to a *Myrtle*-grove the soules repaire
Of deceas'd *Lovers,*) the sad, thoughtfull ghosts
Of *Injur'd Ladyes* meet, where each accoasts
The other with a sigh, whose very breath
Would break a heart, and (*kind Soules !*) love in death.
A thick wood clouds their *walks,* where day scarse peeps,
And on each hand Cypresse and Poppey *sleepes,*
The drowsie Rivers *slumber,* and *Springs* there
Blab not, but softly melt into a teare,   10
A sickly dull aire *fans* them, which can have
When most in force scarce breath to *build* a wave.

80 Eye,) *GC* : Eye, *1651*

On either bank through the still shades appear
A *Scene* of pensive flowres, whose bosomes wear
Drops of a *Lover's* bloud, the *Emblem'd* truths
Of deep despair, and Love-slain *Kings* and *Youths.*
The *Hyacinth*, and self-enamour'd Boy
Narcissus flourish there, with *Venus* Joy
The spruce *Adonis*, and that *Prince* whose flowre
Hath sorrow languag'd on him to this houre ;   20
All sad with love they hang their heads, and grieve
As if their passions in each leafe did *live* ;
And here (*alas !*) these soft-soul'd Ladies stray,
And (oh ! too late !) treason in love betray.
  Her blasted birth sad *Semele* repeats,
And with her *tears* would quench the thund'rers *heats*
Then shakes her bosome, as if fir'd again,
And fears another lightnings *flaming train.*
The lovely *Procris* (here) bleeds, sighes, and swounds
Then wakes, and kisses him that gave her wounds.   30
Sad *Hero* holds a torch forth, and doth light
Her lost *Leander* through the waves and night.
Her *Boateman* desp'rate *Sapho* still admires,
And nothing but the *Sea* can quench her *fires.*
Distracted *Phœdra* with a restless Eye
Her disdain'd Letters reads, then casts them by.
Rare, faithfull *Thysbe* (sequestred from these)
A silent, unseen sorrow doth best please,
For her *Loves* sake, and last *good-night*, poor she
Walks in the shadow of a *Mulberrie.*   40
Neer her young *Canace* with *Dido* sits
A lovely Couple, but of desp'rate wits,
Both dy'd alike, both pierc'd their tender brests,
This with her *Fathers* Sword, that with her *Guests.*
Within the thickest *textures* of the Grove
Diana in her *Silver-beams* doth rove,
Her Crown of stars the *pitchie aire* Invades,
And with a faint light *gilds* the silent shades,
Whilst her sad thoughts fixt on her *sleepie Lover*
To *Latmos*-hill, and his retirements move her.   50
A thousand more through the wide, darksome wood
Feast on their cares, the *Maudlin-Lovers* food,

29 *Procris*] *Pocris 1651*

For *griefe* and *absence* doe but *Edge* desire,
And Death is *fuell* to a Lovers *fire.*

 To see these *Trophies* of his wanton bow
Cupid comes in, and all in triumph now
(Rash, unadvised Boy !) disperseth round
The sleepie Mists, his *Wings* and *quiver* wound
With noise the quiet aire. This sudden stirre
Betrayes his *godship*, and as we from far   60
A clouded, sickly *Moon* observe, so they
Through the *false Mists* his *Ecclyps'd torch* betray.
A hot pursute they make, and though with care,
And a slow wing he softly *stems* the aire,
Yet they (as subtill now as he) surround
His silenc'd course, and with the thick night bound
Surprize the *Wag*. As in a dream we strive
To voyce our thoughts, & vainly would revive
Our Entraunc'd tongues, but can not speech enlarge
'Till the Soule wakes and reassumes her Charge, 70
So joyous of their *Prize*, they flock about
And vainly *Swell* with an *Imagin'd* shout.

 Far in these shades, and melancholy Coasts
A *Myrtle* growes, well known to all the ghosts,
Whose stretch'd top (like a *great man* rais'd by Fate)
Looks big, and scorns his neighbours low estate ;
His *leavy arms* into a *green Cloud* twist,
And on each Branch doth *sit* a lazie mist.
A fatall tree, and luckless to the gods,
Where for *disdain* in life (loves *worst* of *Ods*,) 80
The *Queen* of shades, fair *Proserpine* did rack
The sad *Adonis*, hither now they pack
This little *God*, where, first disarm'd, they *bind*
His skittish wings, then both his hands behind
His back they tye, and thus secur'd at last
The *peevish wanton* to the tree make fast.
Here at adventure without *Judge* or Jurie
He is condemn'd, while with united furie
They all assaile him ; As a thiefe at Bar
Left to the Law, and mercy of his Star,   90
Hath *Bills* heap'd on him, and is question'd there
By all the men that have been rob'd that year,

62 Ecclyps'd] Ecelyps'd 1651 63 they] thy 1651

So now what ever *Fate*, or their own *Will*
Scor'd up in life, *Cupid* must pay the bill.
Their *Servants* falshood, Jealousie, disdain,
And all the plagues that *abus'd Maids* can feign,
Are layd on him, and then to heighten spleen
Their own deaths crown the summe.   Prest thus between
His faire accusers, 'tis at last decreed,
He by those weapons, that they died, should bleed.   100
One grasps an *airie Sword*, a second holds
Illusive *fire*, and in *vain*, wanton folds
Belyes a flame ; Others lesse kind appear
To let him bloud, and from the purple tear
Create a *Rose*.   But *Sapho* all this while
Harvests the aire, and from a thicken'd pile
Of Clouds like *Leucas-top*, spreads underneath
A *Sea* of *Mists*, the peacefull billowes breath
Without all noise, yet so exactly move
They seem to *Chide*, but distant from above   110
Reach not the eare, and (thus prepar'd) at once
She doth o'rwhelm him with the *airie Sconce*.
Amidst these tumults, and as fierce as they
Venus steps in, and without thought, or stay
Invades her *Son*; her old disgrace is cast
Into the *Bill*, when *Mars* and *Shee* made *fast*
In their Embraces were expos'd to all
The *Scene* of gods stark naked in their *fall*.
Nor serves a *verball* penance, but with hast
From her fair brow (O happy flowres so plac'd!)   120
She tears a *Rosie garland*, and with this
Whips the *untoward Boy*, they gently kisse
His *snowie skin*, but she with angry hast
Doubles her strength, untill bedew'd at last
With a thin bloudie sweat, their *Innate Red*,
(As if griev'd with the Act) grew pale and dead.
This *layd* their spleen : And now (*kind soules !*) no more
They'l punish him, the torture that he bore,
Seems greater then his crime ; with joynt Consent
Fate is made guilty, and *he* Innocent.   130
As in a dream with dangers we contest,
And *fictious pains* seem to afflict our rest,
So frighted only in these shades of night
Cupid (got loose) stole to the upper light,

Where ever since (for malice unto these)
The *spitefull Ape* doth either *Sex* displease.
But O that had these *Ladyes* been so wise
To keep his *Arms*, and give him but his *Eyes*!

Boet. Lib. 1. *Metrum* 1.

I whose first year flourish'd with youthfull verse,
In slow, sad numbers now my griefe reherse;
A broken stile my sickly lines afford,
And only tears give weight unto my words;
Yet neither fate nor force my Muse cou'd fright
The only faithfull Consort of my flight;
Thus what was once my green years greatest glorie,
Is now my Comfort, grown decay'd and hoarie,
For killing Cares th'Effects of age spurr'd on
That griefe might find a fitting Mansion;   10
O'r my young head runs an untimely gray,
And my loose skin shrinks at my blouds decay.
Happy the man! whose death in prosp'rous years
Strikes not, nor shuns him in his age and tears.
But O how deafe is she to hear the Crie
Of th' opprest Soule, or shut the weeping Eye!
While treacherous Fortune with slight honours fed
My first estate, she almost drown'd my head,
But now since (clouded thus) she hides those rayes,
Life adds unwelcom'd length unto my dayes;   20
Why then, my friends, Judg'd you my state so good?
He that may fall once, never firmly stood.

Metrum 2.

O in what haste with Clouds and Night
Ecclyps'd, and having lost her light,
The dull Soule whom distraction rends
Into outward Darkness tends!
How often (by these mists made blind,)
Have earthly cares opprest the mind!
   This Soule sometimes wont to survey
The spangled *Zodiacks firie way*
Saw th'early Sun in Roses drest
With the Coole Moons unstable Crest,   10

Met. 1.   5 fate *Er and some copies of 1651*: faith *other copies of 1651*

And whatsoever wanton Star
In various Courses neer or far
Pierc'd through the orbs, he cou'd full well
Track all her Journey, and would tell
Her Mansions, turnings, Rise and fall,
By Curious Calculation all.
Of sudden winds the hidden Cause,
And why the Calm Seas quiet face
With Impetuous waves is Curld,
What spirit wheeles th'harmonious world,   20
Or why a Star dropt in the *West*
Is seen to rise again by *East*,
Who gives the warm Spring temp'rate houres
Decking the Earth with spicie flowres,
Or how it Comes (for mans recruit)
That Autumne yeelds both Grape and fruit,
With many other Secrets, he
Could shew the Cause and Mysterie.
　　But now that light is almost out,
And the brave Soule lyes Chain'd about   30
With outward Cares, whose pensive weight
Sinks down her Eyes from their first height,
And clean Contrary to her birth
Poares on this vile and foolish Earth.

Metrum 4.

Whose calme soule in a settled state
Kicks under foot the frowns of Fate,
And in his fortunes bad or good
Keeps the same temper in his bloud,
Not him the flaming Clouds above,
Nor *Ætna's* fierie tempests move,
No fretting seas from shore to shore
Boyling with Indignation o're
Nor burning thunderbolt that can
A mountain shake, can stirre this man.   10
Dull Cowards then ! why should we start
To see these tyrants act their part ?
Nor hope, nor fear what may befall
And you disarm their malice all.

　　28 Mysterie. *C* : Mysterie, *1651*

But who doth faintly fear, or wish
And sets no law to what is his,
Hath lost the buckler, and (poor Elfe!)
Makes up a Chain to bind himselfe.

Metrum 5.

O thou great builder of this starrie frame
Who fixt in thy eternall throne dost tame
The rapid Spheres, and lest they jarre
Hast giv'n a law to ev'ry starre!
Thou art the Cause that now the Moon
With full orbe dulls the starres, and soon
Again growes dark, her light being done,
The neerer still she's to the Sun.
Thou in the early hours of night
Mak'st the coole Evening-star shine bright,   10
And at Sun-rising ('cause the least)
Look pale and sleepie in the East.
Thou, when the leafes in Winter stray,
Appointst the Sun a shorter way,
And in the pleasant Summer-light
With nimble houres doest wing the night.
Thy hand the various year quite through
Discreetly tempers, that what now
The North-wind tears from ev'ry tree
In Spring again restor'd we see.   20
Then what the *winter-starrs* between
The furrowes in meer seed have seen
The Dog-star since (grown up and born)
Hath burnt in stately, full-ear'd Corn.
  Thus by Creations law controll'd
All things their proper stations hold
Observing (as thou didst intend)
Why they were made, and for what end.
Only humane actions thou
Hast no Care of, but to the flow
And Ebbe of Fortune leav'st them all,   30
Hence th' Innocent endures that thrall
Due to the wicked, whilst alone
They sit possessours of his throne,

The Just are kill'd, and Vertue lyes
Buried in obscurities,
And (which of all things is most sad)
The good man suffers by the bad.
No perjuries, nor damn'd pretence
Colour'd with holy, lying sense   40
Can them annoy, but when they mind
To try their force, which most men find,
They from the highest sway of things
Can pull down great, and pious Kings.
   O then at length, thus loosely hurl'd
Look on this miserable world
Who e'r thou art, that from above
Doest in such order all things move !
And let not man (of divine art
Not the least, nor vilest part)   50
By Casuall evills thus bandied, be
The sport of fates obliquitie.
But with that faith thou guid'st the heaven,
Settle this Earth, and make them even.

Metrum 6.

When the Crabs fierce Constellation
Burns with the beams of the bright Sun,
Then he that will goe out to sowe,
Shall never reap where he did plough,
But in stead of Corn may rather
The old worlds diet, Accorns gather.
Who the Violet doth love
Must seek her in the flowrie grove,
But never when the *Norths* cold wind
The *Russet* fields with frost doth bind.   10
If in the Spring-time (to no end)
The tender Vine for Grapes we bend,
Wee shall find none, for only (still)
Autumne doth the Wine-presse fill.
   Thus for all things (in the worlds prime)
The wise God seal'd their proper time,
Nor will permit those seasons he
Ordain'd by turns, should mingled be

42 find, *C* : find. *1651*

Then whose wild actions out of season
Crosse to nature, and her reason,   20
Would by new wayes old orders rend,
Shall never find a happy End.

Metrum 7.

Curtain'd with Clouds in a dark night
The Stars cannot send forth their light.
And if a sudden Southern blast
The Sea in rolling waves doth cast,
That angrie Element doth boile,
And from the deep with stormy Coile
Spues up the Sands, which in short space
Scatter, and puddle his Curl'd face ;
Then those Calme waters, which but now
Stood clear as heavens unclouded brow,   10
And like transparent glasse did lye
Open to ev'ry searchers Eye,
Look foulely stirr'd, and (though desir'd)
Resist the sight, because bemir'd,
So often from a high hills brow
Some Pilgrim-spring is seen to flow,
And in a straight line keep her Course
'Till from a Rock with headlong force
Some broken peece blocks up her way
And forceth all her streams astray.   20
    Then thou that with inlightned Rayes,
Wouldst see the truth, and in her wayes
Keep without *Errour* ; neither fear
The future, nor too much give ear
To present Joyes ; And give no scope
To griefe, nor much to flatt'ring hope.
For when these Rebels raign, the mind
Is both a Pris'ner, and stark blind.

Lib. 2. Metrum 1.

Fortune (when with rash hands she quite turmoiles
The state of things, and in tempestuous foiles
Comes whirling like *Euripus*,) beats quite down
With headlong force the highest Monarchs crown
And in his place unto the throne doth fetch
The despis'd looks of some mechanick wretch.

So Jests at tears and miseries, is proud,
And laughs to hear her vassals gronc aloud.
These are her sports, thus she her wheele doth drive
And plagues man with her blind prerogative;　　　10
Nor is't a favour of Inferiour strain,
If once kickt down, she lets him rise again.

Metrum 2.

If with an open, bounteous hand
(Wholly left at Mans Command)
Fortune should in one rich flow
As many heaps on him bestow
Of massie gold, as there be sands
Tost by the waves and winds rude bands,
Or bright stars in a Winter-night
Decking their silent Orbs with light,
Yet would his lust know no restraints,
Nor cease to weep in sad Complaints.　　　10
Though heaven should his vowes reguard,
And in a prodigall reward
Return him all he could implore,
Adding new honours to his store,
Yet all were nothing.　Goods in sight
Are scorn'd, and lust in greedy flight
Layes out for more; What measure then
Can tame these wild desires of men?
Since all wee give both last and first
Doth but inflame, and feed their thirst;　　　20
For how can he be rich, who 'midst his store
Sits sadly pining, and believes he's poore.

Metrum 3.

When the Sun from his Rosie bed
The dawning light begins to shed,
The drowsie sky uncurtains round,
And the (but now bright) stars all drown'd
In one great light, look dull and tame,
And homage his victorious flame.
Thus, when the warm *Etesian* wind
The Earth's seald bosome doth unbind,

Straight she her various store discloses,
And purples every Grove with Roses ;   10
But if the Souths tempestuous breath
Breaks forth, those blushes pine to death.
Oft in a quiet sky the deep
With unmov'd waves seems fast asleep,
And oft again the blustring North
In angrie heaps provokes them forth.
   If then this world, which holds all Nations,
Suffers it selfe such alterations,
That not this mighty, massie frame,
Nor any part of it can Claime   20
One certain course, why should man prate,
Or Censure the designs of Fate ?
Why from fraile honours, and goods lent
Should he expect things permanent ?
Since 'tis enacted by divine decree
That nothing mortall shall eternall be.

Metrum 4.

Who wisely would for his retreat
Build a secure and lasting seat,
Where stov'd in silence he may sleep
Beneath the *Wind*, above the *Deep* ;
Let him th' high hils leave on one hand,
And on the other the false sand ;
The first to winds lyes plain and even
From all the blustring points of heaven ;
The other hollow and unsure,
No weight of building will endure.   10
Avoyding then the envied state
Of buildings bravely situate,
Remember thou thy selfe to lock
Within some low neglected Rock ;
There when fierce heaven in thunder Chides,
And winds and waves rage on all sides,
Thou happy in the quiet fense
Of thy poor Cell with small Expence
Shall lead a life serene and faire,
And scorn the anger of the aire.   20

Metrum 5.

Happy that first white age! when wee
Lived by the Earths meere Charitie,
No soft luxurious Diet then
Had Effeminated men,
No other meat, nor wine had any
Then the Course Mast, or simple honey,
And by the Parents care layd up
Cheap *Berries* did the Children sup.
No pompous weare was in those dayes
Of gummie Silks, or Skarlet bayes,   10
Their beds were on some flowrie brink
And clear Spring-water was their drink.
The shadie Pine in the Suns heat
Was their Coole and known Retreat,
For then 'twas not cut down, but stood
The youth and glory of the wood.
The daring Sailer with his slaves
Then had not cut the swelling waves,
Nor for desire of forraign store
Seen any but his native shore.   20
No stirring Drum had scarr'd that age,
Nor the shrill Trumpets active rage,
No wounds by bitter hatred made
With warm bloud soil'd the shining blade;
For how could hostile madness arm
An age of love to publick harm?
When Common Justice none withstood,
Nor sought rewards for spilling bloud.
  O that at length our age would raise
Into the temper of those dayes!   30
But (worse then *Ætna's* fires!) debate
And Avarice inflame our state.
Alas! who was it that first found
Gold hid of purpose under ground,
That sought out Pearles, and div'd to find
Such pretious perils for mankind!

31 worse] worst *1651*

G 2

Metrum 6.

He that thirsts for glories prize,
    Thinking that the top of all
Let him view th'Expansed skies,
    And the Earths Contracted ball,
'Twill shame him then, the name he wan
Fils not the short *walk* of one man.

2.

O why vainly strive you then
    To shake off the bands of Fate,
Though fame through the world of men
    Should in all tongues your names relate,   10
And with proud titles swell that storie
The Darke grave scorns your brightest glorie.

3.

There with Nobles beggers sway,
    And Kings with Commons share one dust,
What newes of *Brutus* at this day,
    Or *Fabricius* the Just?
Some rude *Verse* Cut in stone, or led
    Keeps up the names, but they are dead.

4.

So shall you, one day (past reprieve)
    Lye (perhaps) without a name,   20
But if dead you think to live
    By this aire of humane fame,
Know, when time stops that posthume breath,
You must endure a second death.

Metrum 7.

That the world in constant *force*
Varies her *Concordant course*;
That *seeds* jarring *hot* and *cold*
Doe the *breed* perpetuall hold;
That in his golden Coach the *Sun*
Brings the *Rosie day* still on;
That the *Moon* swayes all those *lights*
Which *Hesper* ushers to *dark nights*

19 shall you, *M*: shall, you *1651*: shall you *GC*

That *alternate tydes* be found
The Seas *ambitious* waves to bound,　　　　10
Lest o'r the wide Earth without End
Their *fluid Empire* should extend;
All this frame of *things* that *be*,
Love which rules *Heaven, Land,* and *Sea,*
Chains, keeps, orders as we see.
This, if the raines he once cast by,
All things that now by turns comply,
Would fall to discord, and this frame
Which now by sociall faith they tame,
And comely orders in that fight　　　　20
And jarre of things would perish quite.
This in a holy league of peace
Keeps King and People with Increase;
And in the sacred nuptiall bands
Tyes up chast hearts with willing hands,
And this keeps firm without all doubt
Friends by his bright Instinct found out.
　　O happy Nation then were you
If love which doth all things subdue,
That rules the spacious heav'n, and brings　　　　30
Plenty and Peace upon his wings,
Might rule you too! and without guile
Settle once more this floting Ile!

Casimirus, Lib. 4. *Ode* 28.

All-mighty *Spirit!* thou that by
Set *turns* and *changes* from thy high
And glorious *throne,* dost here below
Rule all, and all things dost *foreknow;*
Can those *bliud plots* wee here discusse
Please thee, as thy *wise Counsels* us?
When thou thy *blessings* here dost strow,
And poure on *Earth,* we flock and flow
With *Joyous strife,* and *eager care*
Strugling which shall have the best share　　　　10
In thy *rich gifts,* just as we see
Children about *Nuts* disagree.
Some that a *Crown* have got and foyl'd
Break it; Another sees it *spoil'd*

E're it is *gotten* : Thus the *world*
Is all to *peece-meals* cut, and hurl'd
By *factious hands*, It is a *ball*
Which *Fate* and *force* divide 'twixt all
The *Sons* of *men*.   But ô good God !
While these for *dust* fight, and a *Clod*,   20
Grant that poore I may *smile*, and be
At rest, and *perfect peace* with thee.

Casimirus, Lib. 2. *Ode* 8.

It would lesse vex *distressed man*
If *Fortune* in the same *pace* ran
To *ruine* him, as he did *rise* ;
But highest *states* fall in a trice.
No *great Successe* held ever *long* :
A restless *fate* afflicts the throng
Of *Kings* and *Commons*, and lesse dayes
Serve to *destroy* them, then to *raise*.
Good luck *smiles* once an age, but *bad*
Makes *Kingdomes* in a *minute* sad,   10
And ev'ry *houre* of *life* wee drive,
Hath o're us a *Prerogative*.
   Then leave (by *wild Impatience* driv'n,
And *rash resents*,) to rayle at *heav'n*,
Leave an *unmanly, weak complaint*
That *Death* and *Fate* have no restraint.
In the same houre that gave thee *breath*,
Thou hadst ordain'd thy houre of *death*,
But *he* lives *most*, who here will *buy*
With a few tears, *Eternitie*.   20

Casimirus, Lib. 3 *Ode* 22.

Let not thy *youth* and *false delights*
Cheat thee of *life* ; Those *headdy flights*
But wast thy *time*, which posts away
Like *winds* unseen, and swift as they.
Beauty is but meer *paint*, whose *die*
With times *breath* will *dissolve* and *flye*,
'Tis *wax*, 'tis *water*, 'tis a *glasse*
It *melts, breaks*, and *away* doth *passe*

'Tis like a *Rose* which in the *dawne*
The *aire* with gentle breath doth *fawne*   10
And *whisper* too, but in the houres
Of *night* is sullied with smart showres.
Life spent, is wish'd for but in vain,
Nor can past *years* come back again.
  Happy the *Man*! who in this *vale*
Redeems his time, shutting out all
Thoughts of the *world*, whose *longing Eyes*
Are ever *Pilgrims* in the *skyes*,
That views his *bright home*, and desires
To *shine* amongst those *glorious fires*.   20

Casimirus Lyric. Lib. 3. *Ode* 23.

'Tis not *rich furniture* and *gems*
With *Cedar-roofes*, and ancient *stems*,
Nor yet a *plenteous, lasting floud*
Of *gold*, that makes man *truly good*.
Leave to Inquire in what *faire fields*
A *River* runs which *much gold* yeelds,
Vertue alone is the *rich prize*
Can purchase *stars*, and buy the *skies*.
Let others build with *Adamant*,
Or pillars of *carv'd Marble* plant,   10
Which *rude* and *rough* sometimes did dwell
Far under *earth*, and neer to *hell*.
But *richer* much (from *death* release)
Shines in the *fresh groves* of the *East*
The *Phœnix*, or those *fish* that dwell
With *silver'd scales* in *Hiddekel*.
Let others with rare, various *Pearls*
Their *garments* dresse, and in *forc'd Curls*
Bind up their *locks*, look *big* and *high*,
And shine in *robes* of *Scarlet-die*.   20
But in my thoughts more *glorious* far
Those *native stars*, and *speckles* are
Which *birds* wear, or the *spots* which wee
In *Leopards* dispersed see.
The harmless *sheep* with her warm *fleece*
Cloathes *man*, but who his *dark heart* sees
Shall find a *Wolfe* or *Fox* within
That kills the *Castor* for his *skin*.

Vertue alone, and nought else can
A diffrence make 'twixt *beasts* and *man*,   30
And on her *wings* above the *Spheres*
To the *true light* his *spirit* bears.

Casimirus, Lib. 4. Ode 15.

Nothing on *Earth*, nothing at all
Can be exempted from the *thrall*
Of peevish *weariness* ! The *Sun*
Which our *fore-fathers* Judg'd to run
Clear and *unspotted*, in our dayes
Is tax'd with *sullen*, *Ecclips'd rayes*.
What ever in the *glorious skie*
Man sees, his rash, *audacious Eye*
Dares Censure it, and in meer *spite*
At *distance* will condemn the *light*.   10
The *wholsome mornings*, whose *beams* cleer
Those *hills* our *fathers* walkt on here
Wee fancy not, nor the *Moons* light
Which through their *windows* shin'd at *night*,
Wee change the *Aire* each year, and scorn
Those *Seates*, in which we first were *borne*.
Some nice, affected *wand'rers* love
Belgia's mild winters, others remove
For want of *health* and *honestie*
To *Summer* it in *Italie* ;   20
But to no end : The *disease* still
Sticks to his *Lord*, and kindly will
To *Venice* in a *Barge* repaire,
Or *Coach* it to *Vienna's* aire,
And then (too late with *home* Content,)
They leave this *wilfull banishment*.
   But he, whose *Constancie* makes sure
His *mind* and *mansion*, lives secure
From such *vain tasks*, can *dine* and *sup*
Where his *old parents* bred him up.   30
Content (no doubt !) most times doth dwell
In *Countrey-shades*, or to some *Cell*
Confines it selfe, and can alone
Make simple *straw*, a Royall *Throne*.

11 cleer] cheer *G*

Olor Iscanus.

Casimirus, Lib. 4. *Ode* 13.

If *weeping Eyes* could wash away
Those *Evills* they mourn for *night and day*,
Then gladly I to *cure* my *fears*
With my best *Jewells* would buy *tears*.
But as *dew* feeds the growing *Corn*,
So *Crosses* that are grown *forlorn*
Increase with *griefe*, *teares* make *teares* way,
And *cares* kept up, keep *cares* in *pay*.
That *wretch* whom *Fortune* finds to *feare*,
And *melting* still into a *teare*,   10
She *strikes* more *boldly*, but a *face*
Silent and *drie* doth her *amaze*.
Then leave thy *teares*, and tedious *tale*
Of what thou doest *misfortunes* call,
What thou by *weeping* think'st to *ease*,
Doth by that *Passion* but *Increase*;
Hard things to *Soft* will never yield,
'Tis the *drie Eye* that wins the field;
A noble *patience* quells the *spite*
Of *Fortune*, and *disarms* her quite.   20

The Praise of a Religious life by
Mathias Casimirus.
In Answer to that Ode of *Horace*,

Beatus Ille qui procul negotiis, &c.

Flaccus not so: That worldly *He*
Whom in the Countreys *shade* we see
Ploughing his own *fields*, seldome can
Be justly stil'd, *The Blessed man*.
    That title only fits a *Saint*,
Whose free thoughts far above restraint
And weighty Cares, can gladly part
With *house* and *lands*, and leave the smart
Litigious troubles, and lowd strife
Of this world for a better life.   10
He fears no *Cold*, nor *heat* to blast
His *Corn*, for his *Accounts* are cast,

He *sues* no man, nor stands in Awe
Of the *devouring Courts* of Law;
But all his time he spends in *tears*
For the *Sins* of his youthfull years,
Or having tasted those *rich Joyes*
Of a Conscience without *noyse*
Sits in some fair *shade*, and doth give
To his *wild thoughts* rules how to live.   20

He in the *Evening*, when on high
The *Stars* shine in the *silent skye*
Beholds th'*eternall flames* with mirth,
And *globes* of *light* more large then *Earth*,
Then weeps for *Joy*, and through his tears
Looks on the *fire-enamel'd* Spheres,
Where with his *Saviour* he would be
Lifted above mortalitie.
Mean while the *golden stars* doe set,
And the *slow-Pilgrim* leave all wet   30
With his own tears, which flow so fast
They make his *sleeps* light, and soon past.
By this, the *Sun* o're night *deceast*
Breaks in *fresh Blushes* from the *East*,
When mindfull of his former *falls*
With *strong Cries* to his *God* he calls,
And with such *deep-drawn sighes* doth move
That he turns *anger* into *love*.

In the Calme *Spring*, when the Earth *bears*,
And feeds on *Aprils breath*, and *tears*,   40
His Eyes accustom'd to the *skyes*
Find here *fresh objects*, and like *spyes*
Or busie *Bees* search the soft *flowres*
Contemplate the *green fields*, and *Bowres*,
Where he in *Veyles*, and *shades* doth see
The *back Parts* of the *Deitye*.
Then sadly sighing sayes, ,, *O how*
,, *These flowres With hasty, stretch'd heads grow*
,, *And strive for heav'n, but rooted here*
,, *Lament the distance with a teare!*   50
,, *The Honey-suckles Clad in white*,
,, *The Rose in Red point to the light*,
,, *And the Lillies hollow and bleak*
,, *Look, as if they would something speak*,

,, *They sigh at night to each soft gale,*
,, *And at the day-spring weep it all.*
,, *Shall I then only (wretched I!)*
,, *Opprest with Earth, on Earth still lye?*
Thus speaks he to the neighbour trees
And many sad *Soliloquies*   60
To *Springs,* and *Fountaines* doth impart,
Seeking God with a longing heart.
   But if to ease his busie breast
He thinks of *home,* and taking rest,
A *Rurall Cott,* and *Common fare*
Are all his *Cordials* against *Care.*
There at the *doore* of his low *Cell*
Under some *shade,* or neer some *Well*
Where the *Coole Poplar* growes, his *Plate*
Of Common *Earth,* without more *state*   70
Expect their *Lord.*   *Salt* in a *shell,*
Green *Cheese,* thin *beere, Draughts* that will *tell*
No *Tales,* a *hospitable Cup,*
With some *fresh berries* doe make up
His healthfull feast, nor doth he wish
For the fatt *Carp,* or a rare dish
Of *Lucrine Oysters*; The swift *Quist*
Or *Pigeon* sometimes (if he list)
With the *slow Goose* that loves the *stream,*
Fresh, various *Sallads,* and the *Bean*   80
By Curious *Pallats* never sought,
And to Close with, some Cheap unbought
Dish for *digestion,* are the most
And Choicest *dainties* he can *boast.*
   Thus feasted, to the *flowrie Groves,*
Or pleasant *Rivers* he removes,
Where neer some *fair Oke* hung with Mast
He shuns the *Souths* Infectious blast.
On shadie *banks* sometimes he lyes,
Sometimes the open *Current tryes,*   90
Where with his *line* and *feather'd flye*
He sports, and takes the *Scaly frie.*
Mean-while each *hollow wood* and *hill*
Doth ring with *lowings* long and shrill,

     64 rest, *GC* : rest *1651*

And shadie *Lakes* with *Rivers* deep,
Eccho the *bleating* of the *Sheep.*
The *Black-bird* with the pleasant *Thrush*
And *Nightingale* in ev'ry Bush
Choice *Musick* give, and *Shepherds* play
Unto their *flocks* some loving *Lay* ;   100
The thirsty *Reapers* in thick throngs
Return home from the *field* with Songs,
And the *Carts* loden with ripe *Corn*
Come groning to the well-stor'd *Barn.*
   Nor passe wee by as the least good,
A *peacefull, loving neighbourhood,*
Whose *honest Wit,* and *Chast discourse*
Make none (by hearing it) the *worse,*
But *Innocent* and *merry* may
Help (without *Sin*) to spend the day.   110
Could now the *Tyrant-usurer*
Who *plots* to be a *Purchaser*
Of his poor neighbours *seat,* but taste
These *true delights,* ô with what haste
And hatred of his wayes would he
Renounce his *Jewish Crueltie,*
And those *Curs'd summes* which poor men borrow
On *use* to day, *remit* to morrow !

Ad fluvium Iscam.

Isca parens florum, placido qui spumeus ore
    Lambis lapillos aureos,
Qui mœstos hyacinthos, & picti ἄνθεα *tophi*
    Mulces susurris humidis,
Dumჶ novas pergunt menses Consumere Lunae
    Cœlumჶ mortales terit,
Accumulas cum Sole dies, œvumჶ per omne
    Fidelis *Induras* latex,
O quis Inaccessos & quali murmure lucos
    Murumq; *Solaris* nemus!   10
Per te discerpti credo Thracis *ire querelas*
    Plectrumჶ divini senis.

Venerabili viro, præceptori suo olim
& semper Colendissimo M^{ro.}
Mathæo Herbert.

Quod vixi, Mathæe, *dedit* Pater, *hæc tamen olim*
  Vita fluat, nec erit fas meminisse datam.
Ultrà Curâsti Solers, periturâ& mecum
  Nomina post Cineres *das resonare* meos.
Divide discipulum: brevis hæc & lubrica nostri
  Pars vertat Patri, *Posthuma vita* tibi.

Præstantissimo viro, Thomæ Poëllo *in*
suum de Elementis opticæ libellum.

Vivaces *oculorum* Ignes & lumina dia
  Fixit in angusto *maximus* orbe *Deus,*
Ille Explorantes radios *dedit,* & vaga lustra
  In quibus Intuitûs *lex& modus& latent.*
Hos tacitos Jactus, lususq; volubilis orbis
  Pingis in Exiguo, *magne Poëlle,* libro,
Excursusq; situsq;, *ut* Lynceus opticus, *edis*
  Quot& modis fallunt, *quot& adhibenda* fides.
Æmula naturæ manus *! & mens Conscia cœli !*
  Illa videre dedit, *vestra videre* docet.   10

Ad Echum.

O Quæ frondosæ per amœna Cubilia *sylvæ*
  Nympha volas, *luco& loquax spatiaris in alto,*
Annosi numen *nemoris, saltus& verendi*
  Effatum, *cui sola placent* postrema *relatu !*
Te per Narcissi *morientis verba, preces&*
Per pueri Lassatam animam, & Conamina *vitæ*
  Ultima, *palantis& precor* suspiria *linguæ.*
Da quo secretæ hæc Incædua devia *sylvæ,*
  Anfractusq; *loci dubios,* & lustra *repandam.*
Sic tibi perpetuâ *(merito&) hæc regna* Juventâ   10
  Luxurient, *dabitur& tuis, sinè fine,* viretis

Præstantissimo viro.   1 Ignes] *Ignes, El. Opt.*   2 *Deus,] Deus ; El. Opt.*
6 *magne*] docte *El. Opt.*   7 *Excursusq; situsq;* (ut *Lynceus opticus*) edis,
El. Opt.
  Ad Echum.   4 *relatu Er* : *relatûs 1651.*   5 *Te per Er* : *Per te 1651.*

Intactas *Lunæ* lachrymas, & *lambere* rorem
Virgineum, *Cæliḍ* animas *haurire tepentis.*
Nec cedant ævo stellis, *sed* lucida *sempèr*
Et satiata sacro *æterni* medicamine *veris*
Ostendant longè vegetos, *ut Sydera,* vultus *!*
Sic spiret Muscata Comas, & Cynnama *passim !*
Diffundat levis umbra, in funere qualia spargit
Phœnicis rogus *aut Pancheæ* nubila *flammæ !*

OF THE
BENEFIT

Wee may get by our

ENEMIES.

A DISCOURSE

Written originally in the
Greek by *Plutarchus Chæronensis,*
tranſlated in to Latin by *I. Reynolds* Dr.
of Divinitie and lecturer of the Greeke Tongue
in *Corpus Chriſti* College In *Oxford.*

Engliſhed By H : V : *Siluriſt.*

——*Dolus , an virtus quis in hoſte requirat.*
——*fas eſt, et ab hoſte doceri.*

LONDON.
Printed for *Humphry Moſeley* and are to
be ſold at his ſhop at the ſigne of the
Princes Armes in St. Pauls
Church-yard, 1651.

Of the Benefit we may get by our Enemies.

I observe thee; O *Cornelius Pulcher*; though wholly given to
a quiet and calme course of life, Sequestred from all Publique imployments: yet out of that stillnesse, and most private Recession
to afford much fruit and satisfaction to the Publique; while with
so much sweetnes of carriage, and a kind of Native complacency
thou entertainest all comers, whose hazardous affairs cast them of
necessity upon thy most tender Retirements. And (indeed) true
it is, that such a Region, not pestered with Salvages, or Venomous beasts (as the report is of *Crete*) may be easily found; But a
Common-wealth not distempered with Envy, Emulation, Ambitious 10
heates, and Contentions (out of which, Enmity and Warres at last
breake forth) could never yet be found. For if nothing else, yet
in proces of time (which corrupts all things) our very Friendship
and Sociablenes would bring us into Distastes and Enmity. And
this it was that *Chilo* the wise thought upon, when hearing one
affirme That he had not an Enemy in the World, he return'd upon
him this Quere, *If he had ever a Friend?* But in my opinion (as
to the use now to be made of Enemies) there are in that point
many other *Secrets* which more concerne a *Prince*, and (as he is
to sway a Common-wealth burthen'd with a various and vicious 20
multitude) of more advantage and necessity to be considered.
And amongst those, I thinke that not the least, which *Xenophon*
hath left us recorded in this saying; *That it is the part of a Wise*
man, to derive Profit from his very Enemies. Upon this very Consideration (coming but of late into my mind) I resolved to make
some search and discussion, which now finished, in as few words
as the matter would permit, I have sent you to peruse; wherin
also, you shall find this care taken, that (as far as it might be) I
have avoided to touch upon any Observations formerly given you
in my Civill precepts, because I have already found you a very 30
familiar Student in those papers.

24 this *catchword 1651* : his *text 1651*   25 into *G* : nto *1651*

Mankind in that first age of the world thought it well enough with them, if they could but so keep, as not to be hurt by those many fierce, and divers kinds of wild beasts, with which the earth was then replenished; and this was the period of their atchievements, *To defend themselves.* But one day teaching another, and Posterity growing more wary than their Fathers, It was found out, that those very Creatures which their Ancestors deemed noysome and hurtfull, were of speciall use and comodiousnes unto man; so that afterwards they were not only not hurt by them, but very
10 much helpt. They fed upon their flesh, made Garments of their hair, preservatives of their blood, milk, and gaule, and defensive Arms of their skins. So that it is now much to be feared, that if Man were deprived of those Creatures, he would be driven to a subsistance more sordid and rude than the beasts themselves. Seeing then it is sufficient to some, to receive no damage from their Enemies, but the wise (as *Zenophon* affirms) will also derive profit from them; we must not now turn Infidels to his position, or crie it down for a *Paradox,* but rather make diligent Inquirie for that secret, whereby those may acquire some benefit from
20 their Enemies, who (as long as they live) shall not live without them.

The husband-man cannot make every tree fruitfull, nor the hunts-man tame every wild beast; they must therefore assay other remedies, whereby the one may deduce some furtherance from fruitles things, and the other from things untractable. Sea-water is neither good to drink, nor pleasant to the tast; notwithstanding it breeds fish, and feeds them; It serves commodiously to transport men, and maintaines with generall advantage, a rich Commerce, and Exchange of wares. When the *Satyre* upon the first *shine,* and noveltie of the fire would have entertaind it with
30 kisses and embracements, *Take heed goate* (said *Prometheus*) *or it will make thy Chin smart.* If wee kisse fire, it will burn our lips, and yet, it affords us both light and heate, and to (those that can rightly skill it) is the prime Instrument in all learned and reserved arts. I would have thee therefore to think so of thine enemie, and to consider whether his person, which otherwise wilbe ever hurtfull, and (viper-like) cannot be touched without evident danger, may not by some secret meanes be made tractable, and to afford some notable use of himselfe to thy speciall advantage. There are in nature many things unmeete for use, and altogether
40 Inconsistent and repugnant to those very ends for which they may be politickly imployed; so hast thou seene some effeminate,

32 to (those] —to those G

voluptuous constitutions to pretend sicknes, or some other infirmitie, that they might only live at more ease, and deliciousnes.
Others to procure themselves a more hardie health, have volun-
teer'd it in all maner of Drudgerie, and made their bodies subject
to the most slavish and toilesome Imploiments. Some again, as
Diogenes and *Crates*, have made Poverty and Banishment the
meanes to acquire knowledge and retirement. So *Zeno*, when it
was told him, that the ship he had sent to sea with his goods was
cast away, replies presently, *Thou hast done very well Fortune, for
now thou hast taught me to make use again of my thredbare, cast* 10
Coate. For as those living creatures which have the hardiest
stomacks, and the healthiest bodies, feed on Serpents and Scor-
pions, and concoct them, others upon Shells and Stones which by
reason of the vehemencie and heate of their spirits they turn presently into a *Chylus*, and nutriment, while the more infirme and
sickly surfeit on wines, and the best diet; so Weak understandings
corrupt the sincerest Friendship, while the Wise and solid make a
precious use of the most deadly Enmities. And truly in the first
place, that seemes unto me to be most advantagious, than which
(if rightly considered) nothing can be more grievous to our 20
Enemies; and what that is I will shew thee presently. An
Enemy is alwaies watchfull, lying *perdue* (as it were) to all thy
actions, and (seeking an occasion to mischiefe thee) runns over all
thy life with a most curious eye. He doth not only see through
Timber, Stone-walls, and Curtaines as *Lynceus* did, but perhaps
through the Bosomes and inward parts of thy Friend, thy Servant,
and thy Familiar; There (as far as he can see) he apprehends
and reads all thy Actions, dives and screws into thy most hidden
and future Intentions. Our Friends oftentimes while we linger
from them, or neglect them, fall sick, and dye unknowne to us; 30
But our Enemies cannot so much as dream, but most commonly
we inquire into it. Our inward defects, our debts, and domestick
discontents may be sooner hidden from our selves than from our
Enemies, they are the first that prie and search into those maladies.
As Vultures take from far the sent of corrupt carkasses, and
flock to them, but passe by the sound and untainted bodies;
so the diseased and vitious parts of our lives and affections
are alwaies resented by our enemies, they fly upon those soares,
handle them continually, and love to see them bleed afresh.
Let this benefit therefore redound to thee, that thou have a care 40
to live circumspectly, to be attentive to thy selfe, neither speak,
nor act any thing negligently or unadvisedly, but keep thy tongue

and thy hands within the *Lists*, and let thy maners be (as in a strict prescription of diet) uncorrupt, that thy very enemy may find no place for a just Reprehension. For such a caution as this, which bridles the affections of the mind, and drives her home into her selfe, creates in us a kind of virtuous ardour, and a stedfast resolution to lead a life blameles, and incalumniable. As those Cities which are oft-times visited, somtimes chastised by a warlike neighbour and ly subject to incursions and velitations of Armes, retain most commonly the wholesomest lawes, and strict-
10 est form of Government, so those that have their enemies for *Censours*, and are compelled (as it were) to a sober and vartuous vigilancy; though Reason in this point should be dumb, yet Necessity will tell them, that they must avoid all dissolutnes and neglect, do all things seasonably, not suffering themselves to be insensibly led away with custom, but compose and regulate their manners, least at any time they fall into some irrecoverable and destructive delinquency; for where that festivall but fatall verse is alwaies at hand

Sure Priam *will to mirth incline,*   Hom:
20   *And all that are of* Priam's *line.*   Illia:

It lulls asleep all Cautelousnes, and blinds their reason untill at last (*Priam*-like) by their own ruin they procure the mirth, and triumph of their Enemies. Wee see Stage-players in Common assemblies, and their own private assayes, remisse and negligent, not acting so accurately and to the life, as when the Theater is throng'd with judicious spectatours. But when they strive for some prize, or the masterie, they doe not only refine themselves, their habits, and gestures, but with exactest care key all their Instruments, trye every string, and with most nimble and arted
30 motions strik up their most delicious and pleasing strain; so he that knowes himselfe to have an Enemie Competitour both of his life and fame, must be very intentive, weigh all his actions, and make his steps sure and orderly; Especially he is bound to doe it, because vice hath in it this one abominable property, *That those things, wherein wee offend, make our Enemies reverend, and our friends Contemptible.* And therefore it was that *Scipio Nasica*, when some told him that the State of *Rome* was then in saftie, the *Carthaginians*, being quell'd, and *Greece* reduced, gave this answere, *I* (said he) *now is all our daunger, when wee have left us*

---

21 Cautelousnes] Cauteloutnes *1651*
31 Enemie Competitour] enemie, competitour *G*

no Enemy to feare, nor any to reverence. To the same purpose
was that speech of *Diogenes*, most becomming a *Philosopher*, and
worthy the practise of all Common-wealthes, *By what meanes*
(said he) *shall I be avenged of mine Enemie? If thou Diogenes,
will be a good man.* Cowardly, sordid persons if they see us but
well horsed, or sworded, or a faire dog following us, are instantly
cut to the heart; If they see our fields well husbanded, our
mansion-houses, and gardens flowrishing, they break presently into
sighes ; But what thinkest thou, will they doe, if thou shew thy
selfe an honest, prudent, just man, grave in thy words, sincere in 10
thy actions, and temperate in thy diet,

> *Feeding on fruits which in the heavens doe grow,*
> *Whence all divine and holy Counsells flow.*

Those, who are overcome (saith *Pindarus*) have their mouthes so
bung'd up, that they dare not speak ; he saith not this *simply*, nor
of all men, but of those only who are overcome by their Enemies,
either in point of action, honestie, magnanimitie, humanitie, or
good turnes. These are the vertues, which (as *Demosthenes* saith
of them) put the tongue into a traunce, damme up the mouth,
choake the whole man, compell and commaund our silence. 20

> *Excell then if thou canst be not withstood,*
> *But strive, and overcome the evill with good.*

If thou would'st vex thine Enemie, cal him not by way of reproch
an impudent, loose, or intemperate Companion, a knave, or a base
fellow ; but shew thy selfe a man, keepe to moderation, embrace
truth civilitie, and equitie, and in what company soever thou art,
bring those with thee for thy associates. But if at any time thou
art compell'd to rebuke him, have a care that thy own beauty be
not soiled with the same blemishes thou layest to his charge, look
well into thy own bosome, consider the ruins, and dilapidations 30
there, lest happily another more bitter then he, whisper in thy eare
that verse of the Tragedian,

> *You minister to others wounds a Cure,*
> *But leave your own all rotten and impure.*

If he calls thee an ignorant, unlearned, emptie fellow, ply thy
study; if a Coward, stirre up those seeds of valour, and fortitude
which lye asleep in thee ; if wanton, or incontinent, raze out of
thy breast all secret Impressions of lust. For nothing can be
more dishonourable, or bitter, than to have those arrowes wee
shoot at our enemies, to wound our own bosomes. It is commonly 40

26 truth civilitie, and] truth, civilitie and *G*

known, that the repercussion of light is most grievously offensive to sore eys, and those reprehensions which truth casts back
into our own faces give the deepest check, for as the *north-west*
wind gathers clouds, so a dissolute life attracts infamie; wherefore *Plato*, if at any time he lighted upon disorderly Companions,
used always when he was rid of them, to question with himselfe,
have I bin ever as mad as these?   And yet the most busie back-
biter, whose only dialect is slander, did he but consider, and reform
his own life, would from that very office (otherwise the most odi-
10 ous, and basest of all) derive some benefit.   Wee see them commonly derided, who being bald, or crooked themselves, laugh at
those defects in others, And is it not altogether as ridiculous to
charge our Enemies with those very vices, that are most rife in
our selves?   When *Leo Byzantinus* the Philosopher was twitted by
a bunch-backt fellow with the infirmity of his eye-sight, *Thou doest
taxe me* (said he) *with a Common misfortune, but wilt not see that
brand of divine vengeance upon thy own back.*   Wherefore never
object to another his Adulterie, if thou thy selfe burnst with unlawfull Lust; nor his Prodigalitie, or loosenes, if thou beest a
20 Covetous, sordid wretch.   Said *Alcmæon to Adrastus, A kins-
woman of thine hath killed her husband.*   But what did he replie?
He taxed him not with anothers villanie, but his own; *And thou*
(said he) *with thy own hands hast killed thy own mother.*   It was
a question of *Domitius* to *Crassus, Whether upon the death of the
lamprey fed in his fish-ponds he had not mourn'd?   Yea,* (said
*Crassus,) But thou hast buried three wifes without shedding one
teare.*   It is an easie matter to be wittie, lowd, and bitter in our
revilinges, but to be the man upon whom those taunts cannot
justly fasten, there lyes the difficulty.   And truly it seemes that
30 god by that divine Iniunction *Nosce teipsum,* warnes none so much
as those, who are the revilers and rebukers of others, lest happily,
while they take the liberty to speak what they will, they may heare
what they will not; for it happens oft-times to such Companions
according to that saying of *Sophocles, while they give the raines to
their own tongues, they heare from themselves, what they would not
willingly heare from others*; and in this point the reviled and the
reviler have equall advantage.   It was a true saying of *Antisthenes,
That those who would live uprightly, had need either of very honest
friends, or very harsh enemies,* because the one by exhortation, the

---

1 grievously *G*: grievously *1651*
15 bunch-backt *text 1651*: bunch-back *catchword 1651*

other by defamation, will be sure to keep them from offending. But seeing the tongues of friends (as the times now runne) are too short to speak home, too long when they smooth us, and quite dumb to admonish ; it followes that wee can only heare the truth from our Enemies, for as *Telephus* when he could not find a friend to cure him, was glad to have it done with the weapon of his foe, so where our wellwishers will give us no Councell, wee must make use of our Enemies words, and by a discreet application advantage our selves. And in this case wee ought not to consider the malice of the reviler, but the benefit of the reviled. For as that 10 enemie of *Prometheus* by running at him with his sword to have killed him, broke only the Imposthume in his body and so cured him ; In like manner an evill word spoken sometimes out of anger, or enmitie, may cure some ulcer in our manners, which either wee knew not of before, or else neglected. But most men, when they are thus publickly reproach'd, weigh not so much whether they be guiltie, as they doe cast about to learne the vices, and lewd life of their reproacher, and (after the maner of wrestlers) wipe not off those aspersions, which (like dust) they throw one upon the other, but strugling more and more, remain both 20 equally defiled. Whereas (in truth) it concerns him that is so branded, to clear all objections, and that much more then to take a spot of his garment, when 'tis once shewed him. But suppose an Enemy should lay that to our charge, which wee are not guiltie of ? yet must wee examine our selves well, whether wee ever gave any cause for it, or heedlesly let slip our selves into any errour of the like nature, or that had any the least relation or similitude to what wee are taxed with. This was the very *Case* of *Lacides* King of the *Argives*, who for some effeminate Curiositie about his haire, and softnes of apparell was thought wanton, and lascivious. The 30 same thing happened to *Pompey*, * for being ac- * *This was held by* custom'd to scratch his head with one finger only *the Romans for a* (as if he had bin afeard to disorder his locks) he *sure mark of lasci-* was termed effeminate, a vice (in truth) he was *toucheth upon't.—* furthest from, of any. But *Crassus* for being a *huc venient car-* great observer of a vestal virgin, and using often- *pento, et navibus* *omnes Qui digito* times to give her the meeting about some parcell *scalpunt uno Ca-* of land, he would have bought of her, was *put.—* publickly charged to have deflowred her. So *Posthumia* another *Vestall* for her freedome of speech with men, and a 40 jovial, merry nature was accused of incest, And though she was afterwards found Innocent, yet upon her absolution *Spurius*

Minucius then Regent of the *Vestals*, gave her strict charge
that in her after-course of life she should have equall care of her
deportment, as of her chastitie. But what shall wee say of *Themistocles*, that faithful Patriot? who upon a bare point of civilitie for
shewing some kindnes and humanitie to *Pausanias,* and vouch-
safing him a few letters was suspected of treason.   If at any time
therefore thou art falsly accused, slight not, nor neglect the accusation because it is false, but calling thy selfe to an account,
inquire diligently, if there ever happen'd any thing in thy *words*,
10 *actions*, or *Councells*, amongst thy familiars, or elsewhere that
might give a just cause for that calumnie.   And if so, be warie
and avoid it.   For if others by suddaine and unexpected accidents have bin taught to know what is best for them, as *Merope*
tells of her selfe.

> *Chance taking from me things of highest price*
> *At a deare rate hath taught me to be wise,*

What hinders but that wee may learne that lesson from an
Enemie, as from a kind of cheap school-master, whose reprehensions may shew us what wee want, and put us in mind of what wee
20 have forgotten? for an Enemy will sooner see our defects, than
a friend; because the lover (as *Plato* saith) is, in that which he
loves, stark blind, but in hatred there is not only curiositie of
observation, but freedome of speech also.   When *Hjero* was
twitted by his enemie for having an offensive breath, being come
home to his wife, *What is this* (said he) *couldst not thou tell me,
that my breath was not sweet?* but she (a chast and modest
woman) replies, *Indeed I thought that all mens breaths had the like
smell:* So those things which are subject to sense, visible as our
bodies and open to every eye, wee shall sooner know from our
30 enemies and ill-willers, than from our friends and familiars.   Moreover although it is not the least part of vertue to bridle the tongue,
to keep it conformable, and alwayes obedient to reason, yet without
a primarie subduing of thy worst affections, anger, and the rest,
which must be done by a constant practise, premeditation, and per-
severance thou canst never get the masterie over it.   For this vitious
unfolding of our selves, extenuated with an Apologie of *a word
escaped from me,* or, *I slipt a word unawares,* never happens but to
lavish, irresolute persons who by reason of their infirmitie of judgment, or loose Custome of life, stick alwaies in the same errours.
40 Besides Speech though the vainest and emptiest thing under the
Sun, yet (according to the sentiment of divine *Plato*) is usually

punished with the heaviest judgments both by *God* and *Man*.
But silence on the Contrary is alwayes safe, and hath no accusers;
neither doth it only (as *Hippocrates* saith) keep us not thirstie,
but in the presence of a rayling Enemie is full of majesty, wisedome,
and fortitude; And a man so qualified

> *Knaves tongues, and calumnies no more doth price*
> *Then the vaine buzzing of so many flies.*

Certainly there is nothing in the world hath more of worth and
gallantrie in it, than to beare the *big browes* of a base, upstart foe
with a calme and smiling carriage; wee should passe by a tongue 10
given to detraction, as by a rock used to the froth and scumme of
the waves; The benefit will sweeten the practise: for if thou
canst beare quietly the affronts of an Enemie, thou mayest easily
beare with a sharp wife, or any bitter passages from a friend or
brother, and if thy parents chance to strike thee, thou art so
season'd as not to be angrie with them. Thus *Socrates* made it
his frequent practise to beare the stormes of his lowd wife (a
Gentlewoman that for peevishnes and furie out did all her sex) for
said he, If I can *beare* with *Xantippe, I make no question but
I shall bear with all others*. Now, the main end is (after wee have 20
bin thus exercised by the frequent scoffes, reproaches, excessive
anger, and sauciness of our enemies) to accustome our selves to
such a solid temper, and magnanimous patience, as never to be
moved at their weake noise, and detractions. By this means wee
shall shew towards our enemies mansuetude, and a kind of virtuous Contempt; to our friends simplicitie, magnanimitie, and sin-
ceritie. Neither is it so praise-worthy to doe good turnes to our
friends, as it is base to deny them to those that want; But to
forbeare revenge upon an Enemie, when wee opportunely may, is
the highest glory in all humanity; And if any man mourn for the 30
misfortunes of his foe, succour him in his wants, be a support to
his Children, and domestick decayes, who doth not with thanks
accept of such benevolence, acknowledge such a miracle,

> *His deepe, dark heart (bent to supplant)*
> *Is Iron, or else Adamant.*

Said *Cicero* to *Cæsar* (when he commanded the statues of *Pompey*,
that had fallen down, to be erected) *hast thou set up the statues of
Pompey? thou hast established thy own*. This intimates that wee
should keep back no praise, nor any point of honour from a noble
Enemie that may justly claime it; for by bearing testimonie to 40

27 turnes *text 1651*: turns *catchword 1651*

the truth, and fastening Commendations where desert is, wee doe commend our selves.   Nay wee shall have this advantage, that if wee chance afterwards to blame them, wee shalbe believed of all men as disliking their actions, not hating their persons ; and which is most laudable of all, they that use to speak well of their Enemies, without repining at their successe, will hardly envie the prosperity of their friends, or the good parts of their associates.   What better exercise then, or more virtuously fruitfull, or leaving nobler impressions in the soul can wee pitch upon?   It takes away from us all
10 perverse emulations, and puts quite out all fomentations of envie. As in a Common-wealth many things necessarie, (otherwise bad enough) when they are once confirm'd by Custome, or power of law, are not easily forgotten of those whom they have once annoyed ; so hostilitie and variance bringing in with them envie and hatred, leave planted in the mind obtrectation, malevolence, with an Implacable and endles resentment of Injuries.   Adde to this that Couzenage, trecherie, breach of oath, private wiles, and policies which by perverse and bloudie Enemies are held lawfull, where they once begin to be practised, will by a habituation be so per-
20 fectly naturalized, that they can hardly ever be removed, and may afterwards (grown masters by Custome) if not refused against our Enemies, prove hurtfull to our nearest friends.   For this very cause (if I judge right) *Pythagoras* used to abstaine from flesh, and the slaughter of harmles creatures, intreating and sometimes hiring fowlers, not to kill their birds, and Anglers to let goe their fish, and publickly forbad the killing of any tame beast.   Without doubt a generous, just, and solid Enemie will in all Contentions think it the best victorie to bridle an irreligious, insatiable malice, that by teaching his stubbournes to submit to vertue, he may ever after
30 be master of himself.   When *Domitius* was accused by *Scaurus* his Enemie, a servant of his, stept to the barre where *Scaurus* pleaded, about to informe him of some heynous offence done by his master, which *Scaurus* knew not of, but he not suffering him to speak, sent him with a guard back to his master.   So *Cato* when he was drawing up certain heads of an accusation against *Muræna*, had alwaies following him a knot of busie fellows, who of set purpose pryed into his actions ; These oftentimes asked him, if he had yet finished the Charge, or had any more Articles to insert, or witnesses to examine? if he answered, no; They would instantly
40 believe him, and depart ; a great argument of the good opinion they had of *Cato*.   And indeed that which excells all, and is (in truth) most justly preheminent, is the equall administration of

justice to our very Enemies ; for who useth to doe so, can hardly use any fraud, or injustice against his friends. But seeing it is so (as *Simonides* saith) that every lark must have a Crest, and worth, in whomsoever it is, breeds contention, obtrectation, and the envie of fools ; wee shall find no small advantage, if wee put quite from us all sillie and weak ways of revenge even against our most bitter Enemies, and remove them as durt and drosse far enough from our friends. Which very point (in my opinion) *Onomademus* (a very skilfull states-man) made speciall use of ; for living in *Chios*, and happening to be (upon a sudden Insurrection) of that side which then prevailed, he advised his Confederates, that they should not banish all of the adverse partie, but leave some to live amongst them *Lest* (said he) *being rid of our Enemies*, wee *begin to fall out with our friends*. For as long as wee have an Enemy to consume, and weare out our ill affections upon, wee shall give the lesse distast to our friends. It is not convenient (saith *Hesiodus*) that one *Potter* should envie the other, nor ought wee to be troubled at the prosperitie of our brother, or a good neighbour. But if thou canst not otherwise than by doing so, free thy selfe from strif, envy, and Contention, then suffer thy self to fret at the good successe of thine Enemie, and cut him with the edge and keeness of thy anger. For as skilful gardiners think *roses* and *violets* will thrive the better, if *Onions and garlick* be sowed neare them, (because these later attract all harsh qualities that may be in the Compost,) so an Enemie by drawing on himself all the perversnes and morositie in thee, will render thy disposition more mild and pleasing to thy friend. Therefore when wee have any thing to doe with an Enemie either in point of honour, popularitie, or a just benefit, wee must so contend, as not only to be blindly vext because he excells us, but to observe also in what particulars, and by what means he doth so excel. Nor must wee stay there, but with all diligence, industrious sobrietie, and watchfullnes labour to overtake him, after the example of *Themistocles*, whom the victorie of *Miltiades* upon the plaines of *Marathon* would not suffer to sleep. For such a spirit that thinks his Enemie better than himselfe because he hath great offices, patronage, numerous friends, or the favour of Princes, and therefore gives him over and despaires, when he ought rather to be stirring and emulous, doth but pine away with most sordid and cowardly envie. But he that hath a strict eye over him, not blinded with hatred, and stands in the light a discerning spectatour of his life and actions, shall at last find it true, that all those prosperous passages he envied him for,

were brought about by a Judicious care, eminent diligence, and sincere dealings; and having got these virtues for his presidents, he instantly cuts of all dulness and delayes, and treads in the same steps to arrive at the same height.   But if it so happens to any that their Enemies by unlawfull and irreligious means grow powerfull, as by flattery, exactions, perverting of justice, briberie, perjurie or bloud-shed, they ought not so much to mourne, as to rejoyce, considering that they have to oppose to all that rottenness, a sound conscience, unpolluted pietie, and innocent hands.   For (as *Plato*
10 saith) All *the gold above the earth, and under the earth is by no meanes to be compared with a religious Integritie.*   Neither must wee leave them untwitted with that of *Solon*,

> *What though they boast their riches unto us?*
> *Those cannot say, That they are virtuous.*

Let us then neither labour for bribed suffrages, nor bought honours, nor for the chief place with Eunuchs, and Concubines of Kings, or pandars of state; for nothing is amiable, nothing honourable, that is acquird by baseness.   But (as *Plato* saith) *The lover, in that which he loveth is stark blind,* but quick-sighted enough to
20 see the failings of his Enemies; It will become us then, neither to rejoyce at their sins, nor to mourn for what they doe well,
- but wisely to weigh both, that by avoyding the one we may grow *better,* and by imitating the other not grow *worser* then they themselves are.

1 Judicious] text 1651 : Iuditious catchword 1651

FINIS.

OF THE

DISEASES

OF THE

MIND

And the

BODY.

A DISCOURSE

Written originally in the
Greek by *Plutarchus Chæronensis*,
put into latine by *I. Reynolds D.D.*

Englifhed by *H : V :* Silurift.

Omnia perverſæ poterunt Corrumpere mentes.

LONDON.
Printed for *Humphry Moſeley* and are to
be ſold at his ſhop at the ſigne of the
Princes Armes in St. Pauls
Church yard, 1 6 5 1.

Of the Diseases of the Mind and the Body.

When *Homer* had diligently considered the severall kinds of living Creatures, and compared the various dispositions, and provident subsisting of the one with the other, he cryed out,

> *That man for misery excell'd*
> *All creatures which the wide world held.*

A very wretched Prerogative! that excels in nothing, but a calamitous superiority of evils. Seeing then, that by this sentence we are eminent for nothing, but unhappinesse, and in that also more miserable than other creatures, we shall in this discourse (by way of comparison) bring man to a combate with 10 himself about his own calamities; taking the *mind* asunder from the *body* (not vainly, but to a good purpose) that by a distinct examination of both we may come to know from which of these two his miseries flow.

Bodily diseases happen alwaies by a depravation of temperament; but the vitiositie, and taint of the mind, is first the free act of the mind it self, and afterwards its disease. But it would not a little conduce to the ease of the mind, if either that which is infected might be restored; or that which cannot be wholly taken away might be partly mitigated. When *Æsops* fox contended with 20 the *Panther* for variety, after the *Leopard* had bragg'd of the beauteous spots and speckles in his skin, vilifying the other for his sordid, reddish, and ill-sented Coate, *But couldst thou* (said the Fox) *discerne that which is within me, thou wouldst confesse thy selfe lesse various than I am*; Meaning thereby the many fetches and subtilties he had there, and could commodiously use when he pleased. So may we say of our selves. Many diseases truly (O man!) and many infirmities attend on thy Body, some casually and from without, others naturally out of the Body it self: But if thou wouldst but search thy self within, where no eys 30 shine but thy own, what variety of distempers shouldst thou find there? giddie distractions, blind conceits, crooked affections, shuffled wils, and phantastick humours, which lying there as in a Box, or Cabinet, flow not from without, but are Natives and Inhabitants of the place, springing there like so many Wels. Now

33 phantastick] phanstastick *1651*

the diseases of the Body are ordinarily known by the *Pulse*, or beating of the vitall spirits, and a high colour; and those againe are manifested by other *Symptoms*, as excessive heat, wearinesse, and a dangerous aptnesse to faint; But the diseases of the Mind so delude most men, that they are not suspected for maladies, and the case of the patient is then most desperate, when he hath no sense of his paine. But in bodily diseases the judgement remaines sound, and there is still in the patient a very quick and clear perception both of his *time of ease*, and of *accessions*; whereas
10 those that are sick in Mind can find no difference between sicknesse, and health, and indeed how should they, seeing that wherewith they Judge, is the part affected? It is therefore very just that we adjudge this *senslesnesse* to be the most pernicious, and principall of all the diseases of the mind, for by this it comes to passe that many men converse, live, and dye in an uncurable madnesse: for as in ordinary diseases the first step to health is to have a feeling of the disease, for that sets on the patient to inquire for help; so in mentall distempers (wherein men state themselves sound, that are indeed sick,) though they knew a remedy for
20 their disease, yet will they not use it, because they believe, they have no need of it. Of bodily diseases those are most dangerous, which render men senselesse, as *Lethargies, head-akes*, the *falling sicknesse, dead Palsies*, and *Feavers* also, whose vehement Inflammations breed an alienation of mind, and (like unskilfull *Musicians*) put the whole inward harmony out of tune. Therefore honest *Physicians* first wish, that men were not sick at all; Secondly, that if they happen to sicken, they may be sensible of their disease: but in mentall maladies this deliration is so prevalent that it is impossible to remove it; for neither those that
30 rave with some mad conceit, or burne with lasciviousnesse, or delight in doing injuries seeme to themselves to offend, nay, they are so far from it, that they glory in such actions; And yet, who ever gave the name of health to a Feaver, of soundnesse to corruption, of activitie to the Goute, or of Blushes to Palenesse? but to call *anger* fortitude, *love* friendship, *envie* emulation, and *Cowardice* discretion is frequent. Besides, those who have their *Bodies* ill-affected send presently for the *Physician*, because they find themselves to have need of him; but those who have their *minds* so, flye from the *Philosopher*, and will not endure any
40 Precepts of virtue. Moved then with these reasons, I hold an *Outward blindnesse* more tollerable than an *Inward*, and the paine of the *Gout*, than the Dotage of the *mind*; for he that is

diseas'd in his eys, useth his best diligence to have them cured, provides waters, and ointments, breaths a veine, and purgeth his head; but come to mad *Agave*, and you shall heare her singing, having killed her son,

> *A tender Kid (see, where 'tis put,)*
> *I on the Hils did slay,*
> *Now drest, and into quarters cut,*
> *A pleasant, daintie prey.*

Adde to this, that a Patient in the Body takes present notice of his disease, gets him to bed, and while he is in cure, is quiet and 10 tractable, or if he chance to be something wayward and offer to rise thence by reason of wearinesse or a Feaverish heat, yet if a friend say to him, *Lye still,* or *keep in thy Bed,* he will instantly refraine; whereas those that are diseas'd in Mind, are then most restlesse and tumultuous; for from the Commotions of the mind all actions take their beginning, but mentall diseases are the most vehement Commotions, and therefore will not suffer the mind to be in quiet, yea, when a man hath most need to shew patience, silence, and submission of mind, then will these inward maladies most annoy him, giving the rains to anger, contention, lust, and 20 tumults, which dissect and lay him open to his enemies, while he strives to doe many things repugnant to reason, and spits out unseasonable, and dangerous speeches. Therefore, as that tempest at Sea, which keeps us from putting into the Harbour, is more dangerous than that which hinders us to put forth; so those tempests of the mind, which will not suffer us to containe and pacifie our selves, are the most pernicious, for they hurry us away without Pilot or Saile through Gulfs and Quicksands, untill at last upon some rock or other we cast away both our lifes and estates; wherefore in my opinion were there no other Inconvenience but 30 that, it is enough to prove that the disease of the *mind* is far more perillous than the disease of the *body*; though this we shall adde, that the *one* offends only the patient, but the *other* offends all that come neare it.

But to what purpose shall we multiply arguments? seeing the events of the present time sufficiently demonstrate it. You see this numerous and promiscuous multitude here met, justling and shouldring one another from the streets to the Court, from the Court to the Bar, and so out againe; These are come together not to celebrate any works of piety, as sacrifice, or prayer; but a certaine 40 *Epidemicall fit* which once a year all *Asia* shakes of, hath hurryed

them hither about some vaine controversies and matters of Law, which upon a prescript day are here to be heard and determined; for at this one Bar (like the breaking in of so many Rivers) all the Contestations in *Asia* meet, here they are canvased, decided, and grow up into mortall dissentions, betwixt the *undoer* and the *undone*. What Feavers, what Agues, Malignant heats, or Superfluous humours ever so troubled mankind? If aswell as the men, you examine the grounds of their sutes and contentions in Law, you shall find some of them to proceed from a slight word spoken,
10 some from malice, some from anger, others from a mad desire to be contentious, and all of them from *Covetousnesse*.

FINIS

OF THE
DISEASES
OF THE
MIND,
AND THE
BODY,
And which of them is
moſt pernicious.

The Queſtion ſtated, and decided
by *Maximus Tirius* a Platonick Philoſopher, written originally in
the Greek, put into Latine by
John Reynolds D. D.

Engliſhed by Henry Vaughan *Siluriſt.*

LONDON,
Printed for *Humphry Moſeley*, and are to be
Sold at his Shop at the Sign of the
Prince's Arms in St. *Pauls*
Church-yard, 1651.

Of the Diseases of the Mind, &c.

There is sung from all antiquity by some unknowne Poet this following *Hymne* in the stile of a prayer,

> *O Cœlestium princeps Sanitas !*
> *Utinam tecum degere possim*
> *Quod mihi tempus superest vitœ !*

> O health the chief of gifts divine !
> I would I might with thee and thine
> Live all those days appointed mine !

I would gladly be resolved by the Authour of this verse, what kind of health it was, which in those preceding lines he begg'd to 10 have for his Companion in life ; for verily I suspect it was some divine thing worthy the devotion and fervency of prayer ; for sure he could not rashly and upon a suddaine find matter worthy of verse, or being put into verse, it could hardly have past with such generall applause from one age unto another. If it be then such a thing as I suspect, reason it self (instead of the *Poet*,) will give us an answer. For seeing there are but *two things* of which *man* consists, the *Soule*, and the *Body*, if the *Soule* be free from the nature of diseases, it follows of necessity, that, what is petitiond for in this *Hymne* belongs to the *Body*, which naturally useth to 20 fall sick, and to recover againe. But if it be so that both *Soule* and *Body* have from discreet nature a like temperament, which is never disturbed but by a petulant perversitie of parts, when excesse in the one (like a tyrant and his people in a Common-wealth) is destructive to the other, and confounds the genuine harmony, (which excesse wheresoever it is, whether in the soule, or else in the body, we define to be *an impotent Cupidity*, both which as they make up one whole man share equall power, though taken by themselves they bear no proportion at all,) the question now is, to which of these two shall this Celestiall temperament, or 30 Princesse mentioned in the Hymne, be adjudged most necessary ? To resolve this *Quœre* with safety, we must compare the diseases of the *one*, with the diseases of the *other*, that by so doing we may see which of them is most pernicious to the whole man, and then like indifferent Arbiters settle to a righteous judgement.

Man then (as we have said before) is made up of *Soule* and
Body, in which Composure the *Soule* is regent, and the *Body*
obeys, as in a Common-wealth the *Prince*, and his *Subjects*; and
worthily too, for as in this of the *Body*, so in all other Governments the *Prince* is not only the head, or Superiour part of the
Commonwealth, but by a kind of *Sacred affinitie* part also of the
Subject. The question then is, *Whether in a languishing Common-*
wealth the Prince, or the People, the Soule, or the Body, are the
destroying party? I decide it thus: The Common people are
10 sick, but *Pericles* the good Prince is in health, apprehends the
disease, and cures the people: contrariwise, *Dionysius* the *Sira-*
cusian hath the *Kings evill*, but the people, though healthfull
themselves, want strength to restore him. Will you therefore,
that henceforth we substitute for the *Soule*, the *Prince*; and for
the *Body* the *People*? If so, weigh the example, aswell as the
thing.

The People for number exceed the Prince, and the Body the
Soul. The People without a Prince are dead, and heartless; so
is the Body without the Soul. The People consist of many
20 degrees, many voices, and many affections; so hath the Body
diverse, and different parts. The people are in their anger
Merciless, in their desires *vehement*, in their pleasures *dissolute*, in
their troubles *abject,* and in their furie *Mad*; The same vices attend
the Body, for now 'tis lustfull, now winie, anon dejected, and sometimes hurried away with most impetuous, excessive madnes. Let
us see now what Comparatives wee can make between the *Prince*,
and the *Soul*. A *Prince* in a Commonwealth is the fittest person
to govern, as most honourable, and most able; so is the *Soul* in
the *Body*. A *Prince* is by nature provident in his affaires, and
30 prudent in advice; the very same faculties are usually in the Soul.
The *Prince* hath a freedome royall, and is above the Censure of
the people; so is the Soul above the Body. Seeing then that
these Comparisons are true in both, which of these parts (when
diseas'd) shall wee judge the worst, as well in the Commonwealth,
as in Man? surely the best; because the Corruption of things
that are excellent is the most pernicious: For the People though
sick, if the Prince be well, shall have their liberties preserved; but
the disease of the Prince (though the People be in health) brings
inevitable bondage. And that I may in one word summe up all,
40 the Soul is far more excellent than the Body, and the Prince than
the People: Now that *good* which is most excellent, is by somuch
the greater; and that which is repugnant to the *greater good*, must

needs be the *greater Evill* ;—But the health of the *Soul* is a greater good than the health of the *Body* ; therefore the disease of the Soule is a greater Evill than the disease of the Body. The health of the body is restored by Art, but the health of the soul by virtuous Industrie. The disease of the soul is wickednes, that of the body is but sorrow : Wickednes comes by a voluntarie sinning, but calamitie against our wills. If any body hurt us against their will, they deserve our Charitie ; if of set purpose, they deserve our Hatred. Where wee are charitable, there wee relieve ; where revengefull, there wee punish. Those wee relieve are commonly 10 good ; those wee punish, notoriously bad. Again, The health of the soul is full of Chearfullnesse, the body may be in health, and yet want it. The health of the soul leads us to blisse, the other to miserie. The health of the soul hath no iniquitie, the other is wholly vitious. The health of the soule is celestiall, the other earthly ; the one is durable, the other transitorie ; the one eternal, the other mortall. And so much touching their dispositions in that state, let us now consider their diseases. Bodily diseases if not wholly taken off, yet by the help of art may be very much mitigated ; but the mind once infected contemnes the correction 20 of severest Laws. The first (after a few days paine) by making the patient desirous of health, makes him also fitter for cure ; the last by bewitching the mind so hinders the Cure, that it will not somuch as heare of health. The divine mercy may succour the one, but from the other it is alwaies averse. The disease of the body hath never yet occasion'd wars, but that of the mind hath occasion'd many. No man sick in body burns with lust, robs Churches, steales from his neighbour, or doth any other villanie, that disease offends only the patient, the other offends all men. But let us now render this truth more evident by a similitude 30 taken from Civill Government.

When *Pericles* was Duke of *Athens,* a Citie govern'd by *Democracie,* and burthend with a great & populous multitude, large in jurisdiction, powerfull for riches, and stored with many and eminent Commanders, the plague then rife in *Æthiopia* (where it first began) past thence into *Persia,* and afterwards to *Athens,* where having (as it were) taken footing, it increased daily and afflicted the Citie. To augment this miserie, it happend at the same time that they had open war with the *Peloponnesians* ; In this state therefore when the Countrey lay wasted by the Enemie, 40 the Inhabitants tortured, their houses rifled, their armies defeated, and the whole body of the Commonwealth exposed to pillage and

destruction, *Pericles* the good *Prince* being then in health, himselfe
rebuilds the Citie, recruits their armies, restores their Courages,
and dividing himselfe betwixt the Sword and the Pest-house with
the one hand subdued the Infection, and with the other the
Enemie. Thus much for the Soul, let us now find a similitude
for the Body. When the Infection ceased, and the Commonwealth
again took breath, and recovered, those persons in the Citie, who
had the charge of the Republick (as Popular government hath
ever too many) so burnt with hatred, ambition, and Covetousnes
10 one towards another, that they seemed rather to be out of their
witts, than rightly in them. These mentall diseases in a short time
so increased, and dispersed, that all *Athens* was infected, and so
prevalent was the Contagion that it took also the Common people;
And why not? for here they had not one *Cleon* to rave with, or one
Alcibiades to burn with, but (as the nature of *Democracie* is) a hundred, or more; and these (every man as his disease moved him)
plyed severall interests, one this way, another that way, *Alcibiades*
shewed them *Sicilia, Cleon Sphacteria,* another some other territorie,
or *Ocean,* like so many springs to one sick of a feaver. O blessed
20 Statesmen! this was your Reformation! Ruine, Confusion,
prodigious Changes, nationall Miseries, and civill Inflammations
were the religion, and liberty they had from you! so woefully
pernicious is the Maladie of the Soul, if compared with the disease
of the Body. For though the Body lye sick, languishing, and
afflicted, yet if a resolute, immoveable spirit hath the guidance of
it, diseases, Convulsions, and death it selfe can prevail nothing;
A philosopher, and Thus *Pherecides* (though he was * laid quick in
Master to Pythago- the grave, and saw Corruption while he lived)
ras, *he died of the* slighted both the loathsomnes and pain of the
Phthiriasis.
30 disease, wishing only that he might be freed
from that unprofitable body wherewith he was then cloath'd upon.
Nay, I shall not doubt to say, that a soul thus gifted lives in the
body by meere compulsion, for I look upon such a one, as upon
some captive or slave, who seeing the walls of his prison decayed,
and grown ruinous, expects every moment to be set at liberty, that
freed from the darknes and horrour of that dungeon, which
formerly opprest him, he may at last enjoy a cleare aire, and the
comforts of light. Canst thou believe that a hired labourer
accustomed to the hardest, and most toilesome imployments, wilbe
40 any thing astonished to see a suddaine rent, or hole in his

11 witts] wittls *1651*   17 interests] inteterests *1651*
21 Inflammations] Inflammatious *1651*

apparell? or will he not rather cut off that which hangs about him, and leave his body naked to the aire, that he may with more ease and nimblenes prosecute his task? And doest thou think the soul esteemes otherwise of flesh and bones than of a Coat which endures but for a day, or some thred-bare, cheap rags, which sometimes the sword, sometimes the fagot, but most times diseases devoure? Wherefore a generous, and sustaining spirit, when he finds the body begining to undresse, and the bolts of his prison loosed, makes no more account of that Change than a snail doth of her cast shel, or *Vlysses* of the ten yeares suit he wandered in. 10 But the fearefull, and Cowardly soul, stoved in the body, like some lazie beast in his den, will by no meanes be released thence, no, nor somuch as take the aire, but delighting in the passions and miseries of that burthen, is now torn, now burnt, by and by grieves, and alwaies groanes with it. Wee heare *Philoctetes* crying out, *O my foot, I must lose thee!* why, good man, if thou must, lose it willingly, and doe not crie so; Doth it any thing ease thee to raile at thy friends, and make the *Echo* in *Lemnos* mock at thy Complaints? *O Death my only Cure!* well said *Philoctetes*; but if by so saying thou meanest only an Exchange of one Evill for 20 the other, then cannot I approve of thy wish: But if by that Exclamation thou doest acknowledge death the only soveraign remedie, and revenger of a loathsome disease, thou hast spoken right; call, and crie for thy Cure. And now seeing wee have mentioned *Philoctetes* most opportunely will he afford us a very pregnant example. There was heretofore at the siege of *Troy* (for valour and number) an Army of *Grecians* altogether incredible, as many as there be leafes or flowers in the spring, all of them able, hardie, and healthfull bodies lying about the walls and trenches of their Enemies for ten whole yeares, and prevailed 30 nothing; not *Achilles* the pursuer, *Aiax* the defyer, *Diomedes* the slaughterer, *Teucer* the Archer, *Agamemnon* the Counsellour, *Nestor* the Oratour, *Chalcas* the Soothsayer, nor *Vlisses* the Deceiver. But what saies the *Oracle*? *In vain (O noble youths and souldiers of Greece!) in vain I say doe you skirmish, batter, assault, and advize; for never shall you be able to take those walls, before you have to your aid, a mind indeed prudent and healthy, but a body infected, languishing, lame and allmost consumed;* They obey the oracle, and fetch him from *Lemnos*, him (I say) sick in body, but sound in mind. And thus wee see what the Soul can 40 doe in health, let us now consider it when diseased. The mind is infected with sensualitie, it burnes, melts, and pines away.

What will you doe to the patient? what benefit, or advantage can the Body (in this Case) minister to the Soul? *Sardanapalus* lies sick of this disease; Doe not you see, how like an Insatiable *ulcer* it hath taken hold of all the parts of his body? his Colour is gone, his Beauty spent, his Eyes dull'd, and his whole frame burnes with most obscene Impatiencie. *Alcibiades* is in the same case. An outragious, restles fire feedes upon him, overthrowes his reason, hurries him up and down, from **Lycæum* to the * Aristotles *School in* Athens. multitude, from the multitude to the sea, from

10 the sea to *Sicilia*, from *Sicilia* to *Lacedemon*, from *Lacedemon* to *Persia*, from *Persia* to *Samos*, from *Samos* to *Athens*, from *Athens* to *Hellespont*, and from *Hellespont* I know not * *One of the* 30 *ty-rants in* Athens. whither. **Critias* lyes sick, taken with a most grievous, desperate, intolerable disease, and burthensome to a whole Commonwealth. But all these had very healthfull, proper, and handsome bodies; spruce *Sardanapalus*, beautifull *Alcibiades*, and portly *Critias*. But in men of such dispositions I never loved health. Let *Critias* then be sick, untill he may play the tyrant; *Alcibiades* because he cannot bring *Athens* into *Sicilie*; And for

20 *Sardanapalus* let him be sick to death, for it is more manly for him to perish by a disease, than an excessive obscenitie. Yea, and may every one perish, who is only fertill in Continuall evills! for as running ulcers where they once seize, spread further still, and corrupt those parts which are sincerest, dispersing and prevailing against all medicines, untill the very seat and hold of the disease be cut out; So those minds which are used to rotteness, Corruption, and dishonest Intentions will (like infected people) endanger all that have Commerce with them; And therefore in such persons the *strength* and *spring* of the disease should be taken off, as the

30 *hand* of a thiefe, the *Eye* of a leacher, and the *belly* of a glutton. For though against these enormities thou shouldst constitute Iudges, prisons, and tortures, yet would the Evill increase, prevaile, and overflow; for the headines of vice where it finds a predisposition, and growes once habituall, is altogether Incredible, and attended with most desperate licentiousnes, and a frontles audacitie.

FINIS.

THE
PRAISE
AND
HAPPINESSE
OF THE
COUNTRIE-LIFE;

Written Originally in
Spanish by *Don Antonio de Guevara*,
Bishop of *Carthagena*, and
Counsellour of Estate to
Charls the Fifth Emperour
of *Germany*.

Put into English by H. Vaughan *Silurist*.

Virgil. Georg.
O fortunatos nimiùm, bona si sua nôrint,
Agricolas! ——

LONDON,
Printed for *Humphry Moseley*, and are to be
Sold at his Shop at the Sign of the
Prince's Arms in St. *Pauls*
Church-yard, 1651.

The Praise and Happinesse of the Country-Life, &c.

The First Chapter.

Whoever Loves the *Country*, and Lives in it upon his owne Estate, whether *Hereditarie* or *Purchased*, and lends not his Ears to any flatt'ring *allurements* perswading to ambition and greatnesse, but carefully avoids those dangerous *Precipices* and *Quicksands*, I shall not feare to affirme, That such a liver is the *wisest of men*; for he living upon his own, is no mans debtour, and is offensive to none but either a *Courtier*, or a *Citizen*; and therefore is much more happy than if he had Ingrost to himself all *Court favours*,
10 or had bin expert in the *subtiltie* and *Politicks* of all forraign Nations.

He fears no *discontents* to disturbe his *Peace*, but lives well-pleased with what *providence* gives him though never so little. He is free from all fretting *cares*, and is fed with no mans *provision* but his *own*. The *Crop* of his *Land* comes in certainly once a *yeare*, it is got with a *good conscience*, and is ever ready upon any necessity. These are *returns* which he needs not *complement* for, nor be thought troublesome, or rudely *importunate*. A pompous and splendid *fortune* hath seldome *better blessings*; but instead of
20 those lavish and sumptuous *Excesses* she is sometimes accustom'd to, she frequently deceives our hopes with the worst kind of *Exigencies*. A *Nobleman* or *Citizen* living upon the Revenues and accommodations of his Country estate finds more of honour, reputation and authority amongst his Neighbours, than all those *Sycophants* (though outwardly more rich and sumptuous) whom either an antient *descent*, a large *retinue*, or the beauty and spruce-nesse of their *wifes*, hath preferr'd at *Court*. There the lustre of *greater persons* makes theirs to be of no notice; but in his Country-house he is *Lord* alone, and his Wife is *Lady*, there he is
30 really honour'd and admir'd of all. Wherefore it was well said of *Julius Cæsar, That he had rather be the prime Freeholder in a Country Village, than the second Magistrate in the City of Rome.*

Pietie and Religion may be better Cherish'd and preserved in the Country than any where else. While the Husbandman with a *cheerfull* and *holy hope* expects the fruit and recompense of his pains, out of the earth, the Inhabitants of great *Cities* (yea those that have no more than one *garrish suit* of Cloaths, and a very *mean subsistance*) will be reproaching and envying one the other. Hence very many of them are suddenly undone, and by some ambitious attempt of *precedency*, come to lose that little they had gotten, in which ruins their friends also are sometimes involved, whom they had drawn in for greater undertakings than their abilities could bear out. The *Countryman* living private, repines at no man, is alwaies contented, and contributes something towards the relief of the *poor*. But he that seeks after places of Eminency will be sure to find *Envy* and *Competitors*, and these last will be still watching to reduce him to such a condition as shall be far beneath their Envy. To keep a *School*, to be a hir'd *labourer*, or to live by Compounding of *Salves* and *Plaisters*, is a far more blessed and a securer life.

He that lives in his own *fields* and *habitation*, which God hath given him, enjoys true Peace; for no Phantastick, Impudent *Companion* turns in thither to disturbe him, and to seek after a sumptuous entertainment, or to corrupt his family in his absence; the very occasion of *ill-doing* is by his presence taken away. He busieth not himself in a *search* of pleasures, but in regulating, and disposing of his family; in the education of his Children, and Domestick Discipline. No violent tempestuous motions distract his *rest*, but soft gales, and a silent aire refresh and breath upon him. He doth all things commodiously, ordereth his life discreetly, not after the opinion of the people, but by the rules of his own certain experience; he knows he must not live here for ever, and therefore thinks frequently of *dissolution* and the day of *death*. He knows his resting place at night, and is not like *travellours* and *runagates*, sollicitous and uncertaine of his *lodging*, or the manners of *those* that are to entertaine him; he wants no furniture, his *bed* is ready at the time of rest, and his *Horses* and *Sadles* when he rides abroad. He fears not the violence of *Judges*, nor their perverse judgements, which to others is a frequent trouble; And which is a blessing above all, he meets not in the recesse of his fields with any *Impostor, busie-body*, or *lewd-woman*, whose temptations sometimes turne men into beasts, and hurry them into divers lusts, which oftentimes have bin so sadly effectuall as to cause *discord* and *bloudshed*.

He that lives in the Country, hath *time* for his servant, and whatsoever occasions offer themselves (if he be but a *discreet observer* of his *hours*) he can have no cause to complaine that they are unseasonable. Nothing will hinder him from the pleasure of *books*, from *devotion*, or the fruition of his *friends*. If he finds himself remisse and voyd of businesse, there is nothing hinders but he may take either the pleasure of *hunting*, or of visiting some well accomplish'd, pleasing *Companion* ; Whereas those that are *tyed* to businesse, whose *profession* makes their *life* a meer *slaverie*,
10 are alwaies imprison'd (as it were) and barr'd from *recreation*. Sometimes they are driven upon far Journeys against their will, and spend their time of life (which to *Christians* should be most pretious) in the negotiations of others, in *complementing*, *scraping*, *intreating*, *petitioning*, feigned *sighing*, and a ridiculous *humbling* of themselves. Insomuch that the saying of *Augustus Cæsar* to a laborious Citizen of *Rome*, may very well be applyed to them. *I wonder* (said he) *thou doest not leave off, thou art so constant in imployment, thou wilt have no time to dye.*

A *Nobleman* or *Citizen* retyr'd into the Country, may without
20 prejudice to his *honour* walk alone, without the noyse and trouble of *Attendants*, he needs there no *Couches* to stretch upon, nor his *Gentleman* at his back ; and his *Lady* may take the aire without her *Gentlewoman* ; but in *Courts* and great assemblies these *formalities* (with excessive charge and pride) must be kept up to carry the eys of the *multitude*, which are alwaies taken with such vaine *shows* and *Pageantrie*.

We may in the Country, when we please and without offence take the *aire*, walk to the next *neighbourhood*, or *village*, and with an untainted *repute* return home at what houre we shall set to our
30 selves, having no troublesome occasions to entangle and delay us. The Countryman is *slave* to no body, he walks not loaded with *boots* and *spurs*, ready at all *Commands*, as *Souldiers* at the *sound* of the trumpet.

In the Country the *Gentleman* aswell as the *Ploughman* may live, to please himself, and is not bound to a chargeable Imitation of the *fashions* and *foppery* of others. There is no necessity of any thing but a *Cloak* for feare of raine, and a *warme garment* more for health than ostentation. A *bill* to walk his grounds with, a *fish-basket*, an *angling-rod*, or *birding-piece* are his chiefest
40 accoutrements. Yea, the Nobleman in the Country is as much honour'd in his coarsest habit, as he can be elsewhere in his richest and most pompous ornaments.

Of what degree soever he be, that lives in the Country, whether a *Gentleman* or a *Plebeian*, he is not therefore held the more despicable, or unfortunate, because he rides to the market upon his own *working beast*, than the most Lordly *gallant* upon his *great horse*; Yea, more *blessed* is he, that living honestly in the *sweat of his face*, rides his own simple *Asse*, than a rich unconscionable *Tyrant* that furnisheth his great *stable* or *dairie* with the *Cattel* and *Horses* of an innocent, honest *man*.

The Second C H A P T E R.

THE Husband-man never wants *good Corne*, and which in great 10 *Towns* and *Courts* is very rare, he is alwaies furnished with welrellishing *bread* and well baked; for in populous *Cities* their *Corne* is either mouldie, or not wel-grinded, or their *water* with which they knead it, is brackish and unwholesome, which oftentimes is the cause of divers diseases and mortalitie amongst the Inhabitants. But that which is most worthy our observation in this Chapter, is, that in the Country there are more healthfull exercises, and better opportunities and means to spend our time than can possibly be had in Cities and Courts. Frequent *dissimulation*, dangerous *reservednesse*, an evill *eye*, ridiculous *affectation*, *policie*, 20 *revenge*, supercilious *scorns*, a phantastick *gate*, affected *motions*, *Chambering*, splendid and swelling *words*, grosse *calumnie*, *defamation*, *cursing*, *swearing*, (which would make a good *Christian* wish himself deafe) with *ambition* the most poysonous *weed* of the mind are the *plants* which grow in those *Gardens*.

More happy then, yea by much more happy than any *King*, if not nearer to a *divine felicitie* is that person who lives and dwels in the Country upon the Rents and profits of his own grounds. There without danger he may act and speake as it becomes *simplicity* and naked *truth*; he hath liberty and choice in all his 30 imployments; there is no place for flattery, which drives headlong the *bad*, entiseth the *good*, and *Proteus*-like transforms it self into all shapes, and yet at last purchaseth nothing but the hatred of all, especially when it is busied in *tale-bearing* and *back-biting*. In the Country we can have a harmelesse and cheerfull conversation with our familiar friends, either in our *houses* or under some *shade*, not troubling or endangering our selves with the *secret mischiefs* and *designs* of *States-men*. Whereas in publick Company there are many things spoken at randome, which bring more of *wearinesse*, than *pleasure* to the hearers. But the quiet retyr'd *liver*, in 40 that calme silence, reads over some profitable histories or books

17 healthfull] healtfull *1651*   41 profitable] prositable *1651*

of devotion, and very often (stird up by an inward and holy joy)
breaks out into divine praises and the singing of *Hymnes* and
Psalms ; with these sacred recreations (more delightfull than
Romances, and the lascivious Musick of *Fidlers* which only Cloy
and weary the ears) doth he feed his *soule* and refresh his *body*.
Besides by this recesse from places of eminent Confluence, we
avoid the clamours and officious *morning salutations* of such
chargeable *Parasites,* which *strike it up* under every lodging, and
disturbe our rest, that they may have wherewith to be *drunk* and
10 *disorderly*.

Those that live in the Country are much more healthfull, and
are not subject to so many diseases as *Citizens* and *Courtiers,* for
in Cities the *buildings* are high, the *lanes* narrow and durtie, the
aire dull and for want of *rarification* and *motion* breeds many
diseases.   But in the Country the *Villages* are built at a great
distance, the *Inhabitants* are more carefull of their healths, the
aire is quick and fresh, the *Sun* unclowded and cheerfull, the
earth lesse subject to vapours and noysome Exhalations, and
whatsoever *accident* happens either publick or private it is put up,
20 or reconciled without noise and fury.   Severall recreations call the
Countryman abroad, now his *Orchard* and *Gardens,* now his *fallow,*
now his *meadows,* another time his *corne fields,* and when all these
are lookt to, there remains something to be done at *home* ; hence
commeth he to be so *vigorous* and *strong,* so *secure* and *cheerfull,*
and is alwaies accompanied with more *pleasure* than *paine*.   This
Privilege also the Country hath above other places, That there are
in it neither *young Physicians,* nor *old diseases*.   But the *Courtier*
hath his *substance* alwaies divided into *foure parts* ;   The first he
gives to his *flatterers,* the second to his *Sollicitour* and the *devour-*
30 *ing irreligious Lawyer,* the third to his *Apothecary,* and the fourth
to the *Physician*.   O how happy then in comparison of these
wretches is the contented, peacefull Countryman, who never heard
of the *Neopolitan* disease, nor any other *bodily disorders,* the
rewards of an unlimited *lust* !   He knows not what is meant by
the *Canker,* the *Apoplexie,* or the *Gout,* never saw a *Juleb,* a *Purge,*
* *A decoction made*   or an * *Apozeme*.   The peacefull *Country-Life*
of severall herbs.   is seldome broken with so many and so weighty
cares and molestations as may hasten an untimely end, and make
the soule and body part by a forced and painfull dissolution.
40 Briefly so far are the Country people from a pompous Curiositie
and ostentation, that they had not known what *brick* or *lime* is,
but for the necessary use of it to build Stables and Out-houses for

their Cattell. Their own *Cots* are for the most part built with *Tymber* which they cover over with *Clay*, and Thatch with *Straw*. And those few more costly buildings which are to be seen there, for sweetnesse of *situation* and *contrivance*, exceed all regal Palaces, or other sumptuous structures built by Citizens.

The day it self (in my opinion) seems of more *length* and *beauty* in the Country, and can be better enjoyed than any where else. There the *years* passe away calmly, and one *day* gently drives on the other, insomuch that a man may be sensible of a certaine *satietie* and *pleasure* from every *houre*, and may be said to feed 10 upon *time* it self, which devours all other things. And although those that are imployed in the mannaging and ordering of their own estates in the Country, have otherwise, namely by that very imployment, much more pleasure and delights than a *Citizen* can possibly have, yet verily so it is, that one *day* spent in the recesse and privacie of the *Country*, seems more pleasant and lasting than a whole year at *Court*. Justly then and most deservingly shall we account them most happy with whom the Sun stays longest, and lends a larger day. The Husbandman is alwaies up and drest with the morning, whose dawning light at the same instant of time 20 breaks over all the Fields and chaseth away the darknesse (which would hinder his early labours) from every *valley*. If his days task keep him late in the *fields*, yet *night* comes not so suddenly upon him, but he can returne home with the *Evening-star*. Whereas in *Towns* and populous *Cities* neither the *Day*, nor the *Sun*, nor a *Star*, nor the *Season* of the *Year* can be well perceived. All which in the Country are manifestly seen, and occasion a more exact care and observation of *Seasons*, that their *labours* may be in their appointed time, and their *rewards* accordingly.

Another most profitable Prerogative also the Husband-man 30 hath, and that is the cheapnesse of all necessary commodities, as *Wood* for fuell, *Hay*, and *Straw*, which in the *Cities* cannot be had but at a most dear rate. Besides he *Dines* and *Sups* both when and where, and with whom he pleaseth, though not delicately, yet so as to satisfie nature, and not offend his health ; but in Cities and Courts the long *preparation* and *Cookery* makes their meals alwaies *unseasonable* ; and their meat is most commonly either raw, or with long stay lukewarme, and ill-relishing ; which notwithstanding they devoure with so much eagernesse, as if they were half starved. And which is worst of all, they are oftentimes 40 driven to sit at the same Table with their enemies and persecutors, which makes their most dainty morsels relish no better than *gaul*

and *wormewood*. This intemperate manner of feeding is too too often the cause of sudden deaths, or a forward decrepitnesse, with lingring and obstinate diseases. But the Husbandman all this while hath *life* and *health* at will, he keeps good hours, Dines and Sups seasonably, eats cheerfully without *suspition* and a *taster* in the Company of his faithfull friends, which at *Court*, and in *Cities*, are meere *prodigies* and *miracles*. Or if he Dines privately, yet hath he the *comfort* and *societie* of a modest, vertuous *wife*, sweet and healthfull *Children*, a religious and quiet *family*, whose very sight is the best
10 *sauce*, and gives most *content*. And though none of all these feed high & daintily, yet by *Gods* goodnesse they have both healthfull *bodies* and cheerfull *complexions*, and never complaine of *famine* or *scarcitie*. A Messe of *Milk* and a piece of *Cheese* rellish better with them in their own *homes*, than the most sumptuous provisions and banquets in the house of a *stranger*; Yea the coarsest dish their table affords is as welcome to them, as if it were drest with rich *Oils*, rare *Sallads*, and the most costly *Spices*.

This Privilege also (above others) makes the Country-man happy, that he hath alwaies something at hand which is both
20 usefull and pleasant. A blessing which hath never bin granted either to a *Courtier*, or a *Citizen*. They have *enemies* enough, but few *friends* that deserve their love, or that they dare trust to either for *Counsell* or *action*. O who can ever fully expresse the pleasures and happinesse of the Country-life! with the various and delightfull sports of *fishing*, *hunting* and *fowling*, with *guns*, *Greyhounds*, *Spaniels*, and severall sorts of *Nets*! what oblectation and refreshment it is, to behold the *green shades*, the beauty and Majestie of the tall and antient *groves*, to be skill'd in *planting* and dressing of *Orchards*, *Flowres* and *Pot-Herbs*, to temper and allay
30 these harmlesse *imployments* with some innocent merry *song*, to ascend sometimes to the *fresh* and *healthfull hils*, to descend into the *bosome* of the *valleys*, and the fragrant, deawy *meadows*, to heare the *musick* of *birds*, the *murmurs* of *Bees*, the *falling* of *springs*, and the pleasant discourses of the *Old Plough-men*, where without any impediment or trouble a man may walk, and (as *Cato Censorius* us'd to say) discourse with the *dead*, that is read the pious works of learned men who departing this life left behind them their *noble thoughts* for the benefit of *posterity*, and the preservation of their own worthy *names*. Where the Christian
40 pious *Countryman* may walk with the learned Religious *Minister* of his *Parish*, or converse with his familiar faithfull *friends*, avoyding

28 Majestie *text 1651*: Majesty *catchword 1651*

the dissimulation and windinesse of those that are *blown* up with the *spirit,* and under the pretence of *Religion* commit all *villanies.* These are the blessings which only a *Countryman* is ordain'd to, and are in vaine wish'd for by *Citizens* and *Courtiers.*

The third CHAPTER.

The Inhabitants of the Country meet with nothing all the *week* that can make them miserable, and when the *Sabbath day* comes, or other *festivall solemnities,* they enjoy a more sincere and heavenly comfort, than those that live in *Cities* and *Courts*; for such a troop of intricate and numerous *negotiations* take up the *thoughts* and *souls* of those people, that they never make any difference betwixt *working* and *holy days.* O what a pious and beautifull work it is, when *holy* and *solemne days* are observ'd in the Country, according to the *sacred rules* and *Ordinances* of *Religion*! The *doore-keepers* of the *house* of *God* set wide open their *beautifull gates,* The *Church-bels* Ring, and every pious Soule is ravish'd with the *Musick,* and is sick of *love* untill he come into the *Courts* of the *Lord.* The *Temples* and *Communion tables* are drest, and the *beauty of holinesse* shines every where. The poorest *Country-labourer* honours that day with his best *habit*; their *families,* their *beasts,* and their *cattell* rest on that day, and every one in a decent and Christian *dresse* walks Religiously towards his *Parish Church,* where they heare Divine *Service,* performe all *holy duties,* and after Dinner releast from all their labours *rest* in the *practice* of true *piety.* But in *Cities* there are no other signs of *holy days* than to sleep them out, or to see their *Wifes* and their *Daughters* richly cloath'd, with their *haire* artificially combed and curiously tyed up; The men walk out into the *Suburbs,* where they fall to drinking and disorder. And if you enter into their *Churches* you shall find a very thin Company, and most of them either *strangers,* or some inferiour *Trades-men.* The chiefest *Citizens* aswell as the *Courtiers* spend those blessed days in pampering themselves, and obeying their own lusts and devices.

But let us return from this *vitious place* into the *harmles Country*: What dainties are there at Court (omiting the pleasure of taking them) which are not first had from the *Countrey*? The *Courtier* pleaseth his palat with a peece of *stale venison,* but the *Countreyman* by the help of his *bow,* his *nets,* or his *gun,* can have it *fresh,* and consequently more *pleasant* and more *healthie.* He hath not a familie whose necessities must be alwaies furnished out

27 curiously] cuririously *1651*

K 2

of the *shop*, nor their table out of the *market*, but a provident and
gainfull familie ; His provision is alwaies out of his own *store*, and
agreeable with the season of the Yeare ; *Pigeons, Partridges,
Capons, Quists, Hares*, with severall sorts of *fish* and *fowle* he hath
in abundance, and is ever ready to pleasure a friend if call'd upon.
His *sheepe* furnish him and his familie with *wooll* for clothing. His
fat *weathers* and *goates* are numerous and alwaies at hand. He
hath his *Oxen* to plough with, his *kine* and *heifers* yeeld him *milk,
butter*, and *Cheese*; His *Kitchin* is alwaies well stor'd with *Bacon* and
10 *Beefe*, nor wants he any thing that is necessary towards the *breeding*
or the *maintaining* of a familie.   If wee look abroad into his *fields*,
wee shall find him well furnished with young *Cattell* and *Colts*, some
ready for the *Yoke*, and *Sadle*, others fit for the *Market* and *Sale*.
Thus by Gods blessing upon his labours he thrives by an honest
Industrie without supplanting his neighbour, while others out of
an unsatiable madnes and a devlish avarice by meere rapine and
a tyrannicall power, maintaine their abominable greatnes with the
bloud and *teares* of poore Innocents and Orphans, and like *Harpyes*
and *heathens* take the *bread* out of the *mouths* of the helples and
20 harmles *Children*.

In the *Countrey* every *one* finds reverence proportionable to his
worth, and those that have none are accordingly esteemed of.
But in *Citties* and *Courts* it is otherwise, for there, no man is
honour'd for his *worth*, but for his *riches*, nor for his *deserts*, but
for his outward *port* and *greatnes*.   And to such *Swoln outsides*
(though never so *hollow* and *rotten* within) all *Parasites* and *suters*
run like rivers to the sea.   But the honest, plaine Husbandmen, if
there lives amongst them a discreet, learned, and upright Patriot,
faithfull and able to give them advise, can never think themselves
30 thankfull enough, for the good offices, fidelitie, and kindnes they
receive from him ; what ever in their fields, gardens and orchards
is most rare, that they present him with, and all of them from the
lowest to the highest make frequent profession of their love and
duty unto him.   But at Court and in great Cities all honour
is conferred upon subtile dissembling *favorites*, while the wise,
honest, and constant *man* is neglected and past by like a *fruitles
tree*, none but *knaves* and *parasites* being admitted to preferment.
The wicked men there carry all the *rewards*, and the righteous
grone under those *punishments* which are due to the bad.

40 The *Countrey-gentleman* and the *husbandman* breed up and
accustome their *sons* and *daughters* to modest, and virtuous Courses,
lest by any remissnes or Loose Carriage, they might incurre the

danger of an ill name. Equall *matches,* and unforc'd *Affections* make them live *happily,* and the *tyes* of Kinred and marriage so unite all neighbourhoods there, that their affections and Courtesies to one another last equally with their lives, which in greater fortunes use to end with the *marriage-day.* This is a happines which *Cittizens* and *Courtiers* seldome enjoy; for they looking after great fortunes, match their Children far off, and are oftner Troubled with their *absence,* than Comforted with their *presence.*

O too too fortunate, and in every Circumstance most blessed and happy Husband-men! who marry their Children to their 10 neighbours, and live alwaies within the *breath* of their Sons in Law, their grand Children, and their families. Who *reverence, love,* and willingly performe all kind and honest offices for their *superiours,* and which is a speciall Comfort to their soules in their old age, visit, relieve, and cherish the *sick* and the *poore.* Such peacefull private livers as these feare no *fines,* nor *forfeitures,* which many times bring in a *Stranger* or an *Enemie* to be the heire of all our labours under the *Sun.*

It is a singular privilege also which the Countrey hath, that the Inhabitants there are not troubled with any *Importunate Visits,* 20 and yet have no Cause to complaine of *Solitude.* This fashion of *visiting* is in great *townes* and *Courts* grown up to a kind of a politick *vocation;* when their *purses* are emptied of money, then their *heads* are full of gadding thoughts, and they are casting about what acquaintance or friend they shalbe troublesome to, under a pretence of Courtesie; so that they can neither sleep well at *nights,* nor suffer their friends to be quiet in the *day-time.*

How happy then is the Countrey-man which moves only in the Circuite of his own grounds, that is absolute master of his time, and is not compelled to waite at the litigious *bars,* and *Courts* of 30 *Law* by a set houre! that goes not *capping* from Lawier to Lawier for their opinion, and then payes for it, before he hath it. That *Supplicates* not to *door-keepers, Clarks,* and *officers,* nor with much sorrow and more amazement is forced to heare a great deale of invented *barbarisme,* and strange *terms.* That is not driven to make humble requests to ev'ry rotten *Sycophant* and *favourite,* which yet in vaine he often solliciteth, and prostrates himselfe to the *Corrupt Magistrates,* for feare of being devoured by such *Cyclops and harpyes.* Happy I say is the Husband-man, who lives a stranger to all these miseries, and in the shadow of some faire 40 *wood* with unspeakable delight contemplates the beauty of the *fields, meadows, fountaines,* and *rivers* of *water.* He admires and

adores the only wise, and almightie god, who first *created*, and still *preserves* all things in a flourishing and fruitfull condition. With this Consideration of *gods* infinite goodnes he mightily comforts himselfe, and is daily delighted to heare the *bleating* of his *sheepe* and *lambs,* the *lowing* of his *Oxen,* and the *neighing* of his *horses.* Towards *sun setting,* the *nightingale* and other pleasant *birds* caroll to him out of the *wood,* his *dogs* like faithfull attendants walk about him ; The *Rams* leap, the *kids* skip, and his *Yard* abounds with *Pigeons, Turkeys, Capons, ducks* and all sorts of *Poultrie.* In-
10 numerable other pleasing objects greet his Eyes, as the leaping of fish, the flying of *fowles,* and the casuall meeting of wild *beasts,* which steale through the *woods* and pleasant *pastures* to some *green banke,* where they may quench their thirst with the *coole streames.* Happy therefore I say, yea, truly happy is the Husbandman who is every day *feasted* (as it were) with so many and such various delights ; who in a certaine and silent tranquillitie enjoys all these blessings with a thankfull heart. Though he should rest no where else, but on *straw,* or the bare *Earth,* yet are his sleeps unbroken, and far more sweet, than those *naps* which are taken upon *silks,*
20 and *beds* of *down.*

Another advantage which the Husband-man hath is this, That in the Country there is more emulation and striving to be good, and lesse occasion of malice than in *Courts* and places of eminence, where sin and wickednesse find alwaies an open entrance. The Confluence there is at all times populous, few or none exhorting to a virtuous life, and many, yea most of them inciting to vice ; but the most dangerous are those, who doe not so much allure with words as with examples, teaching us to esteeme of every man according to his outside, not considering what he may be within,
30 or how qualified towards *God* and his *neighbour.* These kind of people the wise *Seneca* judged to be the most miserable, compar- ing them to *whited wals* and *painted tables,* whose outward show might deceive a very good judgement ; so easily may an honest man be over-reach'd, though never so wise.

But let us proceed to another consideration. There is not in the Country such frequent miscarriage, and occasion of offence, as in *Cities* and *Courts* ; they justle not, nor overtop one another ; They seek all for a subsistence by manuring their lands, and look- ing to their cattell ; there is no *eminencie* amongst them, and con-
40 sequently no *envy.* There are no *Wine-taverns* nor *Cook-shops* for riotous, lewd livers to frequent; no *night-wanderers* to sit up, drink, and vomit in every corner, making the rooms loathsome, and their

Company lesse tollerable than that of *Swine.* There are no nice, curious *Dames,* that never come abroad without a Guard of Hand-mayds ; no quarrels, no bloodshed, nor provocations to them. There are no voluptuous, lascivious *shows,* no *Arts* to egge men on to impietie and *Epicurisme.* All that can be said to offend there, are a few *gnats* and *flies* ; which notwithstanding are not so troublesome, as that they need to *keep up a troop of horse* to drive them out : But there are *Hornets* elsewhere which sting worse, and a Company of *Drones* whose robbery and greedinesse will admit of no cure at all. 10

We are now come to the last *Prerogative,* which in this short discourse we shall reckon for the Country-Inhabitants, and that is this ; They can with lesse charge maintaine their families, and better their estates, than it can be done in *Cities* and *Courts* ; for it is well known at what vast, and unreasonable expences they live at Court, especially in this age, wherein the excessive charge of *rich habits* and a *luxurious diet* is grown to such a height both in *Courts* and *Cities,* that it seems to call for not only the *censure* of the earthly Magistrate, but the *Divine judgement* it self.

O what *Peace,* what *privacy,* and *securitie* is to be found in the 20 *Country* ! No silken *Curtains,* no costly *Arras,* no *Gold* or *Silver* Plate, no sumptuous *Jewels,* no Embroyderd *Garments,* no *Coaches,* nor *Sedans,* with an unprofitable and troublesome *traine* of atten-dants are there in request. The *expenses* we must be at there, are both *frugall* and *necessary,* there is nothing to incite us to a lavish imitation of every ridiculous *Prodigall,* that claps his Revenues upon his back, and by the way of *bravery* comes at last to *beggery.* The Countrymans *Household-stuffe* is but ordinary, his *Tables* and *Chairs* are of plaine Timber, his *Beds* neither carv'd, nor gilded. The *Cups* he drinks in, are in the *Winter* of wholesome *earth,* or 30 the seasond *Oke,* and in the *Summer* of *glasse.* His richest habit is a plaine *coate,* or *cloke* worne first by his own *sheep,* afterwards *shorne* and *spun* for himself ; an able *horse,* a *man-servant* and a *maid* are all his *retinnue.* And truly this plaine *Husband-man* both in reguard of the *Utensils* of his house, his *provision* and *course* of life, is and ever shalbe in my opinion far more happy than either the *Nobleman,* the *Courtier,* or the *Citizen* ; And if we con-sider him for *uprightnesse,* and *purity* of *conscience,* I believe there is no *man* so *Irrationall,* but will confesse him to exceed them all. As for the *Courtier,* all that ever he gets, comes either by some 40 base, servile *prostitution* of his person, or by *flatterie* and *insinua-tion* ; sometime the rich *donatives* of *Princes* and *Noblemen,*

wearied with their importunate begging and sollicitations, conduce much to their advancement. But *vultures* and *harpies* are more tollerable in a *Common-wealth* than this kind of creatures; for, those feed only upon *Carkasses* & the *dead*; but these prey upon and devoure the *living*. That *God* in whose hand the hearts of Princes are, root out of the earth all such *Caterpillers*, which have occasion'd the ruine of many pious *Kings*, and most flourishing *Kingdomes*. There would be something commendable in them, if they would at last in their *old age* leave off their odious *practices*;
10 but as the Proverb goes, *they are never asham'd to swallow the Oxe and his tayle too.* Good *stomacks* they have, and can convert any thing into *bloud* and *nutriment*. Such, and so fatall is the misery of man, that though he plainly sees the *errours* of his life, yet he neither will *Reforme*, nor use the *means* for *Reformation*. May this *ambition* once perish, and *humilitie* take place, such an *happy* change would (no doubt) have an *holy* end.

FINIS.

THE
MOUNT of OLIVES:
OR,
SOLITARY DEVOTIONS.

By

HENRY VAVGHAN *Silurist.*

With

An excellent Difcourfe of the
bleffed ftate of MAN in GLORY,
written by the moft Reverend and
holy Father ANSELM Arch-
Bifhop of *Canterbury,* and now
done into Englifh.

LUKE 21. v. 39, 37.

*Watch ye therefore, and pray always, that ye may
be accompted worthy to efcape all thefe things
that fhall come to paffe, and to ftand before the
Sonne of Man.
And in the day time he was teaching in the
Temple, and at night he went out, and abode in
the Mount that is called* the Mount of Olives.

LONDON, Printed for WILLIAM LEAKE at the
Crown in Fleet-ftreet between the two
Temple-Gates 1 6 5 2.

TO THE
Truly Noble and Religious
Sr. CHARLES EGERTON
KNIGHT.

SIR,

Though I should have no other *defence*, that near *relation* by
which my *dearest friend* laies claime to your *person*, might in some
measure excuse this otherwise *unhansome adventure* of publishing
these *weake productions* under the *shelter* of your *name*.   But
I was not so much induced to *it* by that *Tye*, though very deare
unto me, as by your *love* to *Religion* and *Learning*, and the
respects due from my selfe to your *person*, and those *reverend years*,
which by a *faire* and *virtuous disposal* of your *time* you have
10 happily attained to, and wherein you *safely* are,

> ——*Cœlo dignus canente senectâ*
> *Consilioque deûm,* ——

I know, *Sir*, you will be pleased to accept of this poore *Olive-leafe*
presented to you, so that I shall not be driven to put forth my
hand to take in my *Dove* againe.   And indeed (considering how
fast and how *soone* men degenerate), It must be counted for
a great *blessing*, that there is yet any left which dares *look* upon,
and *commiserate* distressed Religion.   *Good men* in *bad times* are
very scarce ; They are like the *standing eares of Corne escaped out*
20 *of the Reapers hands*, or the *Vine-dressers last gleanings after the*
first ripe fruits have been gathered.   Such a *precious generation are*
the Just in the *day of trouble*, and their *names* are like to *afflicted*
truth, like the *shadow of a great rock in a weary land*, or a *way-*
faring mans lodge in the waste and howling Wildernesse.   The
Sonne of *God* himselfe (when *he* was *here*,) had no place to put his
head in ; And his *Servants* must not think the *present measure* too
hard, seeing their *Master* himself took up his *nights-lodging* in the
cold *Mount* of *Olives.*

By this time, *Sir*, you may see the *reason* which moved me to
30 take *Sanctuary* at your *name*, and now I will acquaint you with
my *designe.*   To be short, *Sir*, It is no other, but that your *name*
(like the *royall stamp*) may make *current* and commend this *poore*

mite to posterity : And that the unfained *lover* of your *Person* may in these few and *transitory sheets* waite upon your memory in the ages to come ; when your immortal and precious *soule* shall be bound up in the bundle of the living, in the *ever-lasting book* of life ; which is devoutly desired by

SIR,

Newton by *Usk*
this first of
October.
1651.

Your very affectionate

and faithful Servant

VAVGHAN.

TO THE

Peaceful, humble, and pious READER.

I know the world abounds with these Manuals, and triumphs over them. It is not then their scarsity that call'd this forth, nor yet a desire to crosse the age, nor any in it. I envie not their frequent Extasies, *and raptures to the third heaven; I onely wish them real, and that their actions did not tell the world, they are rapt into some other place. Nor should they, who assume to themselves the glorious stile of Saints, be uncharitably moved, if we that are yet in the body, and carry our treasure in earthen vessels, have need of these helps.*

10 *It is for thy good, and for his glory, who in the dayes of his flesh prayed here himselfe, and both taught and commanded us to pray, that I have published this. Thou hast here sound directions and wholsome words, and if thou wilt enquire of the Lord and say,* If the Lord will, I shall live, and do this or that, *thou mayest. Here are* Morning *and* Evening *sacrifices, with holy and apposite* Ejaculations *for most times and occasions. And lastly, here are very faithful and necessary* Precepts *and* Meditations *before we come to the Lords Table. To which last part I have added a short and plaine* Discourse *of Death, with a Prayer in the houre thereof. And*
20 *for thy comfort after thou hast past through that* Golgotha, *I have annexed a* Dissertation *of the blessed state of the righteous after this life, written originally by holy* Anselme *sometimes Arch-Bishop of* Canterbury.

I have purposely avoided to leade thee into this little Book with a large discourse of Devotion, what it is, with the severall Heads, Divisions, and sub-divisions of it, all these being but so many fruitlesse curiosities of Schoole-Divinity, Cui fumus est pro fundamento. *Neither did I thinke it necessary that the ordinary Instructions for a regular life (of which theere are infinite Volumes already extant)*
30 *should be inserted into this small Manuall, lest instead of Devotion, I should trouble thee with a peece of Ethics. Besides, thou hast them already as briefly delivered as possibly I could, in my Sacred Poems.*

And thus, Christian Reader, do I commend it to thy practise, and

31 *Ethics*] *Ethies* catchword and text 1652

To the Reader. 141

the benefit thou shalt finde thereby. Onely I shall adde this short Exhortation: That thou wouldest not be discouraged in this way, because very many are gone out of it. Think not that thou art alone upon this Hill, there is an innumerable company both before and behinde thee. Those with their Palms in their hands, and these expecting them. If therefore the dust of this world chance to prick thine eyes, suffer it not to blinde them; but running thy race with patience, look to J E S U S the Authour and finisher of thy faith, who when he was reviled, reviled not againe. Presse thou towards the mark, *and let the people and their Seducers rage;* be faithful 10 unto the death, and he will give thee a Crowne of life. *Look not upon transitorie, visible things, but upon him that is eternal, and invisible. Choose the better part, yea, that part with Saint* Hierome, *who preferred the poore Coate of* Paul *the Hermite to the purple and pride of the world. Thus with my simple Advise unto thee, I bid thee farewel.*

Thy Christian friend

Henry Vaughan.

7 running] running *1652*   12 *eternal*] etern l *1652*

The Table.

FINIS.

27 *Enemies.*] Enemies *1652*

ADMONITIONS
FOR
Morning-Prayer.

The night (saith *Chrysostome*) was not therefore made, that either we should sleep it out, or passe it away idly; and Chiefly because we see many worldly persons to watch out whole nights for the Commodities of this life. In the *Primitive* Church also the *Saints* of God used to rise at midnight to praise the *Rock of their salvation* with *Hymns and Spiritual Songs.* In the same manner shouldst thou do now, and Contemplate the *Order* of the Stars, and how they all in their several stations praise their Creator. When all the world is asleep, thou shouldst watch, weep and pray and propose unto thy self that *Practise* of the Psalmist, *I am weary of my groaning, every night wash I my bed, and water my Couch with my tears;* for as the *Dew* which falls by night is most fructifying, and tempers the heat of the *Sun;* so the tears we shed in the night, make the soul fruitful, quench all Concupiscence, and supple the hardnesse we got in the day. *Christ* himself in the day-time taught and preach'd, but continued all night in prayer, sometimes in a Mountain apart, sometimes amongst the wild beasts, and sometimes in solitary places.

They, whose Age or Infirmity will not give them way to do thus, should use all Convenient means to be up before the Sunrising, for *we must prevent the Sunne to give God thanks, and at the day-spring pray unto him,* Wisd. 16. It was in the morning that the Children of *Israel* gathered the *Manna*; and of the Just man it is said, *That He will give his heart to resort early to the Lord that made him, and will pray before the most high,* Eccl. 39. So soon therefore as thou dost awake, shut thy door against all prophane and worldly thoughts, and before all things let thy God be first admitted, offer unto him thy first fruits for that day, and commune with him after this manner.

When thou dost awake.

O God the Father! who saidst in the beginning, *Let there be light,* and it was so; *Inlighten my Eyes that I never sleepe in death:* lest at any time my Enemy should say, *I have prevailed against him.*

O God the Sonne! light of light; the most true and perfect light, from whom this light of the Sun, and the day had their

beginning; thou, that art the light shining in darknesse,
Inlightning every one that cometh into this world, expell from me
all Clouds of Ignorance, and give me true understanding, that in
thee, and by thee I may know the *Father*; whom to know is to
live, and to serve is to reigne.

O God the Holy Ghost! the fire that inlightens, and warms
our hearts, shed into me thy most sacred light, that I may know
the true Joyes of Heaven, and see to escape the illusions of this
world. Ray thy selfe into my soul that I may see what an
10 Exceeding weight of glory my Enemy would bereave me of for
the meer shadowes and painting of this world. Grant that I may
know those things which belong unto thee, and nothing else;
Inflame me with thy divine love that with a true Christian
Contempt I may tread upon all transitory Pleasures, and seek
only those things which are eternal.

Most blessed Trinity! and one eternal God! as thou hast this
day awaked me from this bodily sleep, so awake my soule from
the sleep of sin, and as thou hast given me strength after sleep,
now again to watch, so after death give me life, for what is death
20 to me, is but sleep with thee, to whom be ascribed all glory,
wisdome, majesty, dominion and praise now and for Ever, Amen.

When thou dost arise.

Arise O my soul that sleepest, arise from the dead, and Christ
shall give thee light. Arise O daughter of *Sion*, O my soul
redeemed with the blood of Christ! sit no more in the dust of
thy sins, but arise, and rest in that peace which is purchas'd by
thy Saviours merits.

Christ Jesus! my most merciful and dear Redeemer! as it is
thy meer goodness that lifts up this mortal and burthensome body,
30 so let thy grace lift up my soul to the true knowledge and love of
thee; grant also that my body may this day be a helper and
servant to my soul in all good works, that both *body* and *soul*
may be partakers of those Endlesse Joyes, where thou livest and
reignest with the Father and the Holy Ghost, one true God world
without End, *Amen.*

*As soone as thou art drest, before thou comest forth from thy
Chamber, kneel down in some convenient place, and in this, or the
like Prayer commend thy self for that day unto thy Creator's
Protection.*

40 Almighty, eternal God, the Father of our Lord *Jesus Christ,*

34 Father] Faher *1652*

I blesse and praise thy holy name, and with my whole heart give thee all possible thanks, that out of thine infinite goodness thou wert pleased to watch over me this night, to resist my adversary, and to keep me from all perils of body and soul; O thou! that never slumbrest nor sleepest, how careful hast thou been of me! how hast thou protected me, and with thy holy angels, thy ministring spirits sent forth to minister for the heirs of salvation, incompast me about! yea, with what unmeasurable love hast thou restored unto me the light of the day, and rais'd me from sleep and the shadow of death, to look up to thy holy hill; Justly 10 mightst thou, O God, have shut the gates of death upon me, and laid me for ever under the barres of the Earth, but thou hast redeemed me from Corruption, and with thy *Everlasting armes* enlarged my time of Repentance.

And now O Father of mercies, and God of all Consolation, hear the voyce of thy Supplicant, and let my cry be heard in thy highest heavens: As I do sincerely love thee, and beg for thy Protection, so receive thou me under the shadow of thy wings, watch over me with the Eyes of thy mercy, direct me in the wayes of thy Law, and enrich me with the gifts of thy Spirit, that I may passe 20 through this day, to the glory of thy great name, the good of others, and the comfort of my own soul. Keep me, O my God, from the great offence; quench in me all vain Imaginations, and sensual desires; sanctifie and supple my heart with the dew of thy divine Spirit, refresh it with the streams of thy grace, that I may bring forth fruit in due season, and not cumber the ground, nor be cut off in thy anger. And to this end I do here resigne my body and my soul, with all the faculties thou hast bestowed upon both, into thy Almighty hands; Guide thou them in the works of thy Law, turne my eyes from all transitory objects, to the things 30 which are eternal, and from the *Cares* and *Pride* of this world to the *fowles of the aire* and the *Lillies of the field*; And now, O my God, seeing I am but Dust and Ashes, and my Righteousnesse a filthy Rag, having no deserts in my self but what should draw Everlasting vengeance, and the Vials of thy bitter wrath upon my body and soul; behold, I have brought with me thy first-born and onely begotten, the propitiation for my sins, the *Incense* I offer up with my prayers, *Rev.* 8. 3. my Redeemer and Mediatour in whom thou art well-pleased, hear thou him. O look not upon my Leprosie, but on his beauty and perfection! and for the righteous- 40

11 mightst] mighst *1652*
32 *aire G Gu*   aire; *1652*   *field; M: field 1652: field. G Gu*

nesse of thy *Son,* forgive the sins of thy *Servant.* Grant this for his sake, to whom with thee and the Holy Ghost, be all glory and majesty, Dominion and power now and for ever. Amen.

Admonitions when we prepare for any farre Journey.

When thou art to go from home, remember that thou art to come forth into the *World,* and to Converse with an Enemy; And what else is the World but a Wildernesse? A darksome, intricate wood full of *Ambushes* and dangers; A Forrest where spiritual hunters, principalities and powers spread their nets, and
10 compasse it about; wouldst thou then escape these ghostly snares; this *wickednes in high places,* and return home if not better and holier, yet not worse then at thy setting out? Wouldst thou with *Jacob* passe over these *Waters* with thy staffe onely, and in thy return become two bands? *Gen.* 32. 10. Why then, do as he did, begin thy Journey with prayer, and say, *If God will be with me, and keep me in this way that I go, and will give me bread to eate, and raiment to put on, so that I come again to my fathers house in peace: then shall the Lord be my God,* Gen. 28. 20, 21. This was his practise, and the practise of his fathers; *The Lord God of*
20 *heaven* (saith *Abraham*) *who took me from my fathers house, and from the land of my kindred, &c. he shall send his Angel before thee.* Nor must thou pray only at thy setting forth, but all the way, and at all times; Thus *Eliezer* prayed at the Well, *Isaac* in the field, and *Elias* (in his journey to *Mount Horeb*) under a *Juniper* tree in the Wildernesse. This also (if thou wilt imitate these holy men) thou may'st do, and for that pious purpose thou hast here these following Prayers.

When we go from home.

Almighty and everlasting God, who art the *Way,* the *Life* and
30 the *Truth;* look down from heaven, and behold me now betwixt the Assaults of the Devil, the allurements of the World, and my own inclinations; I cannot look abroad, but these flock about me; But O thou that leadest *Joseph* like a sheep, thou most faithful and Almighty guide, lend me thy hand, open mine Eyes, direct my steps, and cause me to walk in thy fear; Thou that didst go out with *Jacob* from *Beer-she-ba* unto *Padan-aran,* guiding him in the *waste plaines,* and watching over him on his *Pillow of stones,* be not now farre from me; Leade me, O Lord, in thy righteous-nesse, make my paths straight, and strengthen my goings, that
40 having finished my Course here, I may sit down in thy Kingdome, an Inheritance undefiled, purchased for me with the blood of my Saviour, and thy beloved Son *Jesus Christ,* Amen.

II.

O thou, that art every where ! *Thou that sittest upon the Circle of the Earth, and all the Inhabitants thereof are as Grashoppers before thee ! Whose Eyes discover the deep things of the night, before whom Hell is naked, and all the Devices of my spirituall Enemies !* Thou that didst leade *Abraham* thy chosen from *Ur* of the *Chaldees* into a land flowing with milk and honey, favour I beseech thee the present harmlesse Enterprise and innocent purpose of thy servant, be unto me in my Journey a Comfort, in the heate a shadow, in stormes a shelter, and in adversity my 10 protection ; That having finished my intended course, I may return in peace full of thy praises, who art near to all those that call upon thee ; Grant this for *Christ Jesus* his sake, *Amen.*

Meditate in the way upon the sojournings and travels of the Patriarchs and Prophets, the many weary journeys of *Jesus Christ* in the flesh, the travels of his Apostles by sea and land, with the pilgrimage and peregrinations of many other precious Saints that wandred in Deserts and Mountains, of whom the world was not worthy.

Admonitions how to carry thy self in the Church. 20

Holinesse (saith the Royall Prophet) *becometh thy house for ever.* When thou art going thither then, carry not the world with thee.

Let vain or busie thoughts have there no part,
Bring not thy *Plough*, thy *Plots*, thy *Pleasures* thither,
Christ purg'd his Temple ; so must thou thy heart.
All worldly thoughts are but Theeves met together
To Cousin thee. Look to thy actions well,
For *Churches* are either our Heav'n or Hell.

These reverend and sacred buildings (however now vilified and shut up) have ever been, and amongst true Christians still are the 30 solemne and publike places of meeting for Divine Worship: There the *flocks feed at noon-day*, there the great *Shepherd* and *Bishop* of their souls is *in the midst of them*, and where he is, that *Ground is holy*; Put off thy shoes then, thy worldly and carnall affections, and when thou beginnest to enter in, say with *Jacob, How dreadful is this place ! sure this is none other then the house of God, and this is the gate of heaven !* Such reverence and religious affection hath in all ages been shew'd towards these places, that the holy men of God detain'd either by Captivity, or other neces- sary occasions, when they could not remedy the distance, yet to 40 testifie their *desire and longing for the Courts of the Lord*, Psal. 84. they would always worship towards them. Thus *Daniel* upon the

Idolatrous Decree signed by *Darius, goes into his house, and his windows being open in his Chamber towards Jerusalem, he kneeled upon his knees, and prayed and gave thanks before his God as he did afore-time,* Dan. 6. 10. which fully proves it to have been his Constant manner of Devotion.   And of *Judith* we read *that about the time that the Incense of that Evening was offered up in* Hierusalem, *she cried unto the Lord,* Iud. 9. 1.   But above all, most pathetical and earnest is that crie of King *David* in the 85. *Psalm.*

> *How amiable are thy Tabernacles O Lord of Hosts!*

10 *My soul longeth, yea even fainteth for the Lord, my heart and my flesh cryeth out for the living God.*

> *Yea the Sparrow hath found an house, and the Swallow a nest for her selfe, where she may lay her young, even thine Altars, O Lord of Hosts, my God and my King!*

> *Blessed are they that dwell in thy house, they will be still praising thee.*

> *For one day in thy Courts is better than a thousand; I had rather be a doore-keeper in the House of my God, than to dwell in the tents of wickednesse.*

20 Let it be thy Care then, when thou art there present to carry thy self like a true worshipper; Give none offence, neither outwardly to thy *Brethren,* nor the *Angels,* 1 Cor. 11. 10.   Nor inwardly to thy God, whose Eyes shine within thee, and discern thy reins and thy heart.   Look seriously about thee, and Consider with thy self how many beauteous, wittie, and hopeful personages in their time lie now under thy feet ; thou canst not tell but thy turn may be next.   Humble thy self in this dust, and all vain Imaginations will flie from thee.   Consider that thou art now in the *Cave of Macpelah,* in a sacred *Repositorie* where the Bodies of
30 Saints are asleep, expecting that hour, *when those that are in the grave shall hear his voyce.*   Do not then stop thy eares against the *Charmer,* but give diligent attention, and hear him while it is yet to day, that in the day of thy death thou mayst rest there in the same hope.   When thy vessell is fill'd with this *Manna,* and thy soul satisfied, go not off without Thanksgiving ; Be not like those nine *Leapers* who never returned to give glory to God ; but come back with the thankfull *Samaritane,* and receive another blessing, *Go in peace.*   Saint *Luke* in the *Acts* of the Apostles making mention of the *Ethiopian Eunuch,* who came up to *Jerusalem* for to wor-
40 ship, tells us, that in his returne he was reading in *Isaiah* the

Prophet; This blessed *Convert* I would have thee to imitate: When thou hast fill'd thy *Hin* with this living water, leave it not behinde thee at the Fountain; spill not thy *Milk* and thy *Wine*, because thou hast it without *money and without price*, but carry it home and use it. Thou mayest have need of it in six dayes, and perhaps shalt not come to draw again, untill thou drinkest it anew with thy Saviour in *his Fathers Kingdom.*

A Prayer before thou goest to Church.

Lord *Jesus Christ*, who out of thy Fathers bosome wert sent into this world to reveal his will unto sinners, and to instruct them 10 in the way of salvation; behold, I am now going to hear thy blessed word, and these many yeers have so done, expecting still thy good pleasure and the Consummation of thy sacred will in me. I have come unto the bread of life, and yet am hungry; into the light, and yet am blind; unto the great Physician, and yet my Issue runs: The former and the later rain of thy heavenly Doctrine falls still without intermission upon my heart, but this bad ground yeelds nothing but Thornes and Briers. Many dayes, many moneths, and many yeers hast thou expected fruit, and found nothing but leaves. It is thy Infinite mercy, O Lord, that 20 thou hast left unto us the seed of thy word, and sendest into thy harvest such upright and faithful labourers; but in vain, O Lord, shall they cry in our Ears, unlesse thou openest and renewest our hearts. Open then, I beseech thee (O blessed Jesu!) the eares of my heart, that not onely the outward hearing, but the inward also may be stirr'd up in me, and what I hear with the eare, I may understand with the spirit. O thou most mild and merciful *Lamb of God!* the onely, and the Almighty sower! grant, I beseech thee, that the seed which falls this day upon my heart, may never be choak'd with the Cares of this world, nor be devoured by the 30 fowles of the aire, nor wither away in these times of persecution and triall: but so Cherish it with the Dew of thy divine spirit, that (as in a good and faithful ground) it may bring forth fruit unto eternal life, to the glory of thy great name, and the Comfort of my poor soul, which thou hast bought with thy most precious and saving blood. *Amen.*

Another when thou art come home, or in the way
if thou beest alone.

Lord *Jesus Christ*, my ever mercifull, and most loving Redeemer! I give unto thee most hearty thanks for this thy heavenly, spiritual 40 provision wherewith thou hast fed and refreshed my soul. Grant

I beseech thee that this Celestial seed may take root in me, and be effectual to my salvation ; Watch over my heart, O Lord, and hedge it in with thy grace, that the fowles which descend in the shadows of the Evening may not pick it out ; But so prepare and fit me for thy love, that I may never forget thy gracious words, thy blessed and saving advice, but may know in *this my day what belongs unto my peace.* It is thy promise by thy holy Prophet, *That as the rain cometh down, and the snow from heaven, and re-*
10 *turneth not thither, but watereth the earth, and maketh it bring forth and bud, that it may give seed to the sower, and bread to the eater: So thy word that goeth forth out of thy mouth, shall not return unto thee void, but shall accomplish that which thou pleasest, and prosper in the thing whereto thou sendest it,* Isai. 55. 10, 11. Even so, Lord *Jesus,* let it be as thou hast promised. Let the words I have heard this day out of the mouth of thy servant, the *Dispenser,* and *Steward* of thy Mysteries prosper in me, and make my life answerable to his Doctrine ; that I may not onely know what thy blessed will is, but performe also and fulfill it ; so that at last by thy mediation and mercies I may attain to thy eternal and
20 most glorious Kingdom. *Amen.*

Admonitions for Evening-Prayer.

Remember that in the *Levitical* Law there is a frequent Com-memoration and Charge given of the two daily Sacrifices, the one to be offer'd up in the morning and the other in the Evening, *Exod.* 30. 7, 8. These offerings by *Incense,* our holie, harmlesse and undefiled High-Priest hath taken away, and instead of them every devout *Christian* is at the appointed times to offer up a Spiritual Sacrifice, namely that of *Prayer* ; for *God is a Spirit, and they that worship him, must worship him in spirit and in truth,* John 4. 24.
30 At these prescribed times (if thou wilt have thy Prayers to ascend up before God) thou must with-draw from all outward occupations to prepare for the inward and divine. To which end thou hast here this following Meditation, that thou maiest therewith season and invite thy soul from thy worldlie imployments to her proper voca-tion, and so come not altogether undrest into the presence of the *King of glory.*

A Meditation at the setting of the Sun, or the Souls Elevation to the true light.

The path of the Just (O my God) is as the shining light,
40 that shineth more and more unto a perfect day of eternity,

Prov. 4. But the wicked neither know, nor understand, they walk in darknesse, and from the inward darknesse of their minds passe at last into the outward, eternal darknesse. O most miserable and undone soul! to whom thy *Sunne* is set; that everlasting glorious *Sun*! which in thy holy Elects never setteth, but is alwaies at the height, full of brightnesse and Consolation. A heavie night sits in the noone-day upon those souls that have forsaken thee; They look for light, and behold darknesse; for brightnesse, and they walk in obscurity. They grope for the wall like the blind, as if they had no Eyes; They stumble at noone-day as in the night, they are in desolate places as dead men. But on those that walk with thee an everlasting day shines; This *Sun* of the firmament hath his Course; it riseth, setteth, comes up again, and again goes down: But thou Lord, knowest no vicissitudes, thou art the *Ancient of dayes*, thou art the *Rock of ages from Everlasting to Everlasting.* O thou, *the same to day and yesterday, and for evermore! Thou bright and morning Starre springing from on high,* illuminate me, who am now sitting in darknesse and in the shadow of death. *O light of light, the brightnesse of thy Fathers glory,* inlighten all inward obscurities in me, that after this life I may never be cast into the outward darknesse. O most blessed, most merciful, and Almighty *Jesu*! abide I beseech thee with me, *for it is towards Evening, and the day is far spent, Luke* 24. As long as thou art present with me, I am in the light, but when thou art gone, I am in the shadows of death, and amongst the stones of emptinesse. When thou art present, all is brightnesse, all is sweetnesse, I am in my Gods bosome, I discourse with him, watch with him, walk with him, live with him, and lie down with him. All these most dear and unmeasurable blessings I have with thee, and want them without thee. Abide then with me, O thou whom my soul loveth! Thou Sun of righteousnesse with healing under thy wings arise in my heart; refine, quicken, and cherish it; make thy light there to shine in darknesse, and a perfect day in the dead of night.

A Prayer for the Evening.

Most gracious, Almighty God! full of loving kindnesse, and long-suffering, whose mercy is above all thy works, and thy glory above the heavens; whose truth reacheth unto the Clouds, and whose words shall never passe away, forgive me, I beseech thee, my transgressions this day, my vain thoughts, idle words, and loose conversation; my exceeding neglect and forgetfulnesse of thee, my head-

5 in] on *G Gu*

long inclinations and lusting after the world, preferring this land
of *Cabul* before the snow of *Lebanon,* and a broken Cistern before
the Well of life.   Justly, O Lord, might'st thou have shewed me
thy back this day, and cut me off from amongst thy people, *Jer.*
18. 17. but thou hast had mercy, and not sacrifice ; thou hast shed
upon me the light of thy Countenance, and removed my sins farre
out of thy sight.   I know, O my God, it is not in man to establish
his own ways, it is thy Almighty arme must do it ; It is thou alone
that hast led me through this day, and kept me both from doing and
10 from suffering evill.   And now, O thou preserver of men ! What
shall I do unto thee ? What shall I render unto my Lord for all the
mercies and loving kindnesses shewed unto thy servant this day,
and all the dayes of my life hitherto ? *I will offer unto thee the sacrifice of thanksgiving, and call upon the name of the Lord.* I will ever
love thee, fear thee, praise thee, and trust in thee ; My song shall
be of thee in the night season, and in the day time I will be
speaking of thy wondrous works, thy most merciful and liberal
arme ; I will make thee my *Delight* in the house of my pilgrimage,
and I shall always with all my strength, with all my heart, and
20 with all my soul ascribe unto thee, all glory, wisdome, majesty,
dominion, and honour this day and for evermore.   *Amen.*

A Prayer when thou art going into bed.

Most glorious, and onely wise God ! to whom the light and the
darknes are the same, whose dwellings are eternal, and in whose
Kingdome there is no need of Candles, nor of the light of the
Sunne ; look, I beseech thee, upon thy servant, who tarries in this
place all night, Gen. 28. 11.   And forasmuch as thou (out of thy
tender love and Compassion on thy Creatures) hast ordained this
time for their repose and refreshing, that having past through the
30 Cares and dangers of the day, they might under the shadow of thy
wings finde rest and security ; keep me, I most humbly beseech
thee, from the hours and the powers of darknesse ; watch over me
this night in thy Almighty providence, and scatter all the rebellions
and devices of my Adversaries.   Inlighten my soul, sanctifie my
body, govern my affections, and guide my thoughts, that in the
fastest closures of my eyelids my spirit may see thee, and in the
depth of sleep be Conversant with thee.   Suffer me not, O my
God, to forget thee in the dark, or to say, *The Lord seeth me not,
The Lord hath forsaken the earth,* Ezek. 8. 12. but so keep me in
40 thy fear, and sanctifie me with thy grace, that all the words of my
mouth, and the meditations of my heart may be alwayes of thee.

Make my soul to thirst for thee, and my flesh also to long after thee. And at what time soever thou shalt awake me from this bodily sleep, awake also my soul in me, make thy morning-star to arise in my heart, and let thy spirit blow upon my garden, that the spices thereof may flow out. Quicken me O Lord, according to thy wonted kindnesse, so shall I seek thee early, and make my prayer unto thee with joyful lips. And now O my most loving and faithful Creatour, take me, I beseech thee, into thy Almighty protection, stretch over me the *Arme* of thy mercy, let thine Eye be towards the work of thine own hands, and the purchased pos- 10 session of thy onely begotten, and my most merciful Redeemer *Jesus Christ*, Amen.

¶ As often as thou dost awake in the night, be sure to lift up thy heart unto God in this or the like short *Ejaculation. Holy, holy, holy, Lord God of Sabbath! heaven and earth are full of the majesty of thy glory.* By resorting thus unto God, thou shalt finde a great furtherance and cheerfulnesse in thy spiritual exercises, and besides it will keep always about thee the *savour of life.* And because thou shalt not be unfurnished upon any incident occasions, I have strowed here this handful of savoury 20 herbs, which thou mayest take up as thou findest them in thy way.

EJACULATIONS.

When the Clock strikes.

Blessed be the houre in which my Lord Jesus was borne, and the houre in which he died! O Lord Remember me in the houre of death!

When thou intendest any businesse, or Journey.

O do well unto thy servant! that I may live and keep thy Word.

When thou art persecuted.   30

Haste thee, O God, to deliver me, make haste to help me, O Lord!

Upon some suddaine fear.

O set me upon the Rock that is higher then I, for thou art my hope, and a strong tower for me against my enemy.

Upon any disorderly thoughts.

Make me a clean heart, O God, and renew a right spirit within me.

Upon any occasions of sadnesse.

Thy rebuke hath broken my heart, I am full of heavinesse, but thou, O Lord, shalt lift me up again.

Upon any Diffidence.

Thou art my hope, O Lord, even from my youth, through thee have I been holden up ever since I was borne ; though thou shouldst kill me, yet will I trust in thee.

When thou dost any good work.

Not unto me, O Lord, not unto me, but unto thy name give the 10 *praise.*

When thou art provoked to anger.

Give thy peace unto thy servant, O God, let no man take away my Crown ; In patience, O Lord, let me possesse my soul.

For thine Enemies.

Lord, lay not this sinne to their Charge ; they know not what they do.

Upon any gracious deliverance, or other mercies conferr'd upon thee.

The Lord is my Shepherd, I shall not want. He maketh me to 20 *lie down in green pastures, he leadeth me besides the still waters. He hath prevented me with the blessings of goodnesse, he hath granted me my hearts desire, and not with-holden the request of my lips. Surely goodnesse and mercy shall follow me all the dayes of my life : And I will dwell in the house of my God for ever.*

Upon any losses, or other adversities.

Shall we receive good at the hand of God, and shall we not receive evill? Naked came I out of my mothers womb, and naked shall I return thither; the Lord gave, and the Lord hath taken away, blessed be the name of the Lord.

30
When thou hearest that any is dead.

Teach me, O Lord, to number my dayes, that I may apply my heart unto wisdome.

Upon thought of thy sins.

Turn away thy face from my sins, O Lord, and blot out all mine offences.

Praise the Lord, O my soul, and forget not all his benefits, who forgiveth all thy sins, and healeth all thine Infirmities.

When thou art weary of the cares and vanities of this world.

Like as the Hart brayeth for the water-brooks, so thirsteth my soul after thee O God.

O who will give me the wings of a Dove, that I may flie, and be at rest.

¶ *Admonitions, with Meditations and Prayers to be used before we come to the Lords Supper.*

All the Sacraments of the New Testament, in those that come to participate them, require a most Exquisite and sincere prepara- tion.   But this Sacrament of the Lords Table, because in *Institu-* 10 *tion* and *Effect* it is the highest of all, requires the most perfect and purest Accomplishments.   Our preparation to this Sacrament is not perfected by Contrition onely and Confession of sins, (both which are unavoidably requisite) but if we will be worthy receivers and partake of those graces which are exhibited unto us in this heavenly banquet, there are many other duties we must necessarily performe, for this Sacrament is of an infinite vertue, having in it the *Wel-spring* of all graces, even *Jesus Christ* with all the merits of his most bitter passion, which admit neither number nor measure.   Wherefore such as our pre-disposition is, such also 20 shall our proportion be of this spiritual *Manna*; for as he that cometh to a Well to draw water, takes no more thence, then what his vessel contains; which yet he cannot impute unto the Well, but unto his Pitcher which could hold no more; so they that come unto this glorious Sacrament, receive onely so much grace as their preparation and holines makes them capable of.   Now there are required of us, before we presume to lay hands upon this bread of life, three things.

{ 1. Purity of Conscience.
{ 2. Purity of Intention.   30
{ 3. Fervent and effectual Devotion.

We must (as far as it lies in us) refrain from all actual sins in thought, word, and deed.   Secondly, We must do it to a good end, not for any private benefit; not by compulsion, or for fear of Censure, or any other Ecclesiastical correction; not out of Cus- tome, nor for any sensual devotion or joy because of the con- fluence and company at these love-feasts.   Thirdly and lastly, we must watch over our owne souls, and take heed that no wind blows upon our garden but the spiritual and eternal; we must

labour for an heavenly setlednesse, sanctified affections, holy
hopes, new garments, a clean heart, and a right spirit.   *Cant.* 2.
The soul must be sick of love, she must long for the banqueting
house, nothing now must appear but flowers, nothing must be
heard but the singing of birds, and the voice of the Turtle.   Lord
God (saith S. *Ambrose*) with what contrition of heart, with what
fountains of tears, with what reverence & fear, with what chastity
of body and purity of mind should this divin mystery be celebrated ! where thy flesh is the meat, where thy blood is the drink,
10 where the creature feeds upon the Creatour, and the Creatour is
united unto the creature, where Angels are spectators, and God
himself both the Priest and the Sacrifice, what holinesse and
humility should we bring thither ?

     O what pure things, most pure, must those hands be
               which bring my God to me !

As therefore some rich, odoriferous water is distill'd out of
many and several sorts of fragrant herbs and flowers, so our devotion at this soveraigne Sacrament should be composed of many
spiritual, acceptable affections with God, as (amongst others) are
20 profound humility, unmeasurable reverence, ardent love, firme
faith, actuall charity, impatient hunger, and an intollerable longing
after this heavenly banquet.

And because we may not touch these white robes with dirty
hands, nor come neer the Rose of *Sharon* with ill sents and
offensive fumes, it hath been ever the Custom of Gods Church to
injoyn and set apart a certain limited time of purification before
this mysterious solemnity, wherein all religious and worthy Com-
municants addressed and prepared themselves in some measure
for this unmeasurable mercy.   Such was in our Church, that more
30 strict and holy season, called *Lent*, and such still are the prepara-
tion-dayes before this glorious Sabbath in all true Churches.
Two dayes were given the *Israelites* to sanctifie themselves, and to
wash their clothes, that they might be ready against the third day,
upon which the Lord was to come downe (in the sight of all the
people) upon Mount *Sinai* ; And this onely at the reception of
the Law which was given by Angels ; much more then ought
we to wash and cleanse our vessels from all vaine affections, idle
words and actions, and to separate our selves from the world for
three dayes at least, that we may be ready against that great and
40 blessed day, wherein we are to come, not to a mountain that
might not be touched, nor to the sound of a Trumpet, nor to the

voice of words spoken to us out of the midst of fire, but to the general assembly, and Church of the first-borne, which are written in heaven, and to *Jesus the Mediatour of the new Covenant, and to the blood of sprinkling, that speaketh better things then that of Abel.* See then that thou refuse not to come to this great marriage of the Kings Son with thy soul, and see withall, that thou comest not without a wedding garment, that is to say, unprepared. *For, whosoever shall eate this bread, and drink this cup of the Lord unworthily, shall be guilty of the body and blood of the Lord ; But let a man examine himselfe, and so let him eate of that bread, and* 10 *drink of that cup of the Lord, for he that eateth and drinketh un-worthily, eateth and drinketh damnation to himselfe, not discerning the Lords body,* 1 Cor. 11. 27, 28, 29. These are the words of a faithful witnesse, and thou maiest beleeve them.

When therefore thou doest intend to be a partaker of this merciful and mysterious Sacrament, be sure for three daies at least not to intermeddle with any worldly businesse, but all that time redeeme those many daies which were vainly spent by thee ; enter into thine owne bosome, examine what thou hast there, and if thou findest any sons of darknesse lurking under those fig-leaves, 20 conceal them not, but turne them out of doors, and wash their Couch with thy teares ; have a care that in the Bridegroomes bed, instead of myrrhe and flowers, thou strowest not thornes and thistles. The Evening before thou art to communicate, feed but moderately, and after supper use no corrupt communication, but converse inwardly with thine own heart, and meditate what an Almighty guest thou art to entertaine there next day. Consider seriously thine own unworthinesse, and desire of him that he would sanctifie and furnish the roome where he is to eate the Passeover with thee. Intreat him to defend thee that night from all sinful 30 Illusions and temptations, and to keep the house cleane and garnished for himself. When thou hast thus commended thy self into his hands, let thy sleep that night be shorter then usual, be up with the day, or rather with thy Saviour, who rose up early, while it was yet dark. Meditate with thy self what miracles of mercy he hath done for thee. Consider how he left his Fathers bosome to be lodged in a manger, and laid by his robes of glory to take upon him the seed of *Abraham,* that he might cloath thee with Immortality. Call to minde his wearisome journeys, con-tinual afflictions, the malice and scorne he underwent, the perse- 40 cutions and reproaches laid upon him, his strong cries and teares in the days of his flesh, his spiritual agony and sweating of blood,

4 *the*] *ehe 1652*

with the Implacable fury of his Enemies, and his own unspeakable humility, humbling himself to the death of the Crosse, a death accursed by Gods own mouth. Consider againe (if thou canst) of what unmeasurable love was he possessed, who having designed and spent his time of life here for thy salvation, did not onely leave thee those divine Oracles and Instructions to be guided by, but to seale up the summe and make heaven sure unto thee, did by his last Testament give himself with all the merits of his life and death to be wholly thine, and instead of them took upon him all 10 thy transgressions, bore all thine iniquities, and to appease the anger, and satisfie the Justice of his Father, became the holy, harmlesse, and undefiled sacrifice and perfect satisfaction for the sins of the world, reconciling all things unto his Father, whether they be things in earth, or things in heaven.

When thou hast thus considered him in his acts of love and humility, consider him again in his glory, take thine Eyes off from *Bethlehem* and *Golgotha*, and look up to the mount of *Olives*, yea, to heaven where he sits now upon the right hand of his Father, Angels, principalities and powers being made subject unto him. 20 Call to minde his Joyful resurrection, his most accomplished conquest, and triumph over the world, death and hell; his most gracious and familiar conversation with his Apostles before his Ascension, with his most loving and comfortable carriage towards them at his departure, *leading them out as farre as* Bethanie, *and lifting up his hands, and blessing them.* Lastly, close up these thoughts with a serious and awful meditation of that great and joyful, though dreadful day of his second coming to judgement, promised by himself, and affirmed at the time of his Ascension by the two men in white apparel. *Ye men of Galilee, why stand* 30 *ye gazing up into heaven? this same Jesus which is taken up from you into heaven, shall so come in like manner as ye have seen him go into heaven.*

Behold! he cometh with clouds, and every eye shall see him, and they also which pierced him, and all kindreds of the earth shall waile because of him. Amen! even so, come quickly, Lord Jesus!

¶ These are the duties required of thee, and which thou must faithfully and punctually performe, if thou wouldst be a worthy Communicant, and receive those sacred and mystical Elements to that blessed end for which they were ordained. But when I speak 40 of three dayes preparation, I do not impose that proportion of time, nor conclude it sufficient, as if it were enough for thee to

recede from thy corrupt inclinations, and the myre of thy sins for
such a terme, with an intention to returne and wallow in it again,
when that holy season is over, for our whole life (had we the
purity of Angels, and the innocence of infants,) bears no proportion at all, nor can it (without an immediate sanctification from
God himself) any way qualifie, or make us fit for the reception of
this unmeasurable mercy. But when I spoke of such a proportion
of time, I did onely propose it to my Readers for the performing
of those holy and necessary duties, which have particular relation
to this solemne Feast, and which (indeed) are required then from 10
every Christian.   And as for a regular, sober, and holy life ; we
should in all places, and at all times labour for it, for *without
holinesse no man shall see the face of God,* much lesse be partaker
of his merits, and by this spiritual eating and drinking become a
member of that body, whose life and head he is.

A Prayer for the grace of repentance, together with a Confession
of sins.

O holy, blessed and glorious Trinity ! three persons, and one
eternal God, have mercy upon me a miserable sinner.

O who will give mine head waters, and mine eyes a fountain of 20
tears ! that I may weep night and day for my infinite transgressions,
ingratitude and rebellion against my most milde and merciful
Creatour ! O God my God be not farre from me ! hide not thy
face from the work of thine hands, reject not my sighing and
mournful spirit, nor the earnest endeavours and desires of mine
undone and miserable soul ! O thou that breakest not the bruised
Reede, nor quenchest the smoking Flax, quench not in me these
weak sparks, this dawne and beginnings of the promised earnest.
Take away, O my God ! this heart of stone, and give me a heart
of flesh, renew a right spirit within me ; cloath me with white 30
raiment, and anoint mine Eyes with Eye-salve, that I may know
and see how wretched, and miserable, and poore, and blinde, and
naked I am, and may be zealous therefore and repent ! O thou
that didst cause the waters to flow out of the stonie rock, and
gavest to *Magdalen* such store of teares that she washed thy
feet with them, give to me true remorse, and such a measure of
repentance as may become a most miserable sinner ! I confesse
dear God, that I am not worthy of the least of thy mercies, much
lesse to appear at this great and solemne Feast, this Feast of
mercy and miracles, where none but with holy hands, pure inten- 40
tions, crucified affections, and renewed spirits should presume to

enter. But as for me I am all uncleannesse, a polluted, vile creature, and nothing belongs unto me at this great day, but confusion of face, and an utter separation from this glorious and saving Communion. I have wasted thy stock, consumed thy talents, and destroyed thy goods. I was restlesse, and unquiet till I had found out wayes to offend thee. I have broken thy Commandments, laid open thine Inclosures, and most grievously trespassed against thy truth, and against the light of mine own Conscience. I have preferred rottennesse and dust to the treasure
10 of thy word, and mine own voluptuousnesse to thy revealed will. And now *O thou preserver of men! What shall I do unto thee? Against thee onely have I sinned, and my transgressions are ever in thy sight.* Lord God! I lay me down at thy footstoole, *and if thou wilt be extreme to mark what is amisse,* I shall from my very heart acknowledge and adore thy Justice. But O my dear Creatour, for Christ Jesus his sake have mercy upon me! look not on my deserts, but on thy glory; O Lord do not refuse me, but reforme and restore me! O Lord hearken, and do, and deferre not, but speak peace to my troubled soul, and send thy loving
20 spirit to strengthen and confirme me in the way of holinesse, bring me home, O Lord, and leade me now unto these living waters, incorporate me into the saving vine, and purge me, that I may bear more fruit. O cast me not away like an abominable and withered branch, but make me to flourish in the Courts of thy house, where thy Children are like Olive-branches round about thy table! O Lord hear, and have mercy, and forgive me, and be reconciled unto me for *Christ Jesus* his sake! To whom with thee and the holy Ghost be glory in the Church through all ages world without end, *Amen.*

30 *A Meditation before the receiving of the holy Communion.*

Holy, holy, holy, is the Lord God of Hosts, the whole earth is full of his glory! Behold to the Moone, and it shineth not, and the Starres are darknesse in his sight. The Pillars of heaven do tremble, and are astonished at his reproof. O who then am I, that I should appear before thee, or *what is man that thou shouldest regard him?* O light of light, the all-seeing light that shineth in darknesse, and the darknesse comprehendeth it not, what will become of me, when I shall appear before thy glorious and searching Eye! What an habitation of darknesse and death wilt thou finde
40 within me? What abominable desolations and emptinesse?

3 glorious] glorions *1652*

What barrennesse and disorders wilt thou see there? Many a time hast thou knockt, and I have shut the doors against thee, thou hast often called, and I would not answer. Sleeping and waking, early and late, day and night have I refused instruction, and would not be healed. And now, O my God, after all this rebellion and uncleannesse, wilt thou come and lodge with me? O Lord, where shall I prepare, and make ready for thee? *What communion can there be betwixt light and darknesse,* purity and pollution, perfection and deformity? O Rose of *Sharon*! thou undefiled and everlasting flower, the glory of the fields, and the first fruits of the dead, shall the wilde Asses and the beasts of the wildernesse feed now upon thee? Wilt thou give the bread of life unto dogs, and cast thy pearls before swine? O *Jesus Christ,* the lover and the redeemer of all humble and penitent souls! Thou that feedest among the Lilies untill the day breaks and the shadows flee, what is there in my heart where onely tares and thistles grow, that thou canst feed upon? Thy blessed body was wrapt in fine and white linen, (which is the righteousnesse of the Saints.) It was laid in a new and undefiled grave, hewen out of a rock, wherein never man was laid before. But all my righteousnesse is a filthy rag, my heart neither new nor undefiled, but a nest of unclean birds, where they have not onely laine, but hatched and brought forth their viperous young ones.

I confesse, dear God, I confesse with all my heart mine own extrem unworthyness, my most shameful and deplorable condition. But with thee, O Lord, there is mercy and plenteous redemption. Thou dost not use to reject and cast off those that unfeignedly repent and return unto thee; the great design and end of thine Incarnation was to save sinners: Thou hadst never come into this world, but for thy love to thy lost sheep, and those thou didst then love, thou dost love still unto the end. Thou didst not come unto the whole, but to the sick. The first (had there been any such,) had no need of a *Physician,* and the last (hadst not thou come to restore them,) had perished for ever. It was thy gracious pleasure (while thou wert here in the world) to receive Publicans and sinners, and though thou art now ascended to thy Father, yet hast not thou changed thy nature. Thou art the same yesterday, to day, and for evermore. Thy life here was nothing else but a pilgrimage and laborious search after sinners, that thou mightst finde them out and make them whole. And how willingly (O blessed Jesus!) didst thou lay down thy robes of glory, and cloath thy self with flesh, that thou mightst afterwards

M

lay down thy life a propitiation for our sins! How many scorching and wearisome journeys didst thou undergo for our sakes! How many cold and tedious nights didst thou watch and spend abroad in prayer, when the birds of the aire lay warme in their nests, and thou hadst not a place to put thy head in! In the day time I finde thee preaching in the Temple, and all night praying in the Mount of *Olives*; a little after on thine own Sabbath travelling for me in the corne-field; Another time (wearied with thy journey) sitting on the Well of *Jacob*, and begging a draught of that cold water from the
10 woman of *Samaria*; Now again I meet thee on the Asse, made infinitely happy by so glorious a rider, by *the God of Jeshurun who rideth on the heavens, and in his excellencie on the skies.* Sure, it was his simplicity and ordinary contempt with man, that made him so acceptable in thy sight. But (Oh!) with what language shall I attempt thy passion? thy bloody sweat, thy deep and bitter agony, thy lingring peece-mealed death, with all the lively anguishments, and afflictions of thy martyr'd Spirit? O my most loving and merciful Saviour! It is onely thy own Spirit, that can fully character thy own sufferings.

20   These miracles of love and most comfortable circumstances encourage me (O my God) to draw neer unto thee: for it is not probable that thou wouldst have subjected thy self to such bitter reproaches, blasphemies, and torments, had not thy love to man (for whose redemption thou didst suffer them,) been as infinite as thy self; *And greater love then this hath no man, that a man lay down his life for his friends.* And lay it down thou didst, for *no man could take it from thee.* Thou couldst have commanded twelve legions of Angels from thy Father, and when thou wentest forth to meet thy murtherers, they went backwards and fell to the
30 ground, and without thy permission (in whose hand their breath was) they could have done nothing. These merciful passages, together with thy own voice and frequent invitation much encourage me to draw neer unto thee.

Come unto me all ye that labour, and are heavy laden, and I will give you rest. Matth. 11. 28.

If any man thirst, let him come unto me, and drink, John 7. 37.

These, with many more, are thy loving Invitations: This is the voyce of the great Shepherd, and thy sheep hear thy voyce. Thus thou didst cry, and these were the words thou didst speak
40 while thou wert here upon earth, and shall I then turn away from thee, *that speakest now from heaven? Thou art a Priest for ever*

24 redemption] redemprion *1652*

after the order of Melchisedech, and thy preaching and Intercession shall last untill the heavens be no more, and woe unto them that refuse to hear thee.

Wherefore, most holy *Jesus,* seeing thou dost invite sinners to thee, and didst die to redeem them, and *art able to save them to the uttermost, that come to God by thee, and dost live for ever to make intercession for them,* Heb. 7. 25, 26. I the most wretched and the worst of sinners in full assurance of thy mercies, and that *thou art touched with the feeling of mine infirmities,* Heb. 4. 15. and wilt have compassion upon my penitent soul, draw neer to thy throne of grace, that I may obtaine mercy, and finde grace to help in time of need.

O Lord be merciful unto me, forgive all my sins, and heal all mine infirmities. Cleanse my heart, sanctifie my affections, renew my spirit, and strengthen my faith, that I may at this great Feast discerne thy blessed body, and eate and drink salvation to my self, to the glory of thy great name, and the comfort of my poor and sorrowful soul, *Amen.*

Now unto him that hath loved us, and washed us from our sins in his own blood, and hath made us Kings and Priests unto God and his Father, to him be glory and dominion for ever, and ever. *Amen.*

A Prayer when thou art upon going to the Lords Table.

In the name of the Father, and of the Son, and of the holy Ghost, *Amen !*

Jesus Christ, the Lamb, the Branch, the bright and morning-Starre, the bread of life that came down from heaven, have mercy upon me ! It is thy promise, that whosoever eateth thy flesh, and drinketh thy blood, he shall have eternal life in him, and thou wilt raise him up at the last day. Behold, O God, I am now coming to thee ; O thou fountain of purgation ! thou Well of living waters wash me cleane ! be unto me the bread of life to strengthen me in my pilgrimage towards heaven ! grant that I may suck salvation from thy *heart, that spring of the blood of God, which flowes into all believers. Thy flesh is meat indeed, and thy blood is drink Indeed. O give me grace to receive both worthily, that I may never incurre thy anger, and eternal condemnation ! Lord *Jesus Christ* ! I beleeve all that thou hast said, and all that thou hast promised, helpe thou

*Cyprian de cænâ domini. Cruci hære-mus, sanguinem fugimus, & inter ipsa redemptoris nostri vulnera figimus linguam.

mine unbelief; thou art the Author, be thou the finisher of my faith; And for thy glories sake, for thine own names sake, leade me in the right way to this great mercy and mystery, *Amen!*

Immediately before the receiving, say,

O Lord I am not worthy of the least of all the mercies, and of all the truth which thou hast shewed unto thy servant, all my life long unto this very day; much lesse am I worthy thou shouldst come now under my roof but seeing it is thy institution and free
10 mercy that will have it so, be jealous, O God, of the place of thine honour, cause me to remember whose Temple I am, and suffer not my last state to be worse then the first. Even so, Lord Jesus, come quickly, *Amen!*

¶ *Admonitions after receiving the holy Communion.*

When you have received the Sacred Elements, you should not presently after spit, nor eate and drink, but refraine untill they are perfectly digested and resolved. You must lay aside all worldly communication, and humane discourses, though never so serious; for judge of your self, what an uncivil part it will be in you, when you have received so great a guest as *Jesus Christ* with all his
20 merits, to turne your back upon him presently, and neither to meditate of him, nor to discourse with him, and keep him company. Wherefore you should all that day be instant in prayer, meditations, thanksgiving, and good works; you should consider and think upon the love of God, who so loved the world, that he gave his onely begotten Son to redeeme it. You should meditate upon his birth, life, doctrine and passion, his death and buriall, resurrection and ascension, and his second coming to judgement. You should pray, that you may be found blamelesse and without spot of him, and so much the more, because you see the day
30 approaching. Tread not under foot the Son of God, and his precious blood wherewith you are sanctified and saved, by returning again to your former sins, like the dog to his vomit, but be sure that you walk warily, and fall not wilfully into the myre. Be not regular and holy for a day or two, but all the dayes of thy life, and number thy dayes, that thou mayst apply thy heart unto wisdome. Cast thy bread upon the waters, (be merciful to the poor) and remember thy Creator, for the dayes of darknesse are many, but the outward darknesse is eternal, and from it there is no redemption.

40 Instead of printed Meditations which are usually prescribed

after communicating, I would advise the pious receiver to read over all these following parcels of Scripture, *John* 6. 22. *to the end, John* 17. *Rom.* 8. 2 *Cor.* 5. *Ephes.* 1. *&* 4. *Heb.* 10. 1 *Pet.* 1. *Rev.* 5.

A Prayer after you have received.

Lord Jesus Christ, very God, and very man, made in all things like unto us, sin onely excepted ; I blesse and praise thy holy name, and with all my heart, with all my strength, and with all my soul give thee all possible thanks for thy infinite love and pity towards lost man. Blessed be the hour in which thou wert born, and the hour in ₁₀ which thou didst die ! Blessed and for ever hallowed be thy most comfortable and glorious name, the name J E S U S C H R I S T, *at which every knee shall bow, of things in heaven, and things in earth, and things under the earth ; for thy name is above every name, and there is no other name by which we can be saved.* O most holy, most humble and harmlesse Lamb ! how didst thou make thy self of no reputation, and becamest obedient to the death of the Crosse for my sake ! And when thou wert to drink the cup of thy Fathers anger due to my sins, didst instead of it ordain and be-queath to me the cup of life and everlasting salvation ! O Lord ₂₀ give me a heart to understand, and eyes to see what thou hast done for me ; O never suffer me to crucifie thee again by return-ing to my former iniquities and pollutions, but write thy sufferings and the price of my redemption in the tables of my heart, set them for a signet upon mine hand, and for a bracelet upon mine arme, that by a continual and careful remembrance of them, I may in the strength of this bread received to day at thy table travel to thy holy mountain, and that this drink which I drank out of the spiritual rock may become a Well of living waters, springing up in me to eternal life. Grant this, O God, for thy glories sake, and for ₃₀ that love and mercies sake which brought thee hither out of thy Fathers bosome to suffer so many things for his Elects sake, *Amen!*

Worthy is the Lamb that was slaine, to receive power, and riches, and wisdome, and strength, and honour, and glory, and blessing ; for he hath redeemed us to God by his blood out of every kindred, and tongue, and people, and nation, and hath made us unto our God Kings and Priests, and we shall reigne on the earth.

Now the God of peace that brought again from the dead my Lord Jesus, that great Shepherd of the sheep, through the blood of the ever-lasting Covenant,

₄₀

23 pollutions] pollutious *1652*   30 O] G *1652*

Make me perfect in every good work, to do his will, working in me that which is well-pleasing in his sight through Jesus Christ, to whom be glory for ever and ever, Amen!

A Prayer in time of persecution and Heresie.

Most glorious and Immortall God, the Prince of peace, unity and order, which makest men to be of one mind in a house, heale I beseech thee these present sad breaches and distractions! Consider, O Lord, the teares of thy Spouse which are daily upon her cheeks, whose adversaries are grown mighty, and her enemies
10 prosper. The wayes of *Zion* do mourne, our beautiful gates are shut up, and the Comforter that should relieve our souls is gone far from us. Thy Service and thy Sabbaths, thy own sacred Institutions and the pledges of thy love are denied unto us; Thy Ministers are trodden down, and the basest of the people are set up in thy holy place. O Lord holy and just! behold and consider, and have mercy upon us, for thy own names sake, for thy promise sake suffer not the gates of hell to prevaile against us; but return and restore us, that joy and gladnesse may be heard in our dwellings, and the voyce of the Turtle in all our land. *Arise O God,*
20 *and let thine enemies be scattered, and let those that hate thee flee before thee. Behold, the robbers are come into thy Sanctuary, and the persecuters are within thy walls. We drink our own waters for money, and our wood is sold unto us. Our necks are under persecution, we labour and have no rest. Yea, thine own Inheritance is given to strangers, and thine own portion unto aliens. Wherefore dost thou forget us for ever, and forsake us for so long a time? Turne thou us unto thee, O Lord, and we shall be turned, renew our dayes as of old. Lord hear, and have mercy, and be jealous for the beloved of thine own bosome, for thy truth, and for the words of thine*
30 *own mouth. Help us, O God of our salvation, and for thine own honours sake deal Comfortably with us,* Amen, Amen.

A Prayer in adversity, and troubles occa-
sioned by our Enemies.

O holy and almighty God, full of goodness and compassion, look I beseech thee with thine Eye of mercy upon my present sad sufferings and most bitter afflictions! Behold, O God, I put my mouth in the dust, and confess I have deserv'd them. I despise not thy Chastenings, but begge grace of thee that I may not faint, and that they may yeild the fruits of righteousnesse unto

36 afflictions] afflctions *1652*

me, who am now exercised by them. Thou seest, O God, how furious and Implacable mine Enemies are, they have not only rob'd me of that portion and provision which thou hadst graciously given me, but they have also washed their hands in the blood of my friends, my dearest and nearest relatives. I know, O my God, and I am daily taught by that disciple whom thou did'st love, that no murderer hath eternal life abiding in him. Keep me therefore, O my God, from the guilt of blood, and suffer me not to stain my soul with the thoughts of recompense and vengeance, which is a branch of thy great prerogative, and belongs wholly unto thee. Though 10 they persecute me unto death, and pant after the very dust upon the heads of thy poore, though they have taken the bread out of the childrens mouth, and have made me a desolation, yet Lord, give me thy grace, and such a measure of charity as may fully forgive them. Suffer me not to open my mouth in Curses, but give me the spirit of my Saviour, who reviled not again, but was dumb like a Lamb before his shearers. O Lord, sanctifie all these afflictions unto thy servant, and let no man take away my crown. Remember those that are in troubles for thy truth, and put their tears into thy bottle. Grant this, O merciful Father, for my dear 20 Saviours sake, and bring me quickly into thy Kingdom, where I shall have all these tears wiped away from mine eyes, Amen, Amen !

M A N
I N
Darknefs,
O R,
A DISCOURSE
O F
D E A T H.

Eccles. 11. 7, 8, 9, & 10.

Truly the light is sweet, and a pleasant thing it is to behold the
Sun.

But if a man live many dayes and rejoyce in them all, yet, let him
remember the dayes of darknesse, for they are many.

Rejoyce, O young man, in thy youth, and let thy heart cheere thee
in the dayes of thy youth, and walk in the wayes of thy heart, and in
the sight of thine eyes, but know thou, that for all these things God
will bring thee into judgement.

10   *Therefore remove sorrow from thy heart, and put away evil from*
thy flesh, for childhood and youth are vanity.

¶

Draw neer, fond man, and dresse thee by this glasse,
Mark how thy bravery and big looks must passe
Into corruption, rottennesse and dust;
The fraile Supporters which betray'd thy trust.
O weigh in time thy last and loathsome state,
To purchase heav'n for tears is no hard rate.
Our glory, greatnesse, wisdome, all we have,
If misimploy'd, but adde hell to the grave:
20   Onely a faire redemption of evill Times
Finds life in death, and buryes all our Crimes.

It is an observation of some *spirits*, that * *the night is the mother of thoughts*. And I shall adde, that those thoughts are *Stars*, the *Scintillations* and *lightnings* of the soul strugling with *darknesse*. This *Antipathy* in her is *radical*, for being descended from the *house of light*, she hates a contrary *principle*, and being at that time a prisoner in some measure to an enemy, she becomes pensive, and full of thoughts. Two great *extremes* there are, which she equally abhors, *Darkness* and *Death*. And 'tis observable, that in the *second death*, when she shall be wholly mancipated to her enemies, those 10 two are united. For those furious and unquenchable burnings of hell (which the *Scripture* calls *the lake of fire*, *&c.*) though they be of such an insuperable *intense heat*, as to work upon *spirits*, and the most subtile Essences, yet do they give no light at all, but burn blacker then *pitch, Cremationem habet, lumen verò non habet.* (Greg. Mor. c. 46.) The Contemplation of *death* is an obscure, melancholy *walk* an Expatiation in *shadows* & *solitude*, but it leads unto *life*, & he that sets forth at *midnight*, will sooner meet the *Sunne*, then he that sleeps it out betwixt his curtains. Truly, when I consider, how I came first into this world, and in what 20 condition I must once again go out of it, and compare my appointed time here with the *portion* preceding it, and the *eternity* to follow, I can conclude my present *being* or *state* (in respect of the *time*) to be nothing else but an *apparition*. The first man that appeared thus, came from the *East*, and the *breath* of *life* was received there. Though then we travel *Westward*, though we embrace *thornes* and swet for *thistles*, yet the businesse of a *Pilgrim* is to *seek his Countrey*. But the *land* of *darknesse* lies in our way, and how few are they that study this *region*, that like holy *Macarius* walk into the wildernesse, and discourse with the skull 30 of a dead man? We run all after the present world, and the Primitive Angelical life is quite lost.

It is a sad perversnesse of *man*, to preferre *warre* to peace, cares to rest, grief to joy, and the vanities of this narrow Stage to the true and solid comforts in heaven. *The friends of this world* (saith a holy father) *are so fearful to be separated from it, that nothing can be so grievous to them as to think of death. They put farre away the evill day, and cause the seate of violence to come neer ; They lie upon beds of Jvory, and stretch themselves upon their Couches ; they eat the lambs* 40 *out of the flock, and the calves out of the midst of the stall ; They chant to the sound of the viol, they drink wine in bowls, and anoint*

*A Proverb in *Italy*, La notte é madre de pensieri.

—Contempsit mori Qui non concupi- scit—

themselves with the chief ointments; they account the life of the righteous to be madnesse, and his end to be without honour, Amos 6. In this desperate and senselesse state they cast away their precious souls, and make their brightest dayes but *dayes of darknesse and gloominesse, dayes of clouds and of thick mists.*   They consider not the day that *shall burne like an Oven, when the heavens being on fire shall be dissolved, and the Elements shall melt with a fervent heat; when the wicked shall be stubble, and all the workers of iniquity shall be burnt up.*   Miserable men! that knowing their masters pleasure, 10 will not do it, that refuse Oyle and balsame to make way for poyson and corrasives.   And why will they call him *Master, Master,* whose precepts they trample on, and whose members they crucifie?   It is a sad observation for true Christians to see these men who would seem to be Pillars, to prove but reeds and specious dissemblers.   For what manner of livers should such *professors* be, seeing they expect and beleeve the dissolution of all things?   With what constant holinesse, humility and devotion should they watch for it?   How should they *passe the time of their sojourning here in fear, and be diligent that they may be found of him* 20 *in peace, without spot, and blamelesse?*   What preparation should they make against the evill day?   What comforts and treasures should they lay up for that long voyage?   For what a day of terrors and indignation is the day of death to the unprepared? How will they lie on their last beds, *like wilde Buls in a net, full of the fury of the Lord?*   When *their desolation shall come like a flood, and their destruction like a whirle-wind; How will they say in the morning, would God it were Even, and at night, would God it were Morning! for the fear of their heart wherwith they shal fear, and for the sight of their Eyes wherewith they shall see?*   This 30 is a truth they will not believe, untill death tells it them, and then it will be too late;   It is therefore much to be wished, that they would yet, while it is life-time with them, remember their last ends, and seriously question with themselves, what is there under the Sun, that can so justly challenge their thoughts as the contemplation of their own mortality?   We could not have lived in an age of more instruction, had we been left to our own choice.   We have seen such vicissitudes and examples of humane frailty, as the former world (had they happened in those ages) would have judged prodigies.   We have seen Princes brought to their graves 40 by a new way, and the highest order of humane honours trampled upon by the lowest.   We have seene Judgement beginning at Gods Church, and (what hath beene never heard of, since it was

redeem'd and established by his blessed Son,) *we have seen
his Ministers cast out of the Sanctuary, &
barbarous persons without *light* or *per-*
fection, usurping holy offices.   A day, an
hour, a minute (saith *Causabone*) is sufficient to over-turn and extirpate the most
settled Governments, which seemed to have
been founded and rooted in Adamant.

* There is extant a little
book called *Speculum Vi-*
sionis printed at *Norim-*
berge 1508, wherein this
fearful desolation and destruction of the Church by
Lay-men is expressely foretold.

Suddenly do the high things of this world come to an end, and
their delectable things passe away, for when they seem to be in 10
their *flowers* and full strength, they perish to astonishment ; And
sure the ruine of the most goodly peeces seems to tell, that the
dissolution of the whole is not far off.   It is the observation of
a known Statesman, (Sir *Water Rawleigh*) *That to all dominions*
God hath set their periods, who though he hath given to man the
knowledge of those wayes, by which Kingdoms rise and fall, yet he
*hath left him subject unto the * affections*
which draw on these fatal mutations in
their appointed time.   Vain therefore and
deceitful is all the pomp of this world,
which though it flatters us with a seeming
permanency, will be sure to leave us even then, when we are most

*N. *Marcellus* de docto-
rum indagine. Potest fatum
morum mutabilitate con-
verti, ut ex iis celeriùs vel
tardiùs aut bonum fiat, aut 20
pessimum.

in chase of it.   And what comfort then, or what security can poor
man promise to himself? whose breath is in the hand of another,
and whose few dayes are most commonly out-lived by every
creature, and sometimes by a *flower* of his own *setting.*   Or what
benefit can these * humane de-
lights though blest with successe,
and a large time of fruition, afford him at his death ? for satisfaction in this point, let us but
have recourse to the ages that
are past, let us aske the *Fathers,*

* Non est, falleris, hæc beata non est,
Quam vos creditis esse, vita non est.
Fulgentes manibus videre gemmas,
Aut auro bibere, & cubare cocco :
Qui vultus Acherontis atri,   30
Qui Styga tristem non tristis videt,
Audétque vitæ ponere finem,
Par ille regi, par superis erit.

& they will tell us.   If we insist upon eminent persons, the rulers
of this world, & the Counsellors of the earth who built *sumptuous*
Palaces for themselvs and filled their houses with silver; we shall have
no better account from them, then if we enquired of the *prisoners*
& the oppressed.   They are gone all the same way, *their pomp &*
the noise of their viols is brought down to the grave, the worms cover
them, and the worms are spread under them.   *Riches* and *power* 40
travel not beyond this life ; they are like *Jobs* friends, *deceitful*
as a brook, and as the stream of brooks they passe away, which

vanish when it is hot, and are consumed out of their place. Hast thou found riches (saith one) then, thou hast lost thy rest. Distractions & cares come along with them, and they are seldome gotten without the worme of conscience. It was an act of *Anacreon* becoming the royalty of a *Poets* spirit : *Policrates* rewards him with five talents ; but he, after he had been troubled with the keeping of them for two nights, carries them back to the owner, telling him, that, *if he had been accustomed to such companions he had never made any verses.* Certainly there is so much of *Mammon* 10 and *darknesse* in them, as sufficeth to shew their *parentage* is low, and not very far from *hell.* Some such thing we may gather from that exclamation of S. *James* against the rich men ; *Your gold and your silver is canker'd, and the rust of them shall be a witnesse against you, and shall eate your flesh as it were fire, you have heaped treasure together for the last dayes.* But to return thither from whence we are digrest : What is become now of these great *Merchants of the earth,* and where is the fruit *of all their labours under the Sun?* Why, truly they are *taken out of the way as all others, and they are cut off as the tops of the eares of corn.* Their 20 dwelling is in the dust, and as for their place here, it lies wast, & is not known : *Nettles and Brambles come up in it, and the Owle and the Raven dwell in it.* But if you will visit them at their *long homes,* and knock at those *desolate doors,* you shall find some remains of them, a heap of loathsomness and corruption. O miserable and sad mutations ! (*Petrarch. de otio Rel.*) Where is now their *pompous & shining train?* Where are their *triumphs, fire-works, and feasts,* with all the *ridiculous tumults* of a *popular, prodigious pride?* Where is their *purple* and *fine linen,* their chains of *massie gold,* and sparkling ornaments of *pearls?* Where are 30 their *Cooks* and *Carvers,* their * *fowlers* and *fishers?* Where are their curious *Utensils,* their *Cups* of *Agate, Chrystal,* and *China-earth?* Where are their sumptuous *Chambers,* where they inclosed themselvs in *Cedar, Ivory,* and *Ebeny?* Where is their *Musick,* their *soft* and *delicate dressings, pleasing motions,* and *excellency of looks?* Where are their rich *perfumes,* costly *Conserves,* with their 40 precious and various store of *forreign* and *domestick* wines ? Where

* Ingeniosa gula est : siculo scarus
æquore mersus
Ad mensam vivus perducitur, inde lucrinis
Eruta littoribus vendunt conchylia cænas
Ut renovent per damna famem.
Jam Phasidos unda,
Orbata est avibus ; mutoque in littore tantum
Solæ desertis aspirant frondibus auræ.

4 (*of Latin*) Phasidos] Phasides *1652*
5 (*of Latin*) tantum] tantũ. *1652*

are their *sons* and their *daughters* fair as the *flowers*, strait as the *Palm-trees*, and *polish'd as the corners of the Temple*? O pittiful and astonishing transformations! all is gone, all is dust, deformity, and desolation. *Their bones are scatter'd* —mors sola fatetur *in the pit, and instead of well-set hair, there* Quantula sunt hominum *is baldnesse, and loathsomnesse instead of* corpuscula.— *beauty*. This is the state of their *bodies*, and (O blessed *Jesus*!) who knowes the state of their *souls*? To have a sad guesse at this, it will not be much out of our way, if we step and visit a *Roman Emperour* upon his death-bed. If you desire his name, 10 it is *Hadrianus*, the most ingenious and learned that ever sate upon the throne of *Cæsar*. You may beleeve, he was royally accommodated, and wanted nothing which this world could afford; but how farre he was from receiving any comfort in his death from that pompous and fruitlesse abundance, you shall learn from his own mouth, consider (I pray) what he speaks, for they are the words of a dying man, and spoken by him to his departing soul,

> Animula vagula, blandula,
> Hospes comésque corporis,
> Quæ nunc abibis in loca? 20
> Pallidula, querula, nudula,
> Nec, ut soles, dabis jocos.

> *My soul, my pleasant soul and witty,*
> *The guest and consort of my body,*
> *Into what place now all alone*
> *Naked and sad wilt thou be gone?*
> *No mirth, no wit, as heretofore,*
> *Nor Jests wilt thou afford me more.*

Certainly, this is the saddest *poetrie*, that ever I met with; and what he thought of his soul in that last *agonie*, when the *pangs* of 30 *death* came *thick* upon him, is enough to draw tears and commiseration from a heart of flint. O happy then, yea Infinitely happy is that religious liver, who is ever meditating upon the houre of death before it comes, that when it is come, he may passe through it with joy, and speak to his * Egredere, quid times? soul in the language of old *Hilarion*, * *Go* egredere anima mea; Sep- *forth, O my soul, go forth; what is it that* tuaginta propè annis Christo *thou art afraid of? Seventy yeers almost* Hieron. in vitâ Hilar. *hast thou serv'd Christ, and art thou now afraid of death?*

Alas! what is *life* if truly and throughly considered, that we 40 should trust to it, and promise to our selves a multitude of years, as if we held *time* by the *wings*, and had the *spirit* of life in our

own *hands*? *Our present life* (saith *Chrysostome*) *is a meere apparition, and differs but very little from a dreame; therefore that minde which is proud of a shadow, and relies upon a dreame, is very idle and childish.* Natural histories tell us of a bird called *Hemerobios* by the river *Hypanis,* which receives his life in the *morning,* sings at *noon,* and dyes at *night.* This *bird* may very well signifie our *life,* and by the *river* we may understand *time,* upon whose brink we are always pearching. *Time* runs faster then any *streame,* and our *life* is swifter than any *bird,* and oft-times
10 all the pomp of it comes to an end in one *day,* yea sometimes in an *houre.* There is no *object* we can look upon, but will do us the kindnesse to put us in minde of our mortality, if we would be so wise as to make use of it. The *day* dyes into *night,* the *spring* into *winter, flowers* have their *rootes* ever in their *graves, leaves* loose their *greenenesse,* and drop under our feete where they *flye* about and *whisper* unto us. The *beasts* run the Common lott with *us* and when they dye by our hands to give us *nourishment,* they are so kinde as to give us *Instruction* also. And if from these *frailer objects* we turne our Eyes to things that are more *permanent,*
20 we may by the doctrine of *contrarieties* make them as useful as any of the former; And this is elegantly done by the *poet,* who was then *serious* and *stayed* enough, though somewhat *passionate.*

> Nam mihi quid prodest quod longo flumina cursu
> Semper inexhaustis prona feruntur aquis?
> Ista manent: nostri sed non mansêre parentes,
> Exigui vitam temporis hospes ago.

> *What is't to me that spacious rivers run*
> *Whole ages, and their streams are never done?*
> *Those still remain: but all my fathers di'd,*
30 *And I my self but for few dayes abide.*

Thus he of the *water-course,* which he saw would out-run him, and will do so with all that come after him. But the quick *tyde* of mans life, when it is once turned and begins to *ebbe,* will never *flow* again. The *Spring* comes constantly once a yeere, and *flowers,* when the *frosts* are past, keep *house* no longer under *ground,* but feel the *Sun,* and come *abroad.* The *leaves* come again to *whisper* over our heads, and are as *green* and as *gay* as ever, *but man dieth and wasteth away, yea man giveth up the ghost, and where is he?* In these sad contemplations was the *Brittish*
40 *Bard,* when he broke out into this Eloquent complaint

1 *Chrysostome*] *Chrystostome 1652*
5 *Hemerobios conj. G Gu* : *Hemerovios 1652*   receives] rceives *1652*
38 *man*] mau *1652*   *wasteth*] wastesh *1652*

𝕸𝖎𝖘 𝖒𝖆𝖜𝖗𝖔𝖔𝖍 𝖗𝖍𝖞𝖔𝖔𝖍𝖎𝖌 𝕬𝖔𝖆𝖗,
𝕻𝖔𝖇 𝖕𝖊𝖙𝖍 𝖞 𝖔𝖔𝖍𝖆𝖜 𝖙𝖗𝖜𝔷 𝖔𝖔𝖍𝖆𝖕𝖆𝖗,
𝕺𝖓𝖔 𝖞 𝖒𝖆𝖗𝖜 𝖒𝖆𝖚𝖗 𝖇𝖞 𝖌𝖆𝖗𝖈𝖍𝖆𝖗.

In March birds couple, a new birth
Of herbs and flowers breaks through the earth,
But in the grave none stirs his head;
Long is th' Impris'ment of the dead.

The dayes of darknesse are many, and he that *goeth down to the grave shall not come up, his place shall not know him, nor shall he returne to his house; he shall not be awaked nor raised out of his sleep, untill the heavens be no more.* These last words were put in for our *comfort,* and imply the *resurrection* or the time of restoring all things. This was manifested to *Ezekiel* by the vision of dry bones with a noise and a shaking amongst them, and they came together bone to bone, and were clothed with sinews, flesh and skin, and the breath of life entered into them, and they stood upon their feet an exceeding great army. We have it also confirmed out of the mouth of *Jesus Christ* himself, *John* 5. 28, 29. his words are these, *Marvel not at this, for the hour is coming, in the which all that are in the grave shall hear his voyce; And they shall come forth that have done good unto the resurrection of life; but they that have done evill unto the resurrection of condemnation.* The *Scripture* is every where full of these *proofs*: But I shall insist only upon *three.*

1. *For I know that my Redeemer liveth, and that he shall stand at the later day upon the earth. And though after my skin worms destroy this body, yet in my flesh shall I see God. Whom I shall see for my self, and mine eyes shall behold and not another, though my reins be consumed within me.* Job. 19. 25, 26, 27.

2. *Thy dead men shall live, together with my dead body shall they arise; Awake and sing ye that dwell in the dust, for thy dew is as the dew of herbs, and the earth shall cast out the dead.* Isa. 26. 19.

3. *Behold (O my people) I will open your graves; and cause you to come up out of your graves; And ye shall know that I am the Lord when I have opened your graves, O my people, and brought you up out of your graves, and shall put my spirit in you, and yee shall live.* Ezek. 37. 12, 13, 14.

And thus have we most full and absolute promises from the *divine spirit,* and from *Jesus Christ,* who is *the life of the world,* for the redemption of our bodies. Nor are we left destitute of very clear and inexcusable demonstrations of it in *nature.* We see mortal

29 19.] 19 *1652*   32 Isa.] Isa *1652*   41 inexcusable] inexcussable *Gu*

men when the *body* and *substance* of *vegetables* is consumed in the *fire*, out of their very *ashes* to make *glasse*, which is a very bright and noble *body*, how much more shall the Immortal and Almighty God (who created all things of nothing) out of dust and corruption, raise us up incorrupt and glorious bodies? *Thou fool*, (saith St. *Paul*) *that which thou sowest is not quickened, except it die first; and that which thou sowest, thou sowest not that body which shall be, but bare grain; but God giveth it a body as he pleaseth.* There are in *nature* many *creatures* which at certain *seasons*, that their
10 *spirit* is inconsistent with, fall into a *dormition*, or *dead sleep* which differs little from *death*, and convey themselves into *secret places*, as *hollow trees*, or some *desolate ruines*, where they may rest in safety during that *season*, as being taught by some *secret informant* that they shall *awake* again. Here have we a clear type of the *resurrection*, for what else is *death* but *sleep*, as the *Apostle* calls it? A great *Philosopher* and *Secretary* to *nature* discoursing of the *resurrection* of the *dead*, tells us, *that he oftentimes lighted upon some of those creatures in that dark state of dormition, and did dissect some of them, and cut off the limbs of others, and yet* (saith he) *could*
20 *I perceive no signe of life at all in them, their arteries and flesh being as hard and as dry as a stick, but casting them into a pot of seething water, they would soften by degrees, and shortly after stir about, and those very parts which were dissected, would give very clear and satisfactory Indications of life.* This is so strong a *Symboll* of the resurrection, that I think it needlesse to make any application. Onely this I shall adde, that the curious observers of nature reckon these creatures amongst those of the *lunar order*; And indeed if we consider well the nature of that *planet* (whose *sphere*

*Omne quod est suprà lunam
30 *æternumque bonúmque*
Esse scias nec triste aliquid cœle-
stia tangit.
Quippe ultra fines lunæ illætabile
nil est;
Cuncta mala in terris posuit Deus,
illáque clausit
In medio, & vetuit sacrum contin-
gere cœlum.
Supra autem lunam lucis sunt
omnia plena
Nec non lætitiæ & pacis; non
tempus & error
Et senium & mors est illîc, nec
40 *inutile quicquam. Mar. Pal.*

is the *veil* or **partition* drawn betwixt *us* and *Immortality*) and whose *relation* to this lower world is more *intimate*, and of a *greater tye* then any of the other *six*, we shall finde that she exactly typifies and demonstrates unto us those two famous *states* of terrestrial bodies, *viz.* their state of *darknesse* and their state of *glory*, their *dissolution* and *restoration*; for she doth *agonizare*, and suffers a monethly *recession* of *light*, and in a short time becomes *full* again. And I pray, are

1 (*of Latin*) bonúmque] bonúmque. *1652*

not *light* and *life* compatriots? What else is *death* but the recession and absence of *life*? or *darknesse* but the absence of *light*?

> *Sic nostros casus solatur mundus in astris.*
> So our decays God comforts by
> The Stars concurrent state on high.

Do not we see divers birds of this *regiment* such as are commonly known to us, with other meaner Creatures as *silk-worms* and the *humble-bee*, which yet are not so contemptible, but they may serve us for noble instances in this point, seeing there is in them a *living spirit*, and that creatures of the same *rank* with them are recorded in Gods own *word*, yea, and are own'd by him as *memorable* and *select Instruments* of his service, as Joshuah *Cap.* 24. *ver.* 12. *And I sent the hornet before you, which drove them out from before you, even the two kings of the Amorites, but not with thy sword, nor with thy bowe.* And Isaiah Chap. 6 ver. 18, 19. *And it shall come to passe in that day, that the Lord shall hisse for the flye that is in the uttermost parts of the river of Egypt, and for the Bee that is in the land of Assyria ; And they shall come, and shall rest all of them in the desolate valleys, and in the holes of the rocks, and upon all thornes, and upon all bushes.* I say then, do not we see that these *birds* and inferiour *creatures* which in the *spring* and *summer* continue here very merry and *musical*, do on a sudden leave us, and all *winter*-long suffer a kind of *death*, and with the *Suns* warmth in the *youth* of the year *awake* again, and *refresh* the world with their *reviv'd notes*? For the singing of birds is *naturalis musica mundi*, to which all *arted strains* are but *discord* and *hardnesse*; How much more then shall *Jesus Christ* the *Sun of righteousnesse rising with healing under his wings*, awake those that sleep in him, and bring them again with a joyful resurrection?

Having then these *prolusions* and strong *proofs* of our *restoration* laid out in *nature*, besides the promise of the *God* of nature, who cannot faile, let us so dispose of this short time of our sojourning here, that we may with joy and sure comforts expect that day of refreshing. Let us number our dayes, and apply our hearts unto wisdome. What ever happens here under our feet, let it not draw down our eyes from the *hill*, whence cometh our help. Let not these sudden and prodigious mutations (like violent *earth-quakes*) shake our foundation; let us hold fast the *faith*, and presse towards the *mark*, that whether absent or present we may be

7 divers] divets *1652*   9 humble] humhle *1652*

accepted of him; for many are already gone astray, and have slipt into the same damnable estate with those *wretches,* whom a very *Heathen* could reprove,

> Sunt qui in fortunæ jam casibus omnia ponunt,
> Et nullo credunt mundum rectore moveri,
> Naturâ volvente vices & lucis & anni.

> *There are that do believe all things succeed*
> *By chance or fortune, &° that nought's decreed*
> *By a divine, wise will; but blindly call*
10 *Old time and nature rulers over all.*

Let us consider him that is *invisible,* and *those that are righteous, let them be righteous still; let them have respect unto the recompence of the reward, for he comes quickly, and his reward is with him. Let us endure unto the end, and overcome, that we may have right unto the tree of life, and may enter in through the gates into the City* : for, *Ex hoc momento pendet æternitas.* Upon our little inch of time in this life, depends the length and breadth, the height and depth of Immortality in the world to come : even two eternities, the one infinitely accursed, the other infinitely blessed. I remember (saith
20 a reverend Author) that I have read (and not without admiration) of some Primitive *Christian,* that considered with himself the eternity of the torments to be endured in hell, after this manner. " *What man living* (said he) *that were in his right minde and reason,* "*if he were offered the most spacious and flourishing Kingdoms of* " France, Spain *and* Polonia, *onely for lying continually upon any* "*one part of his body in a bed of roses for the space of forty yeers,* "*would accept of them upon that condition? And though perhaps* "*such a mad man could be found, as would accept of the offer, yet, it* "*is a thing most certain, that before three yeers would come about, he*
30 "*would get him up, and beg to have the conditions cancell'd. And* "*what madnesse then is it, for the enjoying of one minutes pleasure,* "*for the satisfaction of our sensual, corrupt appetite, to lie for ever in* "*a bed of burning brasse, in the lake of eternal and unquenchable fire?* "*Suppose* (saith the same Writer) *that this whole Globe of earth* "*were nothing else but a huge masse, or mountain of sand, and that* "*a little Wren came but once in every thousand yeers to fetch away* "*but one grain of that huge heap; what an innumerable number of* "*yeers would be spent, before that world of sand could be so fetcht* "*away? And yet* (alas!) *when the damned have laine in that fiery*
40 "*lake so many yeers as all those would amount to, they are no nearer* "*coming out, then the first houre they entered in.* To the same purpose is this *Hymne* of the *Ancients.*

8 *fortune*] *fortnne 1652*   14 *the*] *ehe 1652*

Ex quo poli sunt perfecti
Aude numero complecti
Stellas cœli, stillas roris,
Undas aquei fluoris,
Guttas imbris pluvialis,
Floccos velleris nivalis.
Quot sunt vere novo flores,
Quot odores, quot colores,
Quot vinacios Autumnus,
Poma legit & vertumnus;   10
Quot jam grana tulit æstas,
Frondes hyemis tempestas,
Totus orbis animantes,
Aër atomos volantes,
Pilos feræ, pecus villos,
Vertex hominum capillos;
Adde littoris arenas,
Adde graminis verbenas,
Tot myriades Annorum,
Quot momenta sæculorum: 20
Heus adhuc æternitatis
Portus fugit à damnatis!
Æternum, æternum! quanta hæc duratio, quanta!
Quàm speranda bonis, quámque tremenda malis!

From the first hour the heav'ns were made
Unto the last, when all shall fade,
Count (if thou canst) the drops of dew,
The stars of heav'n and streams that flow;
The falling snow, the dropping showres,
And in the moneth of *May* the flowres,   30
Their sents and colours, and what store
Of grapes and apples Autumne bore;
How many grains the Summer beares,
What leaves the wind in Winter tears;
Count all the creatures in the world,
The motes which in the air are hurl'd,
The haires of beasts and mankind, and
The shores innumerable sand,
The blades of grasse, and to these last
Adde all the yeers which now are past,   40
With those whose course is yet to come,
And all their minutes in one summe.
When all is done, the damneds state
Out-runs them still, and knows no date.

O *Eternity, eternity* (saith a holy *Father*) *whose strength is able*
to bear out thy torments! And the smoke of their torments ascendeth

2 *Aude M*: *Audet 1652*   25 heav'ns] heavn's *1652*

N 2

up for ever & ever! & they have no rest day nor night! O what is this same for ever and ever! Gladly would I speak something of it, but I know not what to speak. All that I know, is this; That it is that, which onely the infinitenesse of the Almighty God doth compass about and comprehend. Seeing then it is so, that eternal pleasures or eternal pains do inavoidably and immediately overtake us after our dissolution, with what unwearied care and watchfulnesse should we continue in well-doing, and *work out our salvation with fear and trembling?* How should we *as strangers*
10 *and pilgrims abstain from fleshly lusts, which warre against the soul? What manner of persons ought we to be in all holy conversation and godlinesse?* With what Christian thrift and diligence should we dispose of every minute of our time that we might make *our calling and election sure?* It is a fearful thing to die without reconciliation; And with what confusion of face and horrour of spirit (if we die in that state,) shall we appear before the *Judge of all the world?* when he shall come in the *Clouds of heaven* with his *holy Angels,* and all mankind from the *first* man created, unto the *last* that shall be borne upon the earth shall appear before his
20 Judgement-seate. Me thinks I see the remisse, lukewarme *professour,* and the *hypocritical, factious pretender* of *sanctity* looking up to the *Clouds,* and crying out, *O that throne! that flaming, white, and glorious throne! and he that sits thereon, with the sharp sickle in his hand and the crown of pure gold upon his head!* Revel. 14. 14, *from whose face the heaven and the earth flye away, and the foundations of the world are brought to nothing. Oh! is he the Lamb that was slain whose blood was poured out like water upon the earth to save his people from their sins? Is he the Prince of life that was crown'd with thornes, scourged, spit upon, crucified, pierced through,*
30 *and murthered, and comes he now to judge the world? Oh! It is he! It is he! miserable wretch that I am! What shall I do, or whither shall I go?*

Such will be the *dreadful agonies* and *concertations* in that *day* betwixt the *Hypocrite* and his *conscience,* betwixt the *enemies* of Gods truth and their *gasping undone souls. When the people that forget God shall go down quick into hell, and the secrets of all hearts shall be disclosed and laid open before Angels and men;* For in that day all their dark and private *lusts,* their *closet-sins, bosome-councels, specious pretences,* and *bloody machinations,* which now (like so many
40 *foul spirits*) lurk in their *gloomy breasts,* shall be forced out, and will appear as visible to all *mankind,* as if they were written with the *beams* of the *Sun* upon the pure and unclouded *firmament.* In

the * mean while the very *fowles of the aire,* and their own *horrid guilt* either in time of *distraction* (which they are alwayes subject to) or in their *sleep* (which is alwayes fraught with *penal visions* and *spiritual tumults*) may make a *full discovery* of their most *secret villanies* before the appointed time.

* Est pœna præsens consciæ mentis pavor, Animúsque culpâ plenus, & semet timens. Scelus aliquis tutum, nullus securum tulit.

It was a blessed and a glorious age the Primitive *Christians* lived in, *when the wildernesse and the solitary places were glad for them, and the desert rejoyced and blossom'd as the rose.* When the blood of 10 *Christ* was yet warme, and the memory of his *miracles* and *love* fresh and vigorous ; what *Zeale,* what powerful *faith,* what perfect *charity,* hearty *humility,* and true *holinesse* was then to be found upon the earth ? If we compare the *shining* and *fervent piety* of those Saints, with *the painted* and *illuding appearance* of it in *these of our times,* we shall have just cause to fear that our *Candlestick* (which hath been now of a long time under a Cloud) is at this very instant upon removing. But I had rather you should be informed of their true *holinesse* and *love* to *Christ,* by an *Eye-witnesse* that was conversant with them, *and went in and out amongst them,* then by a bare 20 relation from my pen. Heare therefore what he saith. *Vidi ego, & verè vidi thesaurum Christi in* Hieron. in vit. Pat.
humanis absconditum vasculis, &c. vidi enim apud eos multos Patres in terra positos cœlestem vitam agentes, & novos quosdam Prophetas tam virtutibus animi, quàm vaticinandi officio imbutos, &c. Non-nullos namque eorum ità ab omni malitia, cogitatione & suspicione vidimus alienos, ut nec si aliquid mali adhuc in seculo gereretur, meminissent, tanta in eis erat tranquillitas animi, tantúsque in eis inoleverat bonitatis affectus, &c. Commanent autem per eremum dispersi & separati cellulis, sed charitatis vinculo connexi. Ob hoc 30 autem dirimuntur habitaculis, ut silentii sui quietem & intentionem mentis nec vox aliqua, nec occursus ullus, aut sermo aliquis otiosus obturbet. Intentis ergo in suo quisque loco animis velut fideles servi adventantem dominum expectant. Omnes hi nullam cibi, aut indu-menti, aut ullius horum sollicitudinem gerunt. Justitiam & regnum Dei requirunt, armis orationum pugnant, & scuto fidei ab inimico insidiante protecti patriam sibi cœlestem conquirunt. "I have seen "(saith he,) and I was not deceived, the treasure of Christ laid up "in earthen vessels ; for amongst those Christians in *Egypt* I have "seen many Fathers who had here upon earth already begun the 40 "heavenly life ; and regenerate Prophets who were indued not "onely with holy habits, but had received therewith the Spirit of

"promise : for I have known many of them that were so free from
"malice, perverse thoughtfulnesse and suspition, as if they had
"never known that there were such evill wayes to be followed in
"the world, Such a great tranquillity of mind, and such a powerful
"love or longing after goodnesse had wholly possessed them.
"They lived dispersed up and down the wildernesse, and separated
"from one another in several Cells or Cots, but knit all together
"in the perfect bond of Charity. The reason of their distinct and
"distant habitations, was, because they would not have the silence
10 "of their retirements disturbed, nor their minds diverted from the
"contemplation of heavenly things by any noyse, sudden occurrence,
"or idle discourse ; for this cause they have every one their par-
"ticular mansion, where with intentive or earnest minds they do
"(like faithful servants) expect and look for the coming of their
"Master. They take no thought for meat and drink and cloathing,
"nor for any such accommodations; they seek onely the Kingdome
"of God and the righteousnesse thereof, they fight with the
"weapons of prayer, & being guarded with the shield of faith
"from the devices of their spiritual enemies, so travel on towards
20 "their heavenly countrey. This was the *old way*, and whether we
are *in it*, or *out* of it, is not hard to be decided. A pretended
sanctity from the teeth outward, with the frequent *mention* of the
Spirit, and a presumptuous assuming to our selves of the stile of
Saints, when we are within full of *subtilty, malice, oppression, lewd
opinions*, and *diverse lusts*, is (I am sure) a convincing argument
that we are not onely *out* of it, but that we have no mind to returne
into it. The *way* to heaven is *wet* and *slippery*, but it is made so with
teares and not with *blood* ; it is through the *vale of miseries, and the
raine filleth the pooles*, Psal. 85. There is no *voyce* in those *shades*
30 *of Palme*, but the *voyce* of the *Turtle*, which is alwayes *groning*, and
Naturalists say, *she hath no gall*. It is ill coming to the *Lamb* of
God in a *Wolfes* skin ; They that do so, must be taught that he
hath another *attribute*, and they shall finde him a *Lion*. It is strange
that (after the experience of almost *six thousand yeares*) men will
hazard so highly, as to purchase a few dayes false honours, with
the losse of eternal and true glory. In what a horrid darknesse
and agony will the pleasures of this world leave us, after we have
cast away our bodies and souls in the acquisition of them ? how
suddenly must the *rich man* leave his *barnes*, and the *oppressour*
40 his ill-gotten *power* ? how do they labour under the load of their
private guilt, and feele the flames of hell while they are yet alive ?
With what gloomy and despairing looks do they passe from hence,

as if that eternal darknesse they are going into, were already in their faces ? It was a sad and a dark reply that *Henry* the *fourth* made to his *hasty son,* when he had taken away the *Crowne* ; *God knowes* (said he and sighed) *what right I had unto it.* Tyrants and oppressors may very well be compared to the *Hyæna* ; while they prosper, and devoure the *prey,* there is nothing to be seene amongst them but *mirth* and *triumphs* ; but when they have drank *blood* enough, when they are full and cloyed, *then they *weepe.* The onely difference is this, that the *Hyæna's* teares are deceitful, but the teares of Tyrants springing from their inward guilt and horrour, are wofully true, though (like *storms* in *harvest*) they are unprofitable and prodigious.

> * Sinnes are not felt, till they are acted. 10

The difference betwixt the *righteous* and the *wicked* is to be seen in their *death.* The good man goes hence like the *Sunne* in the *summers evening* chearful and unclouded, his memory is precious here with men, and his spirit is received into the *joy of his Master.* This Saint *Hierome* saw in the death of *Paul* the *Heremite,* whose *coate* of *Palm-leaves* he preferr'd to the *purple robes* of the proud. *Let me now* (saith he) *aske the great men of this world, whose possessions are numberlesse, and whose dwellings are of marble, what was it, that was ever wanting to this poor old man ? They drink rich wines out of gold, and he drank clean water out of the fountains. They have silk and gold weav'd into their coates, and he had not so much as the coursest wooll. But then is he out of that simple habit carried into Paradise, and they out of their silk and gold into hell.* Paul *the Heremite hath no covering but the* * *common earth ; Their karkasses are laid up in* ¶ *costly Sepulchres of marble and brasse ; but Paul shall be raised to glory, and they to condemnation.* And presently after directing his speech to the Reader, he concludes thus : *Who ever thou art, that shalt reade this Book, I beseech thee to remember* Hieronymus *the* ** *sinner, who (if God would grant him his desire) had rather be master of* Paul *the Heremites coate with his rewards then of the purple robes of Princes with their punishments.* A *dinner of herbes* with a *good conscience* is *heavenly fare,* and *godlinesse is great gaine, if we would be contented therewith.* I do not so

> * Cœlo tegitur, qui non habet urnam. 20
> ¶ Jam ruet & bustum, titulúsque in marmore sectus, —tumulis autem morientibus, ipse Occumbes etiam, sic mors tibi tertia restat. 30
>
> ** Non sanctum dixit, sed peccatorem.
>
> —O quantum bonum est obstare nulli, carpere securas dapes !
>
> Humi ejacentem scelera non intrant casam. 40

7 (*of Latin*) scelera] sclera *1652*   39 *herbes*] herbs catchword *1652*

much admire *Apitius* his feasts, and *Cleopatra's* banquets of *dissolved pearles*, as I do the *Raven* of *Elias*, and *Hilarion's Crow.* Neither can I in this place passe by that *old Cilician* and Countreyman to Saint *Paul*, who (I verily beleeve,) for a reward of his contented and harmlesse life, had the *honor* and the *happinesse* to have it described and left for ever upon record to posterity, by that inimitable *Prince* and *Patriarch* of *Poets*;

Virg. lib. 4. Georgic.

Namque sub Oebaliæ memini me turribus altis
10 Corycium vidisse senem : cui pauca relicti
Jugera ruris erant, nec fertilis illa juvencis,
Nec pecori opportuna seges, nec commoda Baccho.
Hic rarum tamen in dumis holus, albáque circum
Lilia, verbenásque premens, vescúmque papaver,
Regum æquabat opes animo, seráque revertens
Nocte domum, dapibus mensas onerabat inemptis.
Primus vere rosam, atque Autumno carpere poma :
Et cum tristis hyems etiamnum frigore saxa
Rumperet, & glacie cursus frænaret aquarum,
20 Ille comam mollis jam tum tondebat Acanthi
Æstatem increpitans seram, Zephirósque morantes.

Englished thus.

I saw beneath Tarentum's *stately towers*
An old Cilician *spend his peaceful houres :*
Some few bad acres *in a waste, wild* field,
Which neither Grasse, *nor* Corne, *nor* Vines *would yield,*
He did possesse ; There (*amongst* thorns *and* weeds)
Cheap Herbs and Coleworts, *with the common* Seeds
Of Chesboule *or* tame poppeys *he did sowe,*
30 *And* Verveyne *with* white Lilies *caus'd to grow.*
Content he was, as are successeful Kings,
And late at night come home (for long work brings
The night still home,) *with* unbought messes *layd*
On his low table, *he his* hunger *stayd.*
Roses *he gather'd in the* youthful Spring ;
And Apples *in the* Autumn *home did bring ;*
And when the sad, cold winter *burst with frost*
The stones, *and the* still streams *in* Ice *were lost,*
He would soft leaves of Beares-foot *crop, and chide*
40 *The slow West-winds, and lingring Summer tyde !*

Saint *Hierome* in the life of *Antonius*, (who was nobly borne and as tenderly bred) tells us, that about the age of *eighteen* (his parents being then dead,) he gave away all his possessions, & resolving upon a strict, religious life betook himself to the *wildernesse*; where having erected for himself a poore narrow *Cottage*, he digg'd hard by it, and found a *well*, with whose streams he watered a small piece of *ground*, which he did sowe and set with some ordinary *herbs* for his own provision. To this place thus furnished by his industrie, the *wild asses* would in great numbers very often resort, and not contented to borrow of his *water*, they would some times trespasse upon his *garden*, and make bold with his *sallads*. But he upon a time comming amongst them, commanded the *leader* of them, which he had observed to *guide* the *rest*, to stand still, and beating him upon the sides with his hand, reproved him in these words, *What is the reason that thou com'st to eat that which* 10 *thou hast not sowen?* *Et exinde* (saith my Author) *acceptis aquis ad quas potandas ventitabant, nec arbusculam, nec holera unquam contigebant.* We see by these Examples how safe it is to rely upon our *Masters* promise, and how needlesse and superfluous in the Christian state this worldly abundance is. This our Saviour himself hath admonished us of, and upbraids our diffidence with the examples of the *birds* and the *lilies* of the *field.* Certainly it is dangerous medling with the *world*; It is like the * *Torpedo*, he that catcheth it, comes to lose his life by   * *A fish that (as soon as* the bargain. *Love not the world* (saith *ever he is struck,) so be-* 20 St. *John*) *neither the things that are in the* *nums the Angler, that he* *world, if any man love the world, the love*   Arcanas hyemes & cæca *of the Father is not in him.* We should papavera ponti Abdo sinu, therefore be very cautious how we deal necem. with it, or with the followers and favourites of it. *Condescend to men of low estate*, saith the *chosen vessel*; This is good counsel, but it lies so low that most men tread upon it, & very few are they that will stoop to take it up. There is nothing can bring us sooner to it then the serious consideration of our own frailty. This is the *Catharma* that turns away the plague; and as 30 *Physicians* say of *fasting*, that it cures almost all bodily diseases: So may I say of this, that it prevents (if timely applyed) all the *depravations and diseases* of the mind. It will bring down every *high thought* & set us upon even ground,   Qui jacet in terra, non where we shall be in no danger of soul or habet undè cadat. body. Our Saviour was buried in a Rock, and he that builds upon his grave, he that mortifies his affections, and hides his life in him, needs feare no *stormes.* What beauty is there in a *deaths-head* crownd with *roses?* If we carry the *one* about us, we shall be safe enough from the temptations of the *other.* Let sensual *natures* 40 judge as they please, but for my part, I shall hold it no *Paradoxe*

16 upbraids] upraids *1652*   diffidence] dffidence *1652*

to affirme, *there are no pleasures in this world.* Some *coloured griefes* and *blushing woes* there are, which look so clear as if they were *true complexions*; but it is a very sad and a tryed truth that they are but *painted.* To draw then to an end, let us looke alwayes upon this *Day-Lilie* of life, as if the *Sun* were already *set.* Though we *blossome* and *open* many *mornings,* we shall not do so always, *Soles occidere & redire possunt*; but *man* cannot. *He hath his time appointed him upon earth, which he shall not passe, and his days are like the* 10 *days of an hireling.* Let us then so husband our time, that when the *flower* falls, the *seed* may be preserved. We have had many blessed Patterns of a holy life in the *Brittish Church,* though now trodden under foot, and branded with the title of *Antichristian.*

Omnem crede diem tibi diluxisse supremum.

I shall propose but * one to you, the most obedient *Son* that ever his *Mother* had, and yet a most glorious true *Saint* and a *Seer.* Heark how like a *busie Bee* he hymns it to the *flowers,* while in a handful of *blossomes* gather'd by himself, he foresees his own *dissolution.*

* Mr. *George Herbert* of blessed memory; See his incomparable prophetick Poems, and particularly these,
Church-musick,
Church-rents, and schisms
20 *The Church militant.*

I made a Posie while the day ran by:
Here will I smell my remnant out, and tye
   My life within this band,

But time did becken to the flowers, and they
By noon most cunningly did steal away,
   And wither'd in my hand.

My hand was next to them, and then my heart:
I took, without more thinking, in good part
   Times gentle admonition;

30 Who did so sweetly death's sad taste convey,
Making my mind to smell my fatal day;
   Yet sugring the suspition.

Farewel dear flowers! sweetly your time ye spent,
Fit, while ye liv'd, for smell or ornament,
   And after death for cures.

I follow strait without complaint or grief,
Since if my sent be good, I care not if
   It be as short as yours.

15 * Mr.] Mr. *1652*

As often therefore as thou seest the *full* and *ripe corne*, to succeed the *tender* and *flowery Spring*, the *Autumne* again to succeed the *Summer*, and the *cold* and *snowie Winter* to succeed the *Autumne*, say with thy self, *These seasons passe away, but will returne againe: but when I go, I shall returne no more.*

Petrar. *de Contemp. mundi.*
Immortalia ne speres monet
annus, & almum
   Quæ rapit hora diem.
Frigora mitescunt Zephyris,
ver proterit æstas
     Interitura simul
Pomifer Autumnus fruges
  effuderit, & mox
  Bruma recurrit iners.

When thou seest the *Sun* to set, and the melancholy *shadowes* to prevaile and increase, meditate with thy selfe, *Thus when my life is done, will the shadowes of death be stretched over me; And yet this Sun which now leaves me, will be here againe to morrow: but when the Sun of my life sets, it shall not returne to me, until the heavens be no more.*

When the *night* is drawn over thee, and the whole world lies slumbring under it, do not thou sleep it out; for as it is a *portion* of time much abused by wicked livers, so is it of all others the most powerful to excite thee to *devotion*; be stirring therefore, and make special use of that *deepest* and *smoothest current* of *time*, like that vigilant *Pilot* who alwayes mistrusted the *greatest calms*,

Sydera cuncta notat   *And rising at midnight the Stars espi'd*
tacito labentia cœlo.   *All posting Westward in a silent glide.*

When thou also seest those *various, numberles, and beautiful luminaries* of the night to move on in their *watches,* and some of them to *vanish* and *set,* while all the rest do *follow after*, consider that *thou* art carried on with *them* in the *same motion*, and that there is no hope of subsisting for thee, but in *him who never moves, and never sets.*

Consider thy own *posterity* (if thou hast any) or those that are *younger then thy self*, and say, *These are travelling up the hill of life, but I am going head-long down.* Consider thy own *habitation*, how many have been there before thy *time*, whom that place must never know again, and that there is no help, but *thou* must follow. Consider the *works of thine own hands*, the *flowers, trees* and *arbours* of thine own planting, for all those must survive thee; Nay, who knows but thou mayst be gone, before thou canst enjoy those pleasures thou dost expect from them; for the *Poet* in that point proves oftentimes a *Prophet,*

The trees, we set, grow slowly, and their shade
Stays for our sons, while (we the Planters) fade.
       Virg. Georg.

Tarda venit, serísque futura nepotibus umbra.

4 (*of Latin*) simul] simul. *1652*   22 *various,*] various *1652*
39 (*we*] we (*GC*

To be short, acquit thee *wisely* and *innocently* in all thy Actions, live a *Christian*, and die a *Saint*.   Let not the *plurality* of *dayes*, with the numerous *distinctions* and *mincings* of thy *time* into *moneths, weeks, houres* and *minutes* deceive thee, nor be a means to make thee misspend the *smallest portion* of it; let not the *empty honours* and *pompous nothing* of this world keep thee back from the *grapes* of the *brook* of *Eshcol*.   Remember that we must account for every idle *word*, much more for our *actions*. If thou hast lost any *dear friends*, have them alwayes before thine eyes, visit their *graves*
10 often, and be not unkind to a *Jonathan* though in the *dust*. Give eare to *heaven*, and forget not what is spoken to thee from thence. *Behold, I come as a thief; blessed is he that watcheth and keepeth his garments, lest he walk naked, and they see his shame.*   The time of life is short, and *God* (when he comes to see us) *comes without a bell. Let us therefore gird up the loynes of our minds, and be sober, and hope to the end. Let us keep our selves in the love of God as obedient children, not grieving his holy Spirit, by which we are sealed unto the day of redemption.   And let us not give place to the devil, nor be weary of well-doing; but let us be renewed daily in the spirit of our*
20 *mind that when he comes (who will not tarry) we may be found faithful, and about our masters businesse.*

Let us feare God, and forgive men, blesse those that persecute us, and lay up treasure for our selves in heaven, that where our treasure is, there our hearts may be also, and this (if God permits) will we do, and then

> *— We can go die as sleep, and trust*
> *Half that we have*
> *Unto an honest, faithful grave*
> *Making our pillows either down or dust.*

30 Now unto him, who shall change our vile bodies, that they may be fashioned like unto his glorious body, according to the working whereby he is able to subdue all things unto himselfe, even unto *Jesus Christ* the Prince of the Kings of the earth, and the first be-gotten of the dead, be glory and dominion for ever and ever. *Amen.*

A Prayer when thou findest thy self sickly, or when thou art visited with any Disease.

Most merciful, and wise God, who *bringest light out of darknesse,* and true *comforts* out of the greatest *afflictions,* I do in all humility and with all my soule resigne my selfe unto thy divine pleasure,
40 and give thee most hearty and unfeined thanks for this thy present *visitation,* an infallible argument of thy fatherly love, and that

tender care which thou hast of my salvation. Thou gavest me
health, and I took no notice of thy *gift*, and but very little of the
Giver: Thou gavest me dayes of gladnesse and I *numberd them not*.
Wherefore with most true sorrow for my unthankfulnesse, and
with all the *sad Resentments* of a most penitent heart I do acknowledge thy *justice*, adore thy *providence*, and beg thy *mercy*. O
righteous Father! Though I have gone astray, do not thou cast
me off: though *I am no more worthy to be called thy son*, yet have
thou a minde to the work of thine own hands. Confirme my *faith*,
sanctifie my *affections*, give me a lively and enduring *hope*, with 10
an unwearied *patience*; And strengthen me in all my *Agonies*
with the *celestial assistance* and *inexpressible refreshments* of thy
overcoming spirit. Thou that didst give to thy blessed and faithful *Martyrs* such a glorious *measure* of thy Almighty *spirit*, as
encouraged them for thy sake to be *sawed* asunder, to be *burnt*,
stoned and beheaded, give unto me now such a gracious *portion* of
the same *Comforter* as may leade me through *death* unto *life*. Or
if thou wilt in mercy restore me again, and enlarge my time, give
me, I beseech thee, a thankful *heart*, holy *resolutions*, and a stedfast *spirit* to performe them; And for *Jesus Christ* his sake never 20
suffer me to forget thy *tender and fatherly compassion*, or to fall
again into my old sins, and *heap* up for my self thy eternal anger
and most just indignation.

For what end soever thou hast sent this present *sicknesse*,
whether for my *dissolution*, or for a temporal *correction* of my sinful life, grant I beseech thee, that both may be for thy *glory*, and
the salvation of my poore soule, purchased with the *precious blood*
of thine only *Sonne* and my dear *Redeemer*, to whom with thee
and the *holy Ghost* be ascribed by *Angels* and *men*, all wisdome,
dominion and majesty for ever and ever, *Amen!*   30

A Prayer in the hour of Death.

O my most blessed and glorious *Creatour* that *hast fed me all
my life long*, and *redeemed me from all evil*, seeing it is thy merciful pleasure to take me out of this fraile body, and *to wipe away
all teares from mine eyes*, and all sorrowes from my heart, I do
with all humility and willingnesse consent and submit my self
wholly unto thy sacred will. *I desire to be dissolved and to be with
my Saviour.* I blesse and praise thy holy name for all thy great
mercies conferred upon me, from the first day of my life unto this
present hour. I give thee all possible thanks for this gracious & 40
kind *visitation*, in which thou art mercifully pleased to order this

last act of thy *poor creature* to thy *glory,* and the *fruition* of those
heavenly comforts which have already *swallowed* up my whole *spirit.*
O let *all* that come after me speak of thy *wondrous mercies,* and
the *generations* which are yet unborn give praise unto thy *name.*

Lord *Jesus Christ* my most loving Redeemer, into thy saving
and *everlasting Armes* I commend my *spirit,* I am ready my *dear
Lord,* and earnestly expect and long for thy good pleasure ; *Come
quickly,* and receive the soul of thy *servant* which trusteth in thee.

Blessing, and honour, and glory and power be unto him that sitteth
10   *upon the throne, and unto the Lamb and to the holy Ghost for
ever and ever Amen.*

*Glory be to God on high, and on earth peace, good will towards
men !*

Blessed be God alone !
Thrice blessed three in one !

MAN

IN

Glory:

OR,

A Difcourfe of the bleffed
ftate of the Saints in the
New JERUSALEM.

Written in Latin by the moft
Reverend and holy Father

ANSELMVS

Archbifhop of *Canterbury*, and now
done into Englifh.

Printed *Anno Dom.* 1652.

Reader,

Anselmus Archbishop of *Canterbury* lived here in *Britaine,* in the reigne of *Rufus,* and striving to keep entire the Immunities of the Church, (which the spirit of Covetousnesse and Sacriledge did then begin to encroach upon,) he was twice banished, first by *William* the second called *Rufus* or *red-hair'd,* and after by *Henry* the first his youngest brother and successor. Men of fierce and unmanagable spirits they were, and by so much the fitter for the throne. The first was such an infamous lover of money, that the
10 *Neophyte-Jews* were at a constant fee with him, for renouncing *Christianity;* and the later (like a true son of *Ottoman,*) caused
* *Robert* Duke of *Nor-* his eldest * brothers eyes to be pull'd out, *mandy.* who was then his prisoner in the Castle of *Cardiffe.* To avoid the fury of *Rufus* (who had thus banished him,) our Author here retired into *France,* and shelter'd himself in the Abbey of *Clunie,* where by way of discourse with that reverend family, he shed forth this Dissertation, which (at the same time it proceeded from him,) was exactly taken, and put into writing by *Eadinerus,* a Canon regular of the Church of *Canterbury,*
20 and his *Amanuensis* in his banishment. Some brokages and disorderly parcels of it, are to be found in his book *De Similitud,* but the entire and genuine discourse was first made publick at *Paris* 1639. where it took so well, that it was presently translated into French. This much I thought fit to acquaint thee with; and so I shall leave thee to thy owne affaires, which I wish to be such as may bring thee to the fruition of those joyes, which are showne thee here through a glasse darkly, and but in part; untill that which is perfect shall come, and this which is in part shall be done away.

30   *Thy Friend*

HEN. VAUGHAN.

Here holy *Anselme* lives in ev'ry page,
And sits Arch-bishop still, to vex the age.
Had he foreseen (and who knows but he did?)
This fatal wrack, which deep in time lay hid,
'Tis but just to believe, that little hand
Which clouded him, but now benights our land,
Had never (like *Elias*) driv'n him hence,
A sad retirer for a slight offence.
For were he now, like the returning year,
Restor'd to view these desolations here,   10
He would do penance for his old complaint,
And (weeping) say, That *Rufus* was a Saint.

Revel. Chap. 7.

1. *And after this I beheld, and lo a great multitude which no man could number, of all nations and kindreds, and people, and tongues stood before the throne and before the Lamb, clothed with white robes, and palms in their hands.*

2. *And cried with a loud voice, saying, Salvation to our God, which sitteth upon the throne, and unto the Lamb.*

3. *And one of the Elders answered saying unto me, Who are these* 20 *which are arayed in white robes? and whence came they?*

4. *And I said unto him, Sir, thou knowest. And he said unto me, These are they which came out of great tribulation, and have washed their robes, and made them white in the blood of the Lamb.*

5. *Therefore are they before the throne of God, and serve him day and night in his Temple: and he that sitteth on the throne shall dwell among them.*

6. *They shall hunger no more, neither thirst any more, neither shall the Sun light on them, nor any heate.*

7. *For the Lamb which is in the midst of the throne, shall feed* 30 *them, and shall leade them unto living fountains of waters, and God shall wipe away all tears from their eyes.*

7, 8 precede ll. 5, 6 in 1652

Many men, when a holy conversation and good works are proposed unto them, and when they are advised to exercise themselves therein, and not to follow after the vanities of this world,
are wont to question for what end, reward, or retribution shall
they do so? The answer to these men must be this: Because
it is written, *that Eye hath not seen, nor eare heard, neither have
entred into the heart of man, the things which God hath prepared
for them that love him,* 1 Cor. 2. Which words, because they
cannot plainly understand what is meant by them, must be
10 expounded to them by other circumstances, and it must be told
them, that the reward which in the life to come shall be given
unto those that serve God in this life, is, everlasting life, eternal
happinesse, never-ending pleasures, and a fulnesse and sufficiency
of all accommodations to their own desires without any scarcity, or
want at all. When these things are thus told them, they seeme
to be (as they are indeed) very great, and very good. But because,
that neither by this expression they do perfectly apprehend, what
those things are which they shall receive in the life to come; nor
can they of a sudden rightly perceive what is meant by a sufficiency
20 of all accommodations without any want at all, they continue still
in a doubtful minde, and are not effectually drawn to take any
relish or delight in the things so told them. What course then
shall we take to render these eternal rewards more relishing and
delightful to them? I hold that the best way is, to feed them as
Nurses feed their little children; who, (if at any time they give
them a large faire apple, which for the tendernesse of their teeth,
and the narrownesse of their mouths they cannot feed upon) cut
it (according to the capacity of the child) into several bits or parts,
and so give it them to eate by peece-meales.

30   We shall therefore divide this great sufficiencie of all accommodations in the life to come, into several parts or portions, that (by so
doing) they may with those things we shall deliver be fed to eternal life. And because they may appear more plainly to them, we
shall consider what those things are, which the minde of man
most affects in this life; and by those, (as farre as we may) we
shall make it evident that they shall enjoy them after a more
excellent manner in the life to come: if being placed here in the
midst of dangers and worldly temptations, they stick fast to the
precepts of Christ; and when they have kept them, they will of
40 themselves quickly perceive, that by no meanes they shall lose,
nor be deceived of the utmost of their desires. This Course we

shall take in the Explication of this Doctrine, and beginning with the least, passe on to our desired end.

That we may then in the first place briefly summe up all those things which have reference to the body, I suppose them to be such things as are (indeed) desirable of themselves, and for whose service or use all other things are desired of men, and those are Beauty, Activity, Strength, Liberty, Health, Pleasure, & Long Life. But if amongst these we have reckoned, there are some things, which the servants of God have no respect to, but take special care to neglect and avoid them, as (for instance sake) beauty and pleasure are; yet do they not therefore despise them, because that naturally they affect them not, but because they would not offend God in them; for if they certainly knew that by caring for such things, they could not offend God, nor have their affections with-drawn from heavenly things, without doubt they would take more delight in the fruition of them, then in a contrary state. These things being now thus premised, I shall as briefly as I may treat of every one of them distinctly, or by it self, and labour to demonstrate unto you (as God shall enable me) after what manner they shall be enjoyed by us after the resurrection of the body. 20

To begin then, *Beauty* is a certaine good, which all men naturally desire to have. But in the life to come the beauty of the righteous shall shine equally with the Sunne, this the sacred Scripture testifies, *Matth.* 13. *Then shall the righteous shine forth as the Sun in the Kingdome of their Father.* Adde to this, that the body of our Lord Jesus Christ (which none I hope will deny) shall out-shine the brightnesse of the Sun. But by the testimony of the Apostle *we shall be made like unto him*, for he saith, *He shall change our vile bodies, that they may be fashioned like unto his glorious body*, and this is the confession of that authority, which to contradict, is blasphemy. Now if any man would have this proved to him by reason, I beleeve it ought not to seeme incredible to any, that the righteous in that life which is to come, *when this mortality shall be swallowed up of life*, shall shine as bright as the Sun, seeing they are truly *called*, and truly *are* the temple and the seat of God himself, which (as I remember) is no where in sacred Scripture spoken of this visible Sun.

As for *Activity*, which is every way as desirable as *Beauty*, we shall be indued with such a measure of it, as shall render us equall for swiftnesse to the very Angels of God, which in a moment passe from the highest heaven unto the earth, and from the earth again into heaven; which swiftnesse, if it were necessary

to prove it so in the Angels, we might for instance produce that
place of Scripture, where it is written, that the Angel of the Lord
took *Habakkuk* the Prophet by the haire of the head, and carried
him through the vehemency of his spirit (when he was yet in the
flesh) from *Jury* into *Babylon,* and having delivered the dinner
unto *Daniel,* brought him again immediately to his own place.
Therefore I say again, that a swiftnesse every way equal to that
which is in them, shall be given to those, who labour in their
lives here to be like unto them.   The Apostle also, who affirms
10 that our bodies shall in the twinkling of an eye be perfectly raised,
notwithstanding that our limbs be separated or dispersed one from
another, and the distance of place never so great, hath thereby
sufficiently proved, that our very bodies which in that day shall
be raised incorruptible, shall be gifted with the very same swiftnesse ; for he testifies that *this corruptible shall put on incorruption,
and this mortal shall put on immortality,* 1 Cor. 15.   An instance
or demonstration of this swiftnesse we have in the beams of the
Sunne, which as soone as ever the body of that Planet appears
above the earth in the East, passe in a moment to the utmost
20 West.   By this consideration we may conclude that what hath
been spoken touching our velocity in the life to come, is not impossible, especially because that animated bodies have in them
a greater agility, then those which are inanimate.   To this instance of the Sun-beams we may adde another of the like nature,
which we have in our selves ; for the beams or ray of the Eye,
when we open our eye-lids passeth immediately to the utmost
point of the Horizon or visible part of the sky, and when we shut
them returnes wholly and unimpaired into it self.   Again, it is
a thing certainly known, that the souls of the Elect which are in
30 the hand of the Lord, have not yet enjoyed the fulnesse of felicity,
untill their bodies shall be restored unto them incorruptible ;
which when they shall enjoy, there will be nothing more left for
them to wait for and desire.   But these bodies whose redemption
they long and grone for if they would retard or hinder their swiftnesse, they would rather abhorre their fellowship, then long for it ;
therefore it is certain that such a swiftnesse or agility as we have
spoken of shall be given us of God in the life to come.

The next thing we are to treat of is *Fortitude* or *Strength,* which
most men affect, as it is opposite to imbecillity and faint-hearted-
40 nesse.   But they who shall be worthy to walk with the Citizens of
the new *Jerusalem,* shall excell so much in strength, that nothing
can have power to resist them : whether their desire be to remove,

34 for] for, *G*

or over-turn any thing out of its station, or by any other way to divert it, nothing can hinder them ; nor shall they in compassing their desire be put to any more trouble or pains, then we are put to at present when we move an Eye, or turne it towards any object we desire to look upon.   But let us not in this place forget to instance in the Angels, to whom we labour in this life to assimilate our selves ; for if in this branch, or in any of the rest which we are to handle, we can finde no other example or demonstration, we must apply to them.   I suppose there is none will deny, but that the Angels excel so much in strength, as to be able to effect whatsoever shall be enjoyned them.   But here some body may ask, of what use shall this fortitude or strength be unto us in that life, when all things shall be put in such perfect order, that there cannot be a better ; when there shall be no need of mutations, eversions, or reformation wherein this fortitude or strength may be imployed?   Whoever shall ask this question, let him attend a little to me, and consider what use we make at present of the faculties given us in this life ; and he shall finde that we do not alwayes imploy some of those abilities with which we are now gifted in the body ; as the faculty of seeing, our utmost strength, and our knowledge of some select things, with many more ; In the like manner shall it be then with this forti- tude we are now speaking of, for the onely possession of it will be an incredible pleasure and joy unto us, though we shall have no use for it, all things being (as it is said before) in the state of perfection.   If this *objection* be made concerning *velocity*, or any of the other *branches* which are to follow in this discourse ; I hold this *solution* (if we finde not a better) satisfactory enough.

We are now come to the fourth branch, which is *Liberty*, and is no lesse desired then any of the former.   Whoever then shall leade an Angelical life here upon earth, shall without doubt be admitted into an equal liberty with the Angels in heaven.   There- fore as nothing can resist, hinder, or confine the Angels, but that they may passe freely through all things according to their own desires ; so shall there be no obstacle or restraint of the Elects : there shall be no inclosure that can hold us, nor any Element which shall not be pervious or passable for us, when, and how we please.   An eminent and most certain example of this we have left us in the body of our Lord Jesus Christ, to which blessed body (Saint *Paul* affirms) *that our vile bodies shall be fashioned and made like, according to the working whereby he is able to subdue all things unto himself.*   Now the Scripture beares record that he rose from the dead after the Sepulchre was made sure and sealed, and that he came in to his Disciples, the doors being shut upon them, and at the same time caused *Thomas* to thrust his hand into his side ; all which (without doubt) was laid down for a strong and comfortable demonstration to us *of the glorious liberty of the children of God*, Rom. 8.

   In this fifth place comes *Health*, which of all temporal blessings is the principal, and the most to be desired.   And of this what can be better said, then that which hath been already spoken by
10 the Psalmist, *The salvation of the righteous cometh from the Lord*, Psal. 37.   What infirmity then can lay hold upon those, whose health or salvation is from the Lord?   But what example or similitude to introduce, whereby you may perceive what manner of health that shall be which we are to enjoy in the world to come, I do not know ; for neither I in my own body, nor the holiest man that ever lived in the flesh, can finde in himself any state of health which may be compared or liken'd to this eternal and incorruptible health.   For in this life (when we finde our bodies without any paine or disturbance) we conclude that we
20 are in health, and yet are we therein oftentimes deceived.   For it happens very frequently that we are infirme or sickly in some particular member, which yet we can by no means discover, but by motion of the said member, or by touching the place affected. But to come to those that are not thus affected, but seeme to themselves to be in perfect health, what shall we judge of them, that they are in health, or that they are not?   Propose to thy self some one of a most healthful constitution, and that thou shouldst enquire of him concerning the state of his body : he will tell thee, that in his own judgement he finds himself in perfect health.
30 But let his body be examined and felt with a little rigidnesse more then ordinary, or wring him hard in any part of it, he will presently cry out, forbeare, you hurt me.   What is this?   Did not he a little before affirme himself sound, and being now but moderately touched, doth he cry out of paine?   Is this man thinkst thou in health?   Truly I think not.   It is not then such a health as this (which is but a meere remission) that they shall receive in the life to come, whose salvation is expresly promised to proceed from the Lord, *Rev.* 21. *For God shall wipe away all teares from their eyes, and there shall be no more death, neither*
40 *sorrow nor crying, neither shall there be any more paine, for the former things are past away*, Rev. 7. *They shall hunger no more, neither thirst any more, nor shall the Sun light on them, nor any*

heate, for God shall cover them with his right hand, and with his holy arme shall he defend them. What then shall be able to hurt them whose covering and inclosure shall be the arme of God? But what manner of health that shall be, I know for a certain, that neither I, nor any man else, (either by my owne or anothers apprehension or experiment) can possibly expresse. If any man desires to know the qualities of Feavers and diverse other diseases, I can quickly satisfie him, as well by the experience I have had of them in my own body, as by relation from others; but that which neither by my own understanding nor sensation I have never perceived, nor received any knowledge of it from another, how can I say any thing of it? Onely this I shall absolutely assert (and I do verily beleeve it) that this health of the life to come shall fill the whole man with such an immutable, inviolable, and inexpressible sweetnesse and solace, as shall utterly repel and for ever drive away all thoughts of infirmities, their accessions, or revolutions. And let this suffice to have been spoken of our health in the world to come.

The next branch that comes in order to be now spoken of, is *Pleasure*, which by another name, or definition rather, we shall call the *Delectation* of the corporeal senses. And this (truly) most men are very much taken with, because the corporeal senses in every man delight in those things which are adjudged proper or peculiar to them, and withal beneficial or helpful. For (to instance in a few) the sense of smelling is much recreated or pleased with the variety of sweet and comfortable odours; the sense of tasting with the different relishes or gust of several meats, confections, and drinks; And all the rest (as every mans natural appetite carries him) have their several and different delights. But these delectations are not alwayes pleasing; nay, they prove oftentimes distastful and troublesome to their greatest lovers, for they are (indeed) but transitory and bestial. But those delectations or pleasures which in the world to come shall be poured out upon the righteous are everlasting and rational. And for this cause I do not see how it is possible to expresse them so, as to make them intelligible, or subject to our understanding in this life, especially because we cannot find in the pleasures of this life any example or similitude which hath in it any collation with them, or can give us the least light or manifestation of them; for those heavenly delights, the more we enjoy them, will be the more deare and acceptable to us, for the fulnesse of those joyes breeds no surfeit. And such delights as these are, I beleeve no man ever in this world did so far perceive or taste, as to be able to describe unto others the true state or savour of them. Two blessed and two miserable states of man we know to be, the greater and the lesser. His great or perfect state of blisse is in the Kingdome of God; his lesser is that which *Adam* forfeited, the joy of Paradise. As for his states of misery, his great and endlesse one is in the lake of fire and brimstone; and his lesser in the continual travels and afflictions of this present life. Now it is clear, that no man in this life (after *Adam*) did ever taste of 10 either of those two states of blisse. But if we had tried or tasted of (onely) that lesser state of blisse which *Adam* enjoyed in Paradise, we might then perhaps by the mediation or means of the lesser conjecture or guesse at the greater. As now being borne and bred up in the lesser state of misery, we can give many plain and convincing demonstrations of our deplorable condition in the greater. Wherefore seeing the pleasure we speak of, is a branch or portion of that greater state of blisse, I cannot conceive of any possibility to expresse it, unlesse we may do it by some similitudes that are quite contrary to the greater state of 20 misery, and drawne from the lesser. For example, or instance, let us suppose that there stood before us a naked man with hot and flaming irons thrust into the very apples of his eyes, and into every part and member of his body, his veines, nerves and muscles, so that neither his marrow, nor his entrails, nor any the most inward and tender parts were free from the anguish and immanity of the torment, and that he were as sensible of the paine in every member, as he must needs be in the very balls of his eyes. What shall I say now of this man? is he not miserably tormented? And who amongst these dispersed and ubiquitary 30 paines thus inflicted will be so irrational as to think that he can have any ease or pleasure? In the same manner, but by a quite contrary consideration may we conjecture or guesse at the delectations and pleasures of the life to come; for as this man is filled and pained all over with torments, so shall ineffable and endlesse pleasures be poured upon, and over-flow the righteous. Their eyes, their eares, and their hearts, yea their very bones (as the Prophet *David* saith) *shall be glad and rejoyce*; every part and every member of them shall be crowned and replenished with the fulnesse and the life of pleasures. Yea their whole man shall be 40 truly and abundantly satisfied with the fatnesse of Gods house, and he shall make them drink of the river of his pleasures; *for with him is the fountain of life, and in his light shall we see light.*

Man in Glory.

Whosoever then is the happy man that shall be counted worthy to enjoy these heavenly pleasures, I cannot see (as to the comforts of the body) what more he can desire. The onely thing that (in order to what we are to treat of) shall be added to him, is long life. And this shall not be wanting there, for our Saviour testifies, that the wicked shall go into everlasting punishment, but the righteous into life eternal, *Matth.* 25.

Having done now with these blessings bestowed upon the body, there remaine other more excellent gifts, which are every way as desirable, but these belong to the soul as the former did to the body. We shall reduce them all into seven principal heads, and here they follow, 1. *Wisdome.* 2. *Friendship.* 3. *Peace.* 4. *Power.* 5. *Honour.* 6. *Security*, and 7. *Joy.* Our wisdome then, which in this life all men desire, and worthily too, shall be so great in the life to come, that nothing shall be hidden from us, that we have a minde to know; for we shall know all things, which God ordained to be known of man, as well those things which are past, as those which (in this world) are yet to come. There all men shall be known by every man, and every man shall be known by all men. Neither shall any one there be ignorant of what Countrey, Nation, stock or linage every one is descended; nay, he shall know all that ever we did in our life-time. Here some body perhaps may say, how is this? shall all men know the secret sins that I have committed? Is my confession of them come to this? Is it thus that they are blotted out, forgotten, and never more discovered? Well, this is thy objection. But when thou in that state of glory shalt stand in the presence of God, purged from all thy sins, canst thou be unthankful to him for that great mercy shewed thee in the remission of all thy offences? And how canst thou be thankful, if none of those sins for whose forgivenesse thou doest owe those thanks unto him, will be left in thy memory? That therefore thou mayest for ever take delight in the singing of his prayses, thou wilt (I beleeve) have alwayes in thy mind those great transgressions and eternal miseries from which he delivered thee. Seeing then that the consciences of all men shall (in that state) remaine entire to them, I dare affirme that those sinnes for whose remission thou doest then give thanks, shall likewise be openly known, not to thy confusion, but to the glory of God, and the mutual rejoycing of the Saints, for thou shalt be no more troubled then with the remembrance of thy sins, nor be any more ashamed of thy most secret transgressions, then any one is in this life with the memory of some dangerous wounds

or loathsome disease that he is perfectly cured of ; or then we are
in the state of men of those inconveniences we were subject to when
we were little infants in our cradles and swadling-bands ; for in
that life when we shall be blessed with inviolable health, perfect
purity, a full remission and most certain impunity of all our sins,
why should the memory or publike knowledge of them be any
more grievous to us then his denying of *Jesus Christ* is now to
Peter, or his persecution of him to *Paul*, or her sins which were
many to that blessed Convert *Mary Magdalen*, with diverse
10 others whose sins and infirmities are already in this world pub-
likely known of all men ?   And besides all this, by this publike
manifestation of sins, as of thy enormous and loathsome infirmities, the power and wisdome of the great Physician will by
all the Elect be so much the more admired, praised and magnified ;
and the praise and magnificence of the divine glory (if rightly
considered by thee) is thy glory.   But thou wilt say, I consent
indeed that the praise of God is my glory, but when from all
parts of the earth such an exceeding number of innocent and
righteous persons (if compared to me) shall appeare there, who
20 considering the odious obscenity of my life, will (as it is most fit)
abhorre me as a most abominable creature, what shall I say then,
seeing there is a reward as well for unrighteousnesse as for
righteousnesse ?   Thy feare in these circumstances is needlesse,
for it will be otherwise there with thee then thou dost suppose ;
for thou shalt finde, that those Elects which (in comparison of
thee) thou dost hold righteous and innocent, will have no such
thoughts of thee, as thou at present dost suspect.   For they upon
the first sight of thee, will presently know and consider, that by
committing those obscenities thou didst not sin against them, but
30 against God.   And when they see that God hath freely and fully
forgiven thee, they will not so much as have a thought of abhor-
ring, or judging thee in the smallest matter ; for they know, that
if they should any way contemne or censure thee in that state,

What God hath cleansed,   wherein thou shalt be perfectly reconciled
call not thou common,   to the Father and all thy transgressions
Acts 10. 15.   blotted out, they would thereby sin grievously against   the   Lord.   They will   therefore be   the   more
thankful, and have in greater admiration the infinite mercy of
God both towards thee, and towards themselves.   Towards thee,
40 because he brought thee up out of hell, and saved thee from thy
grievous and crying sins.   Towards themselves, because it was his
free grace that saved and held them up from falling into the like

enormities. By praysing God thus they will magnifie and admire in thee after Gods goodnesse, his power and * sure mercies by relying on which *Constantiam. thou didst escape and get out of the pit of perdition ; into which pit (had they been left to themselves) they would have fallen as well as thou didst ; and here they will consider, that had they been in that dangerous state, they should (perhaps) have been utterly cast away, and not break the snare as thou didst. Thou seest now that a publike manifestation of thy sins will in the state of glory be no disgrace nor prejudice at all to thee, and how great a furtherance of divine praise and thanksgiving the knowne remission of them will prove. Yea, if the very Angels should reprove and censure thee (for the heynousnesse of thy sins) to be altogether unworthy of their society, yet hast thou left thee very just reasons wherewith to vindicate and defend thy self. And here perhaps thou wilt aske me, how this may be done? do but give attention, and I will tell thee. Suppose that any one of the Angels should rebuke, or upbraid thee in these words : * dost thou a fraile and mortal creature, made of the dust of the earth, and whose doome was to returne into dust again, after thou hast rebelled against thy Maker, and wallowed in all manner of sins and pollutions, seek now to be like one of us, who never in any thing resisted the divine will?

* This is onely proposed, not asserted, nor (indeed) can it be, for our Saviour himself tels us, That there is joy in the presence of the Angels of God over one sinner that repenteth, *Luke* 15. 10. and their song is, *good will towards men.*

To this Charge thou mayst answer thus. If I (as you say) have been formed out of the dust, it is no wonder then that (being driven up and down by every wind of temptation) I fell at last into the mire of sin ; but afterwards (having first acknowledged, and then believed in the mercies of *Jesus Christ,*) I did renounce and cast off all those courses which I knew to be contrary to his will, and exercised my self in all those wayes which I understood to be well-pleasing unto him. I fainted not, nor refused to under-go and suffer for his glory diverse tribulations and distresses, in hunger, in thirst, in watchings, persecutions, reproaches and manifold afflictions ; And having utterly cast off and contemned all the pleasures of the world, I strongly endeavoured, and earnestly desired to be perfectly reconciled unto my Saviour. But you never suffered any of these things for his sake, you dwelt always in glory, and the joyes of heaven ; The arme of God always sustained and defended you from being assaulted by any sinne, so that you were never stained

3 Constantiam] Constaniiam *1652*

with the least spot of it. Wherefore it is his owne free gift, whose
hand with-held you from it, that hath kept you from falling away
from his will.   But because this way of reasoning may be onely
used by those who have forcibly resisted their owne damnation,
and taken the kingdome of heaven by violence; they that shall
enter into it upon other conditions, must finde another reason by
which they may claime a parity, or equal degree of glory with the
Angels.   And if they desire to know what manner of reason that
is, it may be this which followes: They may tell them that the
10 ground upon which they lay their just claime to an equality of
blisse with them in the kingdome of God, is the free mercy and
donation of *Jesus Christ*; who for that very end vouchsafed to be
made man, and to suffer death upon the Crosse, that being saved
from our sins, and justified through his blood, we might be with
him where he is, and be partakers of his kingdome; consider you
therefore, if the blood of *Jesus Christ* which was shed for us is
not a sufficient price for our salvation, and for an equality of glory
with you.   What reply now can the Angels (who because they are
good of themselves, will be therefore the sooner won with reason)
20 make unto this? truly none at all, unless by way of Confession,
that men redeemed with so high a price may justly claime and
partake with them an equal glorification.   When therefore both
Angels and men, whom thou didst judge more righteous then thy
self shall consent unto thy glory, and hold thee worthy in all
things of those true and eternal honours conferred upon thee,
consider (if thou canst) how acceptable and pleasing such a knowledge will be to thee, which shall make thee known to all men,
and all men to be known of thee.

And shall not consequently out of that mutual and perfect
30 knowledge arise a certaine inestimable and inviolable friendship?
which shall so warm the hearts of every one towards another, that
the love which every one shall have for another, shall be evident
and convincing in the knowledge of all.   Neither do I see how it
can be otherwise, seeing that all in that kingdome are but one
body, and Christ himself (who is very peace,) the head thereof;
neither will they with lesse affection imbrace one another, then the
members of one natural body are united to one another.   Thou
wilt therefore in that state love all men as thy self, and every one
will love thee as dearly as himself.   O (now thinkest thou,) how
40 full of love shall I be towards all men, if I were in that happy

32, 33 evie | dent . . . . knowledg- | *1652*   36 another] anothtr *1652*
37 members] membets *1652*

state? But passe by that Meditation, and consider him, by whose
mediation and grievous sufferings all these blessings were purchased for thee; and thou wilt then perceive that he will love
thee incomparably more then any others; yea, more then thou
canst love thy self; and so wilt thou with a certaine inward,
inexpressible delight come to love him more then any others, yea
infinitely more then thou canst love thy self.

But seeing it fals out very frequently amongst men, that those
persons who continue in a reciprocal and unanimous love, do not
in all circumstances accord and consist, but differ in opinion, and 10
sometimes also in their passions, while that which seems right to
the one, appears clean contrary to the other, and the one may
affect something which the other hath no appetite at all unto; It
follows of necessity that to this perfect friendship in the state of
glory, we must adde perfect concord or agreement. There will be
therefore such perfect agreement and unity there betwixt all, that
none shall dissent from that which another desires. As many as
shall be counted worthy of that kingdome, shall be one body, one
Church, and one Spouse of *Jesus Christ*; and there shall be no
more discord betwixt them, then there is betwixt the members 20
now in the natural body. But as you see in the motion of the
Eyes, that which way soever the one is turned, the other immediately followes, so whatsoever any one in that state shall delight
in, he shall finde all the rest to consent to it. * Seeing then that
God himself with all the Angels and * Here the Translatour
Saints will be propitious and favourable omitted some passages
to thy desires, it is cleare that thou wilt which he conceived not
desire nothing which thou mayst not necessary, and perhaps they
obtaine. So that in a modest sense it may be said, thou shalt be
Almighty in respect of thy will, because the Almighty God will in 30
all things consent to it, for thy will shall be then his will, and his
will shall be thine.

Seeing then that they shall excell so much in power, there is no
doubt to be made, but that an honour proportionable to that
power shall be given unto them. Now what manner of honour
that shall be, we shall labour to demonstrate by this following
similitude. Let us suppose there were laid before our eyes, some
poore begger destitute of all comfort, and smitten in every part
with ulcerous biles, corrupt sores, and all manner of infirmities,
and having not so much as a rag to cover or defend him from the 40
cold: If some mighty and mercifull King passing by, should look
upon this begger lying in so miserable a condition, and having

compassion on him, should give command to heale his infirmities, and being afterwards recovered, should give order to have him cloathed with his own royal apparel, and being brought before him in that habit, should adopt him for his son, and give strict command that he should be received and acknowledged by all men for his son, and that he should be contradicted in nothing by any of his subjects, he having adopted him for his son, and made him coheire with his onely begotten, and calling him after his own name : You would easily grant that this were a great honour to be
10 conferr'd upon so despicable and loathsome a begger. But all this and more will the merciful God most certainly confer upon his faithful servants ; for of his own free mercy will he receive us, who being born of the corruption of the flesh are surrounded with many miseries ; in which we are estated as it were, and destitute of all comforts ; but alwayes subject to, & overcome by many noxious passions, which fill us up with foule and ulcerous sins, and most odious corruptions, from all which he will purge and heale us, and being restored to perfect health, he will cloath us with the ornaments of true righteousnesse and incorruption, and adopt us
20 for his sons, making us his Consorts in his own kingdome, and coheires with his only begotten Son who is in every thing coequal with himself, *changing our vile bodies, that they may be like unto his glorious body,* and commanding every creature to be subject unto us in all things, calling us also by his own name, and making us gods ; for he saith in the Scripture, *I have said you are all gods, and the sons of the most high.* But he himself is the *God deifying,* and we are but *deified,* or *gods* made by him. But perhaps thou wilt say, This reason of mine may stand good in the Apostles and other holy Martyrs, but with thee who art a wretched sinner, and
30 desirest onely to be the least in the kingdome of heaven, thou canst not see how it can consist. Give eare and understand, for God in that recited Scripture, *I have said you are all gods, &c.* excepts none. But that thou mayst more clearly perceive, Consider the nature of fire and of all things that are put therein ; if happily thou canst imagine with thy self after what manner, (in the degree appointed for thee) thou shalt be glorified. The fire (thou seest) is but one, and of nature hot ; put into it either wood, or lead, or iron, or all these together ; when the wood is turn'd into embers, so that nothing appears unto thee but fire, & the lead so
40 melted, that it cannot admit of a greater degree of heat, yet can neither of them be equall to Iron for an intense burning heat, which perhaps hath not yet grown red with the fire. Now although

every one of these doth exceed the other, & is of a more suparla-
tive heat, yet every one of them (as we commonly say) is fire.
So shall it be in that glorious society of the Elect, which we now
speak of; For as those, who are neerer to the *Divine Majesty*, and
therefore better then others, shall be called *gods* : So even those,
who are inferiour to them, because they participate according to
their capacity of the same *Deity* with those that are superiour,
shall be likewise honoured with the same title of *gods*.

When therefore together with so much happinesse, thou hast
attained to so much honour, I do not see with what reason thou 10
canst desire a greater Preferment. Whiles then thou art blessed
with the possession of those high Benefits, which we have mentioned, wilt thou not think thy selfe sufficiently happy? Yes verily,
thou wilt say, well then! but if thou couldst really injoy all those
things as we have described them, but for one short *day*, wouldst
thou not rejoice? No question, but thou wouldst. But if thou
shouldst injoy them for a *moneth*, or one whole *yeare* thou wouldst
rejoyce exceedingly : neither indeed do I thinke it possible to
expresse thy manner of joy. Suppose then if thou shouldst
possesse this happinesse all thy *life-time*, what thou wouldst do. 20
What price wouldst thou give for so great a Blessing? Even willingly all that ever thou hadst : nay, thy very owne selfe, if thou
couldst purchase it at no other Rate.

But if besides all this Fruition, thou wert certaine also of a
perpetuall security, and that all thy life long no accident whatsoever could rob thee of thy happinesse, I will not determine,
whether it were possible for thee to imagine, how great thy joy
would be. Seeing then that in the life to come, thou shalt live for
ever, and together with the possession of all these things, thou
shalt also be eternally secured from all danger of losing them, I 30
beseech thee, how dost thou thinke it will go with thee? I beleeve
truly, that at the very name of security, there springs in thee a
certaine joy of heart, and thou dost greedily desire to know,
whether thou mayst with safety, and for ever injoy such great
and extraordinary Blessings? I tell thee then, if thou art like to
lose these things, thou must either voluntarily, and of thy owne
accord relinquish them, or God must take them from thee whether
thou wilt or no; or else another, who is more powerful then God,
must rob thee of them in spite of God, and thy selfe. But certainly, neither wilt thou reject so great a Blessing, and relapse 40
into those miseries from which thou hast beene graciously
delivered ; neither will God at any time take that away which his

large and mercifull goodnesse hath bestowed upon thee; nor is
there any stronger then God, who should be able to make thee
miserable against thy will, as long as God is thy Protector. Thou
shalt therefore securely, and for ever injoy all these Benefits, nor
shalt thou feare the attempts of any, who would willingly deprive
thee of them.

What dost thou thinke then will thy condition be, when thou
shalt eternally injoy all these things; namely, Beauty, Strength,
Swiftnesse of motion, Liberty, Health, Pleasure, Length of life,
10 Wisedome, Love, Peace, Power, Honour, and a Security of all, as
we have described them: nay, above all humane Description or
Conception, in a more glorious, and a more stately manner, then
we can possibly expresse. Will not thy condition be all Joy,
which is the End and Effect of these Blessings? Verily I cannot
see how that man should not abound with inestimable Joy, who
is compast about with all the riches of eternall happinesse. Thou
shalt therefore most certainly attaine to such a Joy, because
nothing can happen to thee, that should minister occasion of
Grief. For if thou hadst any Friend, whom thou didst love as
20 well as thy selfe, and in whose good thou wouldst rejoyce as in
thy owne, and shouldst see this friend admitted to the same
Heaven, and happinesse with thy selfe; wouldst thou not ex-
tremely rejoyce in his Felicity? But if thou hadst two or three, or
more such friends, and shouldest see them all glorified with a state
equal to thy own, would not thy joyes also exceed, and increase
together with their number? And as formerly, when we discoursed
of Love, we did there shew how all the Inhabitants of the world
to come, should love thee as well as themselves, and thou on the
contrary shouldst love them as thy owne soul: How is it there-
30 fore possible for any man to apprehend the manner of that *mutual
Joy*, seeing there are there above a thousand thousands and ten
thousand times hundreds of thousands: nay, an innumerable
company, and all of them injoying the same Beatitude; nor is
there any one of them, who doth not as much rejoyce in the
happinesse of another, as he doth in his owne. Moreover, they
seeing God love them in a more excellent way then they love
themselves, and againe perceiving themselves (after some inexpressible manner) to love God better then themselves, they do
infinitly triumph in his Glory, and in his wonderful and inex-
40 pressible Joyes. They have Joy therefore within, and Joy without:

3 miserable] miserablee *1652*   27 Inhabitants] Inbabitants *1652*

Joy from above, and Joy beneath : In the Compasse, and Circuit of them there is Joy, and in a word every where.

And this (as we think, and as we have exprest our selves in the beginning of this Book) is that thing which God hath prepared for those that love him, namely *Joy.* Therefore in my opinion, eternal Beatitude, or eternal felicity is nothing else but a suffi-ciency, or fulnesse of all good things, according to our own desire, and without any indigency, which felicity all the friends of God shall fully injoy in the life which is to come. For when we speake of good things, we do not say but that life eternal is farre more great 10 and glorious then this temporal life, which we have mentioned onely by way of Manuduction. Seeing then that the Just shall be rewarded with so great a Felicity, it remaines on the contrary, that the unjust shall be visited with some extraordinary Infelicity. For as we have described the Elect according to those abilities which God gave us : namely that their Beauty, Swiftnesse, and Strength, their Liberty, Health and Pleasure should render them Cheerful and Triumphant : So on the other side a certaine horrible, inestimable deformity, a dulnesse of motion and spirit, together with their Impotencie, and Captivity in Chaines of Dark- 20 nesse, as also their Melancholy, and paine shall make the Repro-bate to mourne and howle. Verily that *Length* of *Life,* which the just shall most joyfully embrace, because it conduceth to their fruition of eternal happinesse, will be very odious, and a meere Curse to the unjust, because it exposeth them to an endlesse sense of ever-lasting tortures. If I look on their *Wisdome,* I know not what to speak of it, unlesse I say, that as to the just it will be great joy and honour, so in the unjust knowledge shall be turned into sadnesse and distraction of spirit. As for Love, whereby the Saints of God shall be link'd together with joy unspeakable : 30 It shall be a meer Affliction to the Impious, for by how much the more they love one another, by so much will they be the more troubled one at anothers punishment. If it be question'd whether they may injoy any peace or concord ? It is answered, they will be at discord with every creature, and every creature with them. Hence in opposition to the power of the Saints, the wicked shall be deprived of all power : They shall never be able to attaine to any thing they would have, and what they can have, even that is it which they would not have. The wicked then in-stead of the honour and eternal happinesse of the Saints shall 40 receive to their portion eternal shame, and now what more shall we say for a Conclusion to these things ? Truly, that as the friends

of God shall alwayes triumph in the security of their everlasting
Beatitude, so the Enemies and Adversaries of God shall utterly
despaire of any redemption from their endlesse Miseries : But in
lieu of the eternal ineffable joyes of the Blessed, they shall inherit
unspeakable everlasting woes; especially such, who because of
their impenitency for their sinnes, shall be condemned to passe
into the society of Devils.

FINIS.

Soli Deo Gloria.

Flores Solitudinis.
Certaine Rare and Elegant
PIECES;
Viz.

Two Excellent Difcourfes
Of { 1. *Temperance, and Patience* ;
{ 2. *Life and Death.*

BY
I. E.   N I E R E M B E R G I U S.

THE WORLD
CONTEMNED;
BY
Eucherius, Bp of Lyons.

And the Life of
PAULINUS,
Bp of *N O L A.*

Collected in his Sickneffe and Retirement
BY
HENRY VAUGHAN, Silurift.

Tantus Amor Florum, & generandi gloria Mellis.

London, Printed for *Humphrey Mofeley* at the
Princes Armes in St *Pauls* Church-yard. 1654.

TO
THE TRUELY NOBLE
And Religious
Sir *CHARLES EGERTON*
Knight.

SIR,

If, when you please to looke upon these Collections, *you will find them to lead you from the Sun into the* shade, *from the open* Terrace *into a private* grove, *& from the* noyse *and* pompe *of this world into a silent and solitary* Hermitage : *doe not you thinke then, that you have descended* (*like the* dead) *in Occidentem &* tenebras, *for in this* withdrawing-roome (*though secret and seldome frequented,*) *shines that happy* starre, *which will directly lead you to the* King *of* light. *You have long since quitted the* Publick, *& to present you now with some thing of solitude* and the contempt of the world, 10 *would looke like a* designe *to Flatter you, were not my* Name, *argument enough for the contrary. Those few that know me, will* (*I am sure*) *be my* Compurgators *; and I my selfe dare assert this,* you have no cause to suspect it. *But what ever the thoughts of men will be, I am already sure of this advantage, that we live in an age, which hath made this very* Proposition (*though suspected of* Melancholie,) *mighty pleasing, and even* meane witts *begin to like it; the* wiser sort *alwaies did, for what* (*I beseech you,*) *hath this world, that should make a wise man in love with it? I will take the boldnesse to describe it in the same character which* Bisselius *did the hansome* 20 *concubine of* Mahomet *the great :*

> *Puella tota quanta, nil erat aliud*
> *Quàm Illecebra picta, delicatus harpago, &c.*

The whole wench (*how compleat soe'r*) *was but*
A specious baite *; a soft, sly, tempting* slut *;*
A pleasing witch ; a living death *; a faire,*
Thriving disease *; a fresh,* infectious aire *;*
A pretious plague *; a furie sweetly drawne ;*
Wild fire *laid up and finely drest in* Lawne.

This delicate, admir'd Inchantresse (*even to those who enjoy her* 30 *after their owne lusts, and at their owne rate,*) *will prove but a very sad bargaine ; she is all deception and sorrow. This* world *and the* prince *of it are the* Canker-Rose *in the mouth of the* fox *;*

Decipit, arefit, pungit. *But those future, supreme* fruitions *which God hath in store for those that love him are neither* Phantasmes, *nor* fallacies; *they are all substantiall and certaine, and in the Apostles phrase,* Καθ᾿ ὑπερβολὴν εἰς ὑπερβολὴν αἰώνιον Βάρος δόξης, a far more exceeding and eternall weight of glory. *Nothing can give that, which it hath not, this transitory, changeable and corrupt world cannot afford permanent treasures. All it gives, and all it shewes us, is but* trash *&* illusion. *The true incorruptible riches dwell above the reach of rust and theeves.*

10 *Man himselfe in his* outward part, *which was taken out of the world, feeles the like passions with the world, he is worn, washed, dissolved and changed, he comes hither, he knowes not how, and goes from hence, he knowes not whither.* Nescio quò vado, valete posteri! *was the* Roman's *Epitaph: One generation commeth, and another passeth away.* Properant & decurrunt in absconditum, *they hasten and drive on to their appointed place, untill the great day of accompt. All the severall* shapes *and* gestures *we see in this wild* Masque *of* time *are but so many* disguises *which the* Spirits *that first assumed them, cast off againe when they have acted their* 20 parts. *Most elegantly did* Augurellius *sing to* Peter Lipomanus *upon the death of his sister* Clara;

Amæna, Petre, cum vides, &c.

Peter, *when thou this pleasant world dost see,*
Beleeve, *thou seest meere* Dreames *and* vanitie;
Not reall *things, but* false: *and through the* Aire
Each where, an empty, slipp'rie Scene, *though faire.*
The chirping birds, *the fresh* woods *shadie boughes,*
The leaves *shrill whispers, when the* west-wind *blowes.*
The swift, fierce Greyhounds *coursing on the plaines,*
30 *The flying* hare *distrest 'twixt feare and paines;*
The bloomy Mayd *decking with* flowers *her head,*
The gladsome, easie youth *by light* love *lead;*
And whatsoe'r heere with admiring eyes
Thou seem'st to see, 'tis but a fraile disguise
Worne *by* eternall things, *a passive* dresse
Put on by beings *that are passiveles.*

All the gay appearances in this life seeme to me but a swift succession of rising Clouds, *which neither abide in any certaine* forme, *nor continue for any* long time; *And this is that, which* 40 makes the sore travell of the sonnes of men *to be nothing else, but a meere chasing of shadowes.* All is vanity (*said the Royall Philosopher,*) and there is no new thing under the Sun.

I present you therefore with a discourse perswading to a contempt

& a desertion *of these* old things which (*our Saviour tells us*) shall passe away; *And with an historicall, faithfull relation of the life and happinesse of a devout, primitive* father, *who gave all that he had upon earth to the poore, that he* might have treasure in heaven. *Some other* Additions *you will finde, which meeting now in this volume under your name, will in their descent to posterity, carry with them this fairest Testimonie,* I loved you. *This (Sir) is my maine and my sole designe in this* Addresse, *without* reservation *and without* flattery, *for which respect, and for no other, I beleeve you will accept of what I have done, and looke upon my* 10 *suddaine and small* Presents, *as upon some forward* flowers *whose kinde hast hath brought them above ground* in cold weather. *The incertainty of life, and a peevish, inconstant state of health would not suffer me to stay for greater performances, or a better season; least loosing this, I should never againe have the opportunity to manifest how much and how sincerely I am*

Newton by   Sir
Uske neare
Sketh-Rock.   Your Servant and
   1653.   well-wisher

                                  Henry Vaughan. 20

To the Reader.

Candidus & medicans Ignis deus est. *So sings the* Poet, *and so must I affirme, who have been tryed by that* white *and* refining fire, with healing under his wings. *Quarrelling with his* light, *and wandring from that fresh and competent* gourd, *which he had shadowed me with, drew those* Sun-beames *upon my head, whose strong and fervent* vibrations *made me oftentimes beg of him, that* I might dye. *In those sad* Conflicts *I dedicated the* Remissions *to thy* use, Reader, & *now I offer them to thy* view. *If the* title *shall offend thee, because it was found in the* woods *and the* wilder-
10 nesse, *give mee leave to tell thee, that* Deserts *and* Mountaines *were the* Schooles *of the* Prophets, *and that* Wild-hony *was his* diet, *who by the testimony of the* Sonne *of* God, *was* the greatest amongst those that are borne of women. *It may be thy spirit is such a popular, phantastick* flye, *as loves to gad in the* shine *of this* world; *if so, this* light *I live by in the* shade, *is too great for thee. I send it abroad to bee a companion of those wise* Hermits, *who have withdrawne from the present generation, to confirme them in their* solitude, *and to make that rigid* necessity *their pleasant* Choyse. *To leave the* world, *when it leaves us, is both* sordid *and* sorrowfull;
20 *and to quitt our* station *upon discontents, is nothing else, but to be the* Apes *of those* Melancholy Schismaticks, *who having burnt off their owne hands in setting the world on fire, are now fallen out with it,* because they cannot rule it. *They are* Spirits *of a very poore, inferiour* order, *that have so much* Sympathy *with worldlie things, as to weepe at* Parting; *And of as low a* Parentage *are those, that will be sick of* Leap-yeares & Sublunarie mutations. *I honour that* temper, *which can lay by the* garland, *when he may keepe it on: which can passe by a* Rosebud, *and bid it* grow, *when he is invited to crop it,*

30 ———— Whose gentle measure
   Complyes and suits with all *estates*;
 Which can let loose to a *Crown*, and yet with pleasure
   Take up within a *Cloyster* gates.
 This Soule doth *Span* the world, and *hang* content
   From either *pole* unto the *center*,
 Where in each *Roome* of the well-furnished *tent*
   He lyes warme and without adventure.

Prince Lewes, *the eldest Son of* Charles *King of* Naples, *at the age of twenty one yeares, and just when he should have been married to*
40 *the youthfull Princesse of* Majorica, *did suddenly at* Barcellon *put on the rough and severe* habit *of the* Franciscans: *The* Queens *and* Princesses *there met to solemnize the marriage of his sister* Blanch

with James *King of* Aragon, *imployed all their* Rhetorick *to dis-swade him from it ; but to no purpose, he loved his* Sackcloth *more then their* silks, *and (as Mounsier* Mathieu *(alluding to that* young Princesse,) *speakes of him,)* Left Roses to make Conserve of thornes. *Resolution,* Reader, *is the Sanctuary of Man, and Saint* Pauls *content is that famous* Elixir, *which turnes the* rudest mettall *into* smooth *and* ductible gold *: It is the Philosophers* secret fire, *that* stomack *of the* Ostrich *which digests* Iron, *and dissolves the hard flint into bloud and nutriment.* It was an honest Reply *that* his Cook *made unto the Duke of* Millain, *when worsted in a great* 10 *battell by the* Florentines, *the over passionate resentment of so unexpected a repulse, made him quarrell with his meate :* If the Florentines (*said he*) have spoyled your tast, that is no fault of mine ; the meate is pleasant, and well drest, but the good success of your Enemies hath made your appetite ill.

I protest seriously unto thee, and without Scepticisme, *that there is no such thing in this world, as* misfortune *; the foolish* testinesse *of man arising out of his* misconstruction *and* ignorance *of the wise method of* Providence, *throwes him into many* troubles. *The* Spouse *tells us, that the fingers of the* Bride-groome *are deckt with* 20 Beryll *and* pretious stones *: what ever falls upon us from that* Almighty *hand, it is a* diamond *; It is celestiall* treasure, *and the matter of some new* blessing, *if we abuse it not.* God (*saith the wise King,*) created not Evill, but man (who was created upright) sought out many inventions : *these indeed beget that* monster *; his ill* digestion *of his* punishment (*which is a kinde of* divine diet,) *makes him to pine away in a sinfull discontent.* If thou art sick of *such an* Atrophie, *the precepts layd down in this little booke (if rightly* understood, *and faithfully* practised) *will perfectly cure thee.* 30

All that may bee objected is, that I write unto thee out of a land of darkenesse, out of that unfortunate region, where the Inhabitants sit in the shadow of death : where destruction passeth for propagation, and a thick black night for the glorious day-spring. If this discourage thee, be pleased to remember, that there are bright starrs under the most palpable clouds, and light is never so beautifull as in the presence of darknes. At least intreat God that the Sun may not goe down upon thy own dwelling, which is hartily desired and prayed for, by

Newton by Usk in South-wales.
April. 17. 1652.

Hen : Vaughan. 40

To the onely true and glorious
God, the Sole disposer of
Life and Death.

O doe not goe, thou know'st I'le dye,
My *Spring* and *Fall* are in thy Booke !
Or if thou goest, doe not deny
To lend me, though from far, one looke !

My sinnes long since have made thee strange,
A very stranger unto me ;
No *morning-meetings* (since this change)
Nor *Evening-walkes* have I with thee.

Why is my God thus hard and cold,
When I am most, most sick and sad ?
Well-fare those blessed dayes of old,
When thou did'st heare the *weeping Lad* !

O doe not thou doe as I did,
Doe not despise a love-sick heart !
What though some *Clouds* defiance bid,
Thy *Sun* must shine in every part.

Though I have spoyl'd, O spoyle not thou,
Hate not thine owne deere gift and token !
Poore *Birds* sing best, and prettiest show,
When their *neast* is fallen and broken.

Deare Lord ! restore thy Ancient peace,
Thy quickning friendship, mans bright wealth,
And if thou wilt not give *me* Ease
From sicknes, Give my *Spirit* health !

Two Excellent

DISCOURSES

Of { 1. Temperance and Patience.
    { 2. Life and Death.

Written in Latin by
Johan : Euseb : Nierembergius.

Englifhed by

HENRY VAUGHAN, Silurift.

—— *Mors Vitam temperet, & vita Mortem.*

LONDON:

Printed for *Humphrey Moſeley*, and
are to be ſold at the *Princes Armes*
in St *Paul's* Church-yard. 1654.

OF

TEMPERANCE

AND

PATIENCE.

The *Doctrine* of good living is short, but the *work* is long and hard to be perswaded, though easie to bee learnt: for to be good, is of all things the most easie, and the most ready, if wee could learne but one other *Art*, which *Antisthenes* termed the most necessary, I will add, the most difficult, and that is, *to forget to doe Evill*. I find that *peace* and *joy* have two *handles*, whereby we may take hold of them, *Patience*, and *Temperance*. Rule thy *Evil* with these, and then thy *will* may rule thee well. Horses are ruled with bridles and spurs. In prosperity use the first, that is,
10 restraine, or keepe in thy selfe. In adversity the last, that is, Incite, and use thy selfe to a gallant *Apathie*, and contempt of misfortunes. Generous and metlesome *Coursers* when they are breathed, or rid abroad, are compelled to trample upon those very things, whose first sight startled and terrified them; doe so with thy selfe: tread under thy feet thy most hideous adversities; so shalt thou forget the feare of fortune, which makes men unfit for vertue. Patience in adversity is temperance in prosperity. Nor can it be easily resolved, which of these two excells: This is most certaine, that noble sufferance is as necessary to man, as the
20 virtue of temperance. Some few Crosses thou canst beare well, but fortune can afflict thee with many, and thou by patience (the greatest of virtues) must afflict her with more; for

> —— *The naked man too getts the field,*
> *And often makes the armed foe to yeeld.*

It costs not much to live well, and it is as cheape to learne it. The whole Art is comprised in these two words, *Patience*, and *Temperance*. In these lies all the *Mysterie* of Peace: you would think it a *Secret* of the Priests of *Ceres*, it is so unknown to any, but sacred minds. These are the Domestick Gods of tranquility,
30 and the tutelar Angels of good men: beleeve with *Epictetus*, that the Quintessence of all Philosophie is squeezed into these two, Ἀνέχου, καὶ ἀπέχου, beare and forbeare. He neither obtaines, nor retaines his joy, that doth not abstain, and sustaine. These are the two

Poles upon which tranquility and vertue move. To obtain peace, you must bear; to retain it, you must forbeare. An odd way of fruition; By refusing you obtaine, and by suffering you preserve: by refusing the favours, and suffering the spite of fortune. By this very carriage did *Diogenes* beleeve that he had quite deposed and overthrown her: hee crowned his temples with branches of *Pine*, the old *Isthmian* ceremonie, and walked like an absolute victour in the Sacred Games. Being required by a crosse fellow, not to usurpe that honour till he had lawfully strived, he answered, that he had overcome two enemies, *Pleasure* and *Griefe*, the one by 10 forbearing, the other by bearing. Make not thy self a Woman: thou hast (if thou wilt use them) both *Temperance* and *Patience*, the best Stratagems, and Countermines against the Wiles of Fortune. Her storms and suddaine furies (which are alwaies clean, and without dissimulation,) thou mayst break and overcome by bearing; Her Arts, her deep and cankerd hatred, by listning to Reason, and a warie, stayd Circumspection, while she spends and wasts with her owne malice. The wrath of furious and hasty persons is sincere, and without artifice; It hath no poyson, but what breakes out presently at the tongue, or the hand: Fortune 20 too, when in this humour, is lesse Noxious, for She makes then an indifferent use of all Tooles, and disposeth of them without Study. But when She begins to hate, She becomes slow and weary, and not contented with open valour, addes to it Treachery. She pines with the Memory of her old favours, and that She may pull down what She built, adornes her most deadly Intentions, as Poverty and grievous Miseries, in the dresse of Felicity. All her projects, machinations and Engines to Torture and vex Man, amount to no more, then to give him what he would not have, and to deny him what he would have. He breaks her neck that 30 abstaines from the *first*, and contemnes the *last*.

But here is our double Disease, by which *Virtue* Conceived for a great end, together with *Felicity*, become both abortive, that wee neither rightly wish, nor rightly abstain, loath, or love, but doe both most absurdly, most preposterously. We Covet most unseasonably, when even necessity is necessary, and this to him that wants, is no more then a wish. We covet, I say, such things as fortune hath not, and in a time when they may not be had. Wee would have *Cherries* in *January*: These wishes are their own Torments: Fortune too most Commonly gives them but cold 40 Comfort. Why should we Covet extraneous Goods? It is better to serve the necessity of the time, then to be a slave to Fortune.

Wee are set upon longing like Woemen with Child, that labour
with strange appetites and depraved stomacks ; that loath healthfull Viands, and (which in them is very strange) abhorre sweet
meats ; That affect raw, absurd compositions, that eat lime, Char-
coles and Ashes, that in the dead of Winter long for Summer-fruits,
and in Summer for Winter-fruits. What dost thou think is bearing
and forbearing ? It is to be even with Fortune, discreetly to abstaine,
discreetly to will, and to covet nothing. Abstain then : otherwise
what wilt thou do by Coveting, but make way for Fortune, and
10 enlarge her Empire ? Though she would not, she must needs hit
thee. Her being blind, hinders not but she may shoote well : When
the mark is *have at all*, and *every where* : an Archer without Eyes
cannot misse it. Though unwilling, her Arrowes cannot wander
from him, whose lust wanders after all things. She will hit him
without Ayming, whose hope aymes at every thing. No Weapon
falls in vaine amongst a multitude. Her scope to hurt, is the same
scope thou takest to wish.

Thou must know that the Command of Fortune over man about
these outward things, lies in the midst of the will, as the hand in
20 the midst of a bended bow. If thou holdest thy will by the middle,
then art thou master of both ends, and mayst doe any thing. If
thou commandst the one halfe, I will not say, thou hast no hold at
all. Liberty hath two Limbs, to *Will*, and to *refraine* : The one is
a stronge *Arme*, the other a weak *Hand* : What thou hast not, thou
mayst refraine from wishing to have, but no man can have what
ever he would have. When you refrain from willing, then have you
Power over all things ; when your will lusteth, then you are subject
to all things. Outward goods are fleeting things, and the faithfull
servants of unfaithfull chance. O how great a treasure, how
30 provident and infallible a supply against these sudden Ebbs and
diminutions is a regular and resolute will ! Why are we troubled
at them ! We are too hard for Fortune, and by much too hard, if
wee command but the one halfe of our will ; that maimed and
halting hand (if I may so speak) will overtake and bring back the
most averse and winged Felicities. It will enrich us sooner and
surer then all the Treasures of *Cræsus* : Those are but beggerie
before thee if thou covet them not, if thy will be not a begger.
Not to will, makes thee securely rich, even when thou wilt, that is,
when thou doest will nothing. Thou makest Fortune poore by
40 leaving her no power over thee, and nothing in her self, wherewith
to please thee ; I meane to deceive thee. Thou wilt be richer than
Attalus by contemning his store, and of greater power than *Midas* ;

for his was placed in fruition and touching, but thine in absence and
emptinesse. By wishing nothing thou hast all, yea those things
which thou seest not : and what wonder then, if those things thou
seekest not, being abundantly enriched by thy most pretious
povertie ? It was Divinely argued by *Eusebius, That he onely should
be esteemed rich, who was perswaded that he had enough. For those
that adde still to what they have already gotten, and never thinke
that they can get enough, though richer than* Midas, *are most poor
and miserable beggers ; because they are nothing rich in their own
minds.* And in another place, *An unreasonable covetousnesse* (saith 10
he) *is sooner driven away with the losse of riches allready gotten, then
by a plenteous and dayly accesse of more treasures.* Wherefore thou
art then only rich, and possessest all things to thy mind, when to
have nothing is in thy will : When ever thou sayest, *It is enough,*
thou hast all. Yea, thou hast more then thou shouldst have. All
that comes afterwards doth but load and overwhelme thee.

Of such an Immoderate use is Temperance, and I Judge
Patience to be of no lesser. Happily it may be easier ; for having
learnt to abstain, we may the better sustain. Impatience ariseth
naturally out of Cupidity, and feare is the Daughter of hope. 20
Cast these away, and you will find, that an adverse Fortune may
be entertained, not onely with Patience, but with much wellcome.
Crates, or *Zeno* (a gallant man, if either of the two) being at Sea
in a great storm, caus'd all his goods (wherewith the Ship was
Loaden) to be thrown over board, and thanked Fortune for the
kindnesse : doe thou the like, and approving of thy misfortunes,
say, *It is well done, Fortune, thou hast read me a good lesson, thou
hast had care of my Soul. I thank thee that thou art Come thy
selfe to fetch these burthens, which I should have brought thee home.
Thou hast dealt courteously to lend me their use, and to prevent their* 30
*Abuse. I like thy Method, and prefer thy advise to thy favours ;
I know thy meaning. I must make a wise use of these crosses,
I must have recourse to virtue, to my self, and to my God. Thou dost
not onely Incite, but compell me to goodnesse. I am brought safe to
shore, by the splitting of the Ship : hereafter I will be better provided.
Behold, thou hast left yet behind thee some moveables, which thou
shouldst have taken with thee, they are thine by right. Thou gavest
me so many things, that thou canst not well remember them.
I desire not to conceale them, take all thy Reliques and appendencies
with thee, all that is here besides my selfe ; I hold thy leavings not* 40
worthy of acceptance from the mind of man. I wish that we would
so deal with Fortune, as a certain old man did with theeves that

came to rob his house. *Take with you* (said he) *all that you see here.* They did so, leaving nothing behind them but an empty purse; which the old man tooke up, and following after, called to them; *Take this also with you, which you forgot to put up.* Fortune perhaps amazed at such a Noble, Serene disposition, would restore all: It is most certaine the Theeves did. But let a Christian reject this figment of Fortune, and in all worldly mutations acknowledge and kisse the divine hand.

But if after all this, thou wilt not excuse the outward and
10 ravenous manners of Fortune; there will be no Just cause for thee to accuse them, having received no damage by her. If thou wilt purge thy mind from wishes and hopes, thou mayst safely place thy selfe before her very Arrowes, and defie them. And truly I believe it will be thy most secure station. When *Stratonicus* saw an unskilfull fellow shooting at *Buts*, he got presently close to the *White*, as the onely place free from danger: and being asked his reason for that unusual Refuge, he answered; *Least that fellow should hit me.* Fortune (we say) is blind; stand then in her way: She hits that the least, which she most aimes at; but if all her
20 shafts should fall upon thee, they can draw no blood from thee, as long as thou art not drawn by covetousnesse. If you break off the point of the Weapon, it cannot hurt you. Our own Covetousnesse is Fortunes edged toole; take that away, and you disarme her, and secure your selfe: blunt weapons wound not to blood.

I suppose now that *Epictetus* his abridgement, or reduction of Philosophy into two words, *Abstain* and *Sustain*, will seeme prolix enough to you. The first we have past through; the second and last, I meane *Sustain*, or the *Art of bearing well*, wee shall find tedious enough. Hee cannot be said to wish for nothing, that
30 finds fault with that which he hath. This bearing well is to desire nothing but what wee have. A Serene, bright Will then, not clouded with thick and muddy desires, will find the burdens of Fortune to be very light: For Fortune of her selfe is very light and easie, but she hath for *pannels* our own Lusts, which are heavier than her *packs*, and without these shee puts not one loade upon us. Nothing tires and weighs us down but our own wishes, which evills (being ignorant that our burthen proceedes from them,) we multiply with an Intent to ease our selves, but in the meane time the weight increaseth. A certain plain Countryman wearied with
40 ploughing, and returning home from the field after his daies task, tyed the Plough to his Asse, and afterwards mounted himself upon his back; but the tyred Asse, and overloaden, could not stirre

from the place; whereupon the Country-man lights, and with the Plough upon his backe remounting the Asse, tells him, *Now I hope thou canst goe well, for it is not thou, but I that carry the Plough.* Wee are every day as ridiculous, though not so harmlesse as this Country-man. Wee study with new cares and new desires to ease and diminish our old lusts; which not onely keepes under, but choaks and presseth to death all the seeds of Joy and Content. This is nothing else, but to retain the former load undiminish'd, and to put another on the top of it. As long as we tolerate these burthens, we become intollerable to our selves, without any 10 exaggeration of Fortune. Let us shake them off, let us cast off hope, that troublesome *Tympany*; so shall we find Fortune light, and be able to bear both her and our selves. All things may be born of him, that bears not future Evills; Those are grievous burthens, which miraculously oppresse us, and so strangly accommodate themselves to our hurt, that they exist in the heart, and vexe it, before they can exist in time. Not onely Evil, but Good, when it is hovering and uncertain, doth afflict us. Of Evills themselves there cannot come so many together upon us, as we can feare: fortune can throw at us but few darts at one time, 20 and were she not still furnished by our lusts, we should quickly see her quiver empty. Abstinence then, or the restraining of our desires is the Nurserie of patience, by a like title as the toleration of evill and good.

But when I name Patience, I speake not of a *Simple* thing; for there is not onely patience in *Evill*, but in *Good* also, and this later is sometimes the most difficult. There is one when we *suffer*, and another when we *act*. There be also other divisions of Patience. Holy *Ephrem* makes it threefold: the *first* towards *god*, the *second* towards the *tempter*, or wicked Angel, and the *third* 30 towards *man*. I shall add a *fourth*, and the most difficult of all, towards our *selves*; or I will make it onely *twofold, first* towards *those* that are *without us*, the *second* and last towards our *selves*, or those *commotions* which fight against us from *within*. This last is the greatest, because it teacheth us to beare those pressures which lean upon us, and bow us down. It is harder to resist those weights which come forcibly upon us from above, then those which come oppositly, or over against us. The beasts can draw more after them, then they can carry upon their backs. Man hath enough to beare within himselfe: but evills are a great familie, and 40 keep aswell without doores as within. Every minute of our

12 Fortune] Fotune *1654*   24 good.] good *1654*

tranquility is purchased with patience; It is the great Sacrament of peace, the Sanctuary of Security, the Herald and the badge of felicity. What will it availe us to be at peace with those that are without, while we suffer intestine warres and tumults within? let us have peace in our selves, and having mastered the rebellion and disorders of the will, let us be the patients of our sadnesse, yea of our Impatience, and some times of our patience.

As nothing is more accidentall to man then to suffer, so should he conclude, that nothing is more necessary for him than patience.
10 It is the naturall medicine for all humane calamities, with which (as the *heart* with *Dittany*) wee pull out the heads and splinters of those arrowes which the *mighty hunters* of this world shoot at us. Nature dealt not more unkindly with man, than with other creatures: The *Boare* is cured with *Ivio*, the *Dragon* with *wild-lettice*, and the *Snake* with *Fennell*. Others have their cure nearer, in their owne members: his *tongue* is the *Balsom* to a wounded *dog*; and the *Catholicon* of man is silence and patience. But did I say that to suffer was accidentall to man? I blot out that errour, and affirme, It is necessary: wherefore patience is most necessary;
20 for by that we are freed from a slavish sufferance, as by a certaine gifted premunition and defensive faculty. By patiently enduring we become impassible. The minde is invulnerable, unlesse in the fits of impatience, as *Achilles* was in the heele. Think not the Art of patience to be any more, then not to suffer voluntarily; at least, not in spight of thy will. Hee that gently endures, doth by a short cut free himself from the tedious labours and numerous punishments of life. Necessities should be chearefully borne. The hands, the feet, and the other limbs will sooner fail to execute their duties, then to be Insensible of paine. The sick, the
30 maimed, yea and the dismembred are not so mortified, but they are subject to sensation. It was an excellent saying of *Herod* the Sophist, when hee was pained with the gout in his hands and feet; *When I would eat,* (said he) *I have no hands; when I would goe I have no feet; but when I must be pained, I have both hands and feet.* So entire and whole are we alwaies to griefe; which sufficiently sheweth, that the soundnesse of man is best seene in his patience; and such a strong necessity of suffering is laid upon us, that when our limbs faile us in their offices, they must not faile of sufferings. Thou wilt aske then what can they suffer, when without spirit and
40 motion? I will tell thee; Not to be apt to suffer, is their suffering. Nothing is lacking to the misery of man, though his limbs should be wanting, his griefe by that defect will abound the more.

Deeply, and into the Inmost Closets of our hearts should that saying of the *Temanite* descend, *Man* (said he) *is borne unto trouble, and the bird to flye.* Observe, if the birds be unfurnish'd of any thing for flight : they are all over arm'd for it; Their Bills are keen and sharp-pointed, and serve like *foredecks* to cut their aire ; Their pinions are two swift *rowers,* and the feathers in both wings placed orderly every one longer then the other represent soe many *oares.* Their traines are the *Sternes,* with which they bend their whole bodies, and govern them in their flights, and with their feete and crooked clawes like *Anchors,* they stick and fasten themselves to the green branches, which are their *Havens,* and 10 shady Harbours. Though thou hadst never seene them use their wings, yet by their very *Structure,* thou would'st Judge that those feathered *Sayles* were design'd for the aire, and flying. Man is every way as well accoutred for trouble. Observe him : Thou shalt find nothing wanting that may conduce to his passion, though he wants much of Patience. Man is every way most exactly trimmed and adorned for trouble ; He was made unfit for labour, that he might be fit for sufferings ; He hath no wings to fly from them, he is poor, infirme, naked, defencelesse ; and (which is worse than all) forsaken of himself : Betwixt nakednesse and 20 poverty he is on all sides exposed and appointed for misery, as the bird is for the flight. Thou shalt observe all this in him ; for wanting all the necessaries which support life, he is surrounded onely with those sad necessities and intanglements which make life grievous and burthensome ; as a *Sparrow* is drest and cloathed all over with those soft habiliments which make his flights easie and pleasant. The onely difference betwixt them is this, that those Instruments of flying may faile the birds, but those of suffering cannot faile Man. So carefull was Nature of Mans condition, that she would not trust Fortune with his relatives. The *Eagle* 30 may casually lose his sharpnesse of sight, the *Roe* her swiftnesse, and the *Lyon* his strength ; but Man while he lives cannot misse of afflictions. There is a greater care had of our affaires ; And to a glorious end are these Calamities made sure unto us, if wee can make them beneficiall.

The first token, and evidence of life is crying. The Prim-roses, or first blossoms of it are teares ; from these it takes its inauguration. Man is not borne before he suffers : Yea, he grones and complaines in his very passage into the World. The first homage he payes to life is sufferance, and from that minute to his last, he becomes 40 (as *Blesensis* saith) *a constant tributary to misery.* I Judge him

37 takes] take *1654*

that murmurs at this payment, that kicks under this generall burthen, to wrong and disesteem the Noblest Nature, I mean Man; and to be worthy of this very punishment, *not to be at all.* He is a most vile abuser of Humane Nature, that thinks it not worth his patience, and values himselfe at a most sordid rate; let him beare in his manhood, what he bore in his Infancie, and not be ashamed of his Investiture, because he felt affliction, before he felt the light. It is the first lesson we are taught here, and the last that wee shall learn. All other Creatures, as soone as they 10 are born, make some use of their strength; but Man knowes no use of any thing but teares: He must afterwards be taught the cause of them. We must teach him every thing, but weeping. All other things are given him for his labour, but teares he can have for nothing. This onely faculty was bestowed upon him *gratis*, all other concessions are the rewards of his paines; but teares were given him freely, because they ease and allay his sorrowes. This convenient *Salve* did nature ordain for some inevitable Sores. She prepared this *Oyle* to allay the aking of those stripes the World gives us, which without this *Native* 20 *Oyntment* would have smarted more: for those wounds, whose anguish is not vented at the Eyes, lie heaviest upon the heart. And by this I am induced to believe, that it is naturall for man to Suffer, because he onely naturally weepes. Every extraneous felicity of this life is violent, or forced; and these constrained, though splendid *Adiuncts* of Fortune are therefore short, because noe violent thing can be perpetuall. To suffer is the naturall condition and manner of man, this is believed to be his misery: without patience, I confesse, it is. Nature never failes us in those things which are needful, much lesse divine providence and grace: 30 Wee shall therefore never faile of Sufferings, because they are the great *Necessaries*, & *Medicines* of Humane Nature. Wee read of many men that never laught, but never heard of any that never wept. *Democritus* himself came weeping into the World; none ever came without labour, none without griefe.

Thou wilt ask, why man, the only creature addicted to beatitude, should bee borne to trouble? why through the vale of teares travells he to the house of joy? why is he alone, being capeable of felicity, made subject unto misery? Because he is borne for virtue, the next and readiest instrument to attaine beatitude. Now troubles, 40 or miserie are the masse, or first matter of virtue, and without this hard rudiment, without this *coyne* of sorrow he cannot purchase it.

3 punishment] puishment *1654*   22 heart.] heart *1654*

Nor are the good offices which these calamities doe for us, either
meane or few; for wherefore flowes, yea overflowes the divine
mercy upon man, but because he is miserable? wherefore is Gods
sure power and saving arme stretched out, but because he is fraile?
wherefore are his comforts and refreshments so plentifully showred
down, but because he is sorrowfull and helplesse? wherefore is
his liberality and most faithful providence seen every minute, but
because he is poore and constantly needy? yea wherefore is Immortality, everlasting pleasures, and a glorious resurrection secured
unto us, but because our bodies are mortal, and subject to death 10
and putrefaction? By this time perhaps you see the appositnesse of
that comparison which *Eliphaz* made betwixt *man* and a *bird.* The
bird by nature lifts himself above the earth upon his wings, he
passeth from hence into the cleare confines and neighbourhood of
heaven, where he dwells for a time, and looks with contempt
upon this inferiour darksome portion of the world: when hee
descends towards the earth, he keepeth still above us, he lodgeth
in the height and freshnesse of the trees, or pitcheth upon the
spires or ridges of our houses, or upon some steepe rock, whose
height & inaccessibleness promise him securitie; something that 20
is eminent and high he alwaies affects to rest upon. Man likewise
ordained for heaven, and the contempt of this spot of earth is by
his very calamities borne up and carried above the world, yea into
heaven, as an Eagle by the strength of his wings ascends above
the clouds. O the depth of the riches of the wisedome of God!
O the mercifull designe, and device of his providence! who
knowing our corrupt nature, hath laid upon us a necessity of
seeking those blessings, whose inestimable value ought to stirre
us up to a most voluntary and diligent searching after them.
To this *necessity* by the same chain of his providence hath 30
hee tyed *utility.* These are sufficient motives to perswade us
to patience. It was wisely said by some *Arabian, that the hedge
about patience was profit:* for he that thinks gaine to be necessary,
must think labour so too. Allthough Fortune should be so
prodigal as to poure all her Treasures into the bosome of one man,
and not repent when she had done; yet would this very man sometimes feele strong exigencies in indigencie. *Pompey,* and *Darius*
were both hardly distrest with thirst; they that were Lords of so
many Rivers, did then wish for one drop of Water. *Alexander*
the *Great,* in some of his expeditions was like to perish with cold, 40
though his Dominion did in a manner extend to the very Sun; for
in the *East* (which I may call the Suns House,) he was such an

absolute Lord, that (bating the Power to forbid the Sun to rise) there was nothing more could be added to his conquests.

Seeing then that labour or troubles are a necessity imposed upon man, it followes, that there are other labours belonging unto him, which are also as necessary; and those I shall terme *Voluntarie Labours.* Of these the Elegant Philosopher *Eusebius* hath excellently spoken; *Voluntary Labours* (saith he) *are necessary, because of future Labours which hang over our heads: he will beare those with more ease when they fall upon him, who of his own* 10 *accord, and beforehand hath exercised himself in them:* But you see that in this course also the maine remedy is patience. He that suffers willingly, suffers not, even that which is necessary to be suffered. One wedge drives out another. Venemous bitings are allayd by Venemous Medecines; therefore in necessary troubles, there is a necessity of voluntary Labours, that *Violent Evills* meet not with *Obstinate Wills:* but the unavoydablenesse of suffering would not be grievous, nor the necessity or Law of Nature any way rigorous, did not we by our owne exaggerations adde to their weight, and our owne pain. Wee helpe to encrease our owne 20 Calamities *by reason of our Inerudition,* as *Diphilus* tells us, who adviseth even *the happy man to learn miseries.* What can wee doe more becomming our fraile condition, then to teach our Mortality the troubles of life, which are certain prolusions, or arguments of death? What is more beneficiall, then to learn great tryalls and dangers, that wee may leave that servile custome of fearing Fortune, whose burthens we ought to bear as willingly, as if wee desired to undergoe them?

It is a great rudiment of patience to suffer willingly, when we least expect sufferings. It is strange, that although wee see 30 nothing in the course of this life more frequent then miseries, yet will wee not be perswaded that they may fall into our share: Our griefes come most commonly before we believe they may come. Nothing can make us believe, that we may be miserable, untill misery it selfe assures it to us. The mind therefore should be tryed and prepared for it, with some lusorie or mock-misfortunes. Nor must we give eare to *Democritus,* whose saying is, *That if there be any things for us to suffer, it is good to learn them, but not to suffer them.* It is good indeed to learn them, but if they must be unavoydably suffered, what will our learning of them avail us? 40 A most ridiculous advise, in my Judgement: And if the Author of it had been wise, he had laught at nothing more then at this his owne Conclusion. It is good to learn to *suffer Evills*, but not to *be evill*. It will benefit us much to learn to suffer them, if not as they are Evills, yet lest wee our selves become Evill; for such we shall be by impatience. Besides the overcomming of reall evills, there remaine other slight hurts, as the discourtesies of nature, chance and furie, of our enemies and our selves also, which we cannot avoyd; but these last are no *evills*, but the *sheaths* or *quivers* of *evills*; out of these either our *opinion*, or our *impatience* draw evills upon our selves. *Bion* used to say, *that it was a great evill, not to be able to beare evills*. Without this ability, life cannot 10 be pleasant to any, and in this consists the skill and knowledge of life.

Let the mind then learne to buckle with these rude toyles of life, and by a frequent velitation or light skirmishing with troubles so improve it selfe, that when we come to deale with the serious hand, and close encounters of fortune, we may receive her *at sharpe*, and like active, vigilant *Duellists*, put by her most Artfull and violent thrusts. One *Salustius* that lived in the time of *Simplicius* did put upon his bare thigh a burning cole, and to keepe in the fire did gently blow it, that he might try how long hee could endure 20 it. I beleeve that fire did put out and quite extinguish all the burnings and raging flames of incensed fortune. If crosses foreseen are alwaies held light, those we tast and make experiment of before they come, must needs be lighter, because after tryall we feare them not: feares are the fore-teeth of miseries, which bite us sorest, and most intollerably. It was a most ridiculous judgement which that *Sybarite* (mentioned by *Serinus*) past upon the valour of the *Spartans*. This tender Citizen travelling by chance into *Lacedemon*, was so amazed at the severe discipline of that manly nation, who brought up their children in all rigorous and laborious 30 exercises, that being returned home hee told the *Fidlers* of * *Sybaris*, that the forwardnesse of the *Spartan* Youths to dye in battell was, because they would not be compelled any longer to such a toylsome life. This soft fellow knew not how much *Industry* could prevaile against *misfortune*, and *patience* against *passion*. That valour of the *Spartans* was not despayre, but the virtue of suffering perfected. Their voluntary labours at home had so excellently

* *A towne in the higher Calabria in Italy 20. miles distant from Rome: the Inhabitants were mightily given to pleasure, and taught their horses to dance to the pipes; which the Crotoniatæ their deadly enemies observing, brought into the field a company of minstrels: the Sybarits horses hearing the pipes* 40 *began to dance, and disordered their Army, by which meanes they were overthrowne to the number of* 300000.

improved them, that they could not onely slight the necessary and common afflictions of life, but overcome also (by a noble *volunteering,*) the very prerogative of fate, violating even the violence of death, while they dyed unconstrayned and undisturbed. *Mithridates* his feare of being poysoned, made him use himselfe to a venomous diet, by which he came at last to disgest all sorts of poysons without any prejudice to his health : so that afterwards when he would have poysoned himselfe in good earnest, he could not possibly doe it. By this destroyer of mankind did he secure
10 himselfe even from himselfe, and by long acquaintance made this deadly enemie a faithfull friend : he fed life with the provision of death. By a like sagacity should we forearme our selves against the conspiracies (if I may so say) of nature. Let us labour against labours ; It will much availe us : our very feares will prove comforts ; by using our selves to sufferance, the Antidote of life, which is Patience, becomes effectuall.

Of such great importance is this assiduous exercise in troubles, that it lets in the nature of *Constancie,* and is a sure manuduction to that sincerest vertue. The *Roman* Fencers, players for prizes,
20 barbarous and dissolute livers, if but indifferently skild, received their wounds without grones, or any alteration of gesture or countenance, because they would not be judged pusillanimous, nor cowardly decliners of danger ; If at any time they fell by the violence of wounds, they sent presently to know their masters pleasures, (because they would satisfie them,) for they themselves were contented to dye ; If their masters (finding them incurable) bad them prepare for death, they would presently hold forth their throats and receive the sword most willingly. O the serious faith of Playes ! O the faith of Players in serious dangers ! It is all one
30 then, whether thou thinkest fortune a meere pageant and pastime, or not ; Thou shouldest obey with an Immortall faith even to the death. Let a wise man execute the commands of his creator, let him like a faithfull souldier of JESUS CHRIST certifie his great master, that he is ready and willing to doe him service, that he will lose his life, & choose rather to dye, then not to submit to his pleasure. The conflicts of a good man with calamities are sacred : he is made a spectacle to the world, to Angels and men, and a hallowed *Present* to the Almighty. Let him in this state overcome his Enemies ! A more glorious garland then the *Olympick*
40 Olive-branches shall crown an enduring Patience, which by an humble, but overcomming Sufferance wearies the hands of those that beat us. It is the part of a wise man, to tire and weare out

the malice of his Enemies. I say not by Suffering, but by Patience, which makes him neither their Patient, nor trampled upon, but a trampling overcomer. This was the glory of *Melancoma*, who lived not one day without an Enemy. In the most vehement season of the yeare, hee judged his single-selfe hard enough for his two Adversaries: He could beare with the *Sun*, his most obstinate *Antagonist*, though fighting against him in the heate of the Summer with so many hands as he had Rayes: When he might have gotten the Victory by Opposition, he would not but by Submission. Hee considered, that the best might be 10 overcome by the worst, if force should take place. That Victory was in his Judgement the Noblest, when the Enemy, yet whole and without any hurt, was compell'd to submit. Then is he overthrown, when not by wounds, but by himselfe.

Therefore what vice, and a spurious Patience did in the *Roman* Fencers, let Virtue and true Patience performe in thee: and what custome and exercise wrought in *Melancoma*, let reason and Judgement worke in thee: What reason effected in *Possidonius*, let grace effect in thy heart, and let not grace which workt mightily a in *Eustathius*, and sufficiently in many others, languish and faile in thee alone. The power of God is perfected in weaknesse, giving us some prelibations (as it were) of it self; whither by bearing with our Infirmities, or by our bearing his Operations. I believe this last: for the glory of an almighty power against a weake thing would be very small; how litle then against Infirmity it selfe? That power is truly glorious, and hath matter for glory, which prevailes against the mind, a free unconfined thing, and holds it firme though surrounded with Infirmities: The power of God Glories more in prevailing against us, then against our infirmities.

But if wee seek for more delicate or easie remedies, and dare not arme our selves against misfortunes with this harnesse of proofe, because we think it too heavy; It remaines that we must make use of either *Hope*, or *Expectation*. Evills that are foreseen, lose much of

a *One of the Courtiers of* 20 *the Emperor* Traian, *and afterwards a most glorious Martyr.*

Being in Chase of a Stagge, he observed betwixt his hornes the signe of the Cross, and heard a voice out of his mouth, speaking to him in the Latin tongue, Cur me persequeris? *Whereupon leaving his game, he retyred presently into his own house, and having called together his wife and children, were all baptized* 30 *and received the Christian Faith. But in the persecution under* Hadrian, *he and his wife* Theophila *for their faithfullnesse to* JESUS CHRIST, *were burnt together in a brasen bull; And so having overcome and endured unto the end, they received the morning star, and crownes of life, which shall never be taken from them. See* Volater lib. 15. 40

their edge: But because we promise our selves the favours of
Fortune (of whom we have alwaies a good opinion, though wee
seldome speak well of her, and she deservs as ill,) our calamities,
while this credulous remissnesse keepes us from looking to them,
find way to surprize and oppresse us at once.   Against violent
misfortunes we may not use violence.   Expectation will sometimes
serve us best, if it be accompanied with a strong and irremisse
beliefe, that the *Crosse* is at hand, and will not delay.   For what
happens in this life more frequent, than unthought of events?
10 Wee meete oftentimes even in one day with matter of grief, and
matter of Patience.   It is strange, that for those two meales we
eat in the day, wee are all the day, and all our life long providing:
But for trouble, for griefes and sadnesse, which take not up two
houres in the day, but all the houres and daies of our lives, wee
never think to make any preparation.   Cast up (if thou canst) how
many things must be had to humor the pride of mans appetite;
more than for a Sacrifice.   It is no small state, nor ceremonie that
the belly is serv'd with: How many men doth this worms-meat
Imploy, Cookes, Bakers, Fishers, Fowlers, Hunters, Sheepfeeders,
20 Herdsmen, Millers, Colliers, and Butchers? How many Instruments, Spits, Pots, Trivets, Cauldrons, Chafing-dishes, Chargers,
Platters, and a thousand other utensils of gluttonie? And to what
end is all this preparation? But to please one palate once in the
day, or twice at most.   O foolish men! Wee are ever providing
for pleasures, but never for troubles, which not twice, but for
a great portion of our time, (if not continually) wee must needs
endure.   Who against the certain approach of an Enemy, will be
secure and quiet, and upon the comming of a friend watchfull and
sollicitous? Why do we provide so much for pleasures and
30 vanitie, and provide nothing against the day of trouble and
miserie? We are guarded about with Cloaths of state, Cano-
pies, Couches, Silk-Curtains, Feather-Beds and Pillowes; wee
arme our selves for delights and softnesse, for sleeping and
eating, because they are every daies works; but hear not
every day telling us, that the Evill day is behind.   We labour to
provide for the backe and the belly, why not for the better part,
why not for our fraile condition? The Sense of the secure
liver is too too delicate: The affliction of the Inconsiderate
or unprepared too bitter.   Chance throwes downe the carelesse
40 violently: and Fortune tires the idle even to vexation.   The
rude and unexperienced in troubles afflicts and macerates
himselfe with an impatient mind in the very midst of his most

affected blandishments, and in the bosome and calme of all his pleasures.

I hold Impatience to be a kind of *Night-Mare* which comes upon us waking, or the *Day-hag* of life: This troublesome disease (for our time of rest is his time of misrule, and when wee are sleeping, then is he stirring,) sets upon us when wee are most at ease, and with a certain strange heavinesse seemes to oppresse and smother us, when in the meane time that weight which so much oppresseth us, is laid on by our owne Imagination: and this sometimes makes us crye out, as if wee were killed; others, ac- 10 cording to *Lucretius*,

> *Struggle & grone as if by* Panthers *torne*
> *Or* Lyons *teeth, which makes them lowdly mourn.*
> *Some others seem unto themselves to dy.*
> *Some clime steep solitudes & Mountains high,*
> *From whence they seeme to fall inanely down,*
> *Panting with fear, till wak'd, and scarce their owne,*
> *They feel about them if in bed they lye,*
> *Deceiv'd with dreams, and nights Imagerie.*

But the greatest trouble of all, is, that without any hope of 20 remedy, they vainly strive and endeavour to shake off this shadow of heavinesse;

> *In vain with earnest struglings they contend*
> *To ease themselves: for when they stir & bend*
> *Their greatest force to do it, even then most*
> *Of all they faint, and in their hopes are crost.*
> *Nor tongue, nor hand, nor foot will serve their turne,*
> *But without speech and strength within they mourne.*

What more expresse Image can there be of Impatience lying heavily especially upon those, who drouse away their time in a 30 vitious rest and Idlenesse? They are opprest, cry out, rage, and vainly resist, without any burthens but what their own fancy layes upon them. They feele the weight the heavier, the more they stirre it, without they shake it quite off. To refuse, or not willingly to undergoe burthens, is the onely burthen of Impatients. But if they would awake to themselves (which of necessity they must, for when can the will be more Rational, than when necessity is unreasonable) all these factitious weights and seeming heavinesse would quickly vanish: Force must not be used against Fortune, but Patience. This excells so much in strength, that it bears all: For it bears 40 what ever it will, and for this very reason because it Wills. *Samson* carryed away the dores, the two posts, and the barre of the Gate of the City of *Gaza*; but this strength lay in his haire,

like the locks of *Nisus* and *Pterelaus.* A miraculous strength; but weakly secured. The strength of Patience is more safely seated; It lyes not in a lock, which may be cut off by some *Dalilah,* or *Comethe,* or *Scylla,* or any womanish and fearfull hand. To *Will,* is the Sanctuary of its strength; by being willing it is not onely enabled to bear, but also beareth. The backe and shoulder of Patience is the *Will.* This voluntary fortitude of the mind will do all its businesse, without the help of outward Engines; It needs not the assistance of the Armes, nor the weak
10 use of wishes. The strength of Virtue is not external, but in it self.

There remain also other necessary Indurances, though not to those that suffer them allready, yet to others that may, or are about to undergoe them: For the preservation of our Country & liberties we ought patiently to suffer even unto death. It is not too deare a rate to pay that debt wee owe to Nature, for the defense of Nature in our publick Persons: To this we want not the Incouragement of examples. What ever hath been suffered heretofore, may be suffered now by us. But if those presidents
20 rather cool, then provoke our Courage, why dare not wee suffer a little, seeing they suffered so much? To teach us this Virtue of Patience, and strengthen our ruinous brittle condition, the motherly love and fatherly care of the eternal, Divine mind, did provide and disperse through certaine spaces and Intervalls of time (like knots for the strengthning of a weak reed,) persons of such eminent Patience and Piety, as might by their examples sustaine and beare up mankind, untill the *Antient of daies,* and Father of Immortality himself should descend into this mortall life, and be born for Patience, and for death. In the meane time,
30 that the populous World might not want a Glasse to dresse themselves by, he sent these to be the substitutes and forerunners of his mighty and inimitable Patience. The first he consecrated to this dignity was *Abel,* in whom *Patience* (saith holy *Aldhelmus*) *was Original, as Sinne was in Adam.* God joyned Patience to his Innocence by a certain Original Justice or claim in him; but to the rest of the Just it descends together with sufferings, by right of Inheritance: to none more, to none better then to the Innocent. But now even by this, those suffer most, that should suffer least, the good and the Just. But those sufferings are most sacred, that
40 are most unjust. *Adam* found out afflictions, and *Abel* Patience; the medicine presently followed the disease. Evills were the Inventions of Sinne, Patience was the Device of Innocence. So

Of Temperance and Patience. 237

that Patience as their peculiar Treasure abounds more, and is more beloved by the Just, then by any else. But that Posthume Cry fo *Abel* proceeded not from Impatience : For God would not have taken to himself the cause of one dying discontentedly, and with Indignation; but as devout *Alexandrinus* saith, Ἀβελ ὁ δίκαιος, *&c.* *Abel the Just dying unjustly was the first of men that shewd the foundations of death to be ruinous ; wherefore he being dead yet speaketh.* Death, whose right came by unrighteousnesse, laid ruinous foundations indeed, because ill-layd, upon the Just dying unjustly. It hath cause to grieve, that it erred so fouly in its first 10 stroke, seeing it might have made a better beginning in wicked *Cain.* But there was *Divinitie* in it, that death taking possession of mankind by the Murther of the Just, might be justly exterminated and swallowed up in Victory by the undefiled *Virgin-Prince* of the Just, who for that end was born of a Virgin. *Ephrem* saith, *that death howled or lamented in her very beginning, which shewed what would be her end.* The *Hern* by instinct of Nature Chatters and mourns, before he becomes the prey of the *Falcon.* Death dyed by him, over whom she had no power. Only there is the night of death, where sin, where corruption lives.   20

Another tie of Constancy laid upon the World, after a convenient space, was *Job*, who retained his Patience after prosperity, and after Innocence. Patience is no where merrier, nor better contented with it self, then in the Innocent. Integrity and Fortune seldome lodge together. Adversity is the Whetstone which keepes it from rust, and makes it shine. No Virtues can subsist without troubles, which are their foode. They live not commodiously, where their Provision is farre from them : Wherefore holy and Just men have adversity alwaies (like a *Well*) at their dores. I shall take up then with that saying of *Eliphaz* : 30 *Affliction comes not forth of the dust, nor doth trouble spring out of the ground ;* but rather from Heaven ; and comes oftner to holy and heavenly livers, then to Worldly and unrighteous persons.

After *Job*, and at a convenient distance from his time was *Tobiah* appointed, who instead of *Celandine*, made use of Patience to heal his Eyes : being blinded by the *Swallows*, he found a more pretious medicine then their *Herbe*, and his glory is more by bearing with the living, than burying the dead. This holy man also after Innocence, though not after prosperity, retained his Patience ; untill at last the *Son* of God himselfe, after *Impassi-* 40 *bility* and *Allmightinesse*, became wofully passible, and humbled himself to the death of the *Crosse* : of so great an example was

Patience worthy, and so necessary was this voluntary passion of God himselfe to our fatall necessity of suffering. By this mighty example of himself he hath sanctified Patience to be the *All-heal* or Universal *Antidote* of Evills, and the Soveraign *Lenitive* of sorrowes.   Divinely did one sing to the blessed *J E S U S.*

Παυσίπονον νηπενθὲς ἔφυς, ἔυαλθες ὄνειαρ.

Thou the Nepenthe *easing griefe*
Art, and the minds healing reliefe.

At this secret Counsel of the Almighty, did the rude Instincts, or
10 hallucinations rather of the old Heathens (proceeding, noe doubt, from their sense of Humane misery) blindly aime.   They dreamt of some Son of God to be the great exemplar of Patience, and pattern of Virtue ; but finding none, they made and proposed to themselves *Hercules* the Son of *Jupiter,* for a president of continuall Patience, Obedience and Virtue : about whose labours and atchievements, Antiquity hath mightily pleas'd it self with lies and Fables.   This (indeed) they rightly apprehended, that labour or troubles are rather repugnant to, then unworthy of Divinity ; they held them becomming Virtue, and withall necessary, that they might adorne
20 Patience with these two Jewells, the reward of suffering, and the dignity of the Sufferer.   But the *Truth* of God hath now outdone the *Fictions* of men ; It hath exceeded all they did licentiously wish, but could not hope for.   Our Patience is now sufficiently instructed by the *S O N N E* of God, who is the pleasant remedy and *Panacea* of Evills.   The blessed *J E S U S* breathed nothing but Patience, nothing but mildnesse in his life, in his Doctrine.

These are the great examples which true *Christians* should follow ; not those of spurious Patience, and a narrow, heathen fortitude, which after it had born some Evills indeed, dyed at the
30 root, and could not bear it self.   *Seneca* (otherwise in many things a very true, and sometimes a Christian Philosopher,) proposeth to his readers the example of *Cato* ; but I utterly reject it ; for he destroyed himselfe, because he could not save his Common-wealth.   What Constancy was here, though in a state that con-cern'd not his private happinesse ? or what manner of Constancy was that, which durst not endure and hold out, but was overcome, not by irrecoverable, fallen affaires, but falling : Not collapsed and ruin'd, but tottering and doubtfull ? I confesse, it was a spectacle, which the Eye of God Intentive to his great and various
40 works might behold with glory : and I confesse him a brave

22 exceeded all] exceede a ll *1654*   37 collapsed] collasped *1654*

Heathen, Ill-disposed. But I see nothing glorious and excellent in him, nothing of true worth, but what I can find as wel in the most degenerate and womanish *Sardanapalus.* If wee look upon *Cato* amidst the publick ruines, wee shall finde him overthrowne and laid along, where an old wall stands up, no Enemy having touch'd him. A most unworthy man! (if he was a man,) to fall thus basely like a Woman; who at the noyse of any thing suddenly thrown down, casts her self to the ground, and squeaks though untouch'd, and far enough from danger. But thou wilt say, *Though all things became subject to one man, though his legions* 10 *possest the Earth and his Navies the Seas, yea though Cæsars own regiment was in the gates, yet* Cato *made his way out.* An honest voice, if it were not flattery: I tell thee he did not make his way, but sneakt and fled out most shamefully: His legs could not carry him off, and therefore hee ran away upon his hands. But it is all one, flye with which he will, it is a plain flight; his busie and searching fear, which in him (by reason of a sudden, unmanly astonishment) was most Sagacious, shew'd him this postern or backdoor, which he most basely fled out at. *But what could that man be afraid of, that had born so often the Assaults of Fortune?* 20 He feared that very same Fortune: *How can that be,* (say'st thou) *seeing he had coped with her so long before?* For that valour let him thank his errour: He believed Fortune (according to her old vogue) to be still inconstant, he expected that the Tyde should turne; but finding her obstinate, and resolved in earnest to the contrary, he feared her last blow, and providing for himself by a most dastardly tendernesse, did with his owne hands dresse and make a wound to his own liking. To be patient, or to suffer as wee please, is not Patience. He could bear the anger, but not the hatred and feud of Fortune. That is poore valour, that bears 30 onely the flourishes and pickearings of an Enemy, but dares not receive his full charge. A weak man will for some time stand under a great burthen; but he that carries it through, and home, is the strongest. *Cato* then was a most base, pusillanimous combatant; hee quitted his ground, and left Fortune in the field, not only unconquer'd, but untir'd, and flourishing with a whole Arme, which hee had not yet drawn bloud from: What Inconstancy can be greater then his, who was more Inconstant than Vertiginous Fortune? Or who more a Coward then he, that fled and ran away swifter and sooner than her wheeles? To call *Cato* 40 then either constant, wise, or good, is most unjust; nay more, it is an Injurie to mankind, to call him a man, who hath deserved so ill of Wisedome and men, by thinking that any *Cause*, or *Chance* in this World can be worthy of a wise mans death. I would he had read the Conclusion of *Theodorus*, not the dissertation of *Socrates*! *Theodorus Cythereus* most truly affirmed, that there never can be cause enough for a wise man to cast away his life; And he proves it by invincible reason: *For him* (saith he) *that contemns humane Chances, to cast away his life because of them, how contrary is it to his own Judgment, which esteems nothing good, but what is Virtuous, nothing vitious but what is evill?*

10 I wish, when he did read *Socrates*, that he had also understood him! for then he should have heard him condemning that αὐτοχειρίαν, or mad refuge of selfemurther, and commanding him not to stirre out of his appointed station without full Orders from the great Generall of life. Why then dost thou cry up *Cato* for a great leader, who was a most cowardly common Souldier, that forsook his Charge, and betrayed the Fort intrusted to him by the *Prince* of Life? But here thou wilt reply, *that his last nights contemplation, just before he quitted it, was Immortality.* The end he did study it for, made it then unseasonable: And I know not 20 (seeing he was but an Imperfect speculator in the Doctrine of Immortality,) why hee should be so hasty to try whither Eternity was perishable, or not, by casting away his own. He should have expected it, as he did expect the change of Fortune, which till that night he alwaies esteemed Mortall: He should have prepared for it by makeing triall of his Constancie before Eternity.

What praise then either of Patience, or Fortitude hath he deserved? he did no more then the most effeminate, *Hemon* and *Sardanapalus.* O the glorious Act of *Cato* then, equall to his, that handled the *Spindles*! An Act of Women, *Evadne, Jocasta,* 30 and *Auctolia.* An Act of Whores, *Sappho* and *Phædra.* An Act of Wenches, *Thysbe, Biblis, Phillis* and *Anaxarete.* An Act of Boyes, *Iphis* and *Damocles.* An Act of Doting, decrepit men, *Ægeus, Sesostris* and *Timathes.* An Act of Crazie, diseased Persons, *Aristarchus* and *Eratosthenes.* An Act of Madmen, *Aristotle, Empedocles, Timagoras* and *Lucretius.* A rare commendation indeed for a wise man, to have done that which Whores, Wenches and Boyes, sick men and Madmen did, whome either the Impatience of their lust, or Fortune made Impatient of life. Whither thou wilt say, that *Cato* kill'd himself to fly from Fortune, 40 or to find Immortality, thou canst in neither deny his Impatience either of Joy, or else of feare, and in both of life. I would he had been as patient now of life, as he was sometimes of thirst! That voice of Honour, upon the Sands of *Libya*, was his! where (the *Roman* Army like to perish with thirst) a Common Souldier that had taken up a litle muddy Water in his Helmet, presenting it to him, had in stead of thanks this bitter rebuke,

> *Base man! & couldst thou think Cato alone*
> *Wants courage to be dry, &, but him, none?*
> *Look'd I so soft? breath'd I such base desires,*
> *Not proofe against this Libyc Sun's weak fires?*
> *That shame and plague on thee more justly lye!*
> *To drinke alone, when all our troops are dry.*   10

Here was a glorious *Voice*, and there followes it a more glorious hand:

> *For, with brave rage he flung it on the Sand,*
> *And the spilt draught suffic'd each thirsty band.*

This manly Virtue he degenerated from in his last *Act*, and all his friends wisely bending to the present necessity, hee onely broke. The people being all taken, he only fled. To see *Cato* a sufferer in the publicke miserie, had been a Publick comfort; they would have judged it happinesse to have been unhappy with him. It is Honour to suffer with the Honourable, and the 20 Tyranny of Fortune is much allayed, and almost welcome to us, when shee equally rageth against the good and Noble, as against our private selves. If, as he refused the remedy of thirst, he had also rejected this ill remedy against misfortune, his glory had been perfect.

Wee must then be the Patients of life; and of this Patience (which I thinke the greatest of any,) wee have two eminent examples in *Job* and *Tobiah*, who not onely provoked by Fortune, but by their wives also, defended their Calamities in the defense of life. For the other Patience in death (which is the least,) the 30 example of *Abel* sufficed, designed by the wonderfull Counsell of God (untill the manifestation of his Son, that great *Arch-type* of Patience in life and death,) to suffer, though Innocent, a violent and unexperienced death, that the first onset of fate (which was most furious,) meeting in him with an unconquerable Patience, might be somewhat tamed, and the weapons of death having their edge dulled in the first conflict, might afterwards be of lesse terrour to mankind. Just *Abel* was the first that shew'd us the way of dying, when the name of death, as yet untri'd, was most formidable unto life; that he might teach man Patience in his 40 death, and leave it to posterity as a Medicine found out by him.

16 onely *G*: onley *1654*

But when men (by a sad experience grown wise,) found out a greater Evill then death, which to religious men was this sinfull life, and to the miserable and Impatient their own lives; then were *Job* and *Tobiah* set forth the convincing examples of Patience in life, who endured a life more bitter than death, lest by not enduring, they should, to their misery, adde sinne. They taught the World that Patience was a better Medicine for Evills than death, and withstood the opinions of the Lunatick people. Falsely did *Euripides* (arrogating a laudable Title to death,) 10 terme it

> *The greatest medicine of Evills,*
> Κακῶν μέγιστον φάρμακον·

As if he in another place had not term'd it the greatest of Evills. If death then be not its own Medicine, how can it be the Medicine of Evills? It is an Evill great enough, that it is not the Medicine of Evills; but that sufficeth not, it is also the greatest Evill. *Æschylus* is in the like errour, for it is called by him

> *The Physician of incurable Evils,*
> τῶν ἀνηκέστων κακῶν ἰατρός·

20 A most ridiculous appellation: How can that be the Physitian of incurable Evills, which is it selfe such an incurable Evill as their owne *Machaon* could not resist? Equally false is that of *Sophocles,*

> *The last Curer of diseases is death.*
> Ἔσθ᾽ ὁ θάνατος λοῖσθος ἰατρὸς νόσων.

If death it selfe be a disease, which must, and shall be healed, how can it be the last curer of diseases? But these men (after the Common manner of *Physicians,*) held the cure of great Evills to consist in desperate remedies, as obstinate diseases are expell'd 30 by strong and *Diaphoretick* Medicines: Health indeed is dear unto us, and death, I confesse, puts an end to all its diseases, and to all Medicaments too. It takes away the disease sooner and oftner then any other remedy; but these *Poets* themselves (as sick men say of their *Potions*) deny not but it is bitter.

> Κακῶς ζῆν κρεῖττον ἢ καλῶς θανεῖν.
> *It is better to live ill, then to dye well,*

Saith *Euripides* himselfe in another place; such a good opinion had hee of death. It had beene but a sorry provision for mankind, if God had given us no other Medicine against Temporal Evills, 40 but death. The cure of our miserable condition had been both imperfect and uncertain, and to our sad necessity there had been added necessarie despair, when the cure of small Evils had been by a greater, and the great Evill it self left incurable.

But (Glory to the blessed *Jesus* !) wee are both fully cured, and faithfully cared for ! That which can cure all Evills, must be something that is not Evill; Therefore death cannot cure them, because it is an Evill; for God created it not, but it came into the World through the envy of the Divell: Good men hold it to be Evill, & the bad find it so. Thou wilt ask then, what is the Medicine of Evills? I answer, it is that, which is the Medicine 10 that strengthens us to bear the violence, and the pangs of death ; that which the very Enemies of it cannot deny to be good, I mean Patience: that which being made Evill by abuse, yet in that state hath been commended by men that were not Evil, by *Seneca* in his *Cato*, *Dion* in his *Melancoma*, and *Philo* in his *Pancratiastes* : So winning and attractive is the Virtue of Patience, that the very shadow of it procures reverence, and makes the very abuse and corruption of it laudable. If then the *Counterfeit* of it could beautifie vice, and make it amiable even to wise men, what wonder is it, if the *Substance* be a protection and ornament to Virtuous 20 persons? This is the Medicine which *Leonides* gave against death. Let those Titles therefore which death usurped, be vindi- cated by the right owner. Patience then is the best medicine of Evills; It is the cure of the Incurable, the last Physitian, the Ease in death, the mollifying Oyle, the gentle purge, the pleasant Potion, and that I may recover its right to another Title which death usurped from the pen of *Boetius*, *It is a sanctuary that lies alwaies open to the distressed*. Lastly, lest I should deny that, which even the envy of Fortune could not deny, *Patience* (as *Zeno* elegantly said,) *is the Queen regent of all things*, yea of that re- 30 bellious changling Fortune. But let us adde to the certainty of the cure, the easinesse of comming by the medicine: We need not send for it into *Forraign Regions*, nor dig it out of *Mines*, nor extract it out of the *Veines* of *Herbs*, or the *vital parts* of *beasts* : Wee need not go for it to the *Apothecary*, nay I shall adde, wee need not wish for it ; It is already in our custody, a manuall *Antidote* that is alwaies about us, and in us, effectuall for all things, and ready for all men. It is a *Physitian* we need not call upon ; not like death, that forsakes the wretched, and those that earnestly long for it, that hath no pitty upon teares, but keeps off, 40

—— *And will not hear the Crie*
Of distrest man, not shut his weeping Eye.

R 2

Hitherto we have taken view but of one side of Patience, and
that halfe of her which she opposeth to *Evills*. Every part of her is
lovely and excellent : and if we remove now from this Collateral
station to a direct, we shall behold her intire beauty, and how well
shee deserves of *good*. The *Sacraments* of this Virtue are two :
To suffer Evill : to do good : Nobly doth she celebrate both ; with
her there is no Evill, without her there is no good. I think her
the *Mart*, and *Mother-City* of all that is good. Every Virtue is
a *Colonie* of Patience, planted and nourished by her. Virtues owe
10 their Original to her, she is part of it, and in every one of them.
She is their *holy fire*, their *Vesta*, and *Lararium*, or private Chappell ; they are her *Nuns* or *Virgins*, what ever they have, either
sacred or glorious, is from her : To the perfection of man there is
nothing more necessary : For as *Brasse* must be first melted, and
afterwards cast ; so the hard and rigid matter of Virtues must be
softned and dissolved by Patience, that man may become a
glorious and living *Statue* of Divinitie. No marvell, that wee
require labour and hardnesse in Virtuous persons, seeing wee expect
it from *Smiths* ; A certain Just Law of all the World hath exacted it
20 to be the price of Virtue. Beare what thou wouldst not, and thou
shalt enjoy what thou wilt. Labour is the good mans purse :
Patience is his Gold : Onely an obstinate, sordid Idlenesse makes
men poor, not onely in body, but in mind also : Without Patience
they cannot possesse their own Soules. Neither Nature, nor
Virtue, nor Fortune (and this last thou wilt perhaps think strange,)
trust us with their goods without this. Prosperity, when it is lent
to man, dispenseth its treasures to none so plentifully, as to the
laborious : Without a blow it stroaks us not. The sweet-meats it
brings are not eaten, but in the sweat of the face. It was truly
30 said of Fortune,

> *Give bread to the poor, but give him thy fists for sauce.*
> Δὸς πτωχῷ ἄρτον, καὶ κόνδυλον ὄψον ἐπ᾽ αὐτῷ.

The *Snake* will easily slip through our hands, unlesse we grasp
her with *Figleaves*, or some knotty, rough grass ; Fortune is very
slippery, and without labour, and a strong hand, she will not be
held. Honest gaine breeds most Joy, I shall adde most security,
when it is gotten with most pain. Labour is the *earnest* we give
for after-Joyes, which are an addition, or consequence rather,
attending the other fruits of it. Though it goes before them, yet
40 it is refreshed with their following after ; As hunger, which is a
Natural sauce, sweetens the meat, and the Joyes of the eater, even

before he eates: Wee look with most delight upon those things which wee think to be our own, and we think them most, which wee have most labour'd for. Patience is a certain *Title* to possession, but labour gives the *Right*. The Mother loves those children best, and as most hers, which shee brought forth with most pain. *Hony* is gathered of *bitter herbes*; they that love not the bitternesse, must not eate of the Honey. *The drones of Attica* (saith *Tzetzes*,) *will not touch the hony of Hymettus, because it is gather'd of Thyme, which the Attic drone cannot endure to light upon.* The Noble *Xenophon* loved no glory, but that which was purchased 10 by his owne Industry.

The glory of God himselfe is not without labour, which he hath shew'd unto us by his works, and amplified in particular natures according to his wisdome, for our example. Wickedly did *Hermogenes* think of that Supreme, eternally active *Mind*, esteeming him to rest, by reason of idlenesse and inefficacie, though elegantly refuted by *Afer* in these words, *his glory is the more in that he hath laboured.* God doth not onely looke upon, and rule the World, he made it also; And which of these, thinkst thou, is most worthy of glory? is it not to have made it? What is more 20 glorious then to have made glory? In the present *Sabbath* and solemnity of Gods rest, the workes which he hath made, declare his glory unto men, whose task also is, *to work*. Besides, this first curious draught of his Almighty hand contributes something to the perfect beauty of his immortal, last one; for the Divine Eye (reflecting upon this *proofe*,) will adorne that building of holinesse and glory with everlasting strength, and an inviolable, Celestial freshnesse. God made not man by a *Fiat*, as he did the rest of the Creatures, but fell to work himself, and like the *Potter* that first tempers, then fashions the Clay, he made him by makeing, 30 not by speaking. That one royall creature capable of felicity, was consecrated for beatitude, and the Divine likenesse with the ceremony of labour: Here man was instructed, before he was made: he received the exemplar of living before he received life: Idlenesse was forbidden him, before he had the Power given him to be active. But when he gave him life, he gave him also with it another *Specimen*, or *Item* of labour, breathing into him, as if he had used respiration (which refresheth the laborious,) to shew man the use of his breath. All things that were created for the service of mankind, were by the manner of their Creation (which was with 40 a *Fiat*, or command,) taught to be obedient and humble: But man was first ordained for Dominion, afterwards for labour; And

God himself, the Lord of all, labour'd in his Creation, that Hee might make him to be in love with his Ordinance, and that God (plotting as it were against himself,) might by that love of man be induced to love him the more, and to esteeme him more his owne Creature then any other, because he onely (like his Creatour) loved Activity, and the use of life. And this I believe is the meaning of *Xenophon*: *Labour* (saith he) *is a certain over-measure, or extraordinary favour of love.*

So glorious an Ornament is Patience, either in suffering, or else in doing, I believe in both (for Labour, without the good of Patience, is good of it selfe,) that for no other end, but to be thought temperate and wise, the *Pythagoreans* commended abstinence, the *Stoicks* severity, the *Cynicks* exceeded to rigour, the *Gymnosophists* to cruelty, and a face of madnesse and despair. Every one of these adorned his *Heresie* with Patience, and all the rude statues they erected to wisedome, were crowned with this Virtue. *Edesius* being sent by his Father to traffick into *Greece*, quitted the *Merchant*, and turn'd *Philosopher*: His Father upon his return receiving him with stripes, and hee patiently bearing them, asked him, what he had learnt in the Schooles of the Philosophers? He answered, *To bear your anger dutifully*: With the same testimony did another Scholer of *Zeno* adorne the *Stoa*: but *Possidonius* was hardlier provoked then either; he was so tortured with bodily pain, as if the disease had maliciously laboured to confute his principles: but how far it prevailed, appeares best by his own words; *It is to no purpose*, (said he) *vex me as much as thou canst, thou shalt never make me give thee an ill word.* So carefull was he of the reputation of his Master. But *Dionysius Heracleotes*, not able to rule his passions, lost the repute of a Philosopher. So much doth that Majesty and tacite reverence wee admire in Virtue depend upon Patience.

Patience doth that for the private man, which their *life-guards* doe for *Kings*: It keepes him safe, and reverenc'd. It is the minds main-guard, that preserves the Authority of Virtue, and secures the Virtuous person, lest Evills should make him Evill. It is in the oppressed a certain tutelar Angel, and the sacred Guardian of their Spirits from Affliction. Most appositely did *Halitargius* call Patience *the Conservatrix of our Condition.* O how great is the Glory of Virtue, whose Guard and attendant is Patience, the Queene of all things! She is not onely the Crown and Ornament of Philosophie, but the badge and Garland of the Christian warriour. She is not onely honour'd by the Impatient

13 *Cynicks*] *Cynick 1654* (?)

themselves, but by the furious and Salvage. *Abraames,* almost
slaine and martyr'd by the *Indian* Infidels, did with this one
weapon not onely resist, but overcome a whole City: And that
with more expedition then *Cæsar,* and with better successe then
Alexander; for to such admiration and reverence of his person did
his patience drive them, that in the very midst of the storme his
persecutors became suddenly calme, begging forgivenesse with
teares, and with the generall consent of the people elected him for
their Patron and President, whom a little before (having not seen
this pearle of Patience,) they design'd for destruction and death. It 10
was the Majesty of this Immoveable, Serene Virtue, that forced
them to this miraculous Election, adjudging it of most royall
Excellencie, and most worthy of Soveraignty.

Leander told the Fathers, met at *Toledo,* that *Patience would
either win, or overcome her adversaries. Solon* knew this: For
being checkt by some standers by, because he suffered an uncivill
fellow to spit upon him, he answered: *Fisher-men, that they may
catch one whiting, suffer themselves to be dashed over with the fome
and flowings of the Sea-waves; and shall not I do the like to catch
a man?* Whither he catched him, or not, I cannot tell: But I 20
am sure, that *John Fernandius,* a Servant of *JESUS CHRIST,*
and a Fisher of men, catch'd a whole Kingdome with that very
baite. Hee preaching to the *Indians* in the street, one barbarous
Infidel, having gathered his mouth full of sordid spittle, came
pressing through the crowd to the place where he stood, and
delivered it just in his face; but he nothing moved therewith, and
neither rebuking the Barbarian, nor discomposing his former
gesture, persisted in his Masters businesse, and preach'd on: His
Doctrine though powerfull, after the silent Rhetorick of this
publick example, might for that time have beene well spared. 30
Here was the foundation of the Churches of *Japan* and *Amangucia:*
This very *Indian* (and none before him) becomming the first fruits
of that region unto *CHRIST.* So glorious a document of
Patience made him envy our Divine Philosophy, that envy made
him Ambitious, and his holy Ambition made him a Christian.
So gainfull an Industry is Patience, and such a compendious Art
of overcomming. Most wholsome is the advice of *Pimenius:
Malice* (saith he) *never overcomes malice, you must overcome malice
with goodnesse:* But if we could overcome one Evill with another,
why will wee not reserve that Glory for Virtue? By such a blood- 40
lesse Victory did *Motois* overthrow his Adversary; from whom he
fled most valiantly, lest he should offend him; I do not say with

his hands, but with his sight; for Patience hath no hands, but shoulders. His Adversary pursues: *Motois* had lockt himself up, & became his own prisoner, esteeming it guilt enough, that another could be angry with him: But hearing that his Enemy was come in (being only Impatient till he had shewed more Patience,) hee breakes open the door, bids him welcome, and like one that had offended, desires to be forgiven, and afterwards feasts him. This story I have touch'd upon, that thou maist see how powerfull an Instrument of tranquillity, and a quiet, happy life, Patience is, that makes peace to beare fruit in another mans soyl, and civilizeth forraigners. How fruitfull then is she at home? How prosperous a dresser of Virtues in himselfe is the patient man, that will not suffer the propagation of Vices in another?

But *Leander* said, that Patience doth either overcome, or else win her Enemies; I say, she doth both win and overcome: She wins men, and overcomes Fortune; nay, she makes her (though unwilling) a most officious servant of Goodnesse. The name of Patience is not an empty, titular Honour; it hath also very large and princely revenues for the maintenance of Virtue. That Fable of the Divine in holy *Maximus* is truth. He saith, *that wise men dwell in the shadow of a tree, which the more the people cut it, growes the more.* It strives, and vies with the *Iron*; or to borrow the *Poets* expression, θανατῷ ζῇ, καὶ τομῇ φύεται,

> *It lives when kill'd, and brancheth when 'tis lopt.*

His own *Mythology* is most elegant: *By this tree* (saith he) *is signified wisedom, which turnes misfortunes into Ornaments, trouble into Virtue, losse into gain, and scars into beauty:* For the Patient and wise liver, like the Serpent of *Lerna*, when he is most mangled, is most entire; he drinkes in fresh spirits through his very wounds, his courage is heightned by them, and his spilt blood, like dew, doth cherish and revive him,

> *Like some faire* Oke, *that when her boughes*
> *Are cut by rude hands, thicker growes:*
> *And from those wounds the Iron made,*
> *Resumes a rich and fresher shade.*

The benefit then wee receive from Patience, is twofold: It diminisheth the sorrowes of the body, and increaseth the treasure of the mind: Or to speak more properly, there is one great benefit it doth us, It turnes all that is *Evill* into *Good.* Most apposite to this, is that of *Nazianzen,*

> *Patience digesteth misery.*

11 home?] home, ? *1654*

Concoction and Digestion of meats are the daily miracles of the stomack : they make dead things contribute unto life, and by a strange *Metamorphosis* turne Herbes, and almost all living Creatures into the Substance of Man, to preserve his particular *Species* : No otherwise doth Virtue by Patience (which is her stomack,) transform and turne all damages into benefits and blessings, and those blessings into it self. *Lupines*, or bitter Pulse, if steep'd in water, will grow sweet and nourishing : Patience doth macerate miseries, to fatten it selfe with them. Certaine Divine Raies breake out of the Soul in adversity, like 10 sparks of fire out of the afflicted *flint*. The lesser the Soule minds the body, the lesser she adheres to sensibility, shee is by so much the more capable of Divinity, and her own Nature. When her Den of flesh is secure and whole, then is she in darkness, & sleepes under it : When it is distressed and broken, then is she awake, and watcheth by some Heavenly *Candle*, which shines upon her through those breaches. The wounds of the Body are the windowes of the Soul, through which she looks towards Heaven ; *light* is her *provision*, shee feedes then upon *Divinity*. Sublime is that rapture of the most wise *Gregory*,   20

————Τροφὴ μία πᾶσιν ἀρίστη
Δαίννσθαι μεγάλοιο Θεοῦ νόον ἠδὲ φαεινῆς
Ἕλκειν ἐκ Τριιάδος σελας ἄπλετον.————

————*one food the best for all*
Is to feed on the great Gods mind, & draw
An Immense light from the bright Trinity.

Death it self, which the *lust* of eating brought into the World *inedible*, or as *Zeno* saith, *indigestible*, is eaten, digested and transubstantiated into life by Patience, begun in *Abel*, and per- fected in *JESUS CHRIST*. So that now, that saying of 30 *Pirrho*, who affirm'd, *that there was no difference betwixt death and life*, is no longer a *Paradox* ; nor need we make use of that shrewd exaggeration of *Euripides* : *who knowes* (said he) *but this which we call life, is death, and death life ? we see, that men, when they are* (as we speak) *alive, are then only sick, but the dead neither sicken, nor suffer any sorrowes* : Certainly the death of a good liver is eternal life.

Every Action of a wise man is a certain emulation of Death ; wee may see it exprest in his patience. The Soul by this Virtue disintangles, and frees her selfe from the troubles of Mortality : For 40

the frivolous flesh burning with *fevers*, or drown'd in *dropsies*, or
any other diseases, the attendants of corruption, which possesse
and fill up the narrow Fabrick of Man ; the Soul (as in great
inundations, when the lower roomes are overflown) ascends to
the battlements, where she enjoyes a secure, healthfull ayre, leaving
the *ground-roomes* to the tumult and rage of the distemper'd
humours. She ascends thither, where griefe cannot ascend.
Carneades, comming to visit *Agesilaus* grievously tormented with
the Gout, and turning his back to be gone, as if impatient of the
10 violence and insolencie of the disease (whose custome it is to shew
litle reverence towards the best men, the prerogative of Virtue
can give no protection to Nature,) *Agesilaus* pointing from his
feet to his brest, calls him back with this Check, *stay* Carneades,
the pain is not come from thence hither. Hee shew'd by this, that
his mind was in health, though his feet were diseased, and that
the pain had not ascended thither, where the Soule sate in-
throned. At this height she hath two priviledges more then
ordinary ; she is lesse affected with the body, because at some
distance from it ; and hovers above griefe, because above sensi-
20 bility ; shee is nearer to God, and dresseth her selfe by his beames
which she enjoyes more freely, as from a kind of *Balconie,* or
refreshing place, having onely a *Knowledge,* but no *Sense* of the
bodies affliction. From this place she overlookes the labours and
conflicts of the flesh, as *Angels* from the windowes of Heaven
behold Warre, and the Slaughter of distracted men. One benefit more shee hath by Patience, that though shut up in the
body, yet shee can have a tast of her glorious posthume liberty.
Death looseth the Soule from the body, it breaks in sunder the
secret bonds of the blood, that she may have the full use of her
30 wings, and be united to Divinity. Patience, though it doth not
quite loosen the chaine, yet it lengthens it, that she may take the
aire, and walk some part of the way towards Home : Though it
frees not the Soul from the body, yet it gives her liberty and
dominion over it. He that is tyed up by a long Cord, is within
the compasse allowed him untyed, and a free man. The Spirit of
man incensed by adversities, and collected into it selfe, is by
a certain *Antiperistasis* made more ardent and aspiring : *Fire* is
never stronger, nor more intense then amongst *Water* ; In the
bosome of a cloud it breakes forth into thunder : So this Divine
40 Spark, which God hath shut up in Vessels of Clay, when all the
passages of pleasures are stopt, his raies (which before were

24 distracted men *G* : distractem en *1654*

diffused and extravagant) returne into it selfe, and missing their usuall vent, break forth with such violence, as carries with it sometimes the very body, and steales the whole man from passion and mortality. The *Levitie* of fire is of greater force, then the *Gravity* and *Massinesse* of Earth: His *Spirit* is unresistable, and the unknown force of it will blow up the greatest *Mountains*, and the strongest *Castles* this earth affords.

Hitherto have I discoursed of outward *Evills*, I shall now consider the Inward, and how Patience is their Antidote. You have seen her Prerogative over Fortune, and reputed *Evills*, which are called *Evills*, because they seem to be so, not because they are so; as disgrace, grief, and poverty. All these are but fictitious *Evils*, which Custom and Humane error have branded with that injurious denomination : for in these contingencies there is no reall *Evill*, but the *Evill* of opinion; neither is any man miserable but in his own conceit, and by comparison. The glory of Patience would be but poor and trivial, if it could doe no more then take away, or beare with such frivolous and fictitious troubles as these : If it prevailed onely against *Evills*, which we do not suffer, but invent. Its true glory is, that it subdues true *Evills* : Not that it bears them, but that it removes them far from us : Not that it endures them, but that it abstaines from them : For truly to suffer *Evil*, is to do *Evil*, whose *Agent* alwaies the *Patient* is, by reason of a most ill impatience : But Patience onely excellent, because it suffers not. This worst kind of *Evil* is therefore the greater, because when 'tis in acting, it is not seen ; and were it not afterwards felt, there would be no place left for Virtue. This is the usuall method of Vice, a flattering, *Comical* entrance, and a *Tragical exit*. The force and malice of Evil Actions may be gathered by their Nature : They are so powerfully hurtful, that when they cease to be, they cease not to torment us : and so malignant, that while we act them, they flatter us, that being Acted, they may afflict us : While we are doing them, they conceal and deny themselves ; but being done, they appear to our sorrow. Wherefore he that will lead a blessed, a joyfull, and a peaceful life, must make it his whole work, to do no work, but what Religion and Virtue shall approve of. What peace and security can he enjoy that will revenge himselfe, (what more would cruelty have?) according to his own lust? What life can he be said to live, that kills himselfe to please his inordinate affections? What joy can he have, whose troubled conscience is his continual Executioner, racking and tormenting him in the

22 but that] but than *1654*

very embraces of smiling Fortune? No outward *Fomentations* will serve turne against that *Indisposition* to which *fevers* and *fire* are but *coolers*. Wee can provide against the violence of winter and Summer-weather when and how we please : But the inward *heats* and *colds*, the raging *accessions* of the *Spirit* admit no cure. Patience, though Fortune should assist her, will never heal the wounds of conscience.

He that suffers by the guilt of Conscience, endures worse torments then the *wheel*, and the *saw* : As that heat which ascending
10 from the liver, and the region of the heart, doth diffuse it selfe through the body, is greater then the united flames of the *dog-star* and the *Sun*. What torturing invention of *Amestris*, *Pherotima*, or *Perillus* did ever so afflict distress'd wretches, as the fury of his owne Conscience did torment *Orestes*, though freed from all men but himself? no Tyrant is so cruel as a guilty spirit: Not *Scylla* with his *prison*, *Sinis* with his *Isthmian pine*, *Phalaris* with his *bull*, *Sciron* with his *Rock*, nor *Faunus* in his *Inne*. The *Pelusians* when they punished *Parricides*, conceived no torture so answerable to the heynousnesse of the crime, as this inward
20 *a Pliny mentions this punishment: the parricide after his apprehension, to augment the horror of his conscience, was first whipt with rods dipt in the blood of his murthered parents: and afterwards together with a dog, an ape, and a cock, (Creatures which shew litle reverence towards their sires) he was thrust alive into a strong sack, and so thrown into the Sea.*
Divine revenge; neither the [a] *Sack*, nor the *Limekil* pleased them so much as this gnawing worm, the terrible and luctual excogitation of the wise *Father* of Nature. They ordered therefore, and enacted it for a Law, that the murtherer for three daies and three nights should be pent up in some narrow roome together with the naked body of the slaine, and be forced to look upon it, whither he would, or not;
30 which was effected by putting him in such a posture, as permitted him not to look any way, but just upon the dead. The *Sicilian* Tyrant himselfe knew that conscience was a more cruell torment then the *bull* of *brasse*. This made him spare the most unnaturall and bloody offenders, that they might be tormented, not with scalding metalls, and glowing Iron, but by a damning conscience. The first penaltie for murther was conscience: The first Actor of a violent death was punished with life : He that first saw, and introduced death, was thought worthy of no other punishment, but the security of life, which he
40 first shewed to be not secure : for it is a more mercilesse punishment then death, to have long life secured with a killing conscience. So he that brought murther first into the World, was first punished

with the terrours of conscience: Which are then most torturing, when health and strength are the capital punishments. The *Protoplasts* themselves, the parents of death, and of mankind too, who gave us death before they gave us life, thought it a greater plague then death, to be still alive, and yet to be guilty of death? They would have fled to death, to flye from themselves. Apposite to this is that of *Marius Victor,*

> ——*They faine would (if they might)*
> *Descend to hide themselves in Hell.   So light*
> *Of foot is vengeance, and so near to sin,*
> *That soon as done, the Actors do begin*
> *To fear and suffer by themselves: Death moves*
> *Before their Eyes: Sad dens, and duskie groves*
> *They haunt, and hope (vain hope which fear doth guide!)*
> *That those dark shades their inward guilt can hide.*

You see now that conscience, even amongst ᶜ the *Pelusians*, was held a legal and politick punishment, that in *Phalaris* it was a Tyrannical devise, in *Cain* the Divine vengeance, and in *Adam* and *Eve*, the Justice of Nature. God, Nature, Reason, and fury it selfe (which in this case must not be defined madnesse,) do all beare witnesse, that selfe-condemnation, or the guilt of conscience is of all others the most bitter and avenging torment.

ᶜ *The inhabitants of Pelusium, a town in the borders of* Egypt, *now called* Damiata; *It was built by* Peleus *the fratricide, from whom the Citizens descended.*

Adde to this, that the certainty of it is as infallible, and inevitable, as the extremity and fiercenesse of it are implacable: there was never any Tyrant so cruel, but would pardon some offender: There was none so severely inquisitive, but some might either escape from him, or deceive him: But the rigour of conscience permits neither favour, flight, nor fraud. It is utterly inexorable, and neither our feete will serve us to run away, nor our hands to free us: whither shall a man run from himselfe, from the secrets of his own spirit, from his life? No man can be an Impostour or dissembler with his own heart, no man can undo what he hath already done: to have sinned is the remediless plague of the Soul. It was a slow expression of *Victor*, that *Vengeance is near to sinne.* It is swifter then so: It is not *consectaneous*, or in chase of it, but *coetaneous* with it, and its *foster-sister*: The punishment hath the same birth with the offence, and proceedes from it; It is both the *Sister*, and the *Daughter* of it: Wickednesse cannot be brought forth without its penalty: The

brest that conceives the one, is big with the other, and when the one is borne, he is delivered of both.   It is a fruitfullnesse like that of *Mice*, whose young ones are included the one in the other, and generate in the very wombe.   Conscience, while man thinkes of Evill, even before he acts, doth rebuke that thought : so that the punishment is præexistent to the crime, though in the reigne of Virtue it is noiselesse and uselesse ; as penal Lawes are dead letters, untill they are quickned by offenders.   It is then in its *minority*, and without a *sting*, or else it is asleep, untill the Cry of
10 Sinne awakes it.   In the state of Evill, Conscience is the first and the last revenger : when smal offences are wiped out, enormous crimes like capital letters will still remain.

No man can find a Sanctuary to save *him* from *himself*.   No evill doer can so fly for refuge, as to be *secure*, though he may be *safe* : Hee will be afraid in that place, where he thought not to fear : Though he fears not the friends of the murthered, yet he finds that within him, which makes him sore afraid : He may escape the Executioner and the sword, but he will be overtaken by himselfe ; and being safe, hee will be afraid even of his safety :
20 Though he may find fidelity in his fellow-Tyrants, yet shall he find none in his own bosome, which is ever clamorous, and spues out blood and guilt.   Nature deviseth such a punishment for evill doers, as that which tyed living Malefactors unto the putrid Carkasses of dead men, that the horrour and stench of them might afflict their spirits, and the quick flesh be infected and devoured by the dead and rotten.   The *punishment* sticks fast unto us after the *offence*, whose carkasse is terrour of Conscience, Shame, and a gnawing remorse, that feeds still upon the faulty, but is not satisfied.   The guilty person can have noe peace,

30   *But night and day doth his owne life molest,*
       And bears his Judge and witnesse in his brest.

Adde to this, that Reason which in all other pressures and misfortunes is the great Auxiliary and Guardian of man, is in an offended Conscience his greatest Enemy, and imploys all her forces to his vexation and ruine.

Fortune therefore is not the onely cause of our contristation ; we our selves do arm adversities, and put a sword into the hand of griefe to wound us with ; we are sticklers against our selves. Evill Actions afflict more then Evill Fortune ; We are not onely
40 troubled that it was *Chaunce*, but that it was our *Choice*.   It is the worst kind of misery, to be made miserable by our owne approbation.   That evill which we procure to our selves, must needs

grieve us more, then that which we casually suffer : Noe damage is so doleful, as a condemning conscience. Truly, I do believe, that the onely misfortune of Man is *Sinne.* And so very bad and mischievous a Cheat it is, that when it is most punished, wee think it most prospers ; neither can Fortune be justly termed Evil, but when she is the Assistant of Evill men, and the surety for Evill doing. This permitted successe makes the affaires of the most unrighteous to be esteemed Just : This is a felicity like that of beasts, which we put into pleasant and well watered pastures, that they may be fed for slaughter. Against this true misfortune, as well as the false and seeming, Patience must be our Antidote ; not by bearing, but by abstaining from it. Patience in this Case must elevate it selfe, and passe into a virtuous anger and contempt of sinfull prosperity : We must be piously impatient of all their proffers and poisonous allurements ; Impatient, I say, that we may patiently overcome them.

Therefore as I have formerly exhibited the *Art* of *bearing well* to be the onely remedy against Fortune : So now I shall demonstrate to you, that the *Art* of *abstaining well,* is the sole medicine against these true and inward misfortunes : Differing diseases must have different cures. Patience is the poyson that kills Fortune, and the Balm that heales her stripes : but a sacred impatience, or abstinence from Sinne is the Antidote of Conscience ; and the *Basis* or foundation of this holy impatience is transcendent and triumphant Patience. To mitigate or overcome Fortune is a trivial trick : Flattery will do it, if we can but descend to approve of, and commend all that she doth. To preserve the peace of Conscience, wee must be rigid, and censorious : We must speak home, and truly : We must examine before we Act, and admit of no Action that wil be a just cause but for to blush. The approaches of Fortune are abstruse : She moves not within the light of Humane wisedome ; or if she doth, the strength of her Prerogative lies betwixt *Willingnesse* and *Constraint* : It is a kind of *fatal fooling* : Man playes with his *Stars* untill they hurt him : But the cause of an evill Conscience is within our view, and may be prevented by Counsell ; For no man can Sinne against his *Will,* or without his *Knowledge.* One naile must drive out another : He that would avoyd damnation, must avoid also those things which are damnable : He cannot grieve too much, that grieves only to prevent Eternal griefe. The helps we use against Fortune are *after-games.* But the *Salves* of Conscience must precede the wound ; the cure of spirituall diseases is their *prevention.* In the affaires of this World the best

man is the experienced: But in the distresses and affaires of Conscience, he is the wisest that is most ignorant. A noxious Knowledge is death, and every Sinner is a Fool. The wisedome of *Doves* is innocence, and that which makes the *light* to shine is its *simplicity*. Light is a Type of Joy, and Darknesse of Sorrow: Joy is the fruit of innocence, and sorrow of Sinne. The sorrow we take for Fortune is hurtfull: Those teares, like tempestuous droppings, if not kept out, will rot the house: But the sorow for sinne is healing. Penitential tears are the *Oile* of the Sanctuary:
10 God gives them, and afterwards accepts them: they both cleanse us and cherish us. When *Marble* weepes, it washeth off the dust: Worldly teares are the waters of *Marah*; the tree that sweetens them, must be shewed by the Lord: The waters of the pool

* the word in the Hebrew signifies, the house of pow-ring out: which in a secret Allegorie may very well con-cerne man.

* Bethesda heal'd not, untill the *Angel* stirred them; without true remorse teares profit not: but if they have that Ingredient, they are showers which the Lord hath blessed, and must not be stopped, although they might. As courage, and a joyfull heart are the *ripe fruits* of
20 innocence, so shame and sorrow are the hopefull *buds* and *prim-roses* of it. Contrition is the infancie of Virtue: Therefore that sadnesse must not be expelled which expelleth Vice. It is an invention of the Deity to destroy Sinnes: That they might be either unfruitfull, or fruitfull onely to their owne destruction: For this we have two instances from Nature, in the *Mule* and the *Viper*: Whereof the one is barren, and the other unhappily fruitfull. Nature is carefull that Evills may not multiply, or if they do, that they may not prosper. The *Mule* is barren, lest there should be an increase of Monsters. Apposite to this, is that
30 saying of *Gregory Cerameus*, Ἡ γάρ κακία &c, *Evils* (saith he) *are denyed from God the power of propagating, as mules have not the faculty to preserve their kind by generating one another.* The *Viper* notwithstanding is a mother, but shee brings forth her owne destruction: The birth of her young ones is her death. So sorrow, that is the child of sinne, is the death of it also. Let therefore this saving destroyer of sins be made much off, let this godly sorrow be still cherished, and never rebuked: he that dryes up his teares, before he is cleansed, takes delight in his filthinesse, and like the lothsome drunkard, would sleep in his vomit:
40 Penitent afflictions should never be resisted but by precaution.

Hee then that would not drink of this *Wormwood*, must be sure to refuse the *sugred venom* of sinne: No man is Evill for nothing. Every defect in life is occasioned by a defect of Patience: because we cannot endure to be constantly good: because we are impatient of continuall holinesse. Two Evills attend upon Sinners, the *Evill* of *sin*, and the *Evill* of *Punishment*, which is the *Evil* of *sorrow*: To escape the last, we must abstain from the first: wee must be either impatient of the first, or else the patients of the last: Unlesse wee will suffer a litle to avoid offences, wee must suffer much after we have fallen into them. A short displeasure is better then a long torment: This previous Patience of abstaining, frees us from two subsequent Evils: The 10 *pain* of *Conscience* untill we repent, and after that the *pain* of *Penitence*: These two are the *Appendants*, or retinue of every sinne; A seasonable, innocent forbearance is the *fense* against them both: one small griefe averts these two great ones: How wholesome and comfortable is that Patience which prevents sinne and sorrow, the Consequent of it? But Virtue, when it is most healthfull, is in the estimation of some reputed to be poyson: For no other reason do they reject it, of whome *Theodotus* elegantly sings,

> *Virtues faire cares some people measure* 20
> *For poys'nous works, that hinder pleasure.*

This Patient abstinence from Evill is the Mother of holy Joy, it keeps the mind pleasant and serene: What is there, or what can there be more beneficial, or delightfull to man, then a pure, innocent conscience, where all the *Virtues* (like busie *Bees*) are in constant action, as in a fair, *flowry field*, or rather in *Paradise*? where all is Divine, all Peacefull, nothing polluted, no feare, no distraction. In this state, as *Theophanes* saith, *The wise man is adorned with a Godlike Conscience, and a mind becomming the very Deity.* What is there more joyful, then to be master of such 30 a Power, as cannot be violated by Tyrants and Torments? It was a golden and Victorious saying of *Tiburtius*: *Every punishment is poor, when a pure Conscience keepes us company:* For as the guilty can receive no comfort: So the Innocent cannot lose his Joy. The Joy of Conscience is Natures recompence, the coalescent reward, or fruite of integrity, an entailed happinesse, the native blandishment of life, and the minds mighty purchase: What happier gaine can be, then to rejoice alwaies, for what wee have done but once? or what greater damage then an unrighteous gain? It was bravely said by *Chilo, that the heaviest losse was to* 40 *bee chosen before base gain:* That will grieve us but once, the

other alwaies. The losse of temporal goods will trouble us but
for a time, but a lost Conscience will torment us Eternally.
What greater liberty can there be, then not to fear any thing?
And what can he be affeard of, that is not frighted by the guilt
of his own spirit? when *Periander* was askèd, *what liberty was?*
he answered, *A good Conscience.* And another saith, that

> *Man should with Virtue arm'd, and hearten'd be,*
> *And innocently watch his Enemy:*
> *For fearlesse freedom, which none can controule,*
> *Is gotten by a pure and upright Soul.*

Sinne makes remisse and cowardly spirits to be the constant
slaves of misery : what liberty, yea, what joy can he have, or what
dares he do,

> *Whose guilty soul with terrours fraught, doth frame*
> *New torments still, and still doth blow that flame*
> *Which still burns him: nor sees what end can be*
> *Of his dire plagues, and fruitful penalty?*
> *But fears them living, and fears more to dye.*
> *Which makes his life a constant Tragedy.*

Therefore to preserve the mirth and peace of Conscience,
righteous, or honest Actions are mainly conducing, and should be
alwaies our imployment ; for this is the appointed *task* of man,
and it is his *mysterie* too. The *hand* is the best *Sacrifice.* The
Antient *Portugals* used to dedicate to their Gods the right hands
of their captives ; but offer thou thine own, and not anothers. To
be onely without Vice, is a vitious commendation : Nay, it is not
commendable at all, but self-indulgence, or a flattering of our
owne corrupt inactivity. To such a passe is man come, that he
is not ashamed to do lesse for Virtue, then the vitious will do for
Vice. It is a most poore and sordid glory, to be onely not
numbred amongst the bad : It is a base degree of praise, to be
reputed only not base. To be without Vice, is not to be good :
Not to be vitious, and to be Virtuous, are two things. To refrain
from Evill, is scarse not Evill, especially if we proceed no further:
For to be able to be good, and not to be throughly so, is, if not
Evill, a neighbourhood to Evill. True praise consists not in a
bare abstinence from Evill, but in the pursuance & the performance of good. It sufficeth not therefore that we doe nothing
which may *afflict* us, but we must withall doe something that may
exhilarate us. This we must remember, that to do good is one

7 hearten'd] hearten,d *1654*

thing, and to become good is another; Although we cannot become good, unlesse wee doe good; But we become good, not because we have done good works, but because we did them well. Discretion, which considers the manner of doing good, orders the Action so excellently, that oftentimes there is more goodnesse in the *manner*, then in the *Action*: What will it availe us to do good, if it be not well done? It is to write faire, and then to poure the Inke upon it. Actions cease to be good, unlesse well acted, they are like excellent *colours* ill-layed on. The more glorious thy intention is, the more carefully thou must manage it. Indiscretion 10 is most evident in matters of importance: One *drop* of *Oyle* upon *Purple*, is sooner seen, then a whole *quart* that is spilt upon *Sackcloath.*

The *Ermyn* keepes his whitenesse unstained with the hazard of his life: Hee values himselfe at a most sordid rate, that esteems lesse of *Virtue*, then this beast doth of his *skin*; that prefers a foule life to a fair death, that loves his blood more then his honour, and his body more then his Soule. *Ennius* saith, *that the way to live, is, not to love life.* Life is given us for another cause, then meerly to live: he is unworthy of it, that would live onely 20 for the love of life; the greatest cause of life is Virtue: what more absolute madnesse can there be, then to make life the cause of sin, yea the cause of death,

> *And for lifes sake to lose the crown of life?*

What greater unhappinesse, then to dye eternally by refusing death? The Virtuous youth *Pelagius*, rather then he would lose his Innocence, suffered the most exquisite and studyed torments of that impure Tyrant *Habdarrhagmanus*: He suffered many deaths before he was permitted to dye: Hee saw his limbs, his hands, and his sinewes cut in sunder, and lying dead by him, 30 while he yet lived. This preservation of their *honour* some chast *beauties* have paid dearly for. It cost *Nicetas* his tongue, *Amianus* his Eye, Saint *Briget* her face, *Apollonia* her teeth, and *Agatha* her breasts: The lovely *Cyprian Virgin* paid her life for it.

> *Nature even for her self doth lay a snare,*
> *And handsome faces their own traitours are.*

The beauty of Chastity is best preserved by deformity, and the purity of life by a contemptible shape.

The *Shoomaker* is carefull of the neatnesse of a *shooe*, which is made to be worn in durt and mire: And shall man be negligent 40 to adorn his Soul, which is made for Heaven, and the service of the deity? Every artificer strives to do his worke so, as none may find fault with it; And shall we do the works of life perfunctorily and deceitfully? All that makes man to be respected, is his worke, as the fruite doth make the Tree: and a good work can never be too much respected. Keepe thy selfe alwaies in respect by doing good: Thy own dignity is in thy own power: If thy works be good, thou shalt be accounted good too; If better then any, thou shalt be acknowledged for the best. Man is the *effect* of his own *Act*, he is made by those things which he himself makes: Hee is the

10 work of his own hands. A rare priviledge, that permits men, and impowers them to make themselves: Thou hast leave to be whatsoever thou wouldst be. God would not limit thy happinesse: He left thee power to encrease it, to polish and beautifie thy selfe according to thy own mind. Thy friend, or thy neighbour cannot do it: Thy owne good must be thy owne industry. Virtue, because she would be crosse to Fortune, is not adventitious. It is our great happinesse, that this great good must not be borrowed. *Blessed be that Divine mercy, which hath given us means to be saved without the assistance of our neighbours, who have endeavoured to*

20 *damn us!* That almighty hand which first Created man in the Image of his Creatour, finished him not, but left some things for him to doe, that he might in all things resemble his maker. It is one thing to be an *Idol*, or *Counterfeit*, and another to be a *lively Figure* and *likenesse*: There are many *Coppies*, which are not assimilant to their *Originals*, like *Pictures* that have not so much as an *ayre* of those *faces* they were drawn by. To the *Politure* and *sweetning* of the Divine *Image*, there are some *lines* expected from thine owne hand. If some expert Statuary, suppose *Phidias* himselfe, should leave unfinished some excellent peece, like that

30 Statue of *Minerva* at *Athens*, and out of an incurious wearinesse, give himself to some obscure and Artlesse imployment, or to meere Idlenesse, wouldst not thou much blame and rebuke him for it? And canst thou deserve any lesse, if by a loose and vitious life thou wilt either totally deface the Image of God in thy selfe, or else leave it unfinished? Doest thou think that God is maimed, seeing thou doest leave his Image without hands, I mean, without good works? Dost thou think that he is blind, seeing thou dost extinguish, or put quite out that discerning light and informing wisdome which hee hath given thee? Hee that doth not integrally

40 compose himself, and will not carefully strive for perfection, would represent God to be imperfect, and a Monster. *Virtuous manners* (saith holy *Maximus*) *are types of the Divine goodnesse, by which*

God descends to be represented by man, assuming for a body those holy habits, and for a soule the Innocent dictates of wisdome in the spirit, by which he makes those that are worthy, to become Gods, and seals them with the true character of Virtue, bestowing upon them the solid riches of his infallible and immortal Knowledge.

Work then while it is day, while it is life-time; work and cease not : Finish this expectation, this great spectacle, not of men onely, but of God and Angels. Remember that the rewards and applause of this World are but a *Paint* of eternity : The solid and permanent glory is given in Heaven, *When every man shall have praise* 10 *of God.* The *Limbner* is carefull to beautifie and shew his utmost skill in that *peece*, which hee knowes to be intended for judicious eyes : Thou art not to paint, but really to make a living Image of the Divine mind, which also must be examined and judged by that searching eye, from which nothing can be hidden : have a care that no *ill mixture*, nothing *disproportionable*, nothing *uneven* or *adulterate* may be found in it. The presents we offer to the true God, must be true and solid works, not the fictitious oblations of *Jupiter Milichus* : Why wilt thou delight in a maimed Soule, or which is worse, in a Soul whose best part is dead ? Thou hadst rather have 20 a member cut off, then hanging dead by thee : Thou wouldst then onely wish for its company, when it would be no hindrance to thee. And canst thou endure the immortal Soul to be sick of death, to be sick in his best part, in the head? wilt thou suffer thy mind to drowse, to be paralytical and senselesse, never thinking of God, nor of doing good? In such a *liver*, the beauty of his immortal part is crusted over with an incurable leprosie ; and reason, which is the Soules *Countenance*, is most ingloriously ecclipsed. The Task of life is to labour, and the Sacrament of the Soule is to work rationally. Idlenesse is a *Parenthesis* in the *line* of life : When 30 we do nothing, wee do not live.

Slothfullnesse is a dead *Existence*, a kind of *sleep* when we are *awake* : That life is empty, that is not filled with the care of living well. It was truly said by *Possidonius, that one day of a learned mans life, was more pleasant, then all the years of the unlearned :* One houre, one minute well spent, is to be preferred before a sinfull, voluptuous *for-ever. Time* is a sacred thing : it flowes from Heaven, it is a thred spun from thence by the motion and circumvolution of the spheres. It is an emanation from that place, where eternity springs. The right use of it, is to reduce it to its Original : 40 If we follow time close, it will bring us to its Fountain. It is a *clue* cast down from Heaven to guide us thither. It is the younger

brother of eternity, the one must be sought in the other.   It hath
some assimilation to Divinity : it is partly knowable, and partly
not : Wee move in it, and wee see it not : It is then most
invisible ; when most present.   If we be carefull of it, the benefit
is ours : If wee neglect it, we cast away our selves.   Hee lives not
at all, that lives not well : And hee that lives ill, shall dye worse :
Hee suffers a living and sensible death : It is death, because it
wants the fruit of life ; and it is sensible, because it is with
losse and punishment.   Many ill livers comfort themselves with
10 a vain conceit, that the state of death is senselesse : But Vice
and Idlenesse are more malitious deaths, they carry with them
the penalty of sense : They are fertill in evills, and barren of
good, like a cursed ground that bringes forth nothing but thornes
and thistles.

You expect *grapes* from your *vines*, & *corn* from your *Fields*, but
no Fruit at all from your selves : Were you made to be good for
nothing ? for shame be your own *dressers, Manure* your selves,
and *prune* your vain and noxious affections.   *Man* himself is his
own pretious *Soile*, his own fruitfull *field*, and thriving *Plant* : let him
20 that expects fruits from extraneous things, tast first of his own.
Good workes are the *apples* of this Heavenly *Plant.*   The *Vine*
and the *Field*, though they bear not for themselves, pay their
annual proventions.   If they had beene left to their first fruitfullnesse
before the *Curse*, they had exceeded in a most uberous, spontaneous
fertility ; if they should yeild nothing now, they would be good for
nothing.   Man bears fruit for himselfe, and may bear as much as
he pleaseth : Wilt thou then keepe backe thy own provision ? Wilt
thou pine thy selfe ? or by burying thy talent in the dust, be an
enemy to thy own soule, and envious towards others ?
30   Virtue in my opinion is like to *Musick* : it pleaseth most of all
the Virtuous man himself ; and it pleaseth also the vitious, whose
Conscience doth force him to admire that in others, which he
neglects in himselfe.   *Musick* delighteth both the *Musician*, and the
unskillfull.   *Musick* built the Walls of *Thebes* ; and *Virtue* must
build the new *Hierusalem*.   Musick and Virtue are the performances of the *hand*, and the Cordials of the *mind*.   Every lover of
Virtue is *Musical*, that is to say, he is pleased with the suffrages
of his own Conscience, and solaced with the Celestiall flights of
his pure Spirit : Hee loves the works of Virtue (not to gain the
40 peoples applause,) but for Virtues sake, whose beauty and power
are best seene in her workes.   Honesty is one of the liberal *Arts*,
it is a trade of Conscience, not of gaine.   Craftsmen shew their

10 conceit] conceir *1654*   37 to] so *1654*

skill in their works : The *Sculptor* in his *Cuts,* the *Painter* in his *limnings,* and the *Goldsmith* in his *Plate.* To do something, not the manner of doing it, is their care : Their worke may be well done, though negligently, and without much *Art.* The *Limner* may give a *stroke* in hast or anger, which neither Judgement, nor curiosity can ever match. *Giotto's* circle, though drawn perfunctorily, surpassed the most elaborate peeces of other *Artists.* Virtue alone makes no use either of errour or chance, and this she doth meerly to oppose Fortune. In virtuous actions, if wee erre in doing, though we do good, yet the worke of Virtue is not well done. 10 In other *Arts,* one *Exemplar,* or *Act* may serve to shew the Artificers skill, though he should never work more : But it is not so in Virtue ; As we cannot know a skillfull *Musician,* unlesse he plaies upon some *Instrument* ; so Virtuous men are not manifested untill they *Act* : He that will give any *proofe* of himselfe, must needs be active ; but to be so once, is not activity.

Virtue is a most usefull thing, and the use of it dyeth not after it is used : For allthough all the actions of man are transitory, yet when they proceed from Virtue, they are permanent. I advise thee therefore to be permanent, yea to be immortal. Care not for 20 those things which the World esteems to be enduring, as Gold, and the Wealth of Fortune ; those will make them wings and fly away, when thou doest least look for it. Care thou for those things which the people, and their Hypocritical rulers value not, because they believe them to proceed from a sheepish and rewardlesse *tamenesse,* and not from *grace,* and the secret dispensations of the God of peace. Care, I say, for Righteousnesse and Innocence ; Care that thy Actions be upright : These are the treasures which the World believing to be transient, shall find one day to be truly solid and permanent. Thou hast read somtimes that advice of 30 the Apostle, *Redeem the times:* That is to say, what thou doest well at one time, thou shalt have it at all times : Thy good Actions, withersoever thou goest, will bear thee company : They are Companions of a most rare fidelity, and will leave thee neither in the hour of death, nor after death. When our friends cannot follow us, then do our good works travell with us, they are then our best friends, and overcome our foes. Envy it selfe is appeased with death, it falls off with the body. Malice knowes no posthume persecution, and the glory of Virtue in that *state* is above the reach of her Enemies : though they may disturb our temporal rights, 40 they are too short to oppose our claime to immortality : The onely peaceful possession of the dead, is his good life, and righteous

24 Hypocritical] Hypocritital *1654*

dealings: what wil it avail the rich oppressours of this World, to have their Carkasses buried in the abundance of their treasures, unlesse they mean by it, to restore that unto the Earth which was digged out of her bowells? Gold and Silver are no ransome for unrighteousnesse. Virtue alone, which survives death, is the refreshment of the dead: He cannot be affeard to dy, who is assured of a better subsistance after death: Their dissolution is onely fearful to those, who lose all by it, and their life to boot. The Posthume Inheritance of man is his righteousnesse and
10 integrity, which death takes not from him, but puts him in possession of them. Thou maist gather, that good or Virtuous works are proper and necessary to the Soul, out of mans natural desire of fame, and that innate appetite of immortality which is planted in his Spirit: Nature desires nothing which is not rational, and her perswasions, even when they degenerate, strain, and point at some primitive delights, and innocent priviledges which she was free to before her corruption. All secular glories dye with the body, goodnesse only is above the power of death: That faire part of life is kin to the Supreme good, and death cannot hurt it; yea
20 it is secured by death, which kills envy, and frees the virtuous both from the malice of their Enemies, and the possibility of failing in themselves.

Therefore the best imployment for man (if he will consider either his own benefit, or the approbation and liking of nature, which aimes also at immortality) is the work of *virtue,* yea far better then the work of *reason.* Many, while they study the reason of virtuous works, passe by virtue it self. By a fruitless study how to do good, they lose their time, and doe none at all. *Theorie* is nothing so beneficial as *Practice.* It is a true saying that *Jamblichus* cites out
30 of *Pythagoras; Every good thing consists of substance and use, and not of meer knowledge.* To be good, is to doe good. The knowledge of a skilfull *Physitian* profits not the *sick,* unlesse he falls to practise, and gives him something towards his cure. Learned *Aphorisms* heal not the diseased, but bitter *Medicines.* That Soul which can reason subtilly, and discourse elegantly, is not saved; but the Soul which doth good works: Knowledge and Faith without actual Charity are both dead.

Neverthelesse there is amongst men a certain covetousnesse of Wisdome and Knowledge, as well as of Money. The acquisition
40 pleaseth them, but they will not set it out to use. As Usurers hoard up their mony, laying it out neither in pious works, nor for their own necessities, but suffer it to lye under rust and darknesse:

42 lye] lye : *catchword 1654*

So some Learned men neither practise those excellent rules of Living which they have learnt, nor will they impart them unto others : They study stil more curiosities, being in the mean time incurious of their salvation. I will say of them, as *Anacharsis* said of the *Athenians, They know no use of money but to count it.* There is no man poorer then the rich miser, and none more un-learned then the unpractised. Nature is contented with mediocrity : The World hath many things in it which humane affairs have no need of. Virtue also is perfected in few precepts : Though we fill the world with our Writings, it is not our *Volumes* that can make us 10 good, but a *Will* to be so. Book-men write out of no other design, but to reform and civilize Mankind : They make several Assayes, numerous attempts, and then renew them. The *Dice* run not well alwaies, the last cast may carry more then all the former. There-fore to stir up and incline the *Will* to goodnesse, many things are necessarie ; but to be good there is nothing needfull but *willing-nesse.* We suffer our selves to be cheated by hope ; we trust that when we have gathered so much knowledge as we covet, then we shall do all that we can desire. O foolish and vain procrastination ! *Alchuvius* terms it a *Palsie,* I am sure it is a *madnesse.* We stay 20 like that foolish Beggar for a Mess from the Kings table, and in the mean time starve. We care not to use this present life which is our own, but study the secrets of another, which as yet is not ours. We would learn Mysteries, and some things that are either out of our way, or else beyond it. Christians should neither wander, nor sit down, but goe on ; *What is that to thee ? follow thou me.* Content is a private sphere, but wants nothing, and is ever calme. They that study the world are (of the two) the worst Speculators. Popular, politick persons live alwayes by events : Their ambition and firienesse makes their lives uneven, and 30 uncertain : innocent, and undisturbed *habits* are the companions of Humility. Giant-spirits, though they may flash sometimes with faire *thoughts,* have alwaies dark and stormy *affections.* Men, or the most part of men, are like *Swans,* whose *feet* though ever in a living *Bath,* are alwaies *black* ; but their *wings* and *doune,* which keep above those streames, are pure *white.* That part of our lives which is ever *padling* with the *current* of Time, is foul and defiled ; but that which soares above it, is fair and holy. Worldly businesse is the Soules Idlenesse.

Man, ordained to be *King* of the Worlds Republick, had been 40 a meer Cypher, if without *Soul-imployment.* He had been created to no *end* without this *Aime.* If he for whom all things

were made, will not endeavour to secure himself being made, he
was made in vain. An ornament to the World he cannot be :
He was not made with any great gaity, & his decaies are both
numerous and hastie. If to be seen only, were the duty of
created things, the *Stars* should have been onely fixt, and not
moving. Stop (if thou canst) the course of the *Sun*, his restlesse
and vast circumvolution : As motion makes him bright and lively
(for hee rejoyceth to run his race) so standing still, and slothful-
nesse would make him sad and sullied ; the beauty of the
10 *Firmament* would be darken'd, the freshnesse of the *earth* would
fade, and the whole *family* of *Nature* missing those cherishing
beames, would pine and decay : *Rivers* would fall asleep, *Minerals*
would prove abortive, and the mourning world would wast away
under darknesse and sterility. But the *Sunne* though he should
not move, would not be uselesse ; his very sight is beneficial.
Hee is the created light of the visible world, a *marvellous vessel*,
and *an ornament in the high places of the Lord*. But man for
whom all these things were made, without he be active and
serviceable to his own Soule, is good for nothing. There is
20 nothing more pleasant, nothing more peacefull, nothing more
needfull then an industrious, *Wise man*, and nothing more im-
pertinent, and uselesse then the sluggard. The *rest* of the mind
is the *motion* of Virtue, and the *idlenesse* of the idle is the *disturbance* of his Spirit. He that doth nothing, is of lesse use, and
by much worse then nothing it selfe. Wouldst thou be reduced
into that unnaturall *Vacuity* of *not being*, which is without form
and void ? Cease to do good, and it is done. The fruitlesse tree
must be cut down : Doest thou ask why ? That it may not be ;
yea, that it may be nothing, and not cumber the ground. *Anni-*
30 *hilation* is more profitable then a fruitlesse *being*. In this *Family*
of Nature, every one hath his *task* : None may be idle. The best
and the Noblest are the most laborious. Consider *Heaven*, the first
Exemplar of agility ; the brightest and the most active *Elements*
are the next to it, and above them move the *Stars*. *Fire* is the
Suburb of *Heaven* : The *Earth* which is cold and dull, like an
Iland lies most remote, and cut off (as it were) from the *neigh-*
bourhood of *light*. Nothing hath commerce with *Heaven*, but
what is pure : he that would be *pure*, must needs be *active* : Sin
never prevailes against us, but in the absence of Virtue, and
40 Virtue is never absent, but when wee are idle. To preserve the
peace of Conscience, wee must not feare sufferings ; if the hand
of man wound us, God himselfe will cure us : But if wee wound

8 slothfulnesse] slothtfulnesse *1654*

our selves by resisting him, the hands of all his creatures will be against us, because *ours* was against *his*.

Having now taught you how to master *Adventitious, Personal Evils,* and to prevent the *Evils* of *Conscience*; It orderly followes, that I should teach you how to subdue and triumph over *Publick Evils,* or *National Calamities.* The sufferings of just persons wound the heart of a wise man, when his own cannot grate upon it. Fortune, that could neither hurt him by force, nor by fraud, drawes blood from him through the sides of others. The right-eous liver is troubled more with the losses of his neighbours, then 10 with his own. Hee whose patience could not be overcome by *passion,* lies open and naked to the assaults of *compassion.* The life of the wise man is the most pretious and profitable, he lives not only for himself, but for others, and for his Country: The safety of the imprudent is his care, as well as his own: Hee is not onely their compatriot, but their patriot and defender. Excellent is that rapture of *Menander,*

> ———*True life in this is shown,*
> *To live for all mens good, not for our own.*

He onely truly lives, that lives not meerly for his own ends. To 20 live is not a *private,* but a *publick* good: The Treasure of good living is diffusive. The *Civil Guardian* lookes to the goods of his *Wards*: but the wise man is the naturall *Tutor* of the people, and lookes to the publick good, and to the *aged* as well as those that are in their *Minority.* It will therefore be worthy our paines, to consider and enquire how such men should carry themselves in popular and grand mutations; Whither they should change their *Nature,* or their *Maners,* or retain them both, when both fortune, knaves and fooles are most changing. In National alterations, a wise man may change his outward carriage, but 30 not his inward: His mind must be dry and unmoved, when his Eyes flow with teares: Hee must bestow a compassionate, Fatherly look upon the afflicted, and those that are soe weak, as to believe that temporal sufferings can make them miserable. But neither his tears, nor those that he bewailes, must work so far upon him, as to break his inward peace by admitting of *fear,* or *hope,* or the *desire* of *revenge*; and though hee himself stands in a secure station, from whence he can both distresse & defeat Fortune, yet must he helpe also to redeem others; he must take the field with his Forces, and set upon her with open valour, 40 *doing good (as Tzetzes saith) to all men, and abolishing every where*

30 wise man] wiseman man *1654*

the power of Fortune. If hee finds that the brests of others are too
narrow to entertaine Royall Reason, hee must labour by Stratagems, by Manuductions, and inducing circumstances to incourage
and strengthen them; Hee must not leave them, untill he hath
secured them. *Antisthenes* said, *that a good man was a troublesome burthen.* Who but insipid wretches, that have no feeling of
their misery, will assent to this position? A good liver is troublesome to none, but to the bad, and he is by so much the more
pretious and desirable. That wound which makes the patient
10 senselesse; is more dangerous then that which smarts and
grieves him. But if their misery when it is made apparent to
them by the good man is thereby diminished, and they acknowledge themselves to have been made so by their own vain
opinion; it is just that they confesse Virtue to be healing, and
that by her meanes they found helpe from a strangers hand, when
their own were infirm and helplesse. O Virtue, the great *lenitive*
of man-kind! Yea of those who are thine Enemies! Thy hand
heals him, that would hurt thee,

As Egypts *drought by* Nilus *is redrest,*
20 *So thy wise tongue doth comfort the opprest.*

Yea, the Evill by whose association thy purity was never
defiled, thou dost helpe by the good. In every virtuous man
I hold that saying to be true, which *Venantius* spoke of the great
Captain *Bonegissus*: *His hand restores, his Counsel secures: whom
Fortune rejects or casts out of her armes, he taketh up and guards
them in his.* And hence I am induced to differ in my opinion
from *Philo*, about that saying of the *Jews* Law-giver, *that a wise
man hath heavy hands.* What wonder is it if they be so, seeing
the imprudent, the afflicted, and the disconsolate, who are grievous
30 and heavy to themselves, do all depend and hang upon his armes,
like Infants upon their mothers?

To help these hangers on, he must needs be bowed, and by
speaking faire to their grievances, begin to redress them. This is
the property, or rather the prerogative of the constant and wise
man; Hee can descend safely from the Sphere of his owne happinesse to mingle with, and to comfort the miserable. Noe man
by standing still can rescue one that is carryed away by a violent
torrent, and ready to be drowned; nor if he also be overcome by
the same stream, can he save the other. It is one thing to be
40 thrown down, and another to be bowed down. He that would
not be thrown down, must look to the liberty of his *Will*, and not

submit it to Fortune. But to restore, or raise up others, it is
necessary that he must bow. No man can take up a Child that
is fallen, but by bending himselfe : To cure the ill-affected, we
must in some things incline to their affections. Comfort is
a *potion* of that nature, that heals not the sick, without an appearance of the same *indisposition* in the very *Physitian* : The *patient*
will otherwise suspect that for *poyson*, which is meant for his
health. Hee that is ill-affected, wil be unwilling to believe that
another which is not so, can have any skill to cure him : And he
that labours with the same disease, can neither cure others, nor 10
himself. Therefore he that would minister comfort unto the
distressed, must of necessity have his *will* above the Tyranny of
Fortune, he must have a mind that is invulnerable, and yet seem
to be very tender and sensible of her lightest strokes. It is one
thing to be subject to these affections, and another to rule them :
To be had of them, and to have them. He that would loose
others, must not be bound himselfe. When *Musonianus* observed
a Troop of horse, that was under his command, to *halt*, and
make a stand, expecting some *Omen* from a bird that had
suddenly pitched before them, he bent his bow, and riding up to 20
the front of the Troop, shot at the bird, and killed him : Then
laughing at their folly, he told them, that *there was but litle
advice or help to be expected from such irrational creatures, that
were not onely ignorant of the destiny of others, but could not foresee
their own ill luck.* Wee must look first to our own safety, afterwards to others : The hand of the helper should make the first
assay upon himself : He that experimentally knowes, he can *swim*,
is fit to save another that is in danger to be *drowned*.

But when I speak of tendernesse, and a seeming complyance
with the weaknesse of others ; I mean not dissimulation. I allow 30
a community of tears, but not of the *cause* of tears. Let the
miserable bewail their misery, and let the wise man mourne with
those that mourn, because they mourne amisse, not because they
suffer. Let him not mourne for the power of Fortune, but for
the weaknesse of man. When a friend of *Solon* found him
weeping, hee told him, *That tears were not the potion against
Fortune, and would therefore profit nothing ; I know it well* (said
Solon) *and that is it which I Lament.* He bewailed the tears of
others, not the cause of their tears : That is it which a wise man
(the enemy and the avenger upon Fortune,) may justly bewail, 40

28 fit to] fi to *1654*   *drowned*] *drtowned 1654. The* t *has slipped
out of place in the original from* fit *in line above*

to see men weep, when weeping availes not. He is troubled, not because they suffer, but because they will not be comforted ; yea, because they will not be men : He thinkes not that it is Evill to suffer worldly afflictions ; Nay, hee knowes it is good, but he knowes withall that worldly sorrowes slay the Soul. This is the consideration that calls forth his tears : Hee wisely distinguisheth, that man is not made miserable by any *outward accidents*, but by his own *opinion* : For no man is made unhappy, because he *exists*, or *is*, but because he thinks himselfe to be so : The wise man 10 bewailes a greater *Evil* then the *Evil* of misfortune, and that is the *inability* of some men to beare *Evil*. Hee mourns not because they are *Patients*, but for their *impatience*. The true or reall *Evil* which he knowes to be in them, is their ignorance of false or reputed *Evills*. That which causeth him to weep, is their causelesse weeping. He that disguiseth his constancie thus, dissembles not. I make not a wise man to be impassible, but enduring and compassionate, yea the *Patient* of compassions : Though I exempt him from the *crowd* and *populacie* ; I place him not above *Humanity* : Though he is no *peere* of the *Multi-* 20 *tude*, yet he *descends* to pitty them : But we doe not therefore disturb his peace and serenity, because he is mercifull and condoling ; but because it is his expectation, his desire. He is not stormy, nor treacherous, nor base, but courteous, liberal and happy ; he is in all estates master of himself ; he is kept fresh and pleasant by the secret Joyes and vivifications of an unoffended Conscience. It was well said by the *School-Divine* ; *That the tears of the righteous were the smiles of their Soules.*

Gregory Nazianzen commended his Brother *Cesarius* for his honest dissimulation with the dissembling Court. He was in- 30 wardly an *Anachorite*, and outwardly a *Courtier*. In publick and splendid affaires (which are more seducing and inconstant then private,) this policie is necessary : Wee should alwaies have a snare ready for them, that we may escape theirs. In the downright blowes of Fortune, that is, in our own domestick losses, We should be sincere and naked ; we should put on nothing but our native complexion, and a serene mind. In this Case, wee should be so undaunted, as to looke upon Fortune, and overcome her without any weapons, we should set naked upon her, not onely without defensive armes, but without cloaths. In the 40 dangers of others, we must deal otherwise ; wee must use all means to secure them : Wee must deal with Fortune as she deals

37 upon] upon upon *1654*

with us, by disguises and stratagems : All her *wares* are but
gilded clouds, a *Superficiall wash* ; they are not that which they
seem to be ; to be true to our selves, wee must be false to these,
wee must not trust them. Shee cannot require more from us, or
better, then what shee gives : Her *Good*, and her *Evill* are both
counterfeits, and he that dissembles with them, offends not.
The riches of this world are not sound within : Wee may not for
their sakes corrupt our Soules, and be made like unto them. Let
the peace of Conscience shine within, upon a white and undefiled
Throne, though wee look mournfull and ragged without. No 10
Man deals better, or more justly with this World, then he that
lends her his *face*, but keeps his *heart*. This is the Nature of the
World, to give us a fair *looke*, and an empty hand. Consider
thy selfe : How often hast thou been that Creature, which thou
didst not seem to be ? All the accoutrements of Fortune, all her
pomp, and the transitory course thereof, when laid out with the
best advantage, seemes to me but a *Stage-play*. Her most glorious
favourits passe by like *Whifflers*, which carry Torches in their
hands onely to shew the deformity of their vizards : They hasten
away, and like   20

To speedy posts, bear hence the Lamp of life.

All the glory of this World, hath darknesse, and treachery in it.
It passeth gloomily by us, like high-way-men that traverse the
road with veiled faces : hee that will be even with this Counterfeit, must clap on a vizard too, and by an honest dissimulation,
preserve himself.

In the funeralls of our friends, our kindred and benefactors,
wee may moderately mourne ; but we must not lose our Patience,
nor that Christian peace, which is the golden fruit of faith and
hope. The great mercy of God hath so provided, that *Evill* 30
when it sets upon us, is but an apparition ; there comes good
presently after it. To live well, we have in our selves more then
enough : we need not any extraneous help ; our very desiring of
it, makes us miserable. So excellently best is our condition, that
the blessed life is ours *gratis*, but misery we must hunt after.
The happy life needes neither riches nor wishes ; Misery cannot
be had without *desiring*, and it is never given without Covetousnesse, which is the price paid for it. Wee suffice of our selves
for a happy life ; why not for meere life, which is something
lesse ? shall we think our selves poor, because we abound with 40

the means of happinesse? As long as the batteries of Fortune
cannot shake the *mind*, nor make the *wil* to fly into shivers; the
heart is whole, and our *peace* is secure: Her musters and preparations seem formidable but to children only: Take off the helmet,
or vizard of *Evil*, and underneath it, you will find *good*: Hast
thou lost a friend that took care for thee like a mother, and
furnished the like a Father? that very losse is an occasion of
greater gain, though at first it appears not.   Parents sometimes to
sport with their Children disguise themselves: The Child at the
10 first sight is dejected, but having taken off the Masque, he findes
his Mother: He laughs, kisseth and embraceth her, and if shee
comes again in that dresse, he fears her not.   Who would not be
astonished at that furious Army of Evils, which fought against
holy *Job*? It was a sad sight to see a Father, after the losse of his
Children, and substance, to lye languishing under the Tyranny of
a devouring Ulcer.   And where? upon a dunghill, the very sink
of uncleannesse and corruption.   But this frighted him not: Hee
was so farre from thinking it an *Evil*, that he played with the
worms, and made that, which his friends esteemed for vengeance
20 and misery, to be his meditation and mirth: Hee was sure that
he was innocent, and retaining his integrity, he could not misse
of joy.   He saw through that *Crust* and *Scab*, the sure mercies of
God: His beautifull and healing *hand*, shined through that
lothsome *Veyle*.   He desired not the comforts of his kinred, nor
his friends: he said to *corruption, thou art my Father*, and *to the
worms, you are my Sisters*.   This was onely a *shel*, or seeming
Evil; but the *kernel*, or substance that lay within it, was solid
and reall *good*.   As Children deal with *nuts*, so good and wise
men deal with *Calamities*; they break the *shell*, and eate the
30 *kernell*: both the *Good* and *Evill* of this World have their *fucus*,
and outside: Hee that knowes that, and knowes how to take it
off, is a knowing man, and knowes how to use them.
   This lesson Saint *Paul* taught the Citizens of *Corinth*.   *Let
them that weep* (saith he) *be as though they wept not: and they that
rejoyce, as though they rejoyced not: And they that buy, as though
they possessed not*.   He allowes onely an illusive and seeming commerce with the World: Hear his *reason*, and you will acknowledge
his *Justice*: *The fashion of this World* (saith he) *passeth away*, or
is transient and deceiving: That which men call *fruition* in this
40 World, is but *face-acquaintance*: All temporall possession is but
a *looking on*, the things themselves passe away.   They are still in
a Cryptical, unperceived motion, when we suppose them to be

fast lockt, and fettered in our armes : They creep from us like
a *mist* or *smoke*, which in confused and silent *Evolutions* steales
out at the top of the chimney, after it hath fouled it within.

> *All worldly things, even while they grow, decay,*
> *As smoke doth, by ascending, wast away.*

Saith *Dionysius Lyrinensis.* The Apostle would have us to put
on the same disposition, and to be even with this great deceiver
by a like deception. Let us. give it but a glimpse, and halfe
a face, as it gives us but a transient and flattering salute. Let us
weep and not weepe, rejoyce and not rejoyce, use it and not use 10
it. This wee can never *Act* handsomly without personating, or
rather mocking this Arch-cheat. When our Eyes flow with tears,
we must keep our Consciences smiling and pleasant : Wee must
have *Heraclitus* his face, and *Democritus* his heart. The forehead
is the *Index* of the mind ; but the Soul of the just must *shine*,
when his face is most *clouded.* Wee must not give our strength
unto the World, that is to say, we must not seriously affect it :
In all our negotiations with it, we must stand at a distance, and
keepe our affection for him, who must be loved with all the heart,
with all the strength, and with all the Soul. Saint *Paul* (when 20
he made use of this expression,) had respect, I believe, unto the
rites of the *Roman Theater,* the *Comick* and *Tragick Lawes* of
their *Poets,* which together with their Government, were dispersed
into all civill climates : He applied to the various representations,
suddain changes and successive showes of the *Stage,* where
Truth moved in *disguise,* and the serious travels of the Sons of
Men, were by *Masquers* and personating *Counterfeits* solidly
Acted : Where the short flourish of humane affaires did wither
by degrees, and ended in a sad *Catastrophe,* while the *Poets plot*
upbrayded the vanity of *States-mens* policie. The *World* is a meer 30
Stage ; the *Master* of the *Revels* is *God ;* the *Actors* are *Men ;*
the Ornaments and flourishes of the *Scenes* are honour, power
and pomp ; the transitory and painted *Streams* of Mortality,
which passe along with the *current* of time, and like *flowers,* do
but onely appeare, when they stay longest : Hee that enjoyes
them most, doth but *smell* to them, and the shortest fruition
permits as much.

What else was the Majesty of the *Assyrian* Empire, but a trac-
titious, vanishing apparition, a slight *Flash* of transient glory ?
It shot by like a falling star, and was presently succeeded by the 40
Medes and *Persians* : after them came the *Macedon,* and last of all

T

the *Roman.* The Kingdomes of mortall men are not Immortal : they are no better then their Rulers. Where is *Ninus* now, where is *Semiramis, Cyrus, Darius, Alexander, Antipater, Ptolomie, Julius Cæsar, Octavian,* and *Tiberius*? Where now are these Patriarchs of ambition, these weak roots of the *Assyrian, Median, Persian, Macedonian, Asian, Egyptian,* and *Roman* greatnesse? What is become of these *Primats* of pride, these eldest Sons of Fortune, these prosperous disturbers of mankinds peace, before whom the world became dumb, like a *Sparrow* before a *Kite*? what a deep
10 Silence! What a thick darkness is now drawn over them! Nothing remaines of them but their names, and the bare *Skeleton* of glory : Their onely *boast,* is, that they have been : Our onely *Knowledge,* is, that they are vanished. Nay, it is most certain, that we

ᵃ Vixere fortes ante Agamemnona multi; sea omnes Illachrymabiles urgentur, ignotique longâ nocte, carent quia vate sacro.

ᵃ know not all their names; those we are acquainted with, are not many : so ruinous a thing is humane glory, though held by mortal men to be immortal. They are deceived : It leaves neither *Reliques,* as their *bodies* do ; nor *Inscriptions,* like their *Sepulchers.* The glory of men
20 is more mortal then their Carkasses. Their bones remain after their Funerals, after the fire, & the Executioner ; And their teeth may be seen, when they can neither snarle, nor bite. But their fame is edible, it is devoured by time without *Fire,* yea, without *Aire* ; for by not reaching posterity, it becomes dumb, and misseth their tongues, by whose speaking it lives. All the felicity of men is a dream, it comes on they know not how, and when it vanisheth, they cannot so much as discern its Back-parts. If these recorded *Empires,* these famous *Yoaks* and *Burthens* of the World came so suddenly to nothing ; what will be the lot of
30 these *petty fetters,* these *leaden manacles* that we are bound with? If those massie and mighty *weights* were so clearly blown off ; what will become of these *loose Packes,* which have nothing to balasse them, but feathers, but chaffe and motes? Those universall *Monarchies* founded upon the principall *Cities* of the World, whose *Colony* was the whole Earth : Those *Cities* whose *bulwarks* did threaten the Clouds, whose *Armies* and *Fleets* made the *Earth* to tremble, and the *Seas* to grone : whose *Lawes* (like *Oracles*) were held sacred and unalterable ; found no security against the *Arm* of God, which tears the *Crowne* from the *Head*
40 and the *Scepter* from the *right hand* of the *Lawgiver. He considers in his dwelling place, like a clear heat upon herbs : he appoints the things that are to come : He sifteth the Nations with the Sive*

21 & the] the *catchword only, not text*

of Vanity: He blowes upon them, and they wither, and shall not be planted. And why think you then that these dry and fading leaves shall flourish for ever ? All temporall triumphs have their date : they passe away in a sure and uninterrupted course, and when they begin to decay and unloade themselves, then they are swiftest. All the pomp of this World, is but gilded emptinesse, a nine daies blossome, whose beauty drops into the same Mould from whence it sprung. It is the Consciousnesse of their delusion, that makes these worldly honours fly from us so fast ; lest if they should stay long, wee should discover their Cosenage ; the *dis-* 10 *coverer* then would be ashamed of his *dotage,* and the *discovered* would blush at his *deceit.*

Therefore Saint *Paul,* in these versible and transitory fashions of the World, would have us to personate *Stage-players,* who when they weep, grieve not ; when they buy, they possesse not ; when they command, they are without authority. Seeing the World is but a *play,* and a *fable,* hee would not have us to *act* in earnest. Players *Act* the lives of others, not their owne : I wish that we could do so too. Excellent is that advice of the *divine,*

To live a stranger unto life. 20

Why should I be troubled with the affaires of others, more then with their *Agues* or *Feavers ?* he that lives without the *Affections* of this life, is master of himself, and looks upon all things, as *Spectators* do upon *Stage-playes,* who are without *passion,* because without *Interest.* The *Actors* care not how the *Scenes* varie : they know, that when the *Play* is ended, the *Conquerour* must put off his *Crown* in the same *Ward-robe* where the *Fool* puts off his *Cap.* Take this wholsome Counsel of resting quiet in the *degree* appointed thee, not from the mouth of *Musonius, Teletes,* or *Epictetus,* who adviseth thee to be a *Pantomime,* or *shifting* 30 *Masquer* in these worldly *Enterludes,* but from the mouth of Saint *Paul,* that great *Doctour* of the *Universe.*

Let every man wherein he is called, therein abide with God.

That Supreme, Eternall mind is the master and deviser of this worldly *Drama :* Hee brings on the *persons,* and assignes them their *parts.* Art thou called to be a servant ? be not troubled at it : Hath he ordained thy life to be short ? desire not to have it lengthned : If poor, desire not to be made rich. What *part* soever he hath appointed for thee, be contented therewith, and Act it faithfully. It is thy duty to represent the *person* thou wert 40 chosen for, and not to choose ; that is the prerogative of thy

great master. If it be his will, that thou shouldst *Act* a begger, a sick man, or an afflicted, let it be thy care to *act* it well, and to meddle with no other action. The *stageplayer* is not commended, because he *acts* the *part* of a *Prince*, but because hee *acts* it well, and like a *Prince*. It is more commendable to *act* a foole, a begger, or a mourner to the life ; then to *act* a King, or a Philosopher foolishly. In the beginning, the midle, and the end of thy Course, keep thou to thy *part*. The best way of *acting* is to make thy *heart* consentaneous to thy *tongue*, thy *deeds* to thy
10 *words*, and thy *conversation* to thy *doctrine*. In all the tumults and combustions of this World, keepe constant to thy *station* ; comfort the *afflicted*, and envy not the *wicked* ; despise not the *one*, and flatter not the *other* : remember thy *Creator*, and forget not thy end.

Gloria tibi mitissime Jesu !

OF
LIFE and DEATH.

The People think Life to be the greatest *good*, and Death the greatest *evill*. They are mightily deceived : And as in the least blessings, so in this, which is the greatest, they greatly erre. For Life, if thou livest not well, is the greatest evill ; and Death, if thou dyest not ill, is the greatest good ; and dye ill thou canst not, unlesse thou livest ill. A life that is not good encreaseth evils and wickednesse ; and the death of the good sets an end to afflictions and miseries. Those that are sick of the *Jaundis*, judge the sweetest honey to be the most bitter : So evil men esteem Death to be evill, because of their evill conscience ; but Death is not so to 10 any, but to those onely, whose evill lives end in the evill of endlesse death. This controversie I shall decide with such reasons as must not be numbred, but weighed. If wee look upon *Philosophy*, it takes part with Death ; and is the first that marcheth into the field against this popular error. It teacheth us that this hideous nothing, this imaginary fear of the multitude should be always contemned, and sometimes desired. How many wise men hath this contempt of Death made Immortall? For those, who by a continual remembrance of death, did compose and regulate their lives, are now by the memory of their virtuous lives vindicated 20 from death. *Socrates* perfected his wisdom by his willingnesse to dye ; *Pythagoras* by his gentlenesse ; *Anaxagoras* dyed merrily ; *Calanus* resolutely ; hee would not stay to be   *One of the* Indian Gymnosophists, *who feeling himself a little sick made a great Bonefire, and in the presence of* Alexander *burnt himselfe therein.* Alexander *a little before asked him,* What he would 30 have? *hee answered,* I shall see thee shortly. *Which fel out, for he dyed at* Babylon *few days after.*
tamely besieged by her, but sallyed out, and took her : he surprized death and all of them despised her. No definitions we can give will suffice to make Death odious, every one will make it desirable. Whither you consider what Death is, or what are the effects, or consequents of it ; whether the *evil* or the *good* attending it ; or whether Death it self be a meer *evill*, or meer *good*, all make for it. For though it should be an *evill*, yet the good that comes by it exceeds that *evill* ; and being evill, it cannot be so great an *evill* as all those *evils* it puts an end to.

14 the] this *catchword 1654* : thus the *G*   25 her : *G* : her. *1654*

What one thing hath Life that is desirable? Contentions, and obstinate, busie miseries, whose frequency and number hath made them lesse feared then Death, which comes but once: Whose assiduity, or daily malice to afflict us, hath by a long custome made us not valiant, but senslesse and blockish. *Orpheus* defined Life to be *the penalty of Soules*; and *Aristotle* added, *That it was a punishment like to that, which tied the living to the dead, mouth to mouth, and breast to breast.* The pure and eternal Soul is tyed to the putrid and wasting carkasse. If God should
10 now suddenly create a man, giving him withall in that very instant the perfect and free use of his mind, and should then bring before him all Mankind (as he did all living creatures before the first man) and shew him in this mixt multitude some weeping and sighing; some without eyes to weep; some without hands; others without legs; some sick and languishing; others eaten up with horrid, impure ulcers; some beging; others quarrelling; some plotting treason, and washing their hands in innocent blood; some old and decrepit, quivering, trembling, and leaning upon staves; some distracted, and bound up in chains; others plun-
20 dered, tortured, murthered, and martyred; their murtherers in the mean time pretending Religion, Piety, and the Glory of God: And after all this outward *Scene*, should so enlighten his eyes, that he might discover another inward one, I meane their secret thoughts, and close devices, their tyranny, covetousnesse, & sacriledge varnished outwardly with godly pretences, dissembled purity, and the stale shift of liberty of Conscience: Is there any doubt to be made, think you, but after such impious, and aston-ishing spectacles, he would quickly repent of his existence or being, and earnestly desire to be dissolved again, that he might
30 rest in peace, and not be cast into this hospital, and valley of villanies which we call the World. It is for this cause, that wise Nature is so slow and niggardly in her dispensations of reason and maturity unto man, lest a sudden perfection should make us loath her, and lest the necessary evils of life understood in grosse, and upon our first entrance into life should discourage us from under-going those miseries which by degrees, and successive conflicts we more willingly struggle with. *Abner* the *Eastern* King, so soon as his son was born, gave order for his confinement to a stately and spatious Castle, where he should be delicately
40 brought up, & carefully kept from having any knowledg of humane calamities; he gave speciall command that no distressed person should be admitted into his presence; nothing sad, nothing

1 desirable] desirarable *1654*

lamentable, nothing unfortunate ; no poor man, no old man, none weeping nor disconsolate was to come near his Palace. Youthful-nesse, pleasures, and joy were alwaies in his presence, nothing else was to be seen, nothing else was discoursed of in his company. A most ridiculous attempt to keep out sorrow with bars and walls, and to shut the gates against sadnesse, when life is an open door by which it enters. His very delights conveigh'd displeasure to him, and grief by a distast of long pleasure found way to invade him. So constant is pleasure in inconstancy, that continual mirth turns it into sadnesse. Certainly though *Abner* by this device might keep 10 all sorrows from the presence of his son, hee could not keep them from his sense : Hee could keep out, and restrain external evils, but could not restraine his inherent affections. His son longed ; this made him sad in the very midst of his joyes. And what thinkst thou did he long for ? Truly, not to be so cumberd with delights. The grief of pleasures made him request his father to loose the bonds of his miserable felicity. This suit of the Son crost the intentions of the Father, who was forced to give over his device to keep him from sadnesse, lest by continuing it, he should make him sad. He gave him his liberty, but charged his 20 attendants, to remove out of his way all objects of sorrow : The blind, the maimed, the deformed, and the old must not come near him. But what diligence is sufficient to conceal the miseries of Mortality? they are so numerous, that they may as soon be taken out of the world, as hidden from those that are in the world. Royal power prevailed lesse here then humane infirmity ; for this last took place in spight of the first. The *Prince* in his Recreations meets with an old man, blind, and leprous ; the sight astonisheth him ; he startles, trembles, and faints, like those that swound at the apparition of a Spirit ; enquires of his 30 followers what that thing might be ? And being inwardly perswaded that it was some fruit of humane life, he became presently wise, disliked pleasures, condemned mirth, and despised life. And that his life might have the least share here, where Fortune hath the greatest, he rejected the hopes and blandishments of life, yea that which is to many the price of two lives, his Kingdom, and royal Dignity : He laboured with all diligence to live so in the world as if he had been dead, that by avoyding sin, the cause of sorrow, he might be, though not safe, at least secure. If this single accident made him so much offended with life, what (think 40 you) would he have done, had his liberty been universal, and unbounded? What if he had seen the inside of those stately

Tombes wee build for the worms to eat us in, where they feed
upon such fat oppressors as have been fed here with the tears and
pillage of the oppressed? What if he had narrowly searched every
corner of the world, and seen those necessary uncleannesses in
which the birth of man is celebrated, in which this miserie is
inaugurated, by the paines of the Mother, and the cries of the
Infant? What if he had entred into their bedchambers and
bosomes, where some sit weeping, others wishing; some surfeited
and sick with fruition? where some mourn for their wives, others
10 for their children; some pine and starve with want, others are full
and vomit; some are troubled with lack of necessaries, and others
are as much vexed with abundance and superfluity? What if after
all this search, and wide disquisition he could not have found one
house without some misfortune, and none without tears? What if
he had been admitted into the breasts of all those, whom either
domestick, hidden griefs, lingring diseases, worldly cares, or an
insatiable covetousness is ever tormenting? Perhaps the sight of
so many evils had driven him to a refusall of life, in which we doe
so dye with miseries, and by which miseries doe so live in us; at
20 least he had earnestly wished and groaned for some means of
redemption from so miserable a bondage. If any had brought
him the joyful news of liberty, and affirmed that some were already
made free, he had certainly envyed them very much, and would
have been impatient to know the means. But when it had been
told him that the device and release was death, I do not onely
think, but I verily beleeve that he had both approved of it, and
would have sought for it more then for hidden treasure. He had
judged it not onely desirable and convenient, but necessary, and
the greatest felicity, and favour that the living could expect.
30 If some solitary travellour, shut up in a wilderness, and
surrounded with wild beasts, should on the one side see a *Tiger*
making towards him, on the other a *Lyon*, and from some third
place a scalie, winding *Serpent*, or a *Basilisk*, which kils with his
very looks,

> *Whose hissings fright all Natures monstrous Ills,*
> *His eye darts death, more swift then poison kils.*
> *All Monsters by instinct to him give place,*
> *They fly for life, for death lives in his face;*
> *And hee alone by Natures hid commands*
40 > *Reigns Paramont, and Prince of all the sands.*

If these, with a thousand more, as *Bears, Leopards, Wolves,*

17 the] thei *1654*

Dragons, *Adders*, and *Vipers* were gathered together about him, and ready to seize upon him, what would not he give to be freed from the violence and rage of such destroyers? What greater felicity could he desire, then to be redeemed from such an horrid and fatall distresse? And is it a lesser blessing to be delivered from greater evils? We are surrounded with calamities, torn by inordinate wishes, hated by the world, persecuted, prest, and trodden upon by our enemies, disquieted with threatnings, which also torture and dishearten some; for in pusillanimous dispositions fear makes words to be actions, and threats to be torments. Death 10 is a divine remedy which cures all these evils. Death alone is the cause that temporal miseries are not eternal. And I know not how that came to be feared, which brings with it as many helps, as the world brings damages. Danger it self is a sufficient motive to make us in love wth security. Death only secures us from troubles: Death heals, and glorifies all those wounds which are received in a good cause. When *Socrates* had drank off his *potion* of *hemlock*, he commanded that sacrifices should be offered to *Æsculapius*, as the *Genius* of *Medicine*. He knew that Death would cure him. It was the *Antidote* against that poysonous *Recipe* of the *Athenian* 20 *Parliament*. Tyranny travels not beyond Death, which is the Sanctuary of the good, and the *Lenitive* of all their sorrows.

Most ridiculous were the tears of *Xerxes*, and worthily checkt by his Captain *Artabazus*; when seated on the top of an hill, and viewing his great Army (wherein were so many hands as would have served to overturn the world, to levell mountains, and drain the seas, yea to violate Nature, and disturb Heaven with their noyse, and the smoak of their Camp) he fell to a childish whining, to consider in what a short portion of time all that haughty multitude, which now trampled upon the face of the earth, would be 30 layd quietly under it. He wept to think, that all those men (whose lives notwithstanding hee hastned to sacrifice to his mad ambition) should dye within the compasse of an hundred yeares The secular death, or common way of mortality, seemed very swift unto him, but the way of war & slaughter he minded not. It had been more rational in him to weep, because death was so slow and lazie, as to suffer so many impious, inhumane souldiers to live an hundred years, and disturb the peace and civill societies of Mankind. If as hee saw his Army from that hill, he had also seen the calamities and mischief they did, with the tears and 40 sorrows of those that suffered by them, he had dried his eyes, and

---

11 evils. *G* : evil *1654*   21 travels] travels *1654*

would not have mourned, though he had seen death seising upon
all those salvages, and easing the world of so vast an affliction.
He would not have feared that, which takes away the cause of
fear : That is not evill, which removes such violent and enormous
evills.   If I might ask those that have made experiment of life
and death, whither they would chuse (if it were granted them)
either to live again, or to continue in their state of dissolution, I
am sure none would chuse life but the wicked, & those that are
unworthy of it ; for no pious liver did ever repent of death, and
10 none ever will.   The Just desire not this life of the unjust, which
(were it offered them,) they would fear it more, (now being at rest,)
then ever they feared death, when they lived.   The story runnes
that *Stanislaus* the *Polonian*, a man of marvellous holinesse and
constancy ; had the opportunity to put this *question*, and the
respondent told him, that *he had rather suffer the paines of dissolution twice over again, then live once* : He feared one life, but did
not fear to dy thrice.

Having this Solution from the experienced, it is needless, and
fruitlesse to question the living.   If Soules were *Præexistent*, as
20 one *Origen* dreamt, as *Cebes, Plato, Hermes,* and other *Philosophers,*
the great Fathers of *Hereticks,* have affirmed ; Wee might have
reason to conclude, that they would obstinately refuse to be
imprisoned in the wombs of women, and wallow in Seminal
humours.   What if it were told them, that they must dwell nine
monthes in a thick darknesse, and more then nine years (perhaps
all the years of their sojourning) in hallucinations, and the darknesse of ignorance ? what if the paines, the exigencies, the hunger
and thirst they must endure, before they can be acquainted with
the miseries of life, were laid before them ? The Infant while he
30 is yet in the womb, is taught necessity.   Quest for foode makes
him violate that living Prison, and force his way into the World.
And now comes he forth, (according to the Sentiment of *Hippocrates,*) to seek for Victualls ; the provision which proceeded from
his Mother, being grown too little for him.   But he comes from
one prison into another, and breaks through the *first* to enlarge his
own, which he carries with him : But if the Soules thus incar-
cerated (like Prisoners through a grate) might behold the various
plagues and diseases of those that are at liberty, as *Palsies, Passions*
of the heart, *Convulsions, Stranguries,* the *Stone,* the *Gout,* the
40 *Wolfe,* the *Phagedæna,* and an hundred other horrid incurable
Evils, such as *Pherecides, Antiochus,* and *Herod* were tormented

38 *Palsies, G : Palsies 1654*

with, or that fearful sicknesse of *Leuthare,* which was so raging
and furious, that she did eat her own flesh, and drink her blood
in the extremity of the pain : Or if they might see those Evills,
which man himselfe hath sought and found out for himself; as
emulations, warres, bloodshed, confusion, and mutual destruction ;
Is there any doubt to be made, think you, but they would wish
themselves freed from such a miserable estate ; or that their intellectuall light were quite extinguished, that they might not behold
such horrid and manifold calamities. *Plato* imputed the *suspension*
of Reason in Infants, and the *hallucinations* of Childhood to the 10
terrour and astonishment of the *Soules,* which he supposed *them*
to be possessed with, because of their sudden translation from the
Empyreal light, into the darke and grosse prisons of flesh, and
this inferiour World ; as if such a strange and unexpected change
(like a great and violent fall,) had quite doated them, and cast
asleep their intellectuall faculties. *Proclus* assisted this conjecture
of *Plato,* with another argument drawne from the mutability, and
the multitude of Worldly Events, which in the uncertaine state of
this life, the Soules were made subject unto. Adde to this, that
the merriest portion of life, which is youth, is in both sexes be- 20
dewed with tears, and the flowers of it are sullied, and fade away
with much weeping, and frequent sadnesse. Children also want
not their sorrowes : The *Rod* blasteth all their innocent joyes, and
the sight of the School-master turnes their mirth into mourning.
Nay that last *Act* of life, which is the most desirable to the Soul,
I mean old Age, is the most miserable.

> *The plenteous Evills of frail life fill the old :*
> *Their wasted Limbs the loose skin in dry folds*
> *Doth hang about ; their joynts are numm'd and through*
> *Their veines not blood, but rheumes and waters flow.* 30
> *Their trembling bodies with a staffe they stay,*
> *Nor doe they breath, but sadly sigh all day :*
> *Thoughts tire their hearts, to them their very mind*
> *Is a disease ; their Eyes no sleep can find.*

Adde to these usuall infirmities, the confluence of adventious
maladies : For all the former distempers and corruptions of life
gather themselves together, and make head in old age ; when the
inward strength, and expulsive power of Nature is decayed, when
wee are almost dead, then do they revive and rage most of all.
Rivers are no where more full, nor more foule then towards the 40
Channell-end. But this generall decay I acknowledge to be
a great benefit, because it drives away all voluptuous and unseemly

20 which] wihch *1654*

delights from the aged, that their Soules may be lively and in health, when the hour of dissolution comes. And indeed it is necessary, that griefes and unpleasantnesse should lay hold upon age, because men (who are alwaies unwilling to think of dying,) may be thereby weaned from the delights of life, and learn to dye before the day of death. Seeing then, that the temporal life is in all its portions so full of misery, it is not irrational to conclude, that Soules (if they were *præexistent*,) would be very unwilling to submit to this sad Bondage of flesh and blood. Nor do I wonder 10 that *Isis*, in his *sacred Book*, writes, that the Soules, when they were commanded to enter into the bodies, were astonished, and suffered a kind of *Deliquium*, or traunce ; and that they did hisse and murmure, like to the suspirations of wind. *Camephes* sets down their complaints : Τί ταῖς δυστήναις ἡμῖν ἀπρεπὲς ὄντως πέπρακται, *&c. Miserable wretches ! in what have we so foulely trespassed, what offense so heinous and worthy of so horrible a punishment have we committed, as to be shut up and imprisoned for it, in these moist and cold carkasses? Our Eyes from henceforth shall not behold the Divine spirits, for wee shall onely peepe through two* 20 *small Spheres made of grosse and corrupt humours. When we look towards Heaven, we shall have onely the liberty to grone for the presence of our Creatour, but see him we may not ; for we shall see then by a Secondary light, which is the light of the lower World, and not be permitted to use our own discerning light, &c. We shall hear our* Kinred *rejoycing in the air, and mourn that we are not partakers of their liberty,* &c. *But thou great Father and maker of Spirits, who doest dispose of all thy works as it pleaseth thee, appoint we beseech thee some terme to our sad bondage, and let this punishment passe quickly over us, that we may be restored again to our celestiall liberty, to* 30 *behold (without obstruction) the perfect beauty of all thy works,* &c. They comforted themselves with the thought of the bodies dissolution, and petitioned before their captivity, that their inlargement might be hastned : when they were excluded from the heavenly life, there was no greater blessing then the death of the body, which sets an end to the earthly. Hee that loves death, hates a transitory corrupt condition, and he that hates his own life here, shall keep it unto life eternall.

I do verily believe, that to him that throughly considers it, no part of life can be desireable. It is altogether so full of sorrowes ; 40 It is a peece weaved of calamities and troubles, yea, life it selfe is its owne vexation. As those that travell in rough, uneven and mountainous roades are alwaies gasping and weary, which makes them sit down often, to recover their spent breath, and refresh themselves, that having reach'd the brow and crown of the hill, they may walk onwards with more delight, and be at leasure to feed their Eyes with the beauteous prospect, and freshnesse of those green & flowry plaines which lye extended before them : So this troublesome and tumultuous life hath need of death, for its ease and repast, as a state in which it doth repaire and strengthen it selfe against the fair Journey and progresse of eternity. Frail and weary life cannot last, and hold out untill the *Indiction* of immortality ; So long a journey cannot be performed without 10 subsiding ; A resting place must be had : Death is the *Inne* where we take up, that we may with more chearfullnesse set forwards, and be enabled to overtake, and to keep company with eternity. Nay, so fraile is life, that it cannot expect, or stay for the day of death without some prevening recreations : It travells by Stages, and Periodical Courses, where it breathes, and gathers strength against the next motion. As tyred travellours make frequent Pauses in the very Roade, and cannot stay for the refreshment of lodging ; So life, by reason of the importunity, and the multitude of humane troubles, cannot endure or hold out till it reacheth the *Inne,* which 20 is death ; but is driven to rest in the shade upon the way-side ; for sleep (the shadow of death) is nothing else but a reparation of weary and fainting life. So much more excellent then life is death, that life is driven to be sustained by so many deaths, that is to say, the mortal life is necessarily preserved by sleep, which is the usher & *Masquerade* of death. Reedes, because they are very weak and brittle, are strengthned with distinct knots or joynts, which makes their length firme, and keepes them from cleaving : So life, if it were not refreshed and mantained still by successive, set alleva- tions of certain prolusions of death, would fall asunder and vanish 30 upon its first appearance.

Hitherto we have discoursed of life, let us now consider death, and compare it with life. If death in its shadow and projection be the recreation of life, how delightfull will it be at home, or in it self ! Wearinesse is a preparative which makes rest pleasant : That *Recipe* which succeedes bitternesse, must needs be sweet. *Charidemus* used to say, *That through all temporal things there was a chaine drawne, whereof one link was* pain, *and the other* pleasure : *That these succeeded one another, and so* (said he) *after great sorrowes there come greater joyes.* What greater sorrowes can there be, then 40 the sorrowes of life ? There is therefore no greater pleasure then the pleasure of death, which succeeds those great sorrows. *Phalaris*

42 succeeds] su cceed *1654*

said, *That men held life to be pleasant, because they suspected death to be grievous and irksome.* He speaks after the sense of the people, and abuseth life, not esteeming it to be good, but because he thinks death to be Evill. I shall crosse his saying, and inferre that death should be esteemed pleasant, because wee are sure that life is painfull : But there is an appearance of something like errour, because we see many here, that passe through their whole lives without any troubles or discontents. That felicity is rare and adulterate, and happens most commonly to
10 those that desire it not : look not upon those few which escape in this storme, but upon those which are drowned : these last are innumerable, though it is thought otherwise, because they are sunk into the bottom, and cannot be seen.

Admit not, I beseech thee, for a testimony against Death, those ejulations and tears which darken Funerals, and make foul weather in the fairest faces. Opinion makes the people compassionate, and they bewail not the party that is dead, but their owne frailty. Call not for evidence to the teares of strangers, because thou knowest not whence they flow ; but call for it to thine own,
20 for none of us is happy or miserable but in his own sense which makes us any thing. What reason hast thou to think life better then death, because others mourne when thou dyest, who when thou wert born, didst weep thy selfe ? It is madnesse to judge our selves miserable, because others think so. The solemnities of death are contrary to the ceremonies of life. At the birth of man others laugh, but he himself weeps. At his death others weep, but surely hee rejoyceth, unlesse his ill life hath made his death deadly. Nor must thou think that his joy is either little or none at al, because it is not manifested unto thee : Thou mayst lye
30 watching by the side of one that dreams of Heaven, & is conversing with Angels, but unlesse hee tells it thee when he is awaked, thou canst discover no such thing while he sleepes. The Infant that is born weeping, learns to laugh in his sleep, as *Odo* and *Augustine* have both observed : So, he that bewailed his birth with tears, welcomes the shadow of his death with smiles : He presaged miseries to follow his nativity, and beatitude his dissolution. Weeping is natural ; tears know their way without a guide : Mirth is rude, and comes on slowly, and very late, nor comes it then without a supporter and a leader : It must be taught, and acquired.
40 Weeping comes with the Infant into the world ; Laughing is afterwards taught him ; the Nurse must both teach, and invite

12 though] thought *1654*

him to it. When he sleeps, then he sips and tasteth joy; when
he dies, then he sucks and drinkes it. Mourning and grief are
natural, they are born with us; Mirth is slow-paced, and negligent
of us: The sense of rejoycing (if we beleeve *Avicenna*) comes not
to the most forward child till after the fortieth day. Men therefore
weep at thy death, because it is an experiment they have not tryed;
and they laugh at thy birth, because the miseries of thy life must
not be born by them. Thou onely art the infallible diviner of
thy own frail condition, who refusest it with teares, which are the
most proper expressions of unwilling, & constrained nature.   10

But as the ceremonies of Life and Death are contrary, so he
that is born, and he that dyes, have different events. Death to
some seems to destroy all, but she restores all: By discomposing
things she puts them in their order: For he that inverts things
that were before inverted, doth but reduce them to their right
Positure. The Funeral rite of the *Tebitenses* (who are certain
East-Indians) is to turn the inside of their garments outward;
they manifest that part which before was hidden, and conceale
that part which before was manifest; by which they seeme, in my
opinion, to point at the liberty of the soul in the state of death, 20
and the captivity of the body, whose redemption must bee expected
in the end of the world. This inversion by death is reparation,
and a preparative for that order wherein *all things shall be made new*.
Most true is that saying of the Royal Preacher, Ἀγαθὸν ὄνομα
ὑπὲρ ἔλαιον ἀγαθὸν, καὶ ἡμέρα τοῦ θανάτου ὑπὲρ ἡμέραν γενέσεος.
*A good name is above precious ointment, and the day of death is
better then the day of ones birth.* But thou wilt ask, To whom is
the day of death better than the day of his nativity? It is in the
first place to him that dies; True (thou wilt say) if he be a just and
holy man; Yea (say I) though he be wicked. Who doubts that 30
there can happen in all their lives a better day to the just and honest,
then the day of death, which frees them both from seeing, and from
feeling the miseries which are in this world? As for the unjust,
it is most certain, that no day can be more beneficiall to them,
then that which sets an end to their impieties, tyranny, perjury, and
sacriledge. To deny a sword to one that would murther himself, is
benevolence; to deny money to a Gamester that would presently
cast it away, is courtesie; and to deny life to those that would use
it to their owne damnation, is Mercy, and not Judgement. But to
whom besides these is the day of death better then the day of 40
life? Certainly to God Almighty; because in that day when the
wicked dye, his Justice on them, and his Mercy towards his own are

conspicuous to all, and acknowledged by all.   And to whom else?
Not to speak of the rich and ambitious, It is good to all men, to
the whole Creation, and to Nature it self: For in that day the
fair order and prerogative of Nature is vindicated from the rage
and rape of lustfull, intemperate persons : It becomes constant,
consonant, and inviolable, by putting off those gross vestiments
wch make her productions subject to the assaults and violence of
man, who is the most perverse and shamelesse defacer of Gods
Image in himself, and the most audacious and abhominable con-
10 temner of his Ordinances in his works, by using them to a contrary
end, and quite different from that which their wise Creator made
them for.

   But let us not consider the goodnesse of death by those evils
onely which it freeth us from, but by the blessings also which it
brings along with it.   Their soules are by some men less valued
then Fortune and temporal power ; Some cast away their lives to
winne a Crowne, yea the Crowne, and the Kingdome of another.
They plot to forfeit a Crown of Eternall glory, by usurping a
transitory one : They murther their owne soules by shedding the
20 blood of some innocent persons, permitted to be overcome by
men, that they might have power with God, and prevail.   Shall the
short soveraignty and sway of some small corners and spots of
earth be compared to the everlasting triumphs in the Kingdom of
Heaven?   The death of the sufferer is in this case the most gainfull ; the more he loseth by it upon earth, his gain is by so much
the greater in heaven.   The shorter our stay is here, our time
above (if reckon'd from the day of our death) is the longer, but
hath no end at all ; and the more our sufferings are, the greater
shall our glory be.   *Hegesias* the *Cyrenian,* when he praised death,
30 promised not these blessings of Immortality, but onely an end of
temporall miseries ; and yet he did so far prevail with his Auditors,
that they preferred death to life ; they contemned the one, and so
lusted after the other, that they would not patiently expect it, but
did impatiently long for it ; they fel upon their own swords, and
forced death to come on, by turning life out of doors before her
lease was out; and had not *Ptolomie* by a special *Edict* silenced
his Doctrine, he had robbed him of more subjects then ever War
or the Plague could have taken from him.   Before the blessed
Jesus had made his entrance through the veile, and opened the
40 way to heaven, the reward of righteousnesse and sanctity was long
life, the peculiar blessing of the *Patriarchs* : It was a favour then
not to appear before *perfect purity,* a *Judge* of infinite, and all-

seeing *brightnesse*, without an *Advocate* or friend to speak for us, in the strength and heat of irregular youthfulnesse, when not so much as time had subdued or reformed the affections; but now because Christ is gone thither before, and hath provided a place for us, the greatest blessing, and highest reward of holynesse, is short life, and an unseasonable, or a violent death: For those harsh *Epithets* (which are but the inventions of fearfull, and sinful livers) are swallowed up of immortality, & an unspeakable heavenly happinesse which crowns and overflowes all those that dye in *Christ.* Wee consider not those blessings which death leads us 10 to, and therefore it is, that we so frequently approve of our most frivolous, worldly wishes, and sit weeping under the burthens of life, because we have not more laid upon us. A certain groundlesse suspition, that death is evill, will not suffer us to believe it to be good, though the troubles of life make us complement, and wish for it every day. This foolish fear and inconstancy of man, *Locmannus* (one of the most antient *Sages* of *Persia,* and admitted also into the Society of the *Arabian Magi,*) hath pleasantly demonstrated in the *person* of an *Old man,* loaded with a great burthen of *Wood*; which having quite tyred him, he threw down, 20 and called for *death* to come and ease him: Hee had no sooner called, but *death* (which seldome comes so quickly to those that call for it in earnest,) presently appeared, and demands the reason, *why he called? I did call thee* (said he) *to help me to lift this burthen of wood upon my back, which just now fell off.* So much are we in love with miseries, that we fear to exchange them with true happinesse: we do so doate upon them, that we long to resume them again, after wee have once shaked them off; being either faithlesse and wavering, or else forgetfull of those future joyes, which cannot be had without the funerall and the death of our 30 present sorrowes.

What man distrest with hunger, if hee sate upon some Barren and Rockie bank, bounded with a deep River, where nothing could be expected but Famine, or the Fury of wild beasts; and saw beyond that stream a most secure and pleasant *Paradise,* stored with all kinds of bearing Trees; whose yielding boughes were adorned and plenteously furnished with most fair and delicate fruites; If it were told him that a little below, there was a boate, or a bridge to passe over, would refuse that secure conveyance, or be affeard to commit himself to the calm and per- 40 spicuous streames, choosing rather to starve upon the brink, then

13 worldly] wordly *1654*

U

to passe over, and be relieved? O foolish men! For Gold, which is digged out of the *Suburbs* of Hell, we trust our selves to the raging and unstable Seas, guarded with a few planks, and a little pitch; *where onely a Tree* (as *Aratus* saith) *is the partition betwixt death and us:* And after many rough disputes with violent perills, and the sight of so many more; wee perish in the unhappy acquisition of false happinesse; the Sea either resisting, or else punishing our covetousnesse. But to passe into our Heavenly Country, into the bosome and embraces of Divinity, into a Realm where
10 Fortune reigns not, wee dare not so much as think of it. Who after long banishment, and a tedious pilgrimage, being now come near to his native Country, and the house of his Father, where his Parents, his brethren, and friends expect him with longing, would then turn back, and choose to wander again, when he might have joy, when he might have rest? God the *Father* expects us, the blessed *Jesus* expects us, the mild and mourning *Dove* doth long and grone for us: The holy Virgin-mother, the Angells our friends, and the Saints our kindred, are all ready to receive us. It is through death that wee must passe unto them: Why grieve
20 we then, yea, why rejoyce wee not to have this passage opened?

But let us grant that death were not inevitable, yea, that it were in the power of man, and that every one had a particular prerogative given him over destinie; So that this greatest *Necessity* were the greatest freedome, yea, that man could not dye, though he desired death: Yet in this very state, would hee be troubled with *Fortune* and *Hope*. He would be a fool that would not venture to dye, to enjoy true felicity: That would choose rather to live alwaies in the changeable state of most unchangeable and lasting miseries, then to put an end to them all by dying once. It is madnesse to
30 feare death, which (if it reigned not upon the Earth) wee would both desire and pray for. It was wisely adjudged by *Zaleucus*, that death ought to be publickly proclaimed, though men had been immortall. Had death been arbitrary, and at every mans pleasure, I believe we had esteemed it as desireable as any other joy; now because it is Imperial, and above us, let it not seem too much, if wee grant it to be tollerable. It was absurdly said by one, *that death was a necessary Evill, and ought therefore to be patiently born.* His *Inference* was good, though from a bad *Principle*: Death is rather a necessary good: And if necessity makes Evils to
40 be tolerable, there is more reason, it should make good so. Death because it is good, should be made much of; and wee should rejoyce that it is necessary, because that makes it certain. How

great a good is that, by which it is necessary that we be not miserable! Which frees the captive without ransome, dismisseth the oppressed without the consent of the oppressour, brings home the banished in spite of the banisher, and heales the sicke without the pain of *Physick* : Which mends all that Fortune marred ; which is most just ; which repaires and makes even all the disorders and in-equalities made by time and chance ; which is the blessed necessity that takes away necessary Evills? He had erred lesse, if he had mentioned a necessity of bearing life patiently, whose more proper definition that sorry proverbe is ; for it casts us into necessary 10 Evills against our will, and is the cause that wee willfully meddle with Evills that are unnecessary. It is a discreet method of nature, that infuseth the Soules into the body in such a state that is not sensible of their captivity, lest they should murmur at the decrees of the great *Archiplast.* What wise man that were neare the terme of his appointed time, if he were offered to have life renew'd, would consent to be born again, to be shut up in flesh, & fed for nine months with excrementitious obscenities, to bear all the ignominies of Nature, all the abuses of Fortune, to resume the ignorance of Infancie, the feares of Childhood, the dangers of 20 youth, the cares of manhood, and the miseries of old age? I am of beliefe that no man did ever live so happily, as to be pleased with a repetition of past life. These Evills which with our owne consent wee would not have reiterated, wee are driven into without our consent : They are necessarily inferred, that they may be willingly borne, to shew the necessity of Patience. Wee are born on condition, that wee must dye. Death is the price or reward of life : It is the Statute-law of mankind, and that ought to be born as a publick good, which (were it not already enacted) would be the spontaneous petition of all men. Certainly if life 30 were without the *Jubile* of death, it were just to refuse it, as a servitude which hath no year of release.

Let us now clearly prove, that death is not Evill, out of her assimilation and conformity to those things, which are most ex-cellently good. None leade a better life, then those that live so, as if they were dead, *Rom. Chap. 6. ver. 7. For he that is dead, is freed from Sinne.* Therefore that which is the exemplar of good-nesse, cannot be Evill : The onely true praise of the living, is to assimilate death : He is the most commendable liver, whose life is dead to the World, and he is the most honest that lives the least 40 to it ; whose Soul listens not to the body, but is at a constant dis-tance from it, as if they were dissolved ; or though it sojournes in

it, yet is not defiled by it, but is separated from sensuality, and united to Divinity. What is the reason (thinkest thou,) that the Divine *Secrets* are revealed to men most commonly in their sleep; because that similitude of death is most pleasing to God. Life is a wild and various madnesse, disturbed with passions, and distracted with objects; Sleepe (like death) settles them all; it is the minds *Sabbath*, in which the Spirit, freed from the Senses, is well disposed and fitted for Divine intimations. The Soul is then alive to it selfe, while the body reigns not, and the affections are
10 ecclipsed in that short *Interlunium* of the temporall life.

Philosophie, or humane Knowledge is nothing else but a Contemplation of death; not to astonish or discourage men, but first to informe, and then to reform them : for the fruit of Philosophy is Virtue, and Virtue is nothing else but an imitation of death, or the Art of dying well, by beginning to dye while we are alive. Virtue is a certain *Primrose*, a *prolusion* or *Assay* of dying. Therefore that by which man becomes immortall and eternall is the *preface*, and the *Inchoation* of death. This is the main drift of *Philosophy*, to make life comfortable by conforming it unto death,
20 and to make death immortality by regulating life. Death is intollerable to him only that hath not mortified his desires, while he yet lives ; but expects to swallow up death, and all the powers of it at once; that is to say, in the hour of death. We cut our meate, and feed on it by bits, lest we should be choaked by swallowing it whole; so death, if it be assayed and practised by degrees, will be both pleasant in the tast, and wholsome in the digestion; if we mortifie one affection to day, and another to morrow. Hee that cannot carry a great burthen at once, may carry it all by portions. *Philosophy* acts the part of death upon
30 the Stage of life : it kills sensuality, and makes death most easie to be born by teaching us to dye dayly. What can be more grievous then death unto him, who together with his own, feeles the paine of a thousand other dying cupidities? We faile not to bewaile the losse of one thing, whither honour, pleasure, or a friend : How much more when we loose all at a blow, and loose eternal life in one short minute? The Soule of the wise man frees her selfe from the body in an acceptable time, she casts off the delectations of the flesh, and the cares of this World while it is day-light, that shee may enjoy her self, and be acquainted with God
40 before the night comes. She finds by experience, that her forces are more vigorous, and her light more discerning, when she is not sullied with Earthly negotiations, and the grosse affections of the

body; she finds that covetousnesse, love and feare permit her not
to see the truth, and that the affaires of the body are the *Remora's*
of the Spirit: and therefore she concludes, that he must neglect
the cryes of the flesh, and be attentive onely to the voyce of God;
and upon these considerations, shee shakes off that Bondage; she
deserts the familiarity and consultations of blood, that she may
advise with, and discerne the most clear light of truth; she casts
off pleasures, by which even Spirits are made subject to sense and
pollution. The truth is most pure, and will not be manifested,
but to the pure and the undefiled: Therefore all the scope and 10
the end of Virtue is, to separate the Soul from the body, and to
come as near death as possibly may be, while wee are yet alive.
This is the cause that wise men do so much love and long for
death, at least they fear it not. How can he feare death, who by
dying passeth into the life of the blessed? Who hath already
delivered himselfe from more feares and inconveniences then
death can free him from? Yea from those dangers which make
death fearfull? Who before his dying day, hath disarmed and
overcome death? Shall he that all his life-time desired to be
separated from the body, repine at the performance and fullfilling 20
of it? It were most ridiculous, if hasting towards home, thou
wouldst refuse the helpe of another to convey thee thither with
more speed, and be angry at thy arrivall in that Port, whither thou
didst bend thy course since the first day thou didst set forth.
There is no man that seeking for a friend, will not rejoyce when
he hath found him. No man will be angry if another perfects
what he did begin, but was not able to finish. Nature by death
perfects that which Virtue had begun in life, and the endeavour
dies not, but is continued, and thrives by a necessary transplanta-
tion. While he yet lived, he denyed himselfe the use of the body, 30
because it hindred the course of the Soul; and the body dying,
he doth but persist in the same just denyall. It is a greater
pleasure to want, then not to use what wee doe not want.

This *Correlation* of *Death* and *Virtue* I shall exhibite, or lay out
to your view, by a discussion of those honours which each of them
procures. As Virtue by the Consideration of death, ordereth and
preserves her Majesty; so by imitating death, she obtaines the
reverence and admiration of all: What more reverend thing can
wee labour for, then that, which by our reverence of it, makes the
worst livers to be reputed not bad? As those who are Evill, are 40
loath to believe themselves to be such, because of an innate
reverence due from every man to Virtue, which makes them love

18 fearfull] fearfull *1654*

the repute of Excellencie, though not inherent, and rejoyce to be accounted good of themselves, or in their own esteem, though they be evill, taking pleasure in that self-deception : So those who have beene vitious in their lives (out of the reverence wee owe to death,) wee dare not speak evill of when they are once dead ; Nay, it is not civil, nor pious, to mention the dead without commendation, either by *praise*, or else by *prayer*, & our *Christian well wishes*, as if they had been most deserving in their lives. So powerfull is the Majesty of death, that it makes the most contemptible, vener-
10 able. Those we most envie while they live, we speak well of when they are dead. Excellent is that observation of *Mimnermus*,

> *Against the Virtuous man we all make head,*
> *And hate him while he lives, but praise him dead.*

Envy pursues us not beyond the grave, and our honour is not free and secure til we are layd in it. That humble and quiet *dust* stops the lying and malicious mouth. *Socrates* foresaw that his *draught* of *hemlock* would (after his death) make his very enemies his worshippers : He saw his *Statues* erected by the same *decree* that did cast him downe : And what was the *motive* (thinkst
20 thou) that made his enemies worship him dead, whom they persecuted living ? There is amongst the people a secret tradition that whispers to them, that *those who are freed from the miseries of this life, live happily in another world.* Now happinesse even in their opinion is worthy of honour ; therefore the honour or veneration which death exacts, is a certain tribute, or a debt rather that is due to happinesse ; and if for this thou wilt advise with thy *Aristotle*, he will not deny it. The *Lacedemonians* bestowed the *Olympick* palms and honours (which whosoever won in his life time, he was accounted most happy) upon all that dyed,
30 without exception, or extenuation ; adorning the *statutes* of some, and the *tombes* of all with the green and flourishing *Laurel*, esteeming every one of the dead as happy as the most fortunate Victor that lived. The antient *Romans* held the greatest honour of the living to consist in the renown of their dead Ancestors : They judged him to be highly honoured, that was enjoyed by any dying persons to perform some extraordinary service for them, as an Embassie, or some other weighty negotiation : And * *Calli-stratus* in his first book of *Questions* affirmes,

* One of the Coun-
sellors of Alexand.
40 *the great.*

That Embassadors so employed are the most honourable ; because that the suffrages and election of dying men is most venerable, as being then upon the borders of

immortality, and discerning more then those who are yet in the
midst of life, and more in the clouds of thick-sighted humanity.
That honour is the greatest which is done us by the honourable.
Nor is this glory of death a *Relative* of the Soul only ; Looke well
upon the body, that provision of the worms, a frail and perishing
object, but ful of Majesty. We are nothing so moved, nor doe we
so gravely compose our selves at the presence of a King, as at the
sight of a dead body. With how much awfulnesse doth it lye along !
with what a secret mysterious command doth it check all about
it ! It is a silent, abstruse *Philosopher*, and makes others so too : 10
Nor is it onely venerable, but sacred, and the *Depositum*, and
Index of an almighty Restauratour. The honour of Sepulture is
a part of Religion.

  Now, if it be argued that goodnesse consists onely in utility,
or benefits, it follows that nothing is good, but that which
profiteth : Death then is the best, and the greatest subordinate
good of all ; for the death of others benefits those that see it,
and their own death is most profitable to those that mind it.
The *Lamæ* (who are the Priests of the *Tebitenses*) are in this point
the most excellent Philosophers in the world : When they prepare 20
to celebrate prayers, they summon the people *The pipes of death*
together with the hollow, whispering sounds of *used by the* Lamæ.
certain Pipes made of the bones of dead men ; they have also
Rosaries, or Beads made of them, which they carry alwayes about
them, and they drink constantly out of a Skull : Being asked the
reason of this Ceremony by *Antonie Andrada*, who first found
them out ; one that was the chiefest amongst them, told him, that
they did it,

                 Ad Fatorum memoriam.

They did therefore pipe with the bones of dead men, that those 30
sad whispers might warn the people of the swift and invisible
approach of death, whose *Musick* they termed it, and affirmed it
to be the most effectuall of any ; That the Beads they wore did
put them in minde of the fraile estate of their bodies, and did in
prayer-time regulate and humble their thoughts ; That a constant
commemoration of death was as beneficial to the Soul as devotion,
& therefore they carryed them alwaies about them as the powerfull
Memento's of their approaching departure out of the Land of the
living. To this he added, that their drinking in a skull did mortifie their affections, represse pleasures, and imbitter their tast, 40
lest they should relish too much the delights of life ; Lastly, he
added that this constant representation of death, was an Antidote

        37 powerfull] powefull *1654*

against all the sinfull Excesses and deviations of man. With the same Medicine they secured themselves from other iniquities : When they were to swear concerning any thing, they laid their hands upon certain *Images* set with the bones of dead men, by which ceremony they were put in mind of the last Judgement, and the Account which the *dead* and the *Quick* must give in that great, that impartiall and censorious day. Certainly this was no barbarous, but a very humane and elegant *Philosophy*, which taught men to season, and redeeme all the daies of their lives,
10 with the memory of the one day of their death. Admirable was the memory of *Mithridates*, who was master of two and twenty Languages, and could readily discourse in every one of them ; and no lesse happy was that of *Cyrus, Themistocles* and *Seneca* ; but a constant memory of mans miseries, and his death exceeds them all. As the rootes of the tree in the Ile of *Maloga*, upon that side which lookes towards the *East*, are an Antidote or preservative, but those which spread *Westward* are poysonous and deadly : So the *Cogitations* of a Christian, which are the *Roots* by which hee stickes to Heaven (for every Christian is a *Tree*
20 reversed,) when they look towards the *West*, or setting point of life, are healing and salutiferous ; but those which reflect still upon temporall things, and his abode in this World are destructive and deadly. Nature doth every minute commend unto us this memoriall of death. *Hermes* in his *sacred book* contends, that respiration was given to man, as a sign of that last efflation, in which the Soul parts from the body. Wee should therefore as often as wee breath, remember death, when we shall breath our last, when the Spirit shall returne unto him that gave it. Our whole life is nothing else but a repeated resemblance of our last expiration ; by
30 the emission of our breath we doe retaine it, and (as I may say) spin it out. God gave it not *continual* and *even*, like fluent *streames*, or the calme and unwearied *Emanations* of light, but refracted and shifting, to shew us that we are not permanent but transitory, and that the Spirit of life is but a *Celestial Gale* lent us for a time, that by using it well, we may secure it Eternally. Another *Hermetist* adviseth us, *Adorare relliquias ventorum*, to make much of, and to honour our Soules, which are the *breathings*, and last *dispensations* of the still fruitful, and liberal creator : This we can never do but by a frequent study of our dissolution, and the frailty of the body. Of
40 such an effectuall goodness is death, that it makes men good before it comes, and makes sure of Eternity by a virtuous disposing of time. Thinke not that evill, which sends from so far the beams

of its goodnesse.   There is no good liver but is a debtor to death,
by whose lendings, and premunitions we are furnished and fitted
for another world.

The certainty of it, and the incertainty of the time and manner,
(which is the onely circumstance that seemes to offend us,) if it
were seriously considered, deserves to be the most pleasing &
acceptable ; for amongst all the wondrous Ordinances of Divine
providence, there is none more Excellent for the Government of
man then death, being so wisely disposed of, that in the height of
incertainty it comprehends and manifests an infallible certainty. 10
God would have us to be alwaies good, to keepe in his likenesse
and Image : Therfore it is his will, that we should be alwaies
uncertaine of our most certain death.   Such is his care of us,
lest the knowledge of a long life, and a late death should encourage
us to multiply our transgressions, as the notice of a swift dissolution might dishearten and astonish us.   But being left now in
a possibility of either, we are taught to live soberly, and to expect
the time of our change in all holynesse and watchfullnesse.   The
possibility of dying shortly, doth lessen the cares of life, and
makes the difficulties of Virtue easie.   Bondage and Slavery (if it 20
be but short,) is to those that suffer it the lighter by so much :
And a large allowance of time makes us slow to Virtue, but a short
portion quickens us, and the incertainty of that very shortnesse
makes us certaine to be good.   For who would weep, and vexe
himself for worldly provisions, if he certainly knew that he should
live but one month ? and how dares he laugh, or be negligent of
his Salvation, that knowes not whither hee shall live to see one
day more, yea, one hour ?   The incertainty of death makes us
suspect life, and that suspition keepes us from sinning.   The
world was never fouler, nor more filled with abominations, then 30
when life was longest, when abused Nature required an Expiation
by waters, and the generall submersion of her detestable defilers.
Theophrastus did unjustly to raile at Nature, and condemne her
of partiality, when he envyed the long life of some *plants* and
inferiour *creatures*, as the *Oake*, the *Hart*, the *Ravens* ; some of
which live to *feed* and *flye* up and down in the World above *five
hundred* years.   He quarrelled with the wise dispensations of
Divinity, because a slight *suite* of feathers, and a renew'd *dresse* of
greene leaves could weare out a building that lodged a rationall
Soul, and the breath of the Almighty.   Both his *wish* and his 40
reason were erroneous : He erred in desiring long life, and in
judging happinesse to consist in the multitude of yeares, and not

the number of good workes. The shortnesse of life is lengthned
by living well: When life was reckond by centuries, the innumerable sins of the living so offended God, that it repented him to
have made impenitent man: Those that sinned out of confidence
of life he punished with sudden destruction. That long-liv'd
generation had made the world unclean, and being polluted by
their lives, it was purged by their deaths. He shorten'd afterwards
the lease of life, reducing it to an hundred and twenty years, that
by the diligence of frequent death, he might reform the past
10 disorders of long life, and prevent them for the future, teaching
both sexes to amend their lives by giving them death for their
next neighbours. So beneficiall is death, so much profits the
certainty of it, and as much the incertainty: The ignorance of the
day of death is in effect the same with the knowledge of it; the
first makes us watch, lest it come upon us unawares; and the last
(though it might name the day to us) yet could it not arme us
better against it, perhaps not so well. This incertainty of dying,
certainly secures us from many errors; it makes us prudent,
provident, and not evill. Death therefore is a device of the
20 Almighty, and a wise instrument of divine policy. *Zaleucus* so
highly approved of it, that he was about to enact and proclaime
a Law for dying, had he not found it already published by the
edict of Nature: And in his Preface to those Laws made for the
Locrenses, he warns them, Τίθεσθαι πρὸ ὀμμάτων τὸν καιρὸν τοῦτον,
&c. To have alwayes before their eyes that time, which is to
every one the end of life, because a hearty repentance for all
former injuries seiseth upon all men that thinke of death, and an
earnest desire or wishing, that all their actions in life had been
just. Wherefore it is expedient that in all our dealings and
30 thoughts death should act a part, and be our familiar counsellor,
ever present with us; so shall we be carefull to doe all things
virtuously and justly. Death then is most necessary to govern
mankinde, because the memory of it keeps us in awe, and conformable to virtue. All Commonwealths that follow the method
of Nature, must approve of this Law of *Zaleucus,* and death in all
their consultations should guide their lives.

Certainly in the Government of the rebellious Generation of
Man, Death hath been the most awfull Engine of the Deity;
without this stern he guided them not: When man was immortall,
40 God saw it necessary to preserve his immortality by death; he
injoyned the Law of Abstinence to *Adam,* under the penalty of
dying, which is continued still by the same artifice of death, lest

iniquities should be immortal, & wickedness should escape punishment : by the patience and submission of his only Son to death
he restored dead men to life, he conferred upon him all his lost
honours, renewd and confirmed his old prerogative, and together
with the salvation of his Soule gave him a sure promise, that his
body allso should be made Immortal ; but in all these favours,
and after full reconciliation, he would not remove death, but continued it still, and the incertainty as well as the certainty of it.
This divine devise of death so pleased God, and was so necessary
for the good of man, that though by the merits of his dying Son 10
he changed all the former things, blotting out ordinances, abolishing Ceremonies, & opening the gates of Heaven to all believers,
yet would not he Exterminate death. It was out of his mercy
that he refused to abrogate it, that while corruption reigned, death
also might reign over it, lest this poyson should want its Antidote.
We have therefore no just cause to complain of death, which is
an Invention conducing to our great good, and the incertainty of
the time (though it most vexeth us) is notwithstanding the most
beneficial Circumstance that attends it. The time of life is
certainly known, & there is but one entrance into the light of this 20
World : The Ceremony of dying is not formal ; It keeps not to
one time, nor one manner, but admits of all times, and many
manners. Life comes into the World but one way, but hath
many waies to go out. It was the benevolence of God to open
so many doors to those that flye for refuge. One way is more
then enough to find out dangers, but to escape them, many are
but necessary. Death is not a burthen of seaven or nine monthes,
but life must have time before it sets forth. And what are the
first encounters of it ? Tears and Bonds. It cannot avoyd Evills,
and it is afeared to bear them ; therefore it delaies time, and 30
when it cannot lurk any longer, it comes forth Crying. Death
leads us forth to joy and liberty : Therefore it stayes not, it seeks
no corners nor protractions. Nor doth death free us onely from
suffering Evills, but keeps us also from doing any : To be good
every day, thou must dye dayly. The incertainty also of the
time of death, and the manner of it, like a busie Monitour, warnes
thee to do good, and to be good at all times, and in every place,
private or publick : And the inevitablenesse of it takes away all
Excuse or pretensions for thy impreparation.

The Glory of death, is also much augmented by its facility, in 40

---

1 immortal,] tall, *catchword 1654*   20 into] to *1654* : in- *catchword*
40 *space for fresh paragraph end of original page* 170. *Catchword* mented
follows space.

redressing the difficulties of life. It is not without the Divine
counsel, and a speciall priviledge that the Soule of man is so
easily parted from the body; the life of beasts is more tenacious,
and will suffer much indignitie and fury before it leaves them.
There is no living creature more fraile, none more weak then
man; the lightest stroake fells him; the Soul is very nice, and
will quickly cast off the body if it persists but in the least Indisposition. A single hair killed *Fabius*, and a Grape *Anacreon*;
these contemptible instruments destroy'd them as effectually as
10 the thunderbolt did *Esculapius.* *Coma* dyed as easily as he
could wish, and *Baptista Mirandulus* as he could think: His
Soule quitted his body without any grudging, without a disease,
without poyson, without violence, or any fatall mischance.
No door can keep death out, it defeats life with its own weapons,
and kills us with the very Cordials and comforts of it. Perhaps
no kind of death is more violent then that which sets upon
us with the forces of life, because it kills when life is most
vigorous and pleasant. Their owne wishes have destroyed many:
And life hath oftentimes perished by her own contrivements.
20 *Clidemus* was killed with honour, *Diagoras* with joy, *Plato* with
rest, and *Philemon* with laughter. This last is both a merry, and
a frequent destroyer, and freed *Sicily* from one Tyrant. Death
also makes use sometimes of our very virtues to exanimate us:
Shame killed *Diodorus*, and the Mother of *Secundus* the Philosopher dyed with blushing, and an excessive modestie. Life is
a fraile possession, it is a flower that requires not rude and high
winds, but will fall in the very whispers and blandishments of fair
weather. It is folly to labour to retain that which wil away; to
fly from that which will meet us every where, yea, in the way we
30 fly, is a vain and foolish industry. Whither we seek death or
avoyd it, it will find us out: Our way to fly, and our very flight
end both in death; by hasting from it, we make hast to it. Life
is a journey, whose end cannot be mist; it is a steady ayming at
dissolution: Though we fetch wide Compasses, and traverse our
way never so often, we can neither lengthen it, nor be out of it:
What path soever we take, it is the Port-roade to death. Though
youth and age are two distant *Tropicks* of life, yet death is as
near to the one, as to the other: And though some live more,
and some lesse, yet death is their equal neighbour, and will visit
40 the young as soon as the old. Death is a Crosse, to which many
waies leade, some direct, and others winding, but all meet in one
Center: It matters not which thou takest, nor whither thou art

young or aged : But if thou beest young, thou maist come sooner thither, then the old, who is both doting and weary. It was necessary that a Sanctuary being provided for the distressed, the way to it should be easie, pervious, and at an indifferent distance from all parts. Good should be diffusive, and the gate that leads to it, must be without doors and bolts. The entrance into this life, is narrow and difficult, it is difficultly attained, difficultly retained, and lyes alwaies in the power of another. Every man may take life from us, none can take death. Life is subject to the Tyranny of men, but death is not ; life makes Tyrants, and death unmakes them. Death is the slaves prerogative royall, and the Sabbath of the afflicted. *Leo Iconomachus* the Emperor, made the birth of both sexes tributary : but death never paid taxation. It was not lawfull in his reigne to get Children without paying for them ; every Infant so soon as borne, was to give him contribution, they paid then the Excise of life. Death onely frees us from these Impositions of Tyrants.

And wilt thou then condemn liberty, and that maturity of death by which it ripens every age? wilt thou the divine liberality blame, because thy life is short, or may be so? thou hast no reason to find fault with the years already given thee, because thou shalt not have more : thou mayst as well quarrel with Nature, because she made not thy dimensions larger, and thy body heavier by eighty or a hundred pounds : he that measured thy proportion, measured thy time too : and too much of this last would have been as troublesome and unweildy as too much of the first : for

> *Long life, opprest with many woes,*
> *Meets more, the further still it goes.*

Death in every age is seasonable, beneficial, and desirable : It frees the old man from misery, the youthfull from sin, and the infant from both. It takes the aged in the fullnesse of their time ; It turnes the flowers of youth into fruit ; and by a compendious secret improvement, matures infancy, leading it into the Gate of Heaven, when it cannot go one step upon Earth, and giving it the wings of a Dove to flye, and be at rest, before it can use its feet.

To these past arguments of the goodnesse of death, I shall adde another. Death in the old world, (before the manifestation of God in the flesh,) was the publick index, or open signe of hidden divinity. It is the gift of God, who gives nothing but what is good. The Divell playing the Ape, and labouring to imitate the Inimitable *Jehovah,* did by asserting death to be the greatest good,

19 the (*space*) 1654 : then (?)

mainly fortifie those abominable rites and honours conferred upon
him by his blind worshipers : When they petitioned him for the
greatest blessing that the Gods could give to man, he (by the permission of the true God whom they had deserted) would within
three daies strangle them in their beds, or use some other invisible
meanes to set an end to their daies.   Thus he served *Triphonius*,
Agamedes, and *Argia* for her three Sons: This miserable mother
requested of him, that hee would give the best thing to her children, that could be given to men : her petition was granted, and
10 within a very short time they received that which she thought to be
the worst, namely death.   So great is the ods betwixt seeming to
be, and being really: betwixt opinion and truth: yea that death
which we judge to be the worst, I meane the immature, is oftentimes the best.

> *What greater good had deckt great* Pompey's *Crown*
> *Then death, if in his honours fully blown,*
> *And mature glories he had dyed? those piles*
> *Of huge successe, lowd fame & lofty stiles*
> *Built in his active youth, long, lazie life*
> 20 *Saw quite demolished by ambitious strife:*
> *He lived to weare the weake and melting snow*
> *Of lucklesse Age, where garlands seldom grow.*
> *But by repining fate torne from the head*
> *Which wore them once, are on another shed.*

Neither could I ever grant that the death of Infants and Children, though commonly bewail'd as unseasonable, were the parents
misfortunes, but the courtesies rather, and mercies of the almighty.
To omit *Amphiaraus*, and other Ethnick instances ; I shall make
use of a true and Christian History, which in these later years,
30 was the great admiration of King *Philips* Court. *Didacus Vergara*,
a most noble hopefull youth, adorned with all those vertues which
beautifie a blooming life, was famous in the mouths of all good
men, and as deare in their hearts.   But what was the reward
(thinkest thou) of his virtuous life?   An immature and almost a
sudden death ; So that it is not to be doubted, but it was a divine
favour.   Being to go into bed, he spoke to his sister, O what
manner of night will this be unto me! I beseech you, deare
sister, furnish me with some candles, and leave one to burn by me.
Abought midnight he suddenly called, so that all the familie was
40 awaked, and got up; to whom he told that he should dye that
night; and desired them to send presently for his Confessour.
They all imagined that he had been troubled with some dream,
especially his Father, a most renowned Physitian, when he

felt his pulse to beate well and orderly. But notwithstanding
all this, they omitted not to send for his Confessour, who
was *Gasper Pedroza*: He (as if touched with some Divine
presension) was at that dead time of the night awake, and being
come to the sorrowfull Father, he told him, that *Didacus* was expected in another World before day, that the Virgin-Queene of
Heaven had revealed so much to him, and that hee would be
gone as soon as the Sacraments could be administred unto him.
It fell out just so: For those sacred solemnities were no sooner
ended, but he was dissolved, as if he had stayed onely for that
spirituall refection to strengthen him in his Journey. He left this
dark and low World towards the first breakings of the day, and
ascending to eternity upon the wings of the morning. He might
have past from thence with lesser noise, and in a shorter time; but
he expired more solemnly then so; and yet without weary accessions, and the Tyranny of sicknesse: He stayed for the saving
institutions of his redeemer, the businesse that detain'd him so
long, was Heaven, and not the tumults of a tyring and obstinate
dissolution; all this proves it to have been the hand of God, and
not an unfortunate, sudden death; the precise Actions of the
deity must be attended with unusuall circumstances.

> *Whome God doth take care for and love,*
> *He dies young here, to live above.*

There is room enough for life within the compasse of few years,
if they be not cast away: Think not that to last long, and to live
long is the same thing: every one that hath stayd long upon
earth, hath not lived long.

Some men find fault with death, because no experiment can be
made of it, without an absolute dissolution: they would dye
twice, to trye what kind of state it is, that they may be fitly
furnished against the second time, when they must dye in earnest.
But this is madness, and were it granted them, the good they
pretend would not be performed. For he that will cast away one
life without preparing for death, wil not fear to hazard another;
desperate malefactors will take no warning by reprieves. Besides,
what benefit would there be by dying twice, seeing that of necessity they must live twice too, and so be twice miserable, if not
twice impious? It is strange, that these men who fear death, and
adjudge it to be evill, should desire to have it doubled, and that
which, by their good will, they would not tast once, they will beg
to chew and swallow downe twice; whereas if death were an Evill,
it would be so much the lesser by comming but once. The

miseries of life are nothing so civill ; they are instant, importunate,
and outragious ; they will reinforce themselves, and set upon us
twice or thrice, yea, a thousand times.   Death is more modest, she
wearies us not as long as wee are well : When our disorders
have turned the harmony of life into discord and noise, then shee
comes to cast those murmurers asleep, and to give the Soul peace :
He is no troublesome guest that comes but once.   But it were
a great happinesse, thou wilt say, if men did experimentally know
what it is to dye : Truely this Felicity is not wanting : Death is
10 a most admirable, ingenious Excogitation : Though we dye but
once, yet do not we dye at once : We may make, yea we do make
many assaies or tryals of dying : Death insinuates it selfe, and
seizeth upon us by peecemeals ; it gives us a tast of it self : It is
the Cronie, or Consort of life : So soon as we begin to be, wee begin
to wast and vanish ; we cannot ascend to life, without descending
towards death : Nay we begin to dye before we appeare to live ;
the perfect shape of the Infant is the death of the *Embryo*, childhood is the death of Infancie, youth of Childhood, Manhood of
youth, and old age of Manhood.   When we are arrived at this
20 last stage, if we stay any long time in it, and pay not the debt we
owe, death requires interest ; she takes his hearing from one, his
sight from another, and from some she takes both : The extent
and end of all things touch their beginning, neither doth the last
minute of life do any thing else, but finish what the first began.
We may know also what death is, by the apparition or Image of
it.   We see it, and make tryal of it assiduously : we cannot act
life one day, but wee must act death at night : Life is a Terrace-
walke with an Arbour at one end, where we repose, and dream
over our past perambulations.   This lesser rest, shewes us the
30 greater ; the Soule watcheth when wee sleepe, and Conscience in
the Just as well as the unjust will be ruminating on the works of
life, when the body is turned into dust.   Sleepe is nothing else
but death painted in a night-peece ; it is a prelibation of that
deepe slumber, out of which we shall not be awaked untill the
Heavens be no more : We go to bed under a Scene of Stars and
darknesse, but when we awake, we find Heaven changed, and one
great luminary giving light to all : We dye in the state of corruption, errours, and mistinesse : But wee shall be raised in glory,
and perfection, when these clouds of blacknesse that are carried
40 about with diverse winds, and every Enemy of truth shall vanish
for ever, and God alone shall be all in all.   We affect sleepe naturally, it is the reparation of man, & a laying by of cares.   The

Coppy cannot match the pattern : if we love sleep then, why should wee hate the Idæa of it ; why should we feare death, whose shadow refresheth us, which nature never made, nor meant to fright us with ? It was her intention to strengthen our hope of dying, by giving us the fruition of this resemblance of death ; lest we should grow impatient with delay, she favour'd us with this shadow and Image of it, as Ladies comfort themselves with the pictures of their absent lovers. There is no part of life without some portion of death, as dreames cannot happen without sleepe, so life cannot be without death. As sleepe is said to be the shadow of death ; So I think dreams to be the shadowes of life, for nothing deceives us more frequent then it : When we shal be raised from death, we shal not grieve so much because the joys of life were not real, as because there were none at all. It was said by one, that he had rather dream of being tormented in Hell, then glorified in *Paradise* : for being awaked, he should rejoyce to find himselfe in a soft featherbed, and not in a lake of unquenchable fire : But having dreamt of Heaven, it would grieve him that it was not reall. *Paracelsus* writes, that the watching of the body is the sleep of the Soul, and that the day was made for Corporeall Actions, but the night is the working-time of Spirits. Contrary natures run contrary courses : Bodies having no inherent light of their own, make use of this outward light, but Spirits need it not. Sunbeams cannot stumble, nor go out of their way. Death frees them from this dark Lantern of flesh. *Heraclitus* used to say, that men were both dead and alive, both when they dyed, and when they lived : when they lived their Soules were dead, and when they dyed, their Soules revived. Life then is the death of the Soule, and the life of the body : But death is the life of the Soule, and the death of the body.

I shall return now to prosecute the Commendations of death, because it comes but once. Death (like the Phœnix) is onely one, lest any should be ill. That which comes but once, is with most longing looked for, and with most welcome entertained. That poor man, the owner of one Ewe, nourished her in his bosome, she did eate of his meat, and drank out of his Cup, as *Nathan* exemplified. The Father that hath but one Son, hath more cares, then he that hath many ; so should we be more carefull to provide for death which comes but once, then for the numerous and daily calamities of life : By providing for that one, wee turne the rest all into so many joyes. Whatsoever is rare, whatsoever is pretious, it is single, and but one. There is nothing

so rare, nothing that is comparable to a good death. But it is
not the universality or diffusivenesse of it that makes it so, but
the contempt and the subduing of it; his death is most pretious,
by whom death is contemned. Dissolution is not a meere merit,
but a debt we owe to nature, which the most unwilling must pay.
That wisedome which can make destiny to be her servant, which
can turne necessity into virtue, Mortality into Immortality, and the
debt we owe to nature into a just right and Title to eternall glory, is
very great. What greater advantage can there be, then to make
10 Heaven due to us, by being indebted to nature, and to oblige
Divinity by paying a temporal debt? *Clemens* called them *Golden
men*, who dyed thus; that is to say, when it was necessary to dye.
They made necessity their free will, when either the publick liberty,
the prerogative of reason, or the word of God called for their sufferings: For though death be a debt due to Nature, yet in these
causes, Nature doth willingly resigne her right, and God becomes
the Creditor. If we pay it unto him before the time of pure
resolution, Nature is better pleased with that anticipation, then if
we kept our set day: He is the best debtour, that paies before
20 the time of payment. The day of payment by the Covenant of
Nature is old age, but the good man paies before the day. If the
noblenesse of thy mind will not incite thee to such a forward
satisfaction; let the desire of gaine move thee, for the sooner
thou payest, the more thou dost oblige. Hee that suffers an
immature death for the good of his Country, for the sacred lawes,
or the vindication of the truth of God, and not for his owne vain
glory, doth free himselfe from the Natural debt, and doth at the
same time make God his debtour, and all mankind? To a man
that dyes thus, all men are indebted: God owes him for the
30 Cause, and men for the effect: The last doth at least set us an
example, and the first improves the faith, and gives life to
Charity.

Adde to this, that this great good of a passive death, is
a voluntary imitation of the Son of God, who laid down his life for
the life of the World: And it is also done without our industry;
this great virtue, this glorious perfection requires not our care and
activity to bring it about. This death is most pretious and the
best, because it is executed by others, and not by our selves: To
suffer death, not to dye, is glorious. If prisoners break their
40 chaines, it is neither their glory, nor their security, but augments
their Guilt, and hastens their condemnation: So he that violates
his own body, and makes way for the Soul to flye out with his own

hands, is damned by the very Act : but if another doth it to him, it is both his Salvation and his Crown.   The heathens esteemed it no honour for Captives to have their bonds loosed : It was their freedome, but not their glory.   When the judge himself did break off their Chaines, that they accounted honorable.   By this Ceremony did *Vespasian* and *Titus* acknowledge the worth of *Joseph* the *Jew* : This vindicated his integrity : By cutting his bonds with their Imperial hand, they freed him both from captivity and disgrace.   *Titus* said, that if they would break off   his fetters, and not stay to take them off, his honour would be so 10 perfectly repaired by it, as if he had been never bound, nor over- come.   The same difference (in point of honour) is betwixt the naturall death and the violent : betwixt dying when wee are full of daies, and the death which Tyrants impose upon us, when we are mangled and grinded by their fury.   This honour is then greatest, when the body is not dissolved, but distorted and broken into peeces.   Certainly the best men have ever perished by the violence of Tyrants ; nature (to preserve her innocence) being very back- ward and unwilling (as it were) to take away such great and needfull examples of goodnesse.   Treachery and violence were 20 ordained for the just in the death of *Abel* ; who dyed by the wicked. This better sort of death was (in him) consecrated to the best men ; those persons whom Nature respects, and is loath to medle with, envy laies hands upon : Whom the one labours to preferre, the other plotteth to destroy.   Nor deals she thus with the good only, but with the eminent and mighty too : thus she served *Hector*, *Alexander* and *Cæsar* : the goodliest object is alwaies her aim. When *Thrasybulus* the Astrologer told *Alexander* the *Roman*, that he should end his daies by a violent death, he answered, that he was very glad of it, for then (said he) I shall dye like an Emperour, 30 like the best and the greatest of men, and not sneak out of the World like a worthlesse, obscure fellow.   But the death of these *Glorioli* was not truly glorious : I have onely mentioned them, because that a passive death (though wanting religion) hath made their honour permanent.   That death is the truly glorious, which is seald with the joy of the sufferers spirit, whose Conscience is ravished with the kisses of the Dove : Who can look upon his tormentour with delight, and grow up to Heaven without diminu- tion, though made shorter on Earth by the head.

   This is the death which growes pretious by contempt, and 40 glorious by disgrace : Whose sufferer runs the race set before him

4 judge] jugde˙*1654*

with patience, and finisheth it with joy. We are carefull that those things which are our own, may be improved to the utmost; and why care wee not for death? what is more ours then mortality? Death should not be feared, because it is simply, or of it self, a great good, and is evill to none but to those that by living ill make their death bad: What ever evil is in death, it is attracted from life. If thou preservest a good Conscience while thou livest, thou wilt have no feare when thou dyest, thou wilt rejoyce and walke homeward singing. It is life therefore that makes thee fear
10 death: If thou didst not fear life, if life had not blasted the joyes of death, thou wouldst never be afraid of the end of sorrowes. Death therefore is of it self innocent, sincere, healthfull, and desirable. It frees us from the malignancie and malice of life, from the sad necessities and dangerous errours we are subject to in the body. That death, whose leaders are Integrity and virtue, whose cause is Religion, is the *Elixir* which gives this life its true tincture, and makes it immortal. To dye is a common and trivial thing, for the good and the bad dye, and the bad most of all: but to dye willingly, to dye gloriously is the peculiar priviledge of good
20 men. It is better to leave life voluntarily, then to be driven out of it forcibly: let us willingly give place unto posterity. Esteem not life for its own sake, but for the use of it: Love it not, because thou wouldst live, but because thou mayst do good works while thou livest. Now the greatest work of life is a good death. If life then ought to be lesse esteemed then good works, who would not purchase a good death with the losse of life? why should we be afeared of politick, irreligious Tyrants, and an arm of flesh though guarded with steele? Nature it selfe threatens us with death, and frailty attends us every hour: Why will we refuse
30 to dye in a good cause when 'tis offered us, who may dye ill the very next day after? let us not promise our selves a short life, when our death assures us of eternal glory.

But if it were granted that death were neither good nor honour-able, but evill and fearfull, why will not we take care for that which we fear? Why do we neglect that which we suspect? Why, if it be evill, do not wee arme and defend our selves against it? we provide against dangerous contingencies, we labour against casuall losses, and we neglect this great and enevitable perill. To neglect death, and to contemn death are two things: none are
40 more carefull of it, then those that contemne it; none feare it more then those that neglect it; and which is strange, they fear it not because they have neglected it, but they neglect it, when they

fear it: they dare not prepare for it, for fear of thinking of it. O the madnesse and Idlenesse of mankind! to that, which they adjudge to be most Evill, they come not onely unprepared, but unadvisedly, and without so much as forethought. What mean we, what do we look for? Death is still working, and wee are still idle, it is still travelling towards us, and we are still slumbering and folding our hands. Let us awake out of this darke and sleepy state of mind, let us shake off these dreams and vain propositions of diverse lusts: let us approve of truth and realities, let us follow after those things which are good; let us 10 have true joy made sure unto us, and a firm security in life, in death.

Sickness and death, you are but sluggish things,
And cannot reach, a heart that hath got wings.

FINIS.

THE WORLD
CONTEMNED,
IN A
Parenetical Epiſtle written by
the Reverend Father

EVCHERIVS,

Biſhop of *Lyons,* to his Kinſman
VALERIANVS.

---

*Love not the VVorld, neither the things that are
in the world. If any man love the world, the love
of the Father is not in him.* 1 Ioh. 2. 15.

*They are of the world, therefore ſpeake they of the
world, and the world heareth them.* Chap. 4. verſ. 5.

*If the world hate you, ye know that it hated me
before it hated you.* Ioh. 15. verſe 18.

*If ye were of the world, the world would love his
own, but becauſe ye are not of the world, but I have
choſen you out of the world, therfore the world hateth
you.* ver. 19.

*Remember the word that I ſaid unto you, the Ser-
vant is not greater than the Lord: if they have perſe-
cuted me, they will also perſecute you : If they have
kept my ſaying, they will keepe yours alſo.* v. 20.

London, Printed for *Humphrey Moſeley,*
at the *Princes Armes* in St *Pauls*
Church-yard. 1654.

Advertisement.

Heribert Ros-weyd *published this peece at* Antwerp 1621. *It is* *mentioned by* Gennadius cap. 63. De Scriptoribus Ecclesiasticis; *and* Erasmus (*long before* Ros-weyd's *Edition*) *writ some Notes upon it. The Author* Eucherius *was a* Roman *Senatour, but being converted to the Faith, he left the* Senate, *and lived in a poor* Cell *by the river* Druentium, *where his Wife* Galla *died. His two daughters,* Consortia, *and* Tullia, *having learnt* Christ, *continued both in the Virgin-life,* & signorum gloriâ claruerunt. *He sate Bishop in the chair of* Lyons (*as I find him placed by* Helvicus) *in the year of our*
10 Lord 443. *Some will have him a Century lower, but that difference weakens not the certainty of it. The peece it self (in the Original) is most elaborate and judicious, and breaths that* togatam elegantiam *which in most of the* Roman *Senatours was not more acquired, then natural. What this* Valerian *was (more then our Authors Kinsman, by whose pen his name lives) is not certainly known. Some will have him to be* Priscus Valerianus, *the Præfect, or Deputy of* France, *mentioned by* Sidonius Apollinaris: *Others are willing to let him passe for that* Valerian, *whose* Homilies *now extant were published by* Sirmondus. *But as it is not determinable, so is it not material:*
20 *This we may safely conclude, that he was a very eminent, noble* Personage, *and one that followed too much after temporal* pomp, *and the* powers *of this* world; *though neither of them could lend him so much* light, *as would keep him from* obscuritie. *To bring down these top-branches,* Eucherius *layes the* Axe *to the root of the tree, by shewing him the* vanity, *and the* iniquity *of* riches *and* honours, *the two grand inticements of* popular spirits. *And this he doth with such powerfull and clear reasons, that to virtuous and peaceful minds he hath renderd them not only* contemptible, *but* odious. *Much more might have been spoken against them, but (seeing the* Age *we*
30 *live in hath made all his* Arguments, Demonstrations) *he hath in my judgement spoken enough.*

H. V. S.

EUCHERIUS

to his Kinsman

VALERIANUS, &c.

They are happily linked in the bond of blood, who are held together by the bond of love. And for this gift (which is descended upon us from the Father of lights,) both you and my selfe may greatly rejoyce: Whom love as well as kindred hath united, and those two faire obligations have betrothed in one entire affection. One of them wee tooke from the Fathers of our flesh, and the other from our private dispositions. This double tye by which (love binding us on the one side, and blood on the other,) we are mutually knit together; hath inforced me to inlarge my selfe in this Epistle with some excesse more then usuall; that I might commend unto your Consideration the Cause of your owne Soul, and assert the work of our profession to be, that Supreme beatitude which is onely true, and capable of those things which are Eternal.

And indeed your own pious propension is not repugnant to the profession of holy living, who already by a forward felicity of manners have in some points prevented, and met with many things which are taught unto us by sacred learning: So that by the meanes of provident and discreet Nature, you seem unto me to have seized upon many duties of Religion; as the Concessions and Indulgences of our good God towards you, whose gift it is, that the Divine wisedome should partly find in you, and partly conferre upon you the riches of his Kingdome.

But although (by the hands of your Father, and Father in law,) you have been allready advanced and seated upon the highest pinnacles of temporall honours, and are still adorned and surrounded with illustrious titles descending from them both; Yet I desire, and long to find in you a thirst of greater and far higher honours, and shall now call you not to Earthly, but Heavenly honours, not to the dignities and splendour of one short age, but to the solid and enduring glories of eternity: For the onely true and indelible glory is, to be glorified in Eternity.

I shall therefore speak unto you, not the wisedome of this

World, but that secret and hidden wisdome which God ordained befor the World unto our glory. I shall speake with much care and affection towards you, and with very little respect or anim-adversion of my selfe; for I have in this attempt considered more, what I wish to see perfected in you, than what I am able to do in my self.

The first duty of Man ordained and brought forth into this World for that end, (my most dear *Valerian*!) is to know his Creatour, and being known, to confesse him, and to resigne or
10 give up his life (which is the wonderfull and peculiar gift of God,) to the service and worship of the giver; that what he received by Gods free donation, may be imployed in true devotion, and what was conferred upon him in the state of wrath and unworthinesse, may by an obedient resignation make him pretious and beloved. For of this saving opinion are we; That as it is most certain, that we came forth first from God, so should we believe it, and presse on still towards him : Whereupon we shall conclude, that he onely, rightly and divinely apprehends the purpose of God in making man, who understands it thus, *That God himself made us for*
20 *himself.*

It is then our best course, to bestow our greatest care upon the Soul; So shall that which is the first and highest in dignity, be not the lowest, and last in consideration. Amongst us *Christians*, let that which is the first in order, be the first cared for; let Salvation which is the chiefest profit be our chiefest imployment· Let the safeguard and the defense of this, take up all our forces; let it be not only our chiefest, but our sole delight. As it sur-passeth all other things in excellencie, so let it in our care and consideration.

30 Our Supreme duty is that which wee owe to God, and the next to it appertaines to the Soul. And yet these two are such loving correlates, that though every one of them is a duty of Supreme con-sequence, and such as by no means we may presume to neglect or omit, yet cannot wee possibly performe any one of them without the other. So that whosoever will serve God, doth at the same time provide for his own Soul; and he that is carefull for his own Soul, doth at the same time serve God. So that the state of these two soveraign duties in man, is by a certain compendious depen-dencie and co-intention rendred very easie, while the faithfull
40 performance of the one, is a perfect consummation of both : For by the unspeakable tendernesse and mercy of God, the good wee

19 understands] understand *1654*

do to our own Soules, is the most acceptable service and sacrifice that we can offer unto him.

Much Physicall curiosity, much care and many strict observations are bestowed upon the body; much pain it undergoes in hope of health; and deserves the Soule no Medicine? If it be but fit and necessary, that diverse helps and means of healing are sought for the body, for the recovering onely of a temporall and transitory health, is it not unjust that the Soul should be excluded, and be suffered to languish and putrifie with deadly and spirituall diseases? Shall the Soul onely be a stranger to those proper and ro pretious remedies ordained for it by the great Physitian? Yea rather, if so many things are provided for the body, let the provision for the Soul be far more abundant: for if it was truly said by some, that this *fleshly frame is the servant, and the Soul the Mistris,* then will it be very undecent and injurious, if we shall preferre and place the servant before the Mistris. It is but a just claim, that the better part should require the better attendance; for with constant and intentive diligence should wee look on that side, where the greater dignity and our most pretious treasure is laid up. It is not agreeable to reason, and it takes from 20 the honour of our imployment, that we should subject it to the unworthier party. The flesh being allwaies inclined to vitiousnesse, drawes us back to the Earth, as to its proper center and Originall: But the Soul being descended from the Father of lights, is like the sparks of fire still flying upwards. The Soule is the Image of God in us, and the pretious pledge of his future munificence. Let us imploy all our innate forces, and all outward Auxiliaries for the preservation of this: if we manage and defend it faithfully, wee take care for, and protect the intrusted pledge and purchased possession of God. What conveniencie can wee have to build, 30 unless we do first of all lay the foundation? but to him that hath design'd a superstructure of true blessings, the fundamentall must be Salvation. And if hee hath not laid that foundation, upon what can the Consequences he hopes for be builded? how shall he be filled with the Increase of those remunerations and after-blessings, that wants the first fruits, and denies the rewarder? what portion can he have in the joyes of Eternity, that will be wanting to his own Salvation? How can he live the life of the blessed, that wil not rise from death? or what will it benefit him to heape up temporal provision, and the materials of this World; 40 when he hath stored up nothing for the comfort of his Soule? Or as our Lord *JESUS CHRIST* hath said, *What is a man*

profited, if hee gain the whole World, and lose his own Soul? There
can therefore be no cause for sparing and laying up, where it is
manifest, that the Soul is already lost ; where Salvation is forfeited,
what gaine or profit can be hoped for? Or wherein shall the true
treasure be laid up, or wherewith shall he receive it, when the
Soules pretious vessell, and the storehouse of Eternal joyes is
utterly ruined and broken? let us therefore while we have time,
labour for true riches, and make earnest hast to that holy and
Heavenly commerce, which is worth our looking and longing
10 after.

Eternall life may be obtained in a very few daies : Which daies
though they should be blest with an inoffensive and untainted
holinesse of life, yet because they are but few, are to be lightly
esteem'd of : for nothing can be rich in value, which is but short
in duration : Nor can that procure any long or durable joyes,
whose time of existence or abode is narrow and transient. The
short Accommodations of this life have but short effects. It seems
therefore but just unto me, that to the joyes of this present life (if
it hath any) we should preferre the true and indubitable joyes of
20 that which is everlasting. For the felicity we enjoy here, is at
best but temporal, but the other is eternal ; and the fruition of
a transitorie, uncertaine happinesse is but a frailty and accident ;
but the possession of inviolable and never ending joyes, is triumph
and security.

It is clear then, that the Eternal life is most blessed ; for what
other thing can be named, or thought upon, that is more happy
then everlasting life? As for this present short life, it is so very
short, that it is withall most miserable. It is prest and assaulted
on every side with surrounding, inevitable sorrowes, it is distrest
30 with many evill defects, and tost to and fro by secret and penal
accidents. For what is there in all the whole World that is so
uncertain, so various, and so replenished with troubles, as the
course of this life? Which is full of labour, full of anguish,
fraught with cares, and made ominous with dangers : which is
distracted with violent and suddaine mutations, made unpleasant
with bodily distempers, afflicted with thoughtfullnesse, and mentall
agonies, and lies naked and open to all the Whirlwinds of time
and Chance? What benefit then, yea, what reason have you to
turne aside, and run away from Eternal joyes, that you may pursue
40 and follow after temporall miseries.

Do not you see, my dear *Valerian,* how every one that is
provident (even in this life,) doth with plenty of all necessaries

furnish that cottage or field, where hee knowes he shall reside? and where he abides but for a short time, his provision is accordingly, where he intends a longer stay, he provides likewise a greater supply? unto us also, who in this present World (being straightned on every side) have but a very short time, are Eternall ages reserv'd in the World which is to come; if so be that wee competently provide for an Eternall state, and seeke onely what is sufficient for the present, not perversely bestowing the greatest care upon the shortest and smallest portion of time, and the smallest care upon the time of greatest and endlesse 10 extent.

And indeed I know not, which should soonest, or most effectually incite us to a pious care of life Eternal, either the blessings which are promised us in that state of glory, or the miseries which we feel in this present life. Those from above most lovingly invite and call upon us; these below most rudely and importunately would expell us hence. Seeing therefore that the continuall Evills of this life, would drive us hence unto a better, if we will not be induced by the good, let us be compelled by the Evill: Both the good and the bad agree to incite us to the best, 20 and though at difference amongst themselves; yet both consent to make us happy. For while the one invites us, and the other compells us, both are sollicitous for our good.

If some eminent and powerfull Prince having adopted you for his Son, and co-partner, should forthwith send for you by his Embassador; you would (I believe) break through all difficulties, and the wearisome extent of Sea and Land, that you might appear before him, and have your adoption ratified. God Almighty, the Maker and the Lord of Heaven and Earth, and all that is in them, calls you to this adoption, and offers unto you (if you will receive 30 it,) that dear stile of a Sonne, by which he calls his onely begotten, and your glorious Redeemer. And will you not be inflamed and ravished with his Divine love? will you not make hast, and begin your Journey towards Heaven, lest swift destruction come upon you, and the honors offered you be frustrated by a sad and sudden death?

And to obtain this adoption, you shall not need to passe through the unfrequented and dangerous Solitudes of the Earth, or to commit your selfe to the wide and perillous Sea: When you will, this adoption is within your reach, and lodgeth with you. And 40 shall this blessing, because it is as easie in the getting, as it is great in the consequence, find you therefore backward or unwilling to attain it? How hard a matter to the lukewarme and the dissembler will the making sure of this adoption prove? for as to the faithfull and obedient it is most easie, so to the hypocrite and the rebellious, it is most difficult.

Certainly, it is the love of life that hath inslaved us so much to a delectation, and dotage upon temporal things. Therefore do I now advise you, who are a lover of life, to love it more. It is the right way of perswading, when we do it for no other end but to obtain that from you, which of your owne accord you desire to
10 grant us. Now for this life which you love, am I an Embassadour; and intreat that this life which you love in its transient and momentary state, you would also love in the Eternal. But how, or in what manner you may be said to love this present life, unlesse you desire to have it made most excellent, perfect, and eternally permanent, I cannot see; for that which hath the power to please you when it is but short and uncertain, will please you much more, when it is made eternal and immutable: And that which you dearly love and value, though you have it but for a time, will be much more deare and pretious to you, when you shall enjoy it
20 without end. It is therefore but fit, that the temporall life should look still towards the Eternal, that through the one, you may passe into the other. You must not rob your selfe of the benefits of the life to come, by a crooked and perverse use of the present. This life must not oppose it selfe to the damage and hurt of the future: For it were very absurd and unnatural, that the love of life should cause the destruction and the death of life.

Therefore whither you judg this temporall life worthy of your love, or your Contempt; my present argument will be every way very reasonable. * For if you contemne it,
An excellent Dilemma.
30 your reason to do so, is, that you may obtain a better: and if you love it, you must so much the more love that life which is eternall.

But I rather desire, that you would esteem of it, as you have found it; and judge it to be (as it is indeed) full of bitternesse and trouble, a race of tedious and various vexations; and that you would utterly forsake and renounce both it, and its occupations. Cut off at last that wearisome and endlesse chain of secular imployments, that one and the same slavery, though in severa negotiations. Break in sunder those cords of vain cares, in whose
40 successive knots you are alwayes intangled, and bound up, and in every one of which your travell is renewed and begun again. Let this rope of sands, this coherencie of vaine causes be taken away:

In which (as long as men live) the tumult of affairs (being still lengthen'd by an intervening succession of fresh cares) is never ended, but runnes on with a fretting and consuming sollicitousness, which makes this present life, that is already of it selfe short and miserable enough, far more short and more miserable. Which also (according to the successe or crosnesse of affairs) lets in divers times vain and sinfull rejoycings, bitter sorrows, anxious wishes, and suspitious fears. Let us last of all cast off all those things which make this life in respect of their imployment but very short, but in respect of cares and sorrows very long. Let us reject, and 10 resolutely contemn this uncertain world, and the more uncertain manners of it, wherein the Peasant as well as the Prince is seldom safe, where things that lye low are trodden upon, and the high and lofty totter and decline. Chuse for your self what worldly estate you please: There is no rest either in the *mean*, or the *mighty*. Both conditions have their miseries, and their misfortunes: The private and obscure is subject to disdain, the publick and splendid unto envy.

Two prime things I suppose there are, which strongly enchain, and keep men bound in secular negotiations; and having be- 20 witch'd their understanding, retaine them still in that dotage; the *pleasure* of *riches*, & the *dignity* of *honours*. The former of which ought not to be called pleasure, but poverty; and the latter is not dignity, but vanity. These two (being joyn'd in one subtile league) set upon man, and with alternate, insnaring knots disturb and intangle his goings. These (besides the vain desires which are peculiar to themselves) infuse into the mind of man other deadly and pestiferous lustings, which are their consequents; and with a certaine pleasing inticement sollicite and overcome the hearts of Mankind. 30

As for Riches (that I may speake first of them) what is there, I pray, or what can there be more pernicious? They are seldom gotten without Injustice; by such an Administrator are they gathered, and by such a Steward they must be kept; for Covetousnesse is the root of all evils. And there is indeed a very great familiarity betwixt these two, Riches * and Vices in their names, as well as in their nature. And ** Divitiæ & Vitia.* are they not also very frequently matter of disgrace, and an evill report? Upon which consideration it was said *[a] Every rich man* by one, that [a] *Riches were tokens of Injuries.* In *is either a tyrant himself, or the son* 40 the possession of corrupt persons they publish *of a tyrant.* to the world their bribery and unrighteousnesse, and elswhere, they allure the eyes, and incite the spirits of seditious men to rebellion, and in the custody of such they bear witnesse of the sufferings, and the murther of innocent persons, & the plundering of their goods.

But grant that these disasters should not happen, can we have any certainty, whither these things that make themselves wings, will fly away after our decease? *He layeth up treasure* (saith the *Psalmist*) *and knoweth not for whom he gathers it.*

But suppose that you should have an heir after your own heart, 10 doth hee not oftentimes destroy and scatter what the Father hath gathered? doth not an ill-bred son, or our ill choice of a Son-in-law prove the frequent ruin of all our labours and substance in this life? What pleasure then can there be in such riches, whose collection is sin and sorrow, and our transmission, or bequeathing of them anxious and uncertaine?

Whither then at last will this wild and devious affection of men carry them? You know how to love accidental and external goods, but cannot love your own self. That which you so much long for is abroad, and without you; you place your affection 20 upon a forraigner, upon an enemy. Returne, or retire rather into your self, and be you dearer, and nearer to your own heart then those things which you call yours. Certainly if some wise man, and skilfull in the affaires of this world, should converse, and come to be intimate with you, it would better please you, that he should affect your person, then affect your goods; and you would choose, that he should rather love you for your self, then for your riches; you would have him to be faithful unto man, not to his money. What you would have another to performe towards you, that doe you for your self, who ought to be the most faithfull to 30 your self. Our selves, our selves wee should love, not those things which wee phantastically call ours.

And let this suffice to have been spoken against Riches.

As for the Honours of this world (to speak generally, and without exception, for I shall not descend to particulars) what dignity can you justly attribute to those things which the base man, and the bad, as well as the noble and good, promiscuously obtain, and all of them by corruption and ambition? The same honour is not conferred upon men of the same merits, and dignity makes not a difference betwixt the worthy and the unworthy, but 40 confounds them. So that which should be a character of deserts, by advancing the good above the bad, doth most unjustly make

22 wise man] wiseman *1654*

them equal; and after a most strange manner there is in no state of life lesse difference made betwixt the worst men, and the best, then in that state which you term honourable. Is it not then a greater honour to be without that honour, and to be esteemed of according to our genuine worth, and sincere carriage, then according to the false gloss of promiscuous, deceiving honours?

And these very things (how big soever they look) what fleeting and frail appearances are they? We have seen of late men eminently honourable, seated upon the very spires, and top of dignity, whose incredible treasures purchased them a great part of the world; their successe exceeded their own desires, and their prodigious fortunes amazed their very wishes: But these I speak of were private prosperities. Kings themselves with all their height and imperiousnesse, with all their triumphs and glory shined but for a time. Their cloathings were of wrought gold, their diadems sparkled with the various flames, and differing relucencies of precious stones; their Palaces were thronged with Princely attendants, their roofs adorned with gilded beams, their Will was a Law, and their words were the rules and coercive bounds of Mankind. But who is he, that by a temporal felicity can lift his head above the stage of humane chances? Behold now, how the vast sway and circumference of these *mighty* is no where to be found! their riches and precious things too are all gone, and they themselves the possessors and masters of those royal treasures! most late, and most famous Kingdoms (even amongst us) are now become a certaine fable. All those things which sometimes were reputed here to be very great, are now become none at all.

Nothing I think, nay I am sure, of all these riches, honours, powers went along with them from hence: All they took with them was the pretious substance of their faith and piety. These onely (when they were deprived of all other attendants) waited on them, and like faithfull, inseparable companions, travelled with them out of this world. With this provision are they now fed; with these riches, and with these honours are they adorned. In these they rest, and this goodnesse is now their greatnesse.

Wherefore, if we be taken at all with honours and riches, let us be taken with the true and durable ones: Every good man exchangeth these earthly dignities for those which are celestiall, and earthen treasures for the heavenly. He layes up treasure there, where a most exact and inconfused difference is made

15 of wrought] of wrought of *1654*

betwixt the good and the bad; where that which is once gotten
shall be for ever enjoyed; where all things may be obtained, and
where nothing can be lost.

But seeing we are fallen into a discourse of the frailty of
temporal things, let us not forget the frail condition of this short
life. What is it, I beseech you, what is it? Men see nothing more
frequently then death, and minde nothing more seldome. Mankinde is by a swift mortality quickly driven into the *West*, or
setting point of life, and all posterity by the unalterable Law of
10 succeeding ages and generations follow after. Our fathers went
from hence before us; we shall goe next, and our children must
come after. As streames of water falling from high, the one still following the other, doe in successive circles break and terminate at
the banks; so the appointed times and successions of men are cut
off at the boundary of death. This consideration should take up
our thoughts night and day; this memoriall of our fraile condition
should keep us still awake. Let us alwayes thinke the time of our
departure to be at hand; for the day of death, the farther we put
i off, comes on the faster, and is by so much the nearer to us. Let
20 us suspect it to be near, because we know not how far. Let us, as
the *Scripture* saith, *make plain our wayes before us.*

If we make this the businesse of our thoughts, and meditate
still upon it, wee shall not be frighted with the fear of death.
Blessed and happy are all you who have already reconciled your
selves unto *Christ*! no great fear of death can disturb them, who
desire to be dissolved that they may be with *Christ*; who in the
silence of their own bosomes, quietly, and long since prepared
for it, expect the last day of their pilgrimage here. They care not
much how soon they end this temporal life, that passe from it
30 into life eternal.

Let not the populacy and throng of loose livers, or hypocriticall
time-pleasers perswade us to a neglect of life, neither be you
induced by the errours of the *many* to cast away your particular
salvation. What wil the multitude in that day of Gods judgement
avail us, when every private person shall be sentenced, where the
examinations of works, and every mans particular actions, not the
example of the common people shall absolve him? Stop your ears,
and shut your eyes against such damnable Precedents that invite
you to destruction. It is better to sow in tears, and to plant
40 eternal life with the few, then to lose it with the multitude. Let
not therefore the number of sinfull men weaken your diligence
of not sinning; for the madnesse of those that sin against their

own soules, can be no authority unto us; I beseech you look alwayes upon the vices of others as their shame, not your example.

If it be your pleasure to look for examples, seek them rather from that party, which though the least, yet if considered as it is a distinct body, is numerous enough: Seek them (I say) from that party, wherein you shall find those ranged, who wisely understood, wherefore they were born, and accordingly while they lived, did the businesse of life; who eminent for good works, and excelling in virtue, pruned and drest the present life, and planted the future. Nor are our examples (though of this rare kind) only copious, but 10 great withall, and most illustrious.

For what worldly nobility, what honours, what dignity, what wisdom, what eloquence, or learning have not betaken themselves to this heavenly warfare? what soveraignty now hath not with all humility submitted to this easie yoke of *Christ*? And certainly it is a madnesse beyond error and ignorance for any to dissemble in the cause of their salvation. I could (but that I will not be tedious to you) out of an innumerable company produce many by name, and shew you what eminent and famous men in their times have forsaken this World, and embraced the most strict rules of 20 *Christian* Religion. And some of these (because I may not omit all,) I shall cursorily introduce.

Clement the *Roman*, of the stock of the *Cæsars*, and the Antient Linage of the Senatours, a person fraught with Science, and most skillfull in the liberall *Arts*, betook himself to this path of the just; and so uprightly did he walk therein, that he was elected to the Episcopal dignity of *Rome*.

Gregorie of *Pontus*, a Minister of holy things, *Gregorius Thauma-* famous at first for his humane learning and *turgus.* eloquence, became afterwards more eminent by those Divine 30 Graces conferr'd upon him. For (as the Faith of Ecclesiastical History testifies,) amongst other miraculous signes of his effectual devotion, he removed a Mountain by prayer, and dried up a deep lake.

Gregory Nazianzen, another holy Father, given also at first to Philosophie and humane literature, declined at last those Worldly rudiments, and embraced the true and Heavenly Philosophy: To whose industry also wee owe no meaner a person then *Basil* the Great; for being his intimate acquaintance, and fellow-student in secular Sciences, he entred one day into his *Auditory*, where 40 *Basilius* was then a Reader of *Rhetorick*, and leading him by the hand out of the School, disswaded him from that imployment with

this gentle reproofe, *Leave this Vanity, and study thy Salvation.*
And shortly after both of them came to be famous and faithfull
Stewards in the house of God, and have left us in the Church,
most usefull and pregnant Monuments of their Christian learning.

Paulinus Bishop of *Nola*, the great
Ornament and light of *France*, a person
of Princely revenues, powerfull eloquence,
and most accomplish'd learning, so highly
approved of this our profession, that *choosing for himself the better*
10 *part*, he divided all his Princely Inheritance amongst the poor, and
afterward filled most part of the World with his elegant and pious
writings.

Thou hast his life annexed to this Epistle: as a precedent after these precepts.

Hilarius of late, and *Petronius* now in *Italie*, both of them out
of the fulnesse of Secular honours and power, betook themselves
to this Course ; the one entring [a] into the
religion, the other into the Priesthood.

[a] Hilarius *about this time (which was* 435. *years after* Christ) *did lead a monastical life: but upon the death of* Honoratus, *he was elected his successour in the Bishoprick of* Orleans,
20 *in which dignity he continued not long, for being addicted to solitarinesse, he resigned it, and turned into the Wildernesse.*

And when shall I have done with this
great cloud of witnesses, If I should bring
into the field all those eloquent Contenders for the Faith, *Firmianus, Minutius,
Cyprian, Hilary, Chrysostome* and *Ambrose*?
These I believe spoke to themselves in
the same words which [a] another of our
profession used as a spurre to drive himselfe out of the Secular life into this blessed and Heavenly vocation ; They said, I believe : *What is this? The unlearned get up,
and lay hold upon the Kingdome of Heaven, and we with our learning, behold where we wallow in flesh and blood.* This (sure) they
said, and upon this consideration they also rose up, and tooke
30 the Kingdome of Heaven by force.

St. Augustine.

Having now in part produced these reverend witnesses, whose
zeal for the Christian faith hath exceeded most of their successours,
though they also were bred up in secular rudiments, perswasive
eloquence, and the Pomp and fulnesse of honours ; I shall descend unto Kings themselves, and to that head of the World, the
Roman Empire. And here I think it not necessary that those
Royal, religious Antients of the old World should be mentioned at
all. Some of their posterity, and the most renowned in our
Sacred Chronicles I shall make use of ; as *David* for Piety, *Josiah*
40 for Faith, and *Ezechias* for Humility. The later times also have
been fruitfull in this kinde, nor is this our age altogether barren of
pious Princes, who draw near to the Knowledge of the onely true

and Immortal King, and with most contrite and submissive hearts acknowledge and adore the Lord of Lords. The *Court*, as well as the *Cloyster*, hath yeelded Saints, of both Sexes. And these in my opinion are more worthy your Imitation, then the mad and giddy Commonalty; for the examples of these, carry with them in the World to come Salvation, and in the present World, Authority.

You see also how the dayes and the years, and all the bright Ornaments and Luminaries of Heaven, do with an unwearied duty execute the commands and decrees of their Creatour; and in a constant, irremissive tenour continue obedient to his ordinances. 10 And shall wee (for whose use these lights were created, and set in the firmament,) seeing we know our Masters will, and are not ignorant of his Commandements, stop our ears against them? And to these Vast members of the Universe it was but once told, what they should observe unto the end of the World; but unto us line upon line, precept upon precept, and whole volumes of Gods Commandements are every day repeated. Adde to this, that man (for this also is in his power) should learn to submit himself to the will of his Creator, and to be obedient to his Ordinances; for by paying his whole duty unto God, he gives withall a good 20 example unto men.

But if there be any that will not returne unto their maker and be healed, can they therefore escape the Arme of their Lord, in whose hand are the Spirits of all flesh? Whither will they fly, that would avoyd the presence of God? What Covert can hide them from that *Eye* which is every where, and sees all things? Let them heare thee, holy *David*, let them heare thee.

Psalm 139.

Whither shall I go from thy presence, or whither shall I flee from thy Spirit? 30

If I ascend up into Heaven, thou art there: if I make my bed in Hell, behold thou art there.

If I take the wings of the morning, and dwell in the uttermost parts of the Sea;

Even there shall thy hand lead me, and thy right hand shall hold me.

If I say, surely the darknesse shall cover me: even the night shall be light about thee.

Yea the darknesse hideth not from thee, but the night shineth as the day: the darkness and the light are both alike to thee. 40

6 Authority.] Authority, *1654*   35 *hand shall*] hand stall *1654*

Therefore (willing or unwilling) though they should absent themselves from the Lord of all the world by their Wills, yet shall they
never be able to get their persons out of his Jurisdiction and
Supreme right. They are absent from him indeed in their love and
affections: But he is present with them in his prerogative and
anger. So then being runagates, they are shut up, and (which is
a most impious madnesse) they live without any consideration or
regard of God, but within his power. And if these being earthly
Masters, when their servants run away from them ; with a furious
10 and hasty search pursue after them ; or if they renounce their
service, prosecute them for it, and become the assertours of their
owne right over them ; why will not they themselves render unto
their Master which is in Heaven his most just right ? Why will
they not stay in his Family, and freely offer themselves unto his
service, and be as impartial Judges in the cause of God as in
their own ?

Why with so much dotage do we fixe our Eyes upon the
deceitfull lookes of temporal things? Why do we rest our selves
upon those thornes onely, which wee see beneath us? Is it the
20 Eye alone that wee live by? Is there nothing usefull about us
but that wanderer? We live also by the eare, and at that Inlet
wee receive the glad tydings of Salvation, which fill us with earnest
grones for our glorious liberty and the consummation of the
promises ; Whatsoever is promised, whatsoever is preached unto
us, let us wait for it with intentive wishes, and most eager desires.
That faithfull one, the blessed Author of those promises assures us
frequently of his fidelity and performance, let us covet earnestly
his best promises.

But notwithstanding this which hath been spoken, if a sober
30 and virtuous use were made of the Eye, we might by that very
faculty be drawn to a certaine sacred longing after Immortality,
and the powers of the World to come ; if that admiration, which by
contemplating the rare frame of the World wee are usually filled with,
were returned upon the glorious Creatour of it, by our praises and
benediction of him ; Or if we would meditate what a copious,
active and boundlesse light shall fill our eyes in the state of Immortality, seeing so fair a luminary is allowed us in the state of
corruption : Or what transcendent beauty shall be given to all
things in that eternall World, seeing this transitory one is so full
40 of Majesty and freshnesse ; There can be no excuse for us, if we
sollicite the faculties of these members to abuse and perversenesse :
Let them rather be commodiously applied to both lifes, and so

minister to the use of the temporall, as not to cast off their duty
to the Eternal.

But if pleasure and love delight us, and provoke our Senses,
there is in Christian Religion, a love of infinite comfort, and such
delights as are not nauseous and offensive after fruition.   There
is in it, that which not onely admits of a most vehement and over-
flowing love, but ought allso to be so beloved; namely, God, blessed
for evermore, the onely beautifull, delightfull, immortal and
Supreme good, whom you may boldly and intimately love as well
as piously; if in the room of your former earthly affections, you 10
entertain Heavenly and holy desires.   If you were ever taken with
the magnificence and dignity of another person, there is nothing
more magnificent then God.   If with any thing that might conduce to your honour and glory; there is nothing more glorious
then him: If with the splendour and excellencie of pompous
showes, there is nothing more bright, nothing more excellent.   If
with fairnesse and pleasing objects, there is nothing more beautifull.
If with verity and righteousnesse, there is nothing more just,
nothing more true.   If with liberality, there is nothing more
bountifull.   If with incorruption and simplicity, there is nothing 20
more sincere, nothing more pure then that Supreme goodnesse.
Are you troubled that your treasure and store is not proportionable
to your mind? The Earth and the fullnesse thereof are under his
lock: Do you love any thing that is trusty and firm? There is
nothing more friendly, nothing more faithfull then him: Do you
love any thing that is beneficial? There is no greater benefactor.
Are you delighted with the gravity or gentleness of any object?
there is nothing more terrible then his Almightinesse, nothing
more mild then his goodnesse.   Do you love refreshments in
a low estate, and a merry heart in a plentifull? Joy in prosperity, 30
and comforts in adversity are both the dispensations of his hand.
Wherefore it stands with all reason, that you should love the giver
more then his gifts, and him from whom you have all these things,
more then the things themselves.   Riches, Honours, and all
things else, whose present lustre attracts and possesseth your heart,
are not onely with him, but are now also had from him.

Recollect your dispersed, and hitherto ill-placed affections,
imploy them wholly in the Divine service.   Let this dissolute love
and compliance with worldly desires become chast piety, and wait
upon sacred affaires.   Call home your devious and runnagate 40
thoughts, which opinion and custome have sadly distracted; and
having supprest old errors, direct your love to his proper object,

bestow it wholy upon your Maker. For all that you can love now is his, his alone, and none else. For of such infinitenesse is he, that those who do not love him, deale most injuriously : because they cannot love any thing, but what is his.

But I would have an impartial judgement to consider, whether it be just for him to love the work, and hate the Workman ; and having cast by, and deserted the Creator of all things, to run and seize upon his creatures every where, and without any difference, according to his perverse and insatiable lust. Whereas it behoved
10 him rather to invite God to be gratious and loving to him, by this very affection to his works, if piously layd out. And now man gives himself over to the lusts and service of his own detestable figments, and most unnaturally becomes a lover of the Art, and neglects the Artificer, adores the Creature, and despiseth the Creator.

And what have we spoken all this while of those innumerable delights which are with him ? or of the infinite and ravishing sweetnesse of his ineffable Goodnesse ? the sacred and inexhaustible treasure of his Love ? or when will it be that any shall be able
20 to express or conceive the dignity and fulnesse of any one Attribute that is in him ? To love him then is not onely delightfull, but needfull : For not to love him, whom even then when we love, we cannot possibly requite, is impious ; and not to returne him such acknowledgements as we are able, whom if we would, we can never recompence, is most unjust : For what shall we render unto the Lord for all his benefits towards us ? What shall we render unto him for this one benefit, that he hath given salvation to man by faith, and ordained that to be most easie in the *fact*, by which he restored hope to the subjected world, and
30 eternal life unto lost man ?

And that I may now descend unto those things which were sometimes out of his Covenant, I mean the Nations and Kingdomes of the Gentiles, doe you think that these were 'made subject to the *Roman* power, and that the dispersed multitude of Mankind were incorporated (as it were) into one body under one head for any other end, but that (as Medicines taken in at the mouth are diffused into all parts of the body) so the Faith by this means might with more ease be planted and penetrated into the most remote parts of the world. Otherwise by reason of different
40 powers, customs, and languages, it had met with fresh and numerous oppositions, and the passage of the Gospel had been much more difficult. Blessed *Paul* himself describing his course

in planting the Faith amongst this very people, writes in his
Epistle to the *Romans, That from Hierusalem and round about to
Illyricum he had fully preached the Gospel of Christ.* And how
long (without this preparation in the fulnesse of time) might this
have been in doing, amongst Nations, either innumerable for
multitude, or barbarous for immanitie? Hence it is that the
whole earth now from the rising of the Sun unto the going down
thereof, from the farthest North and the frozen sea breaks forth
into singing, and rings with the glorious name of *Jesus Christ.*
Hence it is, that all parts of the world flock and run together to 10
the Word of Life: The *Thracian* is for the Faith, the *African* for
the Faith, the *Syrian* for the Faith, and the *Spaniard* hath
received the Faith. A great argument of the divine clemency
may be gathered out of this, that under *Augustus Cæsar,* when
the *Roman* power was in the height, and *Acmie,* then the Almighty
God came down upon the earth and assumed flesh. Therfore
that I may now make use of those things, which you also are
versed in, it may be clearly proved (if any skilled in your Histories
would assert the truth) that from the first foundation of the *Roman*
Empire (which is now one thousand one   *This letter was* 20
hundred and eighty five years ago) what ever *written in the year*
additions and growth it gathered either in the *of our Lord* 435.
reign of their first *Kings,* or afterwards under the administration
of *Consuls,* all was permitted by the onely wise, and almighty God
to prepare the world against the coming of *Christ,* and to make
way for the propagation of the Faith.

But I return thither, from whence I have digrest. *Love not the
world* (saith *St. John*) *neither the things that are in the world;* for
all those things with delusive, insnaring shews, captivate our sight,
and will not suffer us to look upwards. Let not that faculty of 30
the eye which was ordained for light, be applyed to darknesse,
being created for the use of life, let it not admit the causes of
death. Fleshly lusts (as it is divinely spoken by the Apostle) war
against the soul, and all their accoutrements are for the ruin and
destruction of it. A vigilant guard doe they keep, when they are
once permitted to make head, and after the manner of forraign
and expert enemies, with those forces they take from us, they
politickly strengthen and increase their own.

Thus hitherto have I discoursed of those splendid allurements,
which are the chiefest and most taking baits of this subtile world, 40
I mean Riches and Honours. And with such earnestnesse have
I argued against them, as if those blandishments had still some

force. But what beauty soever they had, when cast over heretofore with some pleasing adumbrations, it is now quite worn away, and all that paint and cousenage is fallen off. The world now hath scarce the art to deceive. Those powerfull and bewitching lookes of things, beautiful sometimes even to deception, are now withered, and almost loathsome. In former times it laboured to seduce us with its most solid and magnificent glories, and it could not. Now it turnes cheat, and would entice us with toyes, and slight wares, but it cannot. Reall riches it never had, and now it
10 is so poor, that it wants counterfeits. It neither hath delectable things for the present, nor durable for the future; unless wee agree to deceive our selves, the world in a manner cannot deceive us.

But why delay I my stronger arguments? I affirm then that the forces of this world are dispersed and overthrown, seeing the world it self is now drawing towards its dissolution, and pants with its last gasps, and dying anhelations. How much more grievous and bitter will you think this assertion, that for certain it cannot last very long? What should I trouble my self to tell you that all
20 the utensils and moveables of it are decayed and wasted? And no marvell that it is driven into these defects, and a consumption of its ancient strength, when now grown old and weary it stoopes with weaknesse, and is ready to fall under the burthen of so many ages.

These latter years and decrepitness of time are fraught with evils and calamities, as old age is with diseases. Our forefathers saw, and we still see in these last dayes the plagues of famine, pestilence, war, destruction, and terrours. All these are so many acute fits and convulsions of the dying world. Hence it is that such frequent signs are seen in the firmament, excessive Ecclipses,
30 and faintings of the brightest Luminaries, which is a shaking of the powers of heaven; sudden and astonishing Earthquakes under our feet, alterations of times and governments, with the monstrous fruitfulnesse of living creatures; all which are the prodigies, or fatall *symptomes* of time going indeed still on, but fainting, and ready to expire. Nor is this confirmed by my weak assertions onely, but by sacred authority and the Apostolical Oracles: For there it is written, that *upon us the ends of the world are come*, 1 *Cor.* 10. 11. Which divine truth seeing it hath been spoken so long agoe, what is it that we linger for, or what can we expect? That day,
40 not onely ours, but the last that ever the present world shall see, calls earnestly for our preparation. Every hour tels us of the

coming on of that inevitable hour of our death, seeing a double
danger of two finall dissolutions threatens every one in particular,
and all the world in generall. Wretched man that I am! the
mortality of this whole frame lyes heavily upon my thoughts, as if
my own were not burthensome enough. Wherefore is it that we
flatter our selves against these sure fears. There is no place left
for deviation : A most certain decree is past against us, on the one
side is written every mans private dissolution, and on the other the
publick and universal.

How much more miserable then is the condition of those men 10
(I will not say, in these out-goings, or last walks of time, but in
these decayes of the worlds goodly things) who neither can enjoy
ought that is pleasant at the present, nor lay up for themselves
any hope of true joyes hereafter. They misse the fruition of this
short life, and can have no hope of the everlasting : They abuse
these temporal blessings, and shall never be admitted to use the
eternall. Their substance here is very little, but their hope
there is none at all. A most wretched and deplorable condition!
unless they make a virtue of this desperate necessity, and lay
hold on the onely soveraign remedy of bettering their estate, by 20
submitting in time to the wholesome rules of heavenly and saving
reason. Especially because the goodliest things of this present
time, are such rags and fragments, that he that loseth the whole
fraught, and true treasure of that one precious life which is to
come, may be justly said to lose both.

It remaines then, that we direct and fixe all the powers of our
minds upon the hope of the life to come. Which hope (that you
may more fully and clearly apprehend it) I shall manifest unto you,
under a type or example taken from temporal things. If some
man should offer unto another five peeces of silver this day, but 30
promise him five hundred peeces of gold, if he would stay till the
next morning, and put him to his choice, whither he would have
the silver at present, or the gold upon the day following, is there
any doubt to be made, but he would chuse the greater sum, though
with a little delay? Goe you and doe the like : Compare the
Crummes and perishing pittance in this short life, with the glorious,
and enduring rewards of the eternall : And when you have done,
chuse not the least and the worst, when you may have the greatest
and the best. The short fruition of a little is not so beneficial,
as the expectation of plenty. But seeing that all the fraile goods 40
of this world are not onely seen of us, but also possessed by us :
It is most manifest that hope cannot belong unto this world, in

which we both see and enjoy those things we delight in : For *Hope that is seen is not hope ; for what a man seeth, why doth he yet hope for ?* Rom. 8. *ver.* 24. Therefore however hope may be abused, and misapplyed to temporal things, it is most certaine that it was given to man and ordained for the things that are eternal ; otherwise it cannot be called hope, unlesse something bee hoped for, which as yet (or for the present life) is not had. Therefore the substance of our hope in the world to come is more evident and manifest, then our hope of substance
10 in the present.

Consider those objects which are the clearest and most visible ; when we would best discern them, we put them not into our eyes, because they are better seen and judged of at a distance. It is just so in the case of present things and the future : For the present (as if put into our eyes) are not rightly and undeceivably seen of us ; but the future, because conveniently distant, are most clearly discerned.

Nor is this trust and Confidence wee have of our future happinesse built upon weak or uncertain Authors, but upon our Lord
20 and Master *JESUS CHRIST*, that allmighty and faithfull witnesse, who hath promised unto the just, a Kingdome without end, and the ample rewards of a most blessed eternity. Who also by the ineffable Sacrament of his humanity, being both God and Man, reconciled Man unto God, and by the mighty and hidden mystery of his passion, absolved the World from sinne. For which cause he was manifested in the flesh, justified in the Spirit, seen of Angels, preached unto the Gentiles, believed upon in the World, and received into glory. Wherefore God also hath highly
Philip. Chap. 2. exalted him, and given him a name which is
30 *ver.* 9, 10.   above every name : that at the name of *JESUS* every knee should bow, of things in Heaven, and things in Earth, and things under the Earth. And that every tongue should confesse that the Lord *JESUS* is in glory, both God and King before all ages.

Casting off then the vaine and absurd precepts of Philosophy, wherein you busie your selfe to no purpose, embrace at last the true and saving Knowledge of Christ. You shall find even in that, imployment enough for your eloquence and wit, and will quickly discern how far these precepts of piety and truth surpasse the
40 conceits and delirations of Philosophers. For in those rules which they give, what is there but adulterate virtue, and false wisedom ? and what in ours, but perfect righteousnesse and

sincere truth? Whereupon I shall Justly conclude, that they indeed usurpe the name of Philosophy, but the substance and life of it is with us. For what manner of rules to live by could they give, who were ignorant of the first Cause, and the Fountain of life? For not knowing God, and deviating in their first principles from the Author, and the Wel-spring of Justice; they necessarily erred in the rest: Hence it happened, that the end of all their studies was vanity and dissention. And if any amongst them chanced to hit upon some more sober and honest Tenets, these presently ministred matter of pride and Superstitiousnesse, so that 10 their very Virtue was not free from vice. It is evident then, that these are they, whose *Knowledge is Earthy, the disputers of this world, the blind guides,* who never saw true justice, nor true wisedome. Can any one of that School of *Aristippus* be a teacher of the truth, who in their Doctrine and Conversation differ not from swine and unclean beasts, seeing they place true happinesse in fleshly lusts? whose God is their belly, and whose glory is in their shame. Can he be a Master of Sobriety and Virtue, in whose School the riotous, the obscene, and the adulterer are Philosophers? But leaving these blind leaders, I shall come 20 againe to speak of those things which were the first motives of my writing to you.

I advise you then, and I beseech you, to cast off all their *Axioms,* or general *Maxims* collected out of their wild and irregular disputations, wherein I have knowne you much delighted; & to imploy those excellent abilities bestowed upon you in the study of holy Scripture, & the wholsom instructions of Christian Philosophers. There shall you be fed with various and delightfull learning, with true and infallible wisedome. There (to incite you to the Faith) you shall hear the Church speaking to you, though 30 not in these very words, yet to this purpose, *He that believes not the word of God, understands it not.* There you shall hear this frequent admonition; *Feare God, because he is your Master, honour him because he is your Father.* There it shall be told you, *that the most acceptable Sacrifice to God are justice and mercy.* There you shall be taught, that, *If you love your self, you must necessarily love your neighbour; for you can never do your selfe a greater Courtesie, then by doing good to another.* There you shall be taught, that, *there can be no worldly cause so great, as to make the death of a man legal or needfull.* There you shall hear this precept against 40 unlawfull desires. *Resist lust as a most bitter enemy, that useth to glory in the disgrace of those bodies he overcommeth.* There it will be told you of Covetousnesse, *That it is better not to wish for those things you want, than to have all that you wish.* There you shall hear, that *he that is angry, when he is provoked, is never not angry, but when not provoked.* There it will be told you of your Enemies, *Love them that hate you, for all men love those that love them.* There you shall hear, *that he laies up his treasure safeliest, who gives it to the poor, for that cannot be lost which is lent to the Lord.* There it will be told you, *that the fruite of holy marriage is chastity.* There you shall hear, *that the troubles of this World* 10 *happen as well to the just, as the unjust.* There it will be told you, *that it is a more dangerous sicknesse to have the mind infected with vices, then the body with diseases.* There to shew you the way of peace and gentlenesse you shall hear, *that amongst impatient men, their likenesse of manners is the cause of their discord.* There to keepe you from following the bad examples of others, it will be told you, *That the wise man gains by the fool, as well as by the prudent: the one shewes him what to imitate, the other what to eschew.* There also you shall hear all these following precepts. *That the ignorance of many things is better then their Knowledge;* 20 *and that therefore the goodnesse or mercy of God is as great in his hidden will, as in his revealed. That you should give God thanks as well for adversity, as for prosperity; and confesse in prosperity, that you have not deserved it. That there is no such thing as Fate, and for this let the Heathens examine their owne Lawes, which punish none but willfull and premeditating offenders.* There to keep you stable in faith, it will be told you, *That he that will be faithfull, must not be suspitious; for we never suspect, but what wee slowly believe.* There also you shall hear, *that Christians when they give any attention to the noyse and inticements of their passions,* 30 *fall headlong from Heaven unto Earth.* It will be also told you there, *that seeing the wicked do sometimes receive good things in this world, and the just are afflicted by the unrighteous, those that believe not the final Judgement of God after this life, do (as far as it lies in them) make God unjust,* and far be this from your thoughts. There it will be told you about your private affaires, *that what you would have hidden from men, you should never do, what from God, ye should never think.* There you shall here this rebuke of deceivers; It is lesser damage to be deceived, then to deceive. Lastly you shall hear this reproofe of self-conceit, or a fond 40 opinion of our owne worth; flye vanity, and so much the more, the better thou art: all other vices increase by vitiousnesse, but vanity is oftentimes a bubble that swims upon the face of Virtue.

These few rules, as a tast and invitation, I have (out of many more) inserted here for your use.

But if you will now turn your Eyes towards the sacred Oracles, and come your self to be a searcher of those Heavenly treasures, I know not which will most ravish you, the *Casket*, or the *Jewell*, the *Language* or the *Matter*. For the Booke of God, while it shines and glitters with glorious irradiations within, doth after the manner of most pretious gems, drive the beholders Eyes into a strong and restlesse admiration of its most rich and inscrutable brightnesse. But let not the weaknesse of your Eyes make you 10 shun this Divine light, but warme your Soul at the beames of it, and learne to feede your inward man with this mystical and health-full foode.

I doubt not but (by the powerful working of our mercifull God upon your heart,) I shall shortly find you an unfeyned lover of this true Philosophie, and a resolute opposer of the false ; renouncing also all worldly oblectations, and earnestly coveting the true and eternall. For it is a point of great impiety and impru-dence, seeing God wrought so many marvellous things for the Salvation of man, that he should do nothing for himself : and see- 20 ing that in all his wonderfull works he had a most speciall reguard of our good, we our selves should especially neglect it. Now the right way to care for our Soules, is to yeild our selves to the love and the service of God : For true happinesse is obtained by con-temning the false felicities of this World, and by a wise abdication of all earthly delights, that we may become the Chast and faithfull lovers of the Heavenly. Wherefore henceforth let all your words and actions be done either to the glory of God, or for Gods sake. Get Innocence for your Companion, and she is so faithfull, that she will be also your defendresse. It is a worthy enterprise to 30 follow after Virtue, and to perform something while we live, for the example and the good of others : nor is it to be doubted, but the mind, by a virtuous course of life, will quickly free it selfe from those intanglements and deviations it hath been formerly accustomed to. That great Physition to whose cure and care we offer our selves, will daily strengthen and perfect our recovery.

And what estimation or value (when in this state) can you lay upon those glorious remunerations that will be laid up for you against the day of recompence? You see that God, even in this life, hath mercifully distributed unto all (without any difference) 40 his most pleasant and usefull light. The pious and the impious

are both allowed the same Sunne, all the creatures obediently submit themselves to their service : And the whole Earth with the fullnesse thereof is the indifferent possession of the just and unjust. Seeing then that he hath given such excellent things unto the impious, how much more glorious are those things which he reserves for the pious ? he that is so great in his free gifts, how excellent will he be in his rewards ? He that is so Royal in his daily bounty, and ordinary magnificence ; how transcendent will hee be in his remunerations and requitalls ? Ineffable and beyond
10 all conception are those things which God hath prepared for those that love him ; And that they are so is most certain : For it is altogether incomprehensible, and passeth the understanding of his most chosen vessels to tell, how great his reward shall be unto the just, who hath given so much to the unthankfull and the unbe-lieving.

Take up your Eyes from the Earth, and look about you, my most dear *Valerian* ; spread forth your sailes, and hasten from this stormy Sea of Secular negotiations, into the calme and secure harbour of Christian Religion. This is the onely Haven into
20 which we all drive from the raging Surges of this malitious World. This is our shelter from the lowd and persecuting whirlwinds of time : Here is our sure station and certain rest : Here a large and silent recesse, secluded from the World, opens and offers it selfe unto us. Here a pleasant, serene tranquillity shines upon us. Hither when you are come, your weather-beaten Vessell (after all your fruitlesse toiles) shall at last find rest, and securely ride at the Anchor of the *Cross*.

But it is time now that I should make an end. Let then (I beseech you,) the truth and the force of Heavenly Doctrine
30 Epitomized here by me, be approved of and used by you to the glory of God and your own good. These are all my precepts at present : pardon the length, and acknowledge my love.

Gloria tibi mitissime Jesu !

Primitive Holiness,

Set forth in the

LIFE

of blessed

PAULINUS,

The moſt Reverend, and
Learned Bishop of
NOLA:

Collected out of his own Works,
and other Primitive Authors by

Henry Vaughan, Siluriſt.

---

2 Kings *cap.* 2. *ver.* 12.
My Father, my Father, the Chariot of
Iſrael, *and the Horſmen thereof.*

LONDON,

Printed for *Humphrey Moſeley* at
the *Prince's Armes* in St. *Paul's*
Church-yard. 1654.

TO THE
READER.

If thou lovest Heaven, *and the beauty of Immortality, here is* a guide *will lead thee into that* house of light. *The* earth *at present is not worth the enjoying, it is corrupt, and poysoned with the* curse. *I exhort thee therefore to look after a* better country, an inheritance that is undefiled and fadeth not away. *If thou doest this, thou shalt have a portion given thee here, when* all things shall be made new. *In the mean time I commend unto thee the memorie of that* restorer, *and the* reward *he shall bring with him in the* end of this world, *which truely draws near, if it be not* at the door. *Doat not any more upon a withered, rotten* Gourd, *upon the seducements and falshood of a most odious, decayed* Prostitute; *but look up to Heaven, where* wealth *without* want, delight *without distast, and* joy *without* sorrow (*like undefiled and incorruptible* Virgins) *sit cloathed with* light, *and crowned with* glory. *Let me incite thee to this* speculation *in the language of* Ferarius: Desine tandem aliquando prono in terram vultu, vel præter naturam brutum animal, vel ante diem silicernium videri. Cœlum suspice, ad quod natus, ad quod erectâ staturâ tuendum tenendumque factus es. Immortalia sydera caducis flosculis præfer, aut eadem esse Cœli flores existimato nostratibus Amaranthis diuturniores. *Farewel, and neglect not thy own happiness.*

H. V.

THE LIFE OF
HOLY
PAULINUS,
THE
BISHOP of *NOLA.*

Ben Sirach finishing his Catalogue of holy men (to seal up the summe, and to make his list compleat) brings in *Simon* the Sonne of *Onias*: And (after a short narration of his pious care in repairing and fortifying the Temple) hee descends to the particular excellencies, and sacred perfections of his person. Which to render the more fresh and sweet unto posterity, he adornes with these bright and flowrie *Encomiums.*

1. *He was as the Morning-star in the midst of a cloud, and as the Moon at the full.*

2. *As the Sunne shining upon the temple of the most high, and* 10 *as the Rain-bow giving light in the bright clouds.*

3. *As the flower of Roses in the spring of the year, as Lilies by the rivers of waters, and as the branches of the Frankincense-tree in the time of summer.*

4. *As fire and Incense in the Censer, and as a vessel of beaten gold set with all manner of precious stones.*

5. *As a fair Olive-tree budding forth fruit, and as a Cypresse tree which groweth up to the clouds.*

6. *When he put on the robe of honour, and was cloathed with the perfection of glory, when he went up to the holy Altar, he made the* 20 *garment of holinesse honourable.*

Most great (indeed) and most glorious Assimilations, full of life, and full of freshnesse! but in all this beauty of holinesse, in all these spices and flowers of the Spouse, there is nothing too much, nothing too great for our most great and holy *Paulinus.* The Saints of God (*though wandring in sheep-skins, and goat-skins, in caves, and in mountains*) become eminently famous, and leave behind them a more glorious and enduring memory, then the most prosperous tyrants of this world; which like noysome exhalations, moving for a time in the Eye of the Sun, fall after- 30 wards to the earth, where they rot and perish under the *chaines of darkness.* The fame of holy men (like the *Kingdome of God*) is

a *seed that grows secretly*; the dew that feeds these plants comes
from him, that *sees in secret, but rewards openly.* They are those
trees in the Poet,

Which silently, and by none seen,
Grow great and green.

While they labour to conceal, and obscure themselves, they
shine the more. And this (saith *Athanasius* in the life of *Antonie*
the great) *is the goodnesse of God, who useth to glorifie his servants,*
though unwilling, that by their examples he may condemn the world,
10 *and teach men, that holinesse is not above the reach of humane*
nature. Apposite to my present purpose is all this prolusion,
both because this blessed Bishop (whose life I here adventure to
publish) was a person of miraculous perfections and holynesse,
and because withall he did most diligently endeavour to vilifie his
own excellent abilities, and to make himselfe of no account. But
Pearls, though set in *lead*, will not lose their brightnesse; and
a virtuous life shines most in an obscure livelyhood.

In the explication of his life I shall follow first the method of
Nature, afterwards of *Grace*: I shall begin with his *Birth*,
20 *Education*, and *Maturitie*; and end with his *Conversion, Improve-*
ments, and *Perfection.* To make my entrance then into the
work, I finde that he was born in the City of *Burdeaux* in
Gascoyne, in the year of our Lord three hundred and fifty three,
Constantius the *Arian* reigning in the East, and *Constans* in the

* He subscribed to the damnable heresie of Arius, as both Hierome and A-thanasius testifie a-gainst him. West, and * *Liberius* being Bishop of *Rome*: In
a Golden Age, when Religion and Learning
kissed each other, and equally flourished. So
that he had the happines to shine in an age
that loved light, and to multiply his own by the
30 light of others. It was the fashion then of the *Roman* Senatours
to build them sumptuous houses in their Country-livings, that they
might have the pleasure and conveniency of retiring thither from
the tumult and noyse of that great City, which sometimes was,
and would be yet the head of the World. Upon such an occasion
(without doubt) was *Burdeaux* honoured with the birth of
Paulinus, his Fathers estate lying not far off, about the town of
Embrau, upon the River *Garumna*, which rising out of the *Pyrene*
hils washeth that part of *Guienne* with a pleasant stream, and then
runs into the *Aquitane* sea. By this happy accident came *France*
40 to lay claime to *Paulinus*, which she makes no small boast of at
this day. But his Country indeed (if we follow his descent, which
is the right way to find it) is *Italie*, and *Rome* it self; his Ancestors

were all *Patricians*, and honour'd (by a long succession) with the
Consular *purple*. His Patrimonies were large, and more becomming
a Prince then a private man; for besides those possessions in the
City of *Burdeaux*, and by the River *Garumna*, he had other most
ample Inheritances in *Italy* about *Narbone* and *Nola*, and in *Rome* it
self. And for this we have a pregnant testimony out of *Ausonius*,
who labouring to disswade him from *Evangelical poverty*, and
that obscure course of life (as he is pleased to term it) layes before
him (as the most moving arguments) the desolation of his ancient
house, with the ruin and *sequestration* (as it were) of his large 10
possessions; his words are these.

> *Ne raptam sparsamq̃, domum*, &c.
>
> *Let me not weep to see thy ravish'd house*
> *All sad & silent, without Lord or Spouse,*
> *And all those vast dominions once thine owne,*
> *Torn 'twixt a hundred slaves to me unknown.*

But what account he made of these earthly possessions, will
appeare best by his own words in his fifth Epistle to *Severus*:
Ergo nihil in hunc mundum inferentibus substantiam rerum tem-
poralium quasi tonsile vellus apponit, &c. "God (saith he) layes 20
"these temporal accommodations upon us that come naked into
"this world, as a fleece of wooll which is to be sheared off. He
" puts it not as a load to hinder us, whom it behoves to be born
" light and active, but as a certain matter which rightly used may
" be beneficial. And when he bestoweth any thing upon us, that
" is either dear or pleasant to us, he gives it for this end, that by
" parting with it, it may be a testimonial, or token of our love and
"devotion towards God, seeing we neglect the fruition of our best
"present things for his sake, who will amply reward us in the
" future. 30

He had conferred upon him all the ornaments of humane life
which man could be blest with. He was nobly born, rich, and
beautifull, of constitution slender and delicate, but every way fitted
for virtuous imployment; of an excellent wit, a happy memory,
and, which sweeten'd all these gracious concessions, of a most
mild and modest disposition. To bring these seeds to perfection,
his Father (having a care of him equall to his degree) caused him
to be brought up under the regiment of *Decius magnus Ausonius*,
a famous *Poet* and *Oratour*, who at that time kept a School of
Grammar and *Rhetorick* in the City of *Burdeaux*. The Ingenuity 40
and sweetnesse of *Paulinus* so overcame and ravished *Ausonius*,
that he used all possible skill and diligence, to adorne and perfect

those natural abilities which he so much loved and admired in
this hopefull plant. The effect was, that he exceeded his Master.
Ausonius upon this being called to the Court by the old Emperor
Valentinian; *Paulinus* gave himselfe to the study of the *Civill
Law*, and the acute and learned pleadings of that age, wherein he
was so excellent, that the Emperor taking notice of his Abilities,
took order for his Election into the *Senate*, and this a very long
time before his *Tutor* attained to that honour.   This præcedence

10

** Cedimus ingenio
quantum præcedi-
mus ævo, Assurgit
Musæ nostra Ca-
mæna tuæ. Sic &
fastorum titulo pri-
or, & tua Romæ
Præcessit nostrum
sella curulis ebur.*

of eloquence and honour ** Ausonius* himself
confesseth; but having a greater witnesse, I
shall leave his testimony to the *Margin*, to make
room for the other. Take then (if it please you)
the Judgement of that glorious and Eloquent
Doctour Saint *Hierome*, for thus he writes in his
thirteenth Epist. to *Paulinus*, *O si mihi liceret*

*istiusmodi ingenium non per Aonios montes & Heliconis vertices, ut
poetæ canunt, sed per Sion*, &c.   "O that I were able (saith he) to
"extoll and publish your ingenuity and holy learning, not upon
"the *Aonian* hills, or the tops of *Helicon* (as the Poets sing) but

20

"upon the Mountaines of *Sion* and *Sinai*; that I might preach
"there what I have learnt from you, and deliver the sacred
"mysteries of Scripture through your hands; I might then have
"something to speak, which learned *Greece* could never boast of.
"And in another place, A most pregnant wit you have, and an
"infinite treasure of words, which easily and aptly flow from you,
"and both the easinesse and the aptness are judiciously mixt.

To these Divine favours already conferred upon him, God
added another great blessing, the Crown of his youth, and the
Comfort of his age; I meane *Therasia*, a Noble *Roman* Virgin,

30

whom he tooke to wife in the midst of his honours, and who
afterwards (of her owne free will) most joyfully parted with them
all, and with her own pleasant possessions to follow *Christ* in the
regeneration.

At this height of honours, & growing repute, he was employ'd
(upon some concernments of the *Empire*) into *Italy*, *France*, and
Spain; Where he was detained (together with his dear consort)
for the space of almost fifteen years; during which time, he
secretly laboured to make himself acquainted with the glorious
Fathers of that age, and (the Spirit of God now beginning to

40

breath upon him) hee was strongly moved to embrace the
Christian Faith.   In these travells of his, it was his fortune to

3 *(note) ævo*] *ayo* 1654

arrive at *Millaine*, where Saint *Augustine*, and *Alypius*, the Bishop of *Tagasta* in *Africk*, did then Sojourne ; here by accident he was known of *Alypius*, though unknown to him ; as we see it often fall out, that great persons are known of many, which to them are unknown.

Much about this time (which was the eight and thirtieth year of his age,) he retired privately with his wife into the City of *Burdeaux*. And the hour being now come, that *the singing of birds should be heard, and the lips which were asleep should speak* : Hee was there by the hands of holy *Delphinus* (who then sate Bishop in the *Sea* 10 of *Burdeaux*,) publickly baptized, from which time forward he renounced all his Secular acquaintance, associating himself to the most strict and pious livers in that age, especially to Saint *Ambrose* the Bishop of *Millan*, and Saint *Martin* the Bishop of *Tours*. That he was baptized about the eight and thirtieth yeare of his age, is clear by his owne words in his first Epistle to Saint *Augustine*, *Nolo in me corporalis ortus, magis quam spiritalis exortus ætatem consideres*, &c. "I would not (saith he) that you consider my "temporall age, so much as my spiritual ; my age in the flesh is "the same with that Cripple, who was healed in the beautifull gate 20 "by the power of Christ working by his Apostles ; but my age in "the regeneration is the same with the blessed Infants, who by "the wounds intended for Christ himself, became the first fruits "unto Christ, and by the losse of their innocent blood, did fore- "shew the slaughter of the Lamb, and the passion of our Lord. Now for the first, Saint *Luke* tells us, *That the Cripple upon whom this miracle of healing was shown, was above forty years of age* (Acts Chap. 4. ver. 22.) and for the Infants, the *Evangelists* words are, that *Herod sent forth his messengers, and slew all the Male Children that were in* Bethlem, *and the Coasts thereof, from two years old and under.* 30 So that considering all the Circumstances which offer themselves for the clearing of this point, it will evidently appear, that he was baptized (as I have said before) in the eight and thirtieth year of his age. The onely Instrument which God was pleas'd to ordain, and imploy upon the Earth for his Conversion, was his dear and Virtuous Wife *Therasia* ; Which makes me conjecture, that she was borne of Christian parents, and had received the faith from her infancie. This *Ausonius* his old *Tutor*, (who was scarce a good Christian,) forgat not to upraid him with in most injurious termes, calling her *Tanaquil*, and the *Imperatrix* of her Husband : 40 To which passionate passages (though sadly resented) *Paulinus*

3 *Alypius*] *Alpyius 1654*   39 Christian] *Chrihian 1654*

replyed with all the humanity and sweetnesse which language could expresse. Thus *Ausonius* barks at him.

> *Undè istam meruit non fœlix Charta repulsam ?*
> *Hostis ab hoste tamen,* &c.

> —— how could that paper sent,
> That luckless paper, merit thy contempt ?
> Ev'n foe to fo (though furiously) replies ;
> And the defied, his Enemy defies :
> Amidst the swords and wounds ther's a Salute.
> 10 Rocks answer man, and though hard, are not mute.
> Nature made nothing dumb, nothing unkind :
> The trees and leaves speak trembling to the wind.
> If thou doest feare discoveries, and the blot
> Of my love, *Tanaquil* shal know it not.

To this Poetical fury, *Paulinus* reposeth with that Native mildnesse, which he was wholly composed of.

> *Continuata meæ durare silentia linguæ,*
> *Te nunquam tacito memoras ; placitamᵭ latebris*
> *Desidiam exprobras ; neglectæᵭ insuper addis*
> 20 *Crimen amicitiæ ; formidatamᵭ Jugalem*
> *Objicis, & durum iacis in mea viscera versum,* &c.

> Obdurate still, and tongue-tyed you accuse
> (Though yours is ever vocall) my dull muse ;
> You blame my Lazie, lurking life, and adde
> I scorne your love, a Calumny most sad ;
> Then tell me, that I fear my wife, and dart
> Harsh, cutting words against my dearest heart.
> Leave, learned Father, leave this bitter Course,
> My studies are not turn'd unto the worse ;
> 30 I am not mad, nor idle ; nor deny
> Your great deserts, and my debt, nor have I
> A wife like *Tanaquil*, as wildly you
> Object, but a *Lucretia*, chast and true.

To avoid these clamours of *Ausonius*, and the dangerous sollicitations of his great kindred and friends, he left *Burdeaux* and *Nola*, and retyred into the Mountanous and solitary parts of *Spaine*, about *Barcinoe* and *Bilbilis* upon the River *Salo*. Two journeyes he made into *Spain*, this last, and his first (before his baptism) upon the Emperours affairs ; he Sojourned then in new 40 *Castile*, in the City of *Complutum* now called *Alcala de henares*, where his wife *Therasia* was delivered of her onely Son *Celsus*, who died upon the eighth day after his birth. Holy *Paulinus* in his *Panegyrick* upon the death of *Celsus* the Son of *Pneumatius*,

3 *Undè*] *Unde catchword* 1654   15 reposeth] reponeth *Gu*

by his Wife *Fidelis*, takes occasion to mention the early death of
this blessed infant,

> *Hoc pignus commune superno in lumine Celsum*
> *Credite vivorum lacte favisĝ frui.*
> *Aut cum Bethlæis infantibus in Paradiso*
> *(Quos malus Herodes perculit invidiâ,)*
> *Inter odoratum ludit nemus, &c.*

This pledge of your joint love, to Heaven now fled,
With honey-combs and milk of life is fed.
Or with the *Bethlem*-Babes (whom *Herods* rage   10
Kill'd in their tender, happy, holy age)
Doth walk the groves of Paradise, and make
Garlands, which those young Martyrs from him take.
With these his Eyes on the mild lamb are fixt,
A Virgin-Child with Virgin-infants mixt.
Such is my *Celsus* too, who soon as given,
Was taken back (on the eighth day) to Heaven,
To whom at *Alcala* I sadly gave
Amongst the Martyrs Tombes a little grave.
Hee now with yours (gone both the blessed way,)   20
Amongst the trees of life doth smile and play;
And this one drop of our mixt blood may be
A light for my *Therasia*, and for me.

These distant and obscure retirements he made choice of,
because he would not be known of any, nor hindred in his course;
Which at *Nola*, and the adjacent parts of *Rome* (where his Secular
honours and antient descent made all the people obsequious to
him) could not possibly be effected. Besides very few in those
Western parts (especially of the Nobility) had at that time received
the *Christian* Faith; for they look'd upon it as a most degenerate, 30
unmanly profession: such a good opinion had those rough times
of peace and humility. This made him lesse looked after by the
Inhabitants of those parts; and his own friends not knowing what
became of him, began to give him over, and not onely to withdraw
from him in their care, but in their affections also, giving out that
he was mad, and besides himself. But all this moved him not:
he was *not ashamed of the Gospel of Christ, he counted all things
dung that he might gaine* his Saviour, and hee fainted not, but
endured, as seeing him that is invisible. The first step to Christianity (saith Saint *Hierome*) is to contemne the   *St. Hierome Ep.* 26. 40
censures of men. This foundation he laid, and
upon this he built; he had given himselfe wholly to *Christ*, and
rejected the world; he tooke part with that *man of sorrowes*, and
suffered the scoffs and reproaches of these men of mirth. The

people are the many waters, he turn'd their froth and fome into pearls, and wearied all weathers with an unimpaired *Superstitie.* Hee was founded upon that Rock, which is not worne with time, but wears all that oppose it. Some dispositions love to stand in raine, and affect wind and showers beyond Musick. *Paulinus* sure was of this temper; he preferred the indignation and hatred of the multitude to their love, he would not buy their friendship with the losse of Heaven, nor call those Saints and propagators, who were Devills and destroyers. What courage he had in such
10 tempests, may be seen in every line almost of his workes; I shal insert one or two out of his 6th Epistle to *Severus: Utinam, frater mi, digni habeamur qui maledicamur, & notemur, & conteramur, atque etiam interficiamur in nomine Jesu Christi, dum non ipse occidatur Christus in nobis.* &c. "I would (saith he) my dear "brother, that we might be counted worthy to suffer reproach, to "be branded and troden upon; Yea, and to be killed for the "name of Christ, so that Christ be not killed in us. Then at last "should we tread upon the Adder, and the Dragon, and bruise "the head of the old Serpent. But (alas!) wee as yet relish this
20 "World, and do but pretend to love Christ; we love indeed to be "commended and cherished for professing his name, but wee love "not to be troubled and afflicted for his sake. And in his first "Epistle to *Aper;* O blessed displeasures (saith he) to displease "men by pleasing Christ! Let us take heed of the love of such, "who will be pleased without Christ. It is an observation of the Readers of Saint *Cyprian, quod in ejus scriptis singula propè verba Martyrium spirant,* that through all his writings, almost every word doth breath Martyrdome. His expressions are all Spirit and Passion, as if he had writ them with his blood, and conveyed the
30 anguish of his sufferings into his writings. I dare not say so much of *Paulinus,* nor of any other Father of the Church; but I fear not to say that *Paulinus* both durst, and (had he beene called to it) would have laid downe his life for the love of Christ.

Four yeares hee spent in these remote parts of *Spain,* during which time, he did lead a most solitary and austere life, labouring by all meanes to conceale and vilifie himself. *But a City that is built upon a hill cannot be hidden;* his holinesse and humility had so awaked the Common people dwelling about the place of his abode, that they would not rest again till they had him for their
40 Minister. This most honourable and sacred charge he would by no meanes adventure to undergo, judging himselfe a most unworthy vile sinner, not fit to deale in holy Scripture, much lesse to handle

3 worne] worn *catchword 1654*

and administer the mystical Elements of life. But God, who had
ordained him for it, would not suffer this. For the people (not
without violence and some rudeness,) carried him away to *Barcinoe*,
where holy *Lampius*, then Bishop of that Sea, did upon *Christmasse*
day by the laying on of his hands, consecrate him a faithfull
steward and learned dispenser of the Mysteries of God. This
passage we have fully related in his sixth Epistle to *Severus, Nos
modo in Barcinonensi (ut ante Scripseram) civitate consistimus*, &c.
"I live now (saith he) as I formerly writ to you in the City of
"*Barcinoe*, where (since the last letters received from you) I was by 10
"the violence of the people (God, I believe, having foreordained
"it) compell'd to enter into holy Orders upon that day in which
"our Lord was born. I confesse it was done against my will, not
"for any dislike that I have to the place (for Christ is my witnesse,
"that my highest desire was to begin my imployment in his house
"with the office and honour of a door-keeper) but having designed
"my selfe (as you know) * elsewhere, I was   * *For Nola.*
"much terrified with this sudden and unexpected
"pleasure of the Divine will : However I refused it not, but
"submitted with all humility, and have put my necke into the 20
"Yoke of Christ, though altogether unworthy and unable. I see
"now that I have medled with things that are too wonderful for
"me ; I am made a Steward of the Secrets of the Almighty, and
"honour'd with the dispensation of Heavenly things, and being
"called nearer to my Master, I am exercised about the Body,
"about the Spirit, and the glory of Jesus Christ. The narrownesse
"of my understanding cannot comprehend the signification of
"this high and sacred dignity, and I tremble every minute (when
"I consider my own infirmities) to thinke of the great burthen
"that is laid upon me. But he that gives wisedome to his little 30
"ones, and hath perfected praise out of the mouths of babes and
"sucklings, is able to finish what he begun in me, that by his
"mighty working, I may be made worthy, who was most unworthy
"to be called. The Priesthood is an Office belonging to the
Kingdome of Heaven. It is an honour that is ranged upon holy
ground, and by it selfe. Worldly dignities, which are but humane
inventions, are, and may be acquired (with lesse offence) by
humane meanes, as bribery, ambition, and policie. But to take
hold of this white robe with such dirty hands, is nothing lesse
then to spit in the face of *Christ*, and to dishonour his Ordinance. 40
He that doth it, and he that permits it to be done, agree like
Herod and *Pilate*, to dispise and crucifie him. They that

Countenance and ratifie such disorders, take care to provide so many *Judasses* to betray Christ, and then vote the treason to be lawfull. Every man can speak, but every man cannot preach : Tongues and the gift of tongues are not the same things : The wisdome of God hath *depth* and *riches*, and *things hard to be spoken*, as well as *milk*, and *the first principles of his Oracles*. Wee have amongst us many builders with *hay and stubble*, but let them, and those that hired them, take heed how they build ; The tryal will be by fire, and by a consuming fire. The *hidden things of*
10 *dishonesty, the walking in Craftinesse*, and *the handling deceitfully of the word of God* they are well versed in ; but true sanctitie, and the Spirit of God (which Saint *Paul* thought he had) I am very sure they have not.

A modest reader would now thinke that *Paulinus* had removed himselfe farre enough from the elaborate temptations, and clamorous pursuits of *Ausonius* ; But even in this will he be deceived. For at the fourth years end, did the Incantations of this busie and obstinate Charmer find him out. God (no doubt) providing for the security of his servant all that while, by delaying them in severall
20 regions, or else by concealing the abode of his beloved votary, from this pursuer of Soules. For with all the artifice and strength of wit, did he set upon him in this last letter, which the divine providence suffered not to come into his hand, till he had set both his *hands to the plough*, and seald his conformation with that indelible Character. And now having set a hedge about his beloved, he suffered this *Fowle* of the Evening to fly over, which chattered to him in these melodious numbers.

> *Vertisti*, Pauline, *tuos dulcissime mores ?* &c.
> *Sweet* Paulinus, *is thy nature turn'd ?*
30 > *Have I so long in vaine thy absence mourn'd ?*
> *Wilt thou, my glory, and great* Romes *delight,*
> *The Senates prop, their oracle, and light,*
> *In* Bilbilis *and* Calagurris *dwel,*
> *Changing thy Ivorie-chair for a dark Cell ?*
> *Wilt bury there thy Purple, and contemn*
> *All the great honours of thy noble stem ?*

To this *Roman Magick*, and most pernicious Elegancy, *Paulinus* replyed with a certain sacred and serene simplicity, which proved so piercing, and powerful, that he was never after troubled with
40 the Poetry of *Ausonius*.

> ——*Revocandum me tibi credam,*
> *Cum steriles fundas non ad divina precatus ?*
> *Castalidis supplex averso numine musis,* &c.

42 *precatus*] *percatus 1654*

Shall I beleeve you can make me return,
Who pour your fruitless prayers when you mourn,
Not to your Maker ? Who can hear you cry:
But to the fabled Nymphs of *Castalie*?
You never shall by such false Gods bring me
Either to *Rome,* or to your company.
As for those former things you once did know,
And which you still call mine, I freely now
Confesse, I am not he, whom you knew then ;
I have dyed since, and have been borne agen.   10
Nor dare I think my sage instructor can
Believe it errour, for redeemed man
To serve his great redeemer. I grieve not,
But glory so to erre. Let the wise knot
Of worldlings call me fool ; I slight their noise,
And heare my God approving of my choice.
Man is but glass, a building of no trust,
A moving shade, and, without *Christ,* meer dust :
His choice in life concerns the Chooser much :
For when he dyes, his good or ill (just such   20
As here it was) goes with him hence, and staies
Still by him, his strict Judge in the last dayes.
These serious thoughts take up my soul, and I
While yet 'tis day-light, fix my busie eye
Upon his sacred Rules, lifes precious sum,
Who in the twilight of the world shall come
To judge the lofty looks, and shew mankind
The diff'rence 'twixt the ill and well inclin'd.
This second coming of the worlds great King
Makes my heart tremble, and doth timely bring   30
A saving care into my watchfull soul,
Lest in that day all vitiated and foul
I should be found : That day, times utmost line,
When all shall perish, but what is divine.
When the great Trumpets mighty blast shall shake
The earths foundations, till the hard Rocks quake,
And melt like piles of snow, when lightnings move
Like hail, and the white thrones are set above.
That day, when sent in glory by the Father,
The Prince of life his blest Elect shall gather ;   40
Millions of Angels round about him flying,
While all the kindreds of the earth are crying,
And he enthron'd upon the clouds shall give
His last just sentence, who must die, who live.
    This is the fear this is the saving care,
That makes me leave false honours, and that share
Which fell to mee of this fraile world ; lest by
A frequent use of present pleasures I
Should quite forget the future, and let in
Foul Atheism, or some presumptuous sin.

Now by their loss I have secur'd my life,
And bought my peace ev'n with the cause of strife.
I live to him, who gave me life & breath,
And without feare expect the houre of death.
If you like this, bid joy to my rich state,
If not, leave me to *Christ* at any rate.

Being now ordained a Minister of holy things, and a feeder of
the flock of *Christ*, that he might be enabled to render a joyfull account at the appearance of the great Shepheard, he resolved
10 with all convenient expedition to sell and give away all his large and
Princely Possessions in *Italy* and *France*, which hitherto he had not
disposed of; for he looked upon his great Patrimonies as matters of
distraction and backsliding, the thoughts and solicitousnesse about
such vast revenues disturbing his pious affections, and necessarily
intruding into his most holy exercitations. Upon this rare resolution
he returnes with his faithfull Consort into *France*, leaving *Barcinoe*
and holy *Lampius* in much sorrow for his departure. For though
hee had entred there into the Ministery, yet was he no member of
that Diocesse. And here (saith *Uranius*, who was his Presbyter,
20 and wrote a brief narration of his life) did he open his Treasuries
to the poor and the stranger. He did not only refresh his neighbours, but sent messengers into other remote parts to summon the
naked, and the hungry to this great Feast, where they were both
fed and cloathed with his own hands. He eased the oppressed,
freed the captives, payd the debts of whole families, and redeemed
divers persons that were become bondslaves to their creditors.
Briefly, he sold all that he had, and distributed the money amongst
the poor, not reserving one penny either for himself, or his dear
Therasia. Saint *Ambrose* in his thirtieth Epistle to *Sabinus* con-
30 firmeth this relation : *Paulinum splendore generis in partibus
Aquitaniæ nulli secundum, venditis facultatibus tam suis quam etiam
conjugalibus, &c.* "*Paulinus* (saith he) the most eminent for
" his Nobility in all the parts of *Aquitane*, having sold away all his
" patrimonies, together with the goods of his wife, did out of pure
" love to Jesus Christ divide all that vast Summe of Money amongst
" the poor ; and he himself from a rich Senator is become a most
" poor man, having cast off that heavy secular burthen, and forsaken
" his own house, his country, and his kindred, that he might with
" more earnestnesse follow Christ. His Wife also, as nobly de-
40 " scended, and as zealous for the Faith as himself, consented to all
" his desires, and having given away all her own large possessions,
" lives with her husband in a little thatch'd cottage, rich in

32 (saith *text 1654* : saith *catchword 1654*

"nothing but the hidden treasures of Religion and holinesse. Saint *Augustine* also in his first book *de Civitate Dei*, and the tenth Chapter, celebrates him with the like testimony: "Our *Paulinus* "(saith hee) from a man most splendidly rich, became most poor "most willingly, and most richly holy. He laboured not to adde field unto field, nor to inclose himself in Cedar and Ivory, and the drossie darke gold of this world, but to enter through the gates into the precious light of that City, which is of *pure gold like unto cleare glasse.* He left some few things in this world, to enjoy all in the world to come. A great performance certainly, and a most fair approach towards the Kingdom of heaven. He that fights with dust, comes off well, if it blinds him not. To slight words, and the names of temptations, is easie, but to deale so with the matter, and substance of them, is a task. Conscience hath Musick, and light, as well as discord and darknesse: And the triumphs of it are as familiar after good works, as the Checks of it after bad. It is no heresie in devotion to be sensible of our smallest Victories over the World. But how far he was from thinking this a Victory, may be easily gathered out of his owne words in his second Epistle to *Severus*; *Facilè nobis bona*, &c. "The "goods (saith he) I carried about me, by the slipping of my skirt "out of my hand, fell easily from me: And those things which "I brought not into this World, and could not carry out of it, being "only lent me for a time, I restored again. I pulled them not "as the skin off my back, but laid them by, as a garment I had "sometimes worne. But now comes the difficulty upon me, "when those things which are truly mine, as my heart, my Soul, "and my works must be presented and given a living Sacrifice "unto God. The abdication of this World, and the giving of our "temporall goods amongst the poore, is not the running of the race, "but a preparing to run; it is not the end, but the beginning, and "first step of our Journey. Hee that striveth for masteries, shall "not be crowned, except he first strive lawfully; And he that is "to swimme over a River, cannot do it by putting off his "cloathes onely, he must put his body also into the stream, and "with the motion of his armes, his hands and feete, passe through "the violence of the Brook, and then rest upon the further side "of it. And in his 12th Epistle, he cries out, "O miserable and "vaine men! Wee believe that wee bestow something upon the "poor: wee trade and lend, and would be counted liberall, when "we are most covetous. The most unconscionable userers upon

" Earth are not so greedy as we are, nor their interest and exactions
" so unreasonable as ours. We purchase Heaven with Earth,
" happinesse with misery, and immortality with rust and rotten-
" nesse. Such another Divine rapture is that in his Poems.

> ———— *Et res magna videtur,*
> *Mercari propriam de re pereunte salutem ?*
> *Perpetuis mutare caduca ?* &c.

> ———— And is the bargain thought too dear,
> To give for Heaven our fraile subsistence here?
> To change our mortall with immortall homes,
> And purchase the bright Stars with darksome stones?
> Behold ! my God (a rate great as his breath !)
> On the sad crosse bought me with bitter death,
> Did put on flesh, and suffer'd for our good,
> For ours, (vile slaves !) the losse of his dear blood.

Wee see by these *Manifesto's* what account he made of this
great deed ; so great, that none now adaies thinke of doing it. *Go
thy way, sell whatsoever thou hast, and give to the poor,* is a com-
mandement, as well as, *take up the Crosse and follow me.* This last
cannot be done, but by doing the first. Wee sell oftentimes, but
seldome give : and happily that is the reason we sell so often. He
that keeps all to himselfe, takes not the right way to thrive. The
Corn that lies in the Granarie will bring no harvest. It is most
commonly the foode of vermine, and some creatures of the night
and darknesse. Charity is a relique of Paradise, and pitty is
a strong argument that we are all descended from one man : He
that carries this rare Jewell about him, will every where meete with
some kindred. He is quickly acquainted with distressed persons,
and their first sight warmes his blood. I could believe, that the
word *stranger* is a notion received from the posterity of *Cain,* who
killed *Abel.* The *Hebrewes* in their own tribes, called those of the
farthest degree, *brothers* ; and sure they erred lesse from the law
of pure Nature, then the rest of the Nations, which were left to
their owne lusts. The afflictions of man are more moving then of
any other Creature ; for he onely is a stranger here, where all things
else are at home. But the losing of his innocency, and his device
of Tyranny have made him unpittied, and forfeited a prerogative,
that would have prevailed more by submission, then all his posterity shall do by opposition. Not to give to one that lacks, is
a kind of murther : Want and famine are destroyers as well as the
sword, and rage very frequently in private, when they are not

14 suffer'd] suffe'rd *1654*   18 *whatsoever] whatsover 1654*   20
Wee *M*: Well *1654*: We'll *G Gu*

thought of in the Publick. The blessed *JESUS* who came into the World to rectifie Nature, and to take away the inveterate corruptions of man, was not more in any of his precepts, then in that which bids us *Love one another.* This is the cement not onely of this World, but of that other which is to come. *Blessed are the mercifull;* and, *give to him that asketh thee,* proceeded from the same lips of truth. And in his description of the last judgement, he grounds the sentence of condemnation pronounced against the wicked upon no other fact, but because they did not *cloath the naked, feed the hungry, and take in the stranger. Love covers a multitude of sins, and God loves the chearfull giver.* But this is not our whole duty: though we give our bodies to be burnt, and give all our goods unto the poor, yet *without holinesse we shall never see the face of God.* Darknesse cannot stand in the presence of light, and *flesh and blood cannot inherit the Kingdome of God.* The great difficulty then (as our holy Bishop here saith) is to become a living sacrifice; and truly the next way to it, is by an Evangelical disposing of these outward incumbrances; this will open and prepare the way before us, though it takes nothing from the length of it. The Hawke *proines* and *rouseth* before she flyes, but that brings her not to the *mark*: Preparations, and the distant flourishes of *Array* will not get the field, but action, and the pursuance of it.

His Estate in *France* being thus disposed of, he retyred into *Italy*; where having done the like to his Patrimonies there, hee came to *Millaine*, and was honourably received by holy *Ambrose*, then Bishop of that *Sea.* But these gay feathers of the World, being thus blown off him, by the breath of that Spirit which makes *the dry tree to become green*, and *the spices of the Garden to flow out*, all his kindred and former acquaintance became his deadly Enemies. Flyes of estate follow Fortune, and the Sun-shine; friendship is a thing much talked off, but seldome found; I never knew above two that loved without selfe-ends. That which passeth for love in this age, is the meere counter to it; It is policie in the cloathes of love, or the hands of *Esau* with the tongue of *Jacob*. These smooth Cheats the World abounds with: There is *Clay enough for the potter, but little dust whereof commeth Gold.* The best direction is Religion; find a true Christian, and thou hast found a true friend. He that fears not God, will not feare to do thee a mischiefe.

From *Millaine* he came to *Rome*, where he was honourably entertained by all, but his own kindred, and *Siricius* the great Bishop. It was the ill Fortune of this zealous Pope, to be offended

not onely with *Paulinus*, but with that glorious Father Saint *Hierome*.
It was a perillous dissolutenesse of some Bishops in that Century,
to admit of Lay-men, and unseason'd persons into the Ministry.
This rash and impious practice *Siricius* had, by severall strict
Sanctions or decrees, condemned and forbidden ; and it is probable that the reason of his strange carriage towards *Paulinus* and
Hierome was, because he would not seem to connive at any persons
that were suddenly ordained, though never so deserving, lest he
should seeme to offend against his own edicts. It is a sad truth that
10 this pernicious rashnesse of Bishops (fighting *ex diametro* with the
Apostolical cautions) hath oftentimes brought boars into the Vine-
yard, and Wolves into the sheep-fold ; which complying afterwards
with all manner of Interests, have torne out the bowels of their
Mother. Wee need no examples : Wee have lived to see all this
our selves. Ignorance and obstinacie make *Hereticks* : And
ambition makes *Schismaticks* ; when they are once at this passe,
they are on the way toward *Atheisme*. I do not say that *Ecclesiastical polity* is an inviolable or sure fense against Church-rents ;
because there is a necessity that *offences must come*, though *wo to*
20 *them by whom* ; but rules of prevention are given, and therefore
they should not be slighted. The Bridegroom adviseth his spouse
to *take these foxes while they are litle.*

In a pleasant field halfe a mile distant from *Nola* lies the
Sepulcher of the blessed Martyr *Felix*. To this place (which from
his youth hee was ever devoted to,) did *Paulinus* now retire. It
was the custom of holy men in that age, not onely to live near
the Tombs of the Martyrs, but to provide also for their buriall in
those places ; because they were sure, that in the Resurrection,
and the terrours of the day of Judgement God would descend upon
30 those places in *the soft voyce*, that is to say in his love and mercies.
Eusebius in his fourth Book, and the sixth Chapter of the life of
Constantine tells us, how that great Emperour gave strict order for
his buriall amongst the Tombes of the Apostles, and then adds,
Ὠφέλειαν ψυχῆς ὀνησιφόρον τὴν τῶνδε μνήμην ποιεῖσθαι αὐτῷ
πιστεύων. Saint *Chrysostome* in that homilie which hee writ to
prove that *Christ is God*, gives the same relation, Καὶ ἐν τῇ
Κωνσταντίνου πόλει δε, &c. The Emperors of *Constantinople*
(saith he) esteeme it for a great honour, if they be buried not
within the shrines of the Apostles, but at the Gates of their
40 Temple, that they may be the door-keepers of those poor fishers.
So *Marcellina*, descended from the consular Nobility of *Rome*,

15 *Hereticks*] *Heretick catchword 1654*   31 in] is *1654*

refused to be buried amongst her Ancestors, that she might sleepe at *Millaine* with her great Brother Saint *Ambrose,* where shee lies under this *Epitaph.*

> *Marcellina, tuos cum vita resolveret artus ;*
> *Sprevisti patriis,* &c.

> Life, *Marcellina,* leaving thy faire frame,
> Thou didst contemne those Tombes of costly fame,
> Built by thy Roman Ancestours, and lyest
> At *Millaine,* where great *Ambrose* sleeps in Christ.
> Hope, the deads life, and faith, which never faints,   10
> Made thee rest here, that thou may'st rise with Saints.

To this place therefore near *Nola* in *Campania* (a Country lying within the Realm of *Naples,* and called now by the Inhabitants *Terra di Lavoro,*) as to a certain Harbour and recesse from the clamours of their friends, and the temptations of the World, did *Paulinus* and *Therasia* convey themselves. *Paulinus calls him* His affection to this holy [a] Martyr was very *a Martyr, quia* great: for frequenting *Nola,* when he was yet *multa pro Christo passus, etsi non oc-* a youth, he would oftentimes steale privately to *cisus.* visit his Sepulcher : and he loved the possessions which his 20 Father had left him in those parts above any other, because that under pretence of looking to his estate there, he had the convenience of resorting to the Tombe of *Felix* ; where he took in his *first love,* and in the seaven and twentieth year of his age, made a private vow to become a Servant of *Jesus Christ.* This *Felix* was by descent a *Syrian,* though born in *Nola,* where his Father (trafficking from the *East* into *Italie,*) had purchased a very fair estate, which he divided afterward betwixt him and his Brother *Hermias* ; but *Felix* following *Christ,* gave all to his brother. The frequent miracles manifested at his Tombe, made 30 the place famous, and resorted to from most parts of the world. Saint *Augustine,* upon a Controversie betwixt his Presbyter *Boniface,* and another fellow that accused him, when the truth of either side could not be certainly known, sent them both from *Hippo* to *Nola,* to have the matter decided upon Oath, before the Tombe of *Felix* ; and in his 137th Epistle, hee sets down the reason, why he sent them so farre. His words are these : *Multis notissima est sanctitas loci, ubi Felicis Nolensis corpus conditum est, quò volui ut peragrent, quia inde nobis facilius fideliusque scribi potest, quicquid in eorum aliquo divinitus fuerit propalatum.* "The 40 "holinesse (saith he) of that place where the body of *Felix* of

1 *(note) Paulinus*] *Paulininus 1654* 15 temptations] t mptations *1654* (?)
27 *Italie,*)] *Italie, 1654*

"*Nola* lies interred, is famously knowne to many; I have there-
"fore sent them thither, because that from thence, I shall be
"more easily and truly informed about any thing that shall be
"miraculously discovered concerning either of them.

Paulinus had not lived very long in this place, but it pleas'd
God to visit him with a very sharpe and tedious sicknesse. Hee
had now (upon Earth) no Comforter but *Therasia*; His Estate
was gone, and his contempt of that made the World contemne
him. In this solitude and poverty, he that tries the reines and
the heart, begins to take notice of this his new servant, and the first
favour he conferred upon him was a disease. Good Angels doe
not appeare without the Ecstasie and passion of the Seere:
without afflictions and trialls God will not be familiar with us.
Fruit-trees, if they be not pruned, will first leave to beare, and
afterwards they will dye. Nature, without she be drest by the
hand that made her, will finally perish. He that is not favour'd
with visitations, is (in Saint *Pauls phrase*) a bastard, and no Son
of the Superiour *Jerusalem*. *Paulinus* had put from him all
occasions of worldly sorrowes, but he wanted matter for Heavenly
Joyes. Without this disease, hee had not known so soone, how
acceptable his first Services were unto his Master. This sicknesse
was a pure stratagem of love, God visited him with it for this very
purpose, that he himselfe might be his Cordial.

Man and the *Eagle* see best in the day-time, they see by the
light of this World: but the ᵃ *night-Raven*
is a bird of Mysterie, and sees in the darke
by a light of her own. *Paulinus* thought
now (like the servant of *Elisha*) that hee
had not a friend in all the World to be of
his side; but God removes the mist from
his Eyes, and shewed him a glorious Army
of *Saints* and *Confessours*, who during the
time of his sicknesse, did so throng and
fill up his Cottage, and the fields about it,
that neither his Palace in *Rome*, nor his

ᵃ *Paulinus will have the word which is commonly used in the Latin, to be* Nicticora, *from* νύξ *and* χορή, *which signifies the apple or candle of the eye, and not from* χορά. *And this he saith was told him by a holy man, that had lived a long time in the deserts of* Egypt, *where he observed the nature of this bird of night, and the* Pelican.

house in *Burdeaux* could ever boast of such a number. These
Comforters he hath recorded with his own pen in his first Epistle
to *Severus*; *viderant pueri tui*, &c. "Your men (saith he) that
"were here with me, have seen, and can tell you with what
"constant diligence all the Bishops, and my brethren the Clergy,
"with the common people my neighbours, did minister unto me

8 (*note*) χορα̃.] χορα̃ *1654*   14 , if] if, *1654*   27 thought] hought *1654*

"all the time of my sicknesse. Unto you, who are unto me as
"my own soul, I take leave to boast and glory in this mercy of
"the Lord, whose goodnesse it is, that I am so plentifully
"comforted. There is not one Bishop in all *Campania* that did
"not come personally to visit me, and those whom either a farther
"distance, or their own infirmities would not permit to travel,
" fail'd not to visit me by their Presbyters & letters. The Bishops
"of *Africk* allso with the beginning of the spring, sent their
"particular letters and messengers to comfort me. Thus *he that
forsakes houses and brethren, and lands to follow Christ, shall* 10
*receive an hundred fold even in this World, and in the world to
come life everlasting.*

As touching the letters, or Embassage rather of the *African*
Bishops to *Paulinus*, it happened on this manner. *Alypius*, the
Bishop of *Tagasta* in *Africk*, had at *Millain* (as I intimated
before) taken speciall notice of *Paulinus*: And the rumour of his
Conversion (as the actions of eminent and noble personages passe
quickly into the most distant regions,) had filled with joy not
onely the Churches of *Africk*, but the most remote corners of
Christianity, even the very wildernesse and the scattered Isles, 20
which in those daies were more frequented by Christians, then
populous Continents and splendid Cities. *Alypius* upon this
(because he would not loose so fair an opportunity to ground his
acquaintance,) dispatcheth a letter from *Tagasta* to *Paulinus*, to
gratulate his conversion to the Faith; encouraging him withall
to hold fast his Crown; and for a token, sent him five of Saint
Augustines bookes against the *Manichæans*, which in that age
(when the Invention of the *Presse* was not so much as thought
of,) was a rich present. *Paulinus* was so taken with the reading
of these Volumes, that he conceived himself not onely engaged to 30
Alypius, but to *Augustine* also. Whereupon he sent his servant
from *Nola* with letters full of modestie and sweetnesse to them
both, and with particular commendations to other eminent lights
of the Church then shining in *Africk*. These letters received by
Augustine and *Alypius*, and communicated by them to the other
Bishops, and the *African* Clergy, were presently Coppied out by
all, and nothing now was more desired by them, then a sight of
this great Senatour, who was turned a *poor Priest, and a fool* (as
Saint *Paul* saith) *for Christ his sake*, and *the off-scouring of the
World*. But above all, the Soules of holy *Augustine* and *Paulinus* 40
(like *Jonathan* and *David*, or *Jacob* and *Joseph*) were *knit together*,

7 fail'd] fai'd *1654*

and *the life of the one was bound up in the life of the other*. The perfect love and union of these two, can by none be more faithfully, or more elegantly described, then it is already by Saint *Augustine* himself. I shall therefore insert his own words, the

August. Epistol. 22. words of that tongue of truth and Charity; *O*
ad Paulin. *bone vir, O bone frater! latebas animam meam;*
& ei dico ut toleret, quia adhuc lates oculos meos, & vix obtemperat,
immo non obtemperat. Quomodo ergo non doleam quod nondum
faciem tuam novi, hoc est, domum animæ tuæ, quam sicut meam
10 *novi? legi enim literas tuas fluentes lac & mel, præferentes simpli-*
citatem cordis, in quâ quæris dominum, sentiens de illo in bonitate,
& afferens ei claritatem & honorem. Legerunt fratres & gaudent,
infatigabiliter & ineffabiliter tam uberibus & tam excellentibus
donis dei, bonis tuis. Quotquot eas legerunt, rapiunt; quia rapiun-
tur, cum legunt. Quàm suavis odor Christi, & quàm fragrat ex eis?
dici non potest, illæ literæ cum te offerunt ut videaris, quantum nos
excitent ut quæraris: nam et perspicabilem faciunt, & desidera-
bilem. Quantò enim præsentiam tuam nobis quodammodò exhibent,
tantò absentiam nos ferre non sinunt. Amant te omnes in eis, &
20 *amari abs te cupiunt. Laudatur & benedicitur deus, cujus gratiâ*
tu talis es. Ibi excitatur Christus, ut ventos & Maria tibi placare
tendenti ad stabilitatem suam dignetur. Ibi conjux excitatur, non
dux ad mollitiem viro suo, sed ad fortitudinem redux in ossa viri sui:
quam in tuam unitatem redactam, in spiritualibus tibi tantò firmiori-
bus quantò castioribus nexibus copulatam, officijs vestræ sanctitati
debitis in te, uno ore salutamus. Ibi cedri Libani ad terram depositæ,
& in arcæ fabricam compagine charitatis erectæ, mundi hujus fluctus
imputribiliter secant. Ibi gloria ut acquiratur, contemnitur; & mun-
dus, ut obtineatur, relinquitur. Ibi parvuli, sive etiam grandiusculi
30 *filij Babylonis eliduntur ad petram, vitia scilicet confusionis, super-*
biæque secularis. Hæc atque hujusmodi suavissima & sacratissima
spectacula literæ tuæ præbent legentibus; literæ illæ, literæ fidei
non fictæ, literæ spei bonæ, literæ puræ charitatis. Quomodo
nobis anhelant sitim tuam, & desiderium defectumque animæ tuæ
in atria domini? Quid amoris sanctissimi spirant? Quantam
opulentiam sinceri cordis exæstuant? Quas agunt gratias deo?
Quas impetrant â deo? blandiores sunt, an ardentiores? luminosiores,
an fæcundiores? Quid enim est, quòd ita nos mulcent, ita accendunt,

5 *So Vita. Misprinted in 1654 as follows: O bone vir, O bone frater!*
lei dico ut toleret, quia adhuc lates oculos meos, latebas animâ meâ, & & vix
obtemperat immo,
32 *legentibus; literæ illæ, Vita: legentibus; 1654*

ita compluunt; & ita serenæ sunt? Quid est, quæso te, aut quid tibi pro eis rependam, nisi quia totus sum tuus in eo, cujus totus es tu? si parùm est, plus certê non habeo. "O good man, O good "brother! you lay hidden from my Soul, and I spoke to my "Spirit, that it should patiently bear it, because you are also "hidden from my Eyes; but it scarse obeyes, yea it refuseth to "obey. How then shall I not grieve, because I have not as yet "knowne your face, the habitation of your Soul, which I am as "well acquainted with as my owne? For I have read your letters "flowing with milk and honey, manifesting the simplicity of your "heart, in which you seek the Lord, thinking rightly of him, and "bringing him glory and honor. Your brethren here have read "them, and rejoyce with an unwearied and unspeakable Joy, for "the bountifull and excellent gifts of God in you, which are your "riches. As many as have read them, snatch them from me; "because when they read them, they are ravished with them. "How sweet an Odour of Christ, and how fragrant proceeds from "them? It cannot be exprest how much those letters, while they "offer you to be seen of us, excite us to seek for you: They "make you both discerned and desired: For the more they "represent you unto us, wee are the more impatient of your absence. "All men love you in them, & desire to be beloved of you. God "is blessed and praised by all, through whose grace you are such. "There do we find that Christ is awaked by you, and vouchsafeth "to rebuke the winds and the Seas, that you may find them calme "in your Course towards him. There is your dear wife stirred "up, not to be your leader to softnesse and pleasures, but to "Christian fortitude; becomming Masculine again, and restored "into the bones of her Husband: whom we all with one voice "salute and admire, being now united unto you, serving you in "spiritual things, wherein you are coupled with mutuall embraces, "which the more chast they be, are by so much the more firm. "There do we see two Cedars of *Libanus* fell'd to the Earth, "which joyned together by love, make up one Arke, that cuts "through the Waves of this World without detriment or putre- "faction. There glory, that it may be acquired, is contemned; "and the World, that it may be obtained, is forsaken. There the "Children of *Babylon*, whither litle ones, or of Maturer age; "I mean the Evils of Confusion and secular pride, are dashed "against the stones. Such sacred and delightfull spectacles do "your letters present unto us: O those letters of yours! Those

2 *cuius*] *cu us* 1654

" letters of an unfained faith, those letters of holy hope, those letters
" of pure Charity! How do they sigh and gaspe with your pious
" thirst, your holy longings, and the Ecstatical faintings of your Soul
" for the Courts of the Lord? What a most sacred love do they
" breath? with what treasures of a sincere heart do they abound?
" How thankfull to God? How earnest for more grace? How
" mild? How zealous? How full of light? How full of fruite?
" Whence is it that they do so please us, and so provoke us, so
" showre and raine upon us, and yet are so calm and so serene?
10 " What is this I beseech you? or what shall I returne unto you
" for these letters, unlesse I tell you, that I am wholly yours in
" him, whose you are altogether? If this be too little, in truth
" I have no more.

These were the first effects of *Paulinus* his letters; but shortly
after, St. *Augustine* sent him others, nothing inferiour to this first,
either in affection, or Piety. And the year following, being
elected by *Valerius* to sit his Coadjutor in the Sea of *Hippo*, where
he afterwards succeeded him; It was resolved by them all, namely
by *Valerius, Augustine, Alypius, Severus,* and *Profuturus,* the
20 *African* Bishops, that a messenger should be dispatched into
Campania to present *Paulinus* with their several letters, and the
sincere gratulations of their respective Clergy; which accordingly
was performed.

In the beginning of this year, which was the three hundred
ninety and fifth after *Christ, Theodosius Augustus* the first,
a most pious Emperour, and a *Nursing Father* of the Church
departed this life. The *Ethnick* writers hating his memory as
virulently as his person, laboured with all manner of lyes and
Libels to render him odious and detestable to posterity. Holy
30 *Endelechius* awaked with these scandalous clamours, and the
insolent aspersions cast upon so religious an Emperour, writes
earnestly to *Paulinus,* and prevailes with him, to imploy those
excellent abilities bestowed on him, in the defense of this faithfull
Souldier of *Jesus Christ,* and Champion of his Spouse. This task
Paulinus performed, as appears by his owne words in his 9th
Epistle to *Severus,* to whom hee sent a Coppy of his learned
Panegyrick; however posterity have suffered in the losse of it. But
we want not another witnesse: That learned Father, and happy
translator of the booke of God in his thirteenth Epistle to *Paulinus,*
40 gives us a very fair and full account of it. *Librum tuum quem
pro Theodosio principe prudenter ornateque,* &c. " Your booke

7 light?] light?? *1654*   8 so showre *Gu*: to showre *1654*   37 *Panegyrick*]
Panegygick 1654   41 booke] Book *catchword 1654*

"(saith he) which elegantly and judiciously you composed in the
"defense of the Emperor *Theodosius*, and sent to me by ᵃ *Vigi-*
"*lantius*, I have with much delight read over.   ᵃ *He proved after-*
"What I admire in it, is your Method : For *wards a most detes-*
"having excelled all other writers in the first parts, *table Heretick.*
"you excell your selfe in the last.   Your stile is compact and
"neat, and with the perspicuity and purenesse of *Cicero*, and yet
"weighty and sententious ; for that writing which hath nothing
"commendable in it, but words, is (as one saith) meer prating.
"The consequence besides is very great, and the coherence exact. 10
"What ever you infer, is either the confirmation of the antece-
"dent, or the inchoation of the subsequent.   Most happy *Theo-*
"*dosius*, to be vindicated by such a learned Oratour of *Christ*!
"You have added to the glory of his Imperial robe, and made the
"utility of his just lawes sacred to posterity.   But this rare peece,
with many more mentioned by *Gennadius*, either through the
envie of the Heathen, or the negligence of our own, are unfortunately lost ; especially a *Volume of Epistles* written to his *Sister*,
with some *controversial peeces* against the *Ethnick* Philosophers,
mentioned also by Saint *Augustine* in his four and thirtieth 20
Epistle ; and a most learned *Treatise of true Repentance*, and *the
glory of Martyrs.*

Much about this time, the name of *Paulinus* began to be
famous in the *East* ; and not onely there, but in all parts of the
Christian World.   It is almost incredible (especially in this age
of Impieties and Abominations) how much the example of this
one man prevailed over all.   The Course he ran, drew another
wealthy and noble *Roman* (I mean *Pammachius*) from the Senate
to the Cell ; and all the Fathers of that age, when they prest any
to holy living, and a desertion of the World, brought in *Paulinus* 30
for their great exemplar, and a star to lead them unto *Christ*.
St. *Augustine* propounds him to *Romanianus* & *Licentius*, Saint
Hierome to *Julian*, and the Daughters of *Geruntius* ; and Saint
Chrysostome in his thirteenth homily upon *Genesis*, sets him
downe for a pattern to the husbands, and *Therasia* to the wives.   The
reverend Bishop of *Hippo* did very earnestly sollicite him to come
over into *Africk*, & he gives his reason for it in these words : *Non
imprudenter ego vos rogo, & flagito, & postulo*, &c.   "Not un-
"advisedly doe I intreat and earnestly desire, and require you to
"come into *Africk*, where the Inhabitants labour more now with 40
"the thirst of seeing you, then with the famous thirstinesse of the

1 which] whihc *1654*

"Climate. God knowes, I ask it not for my private satisfaction, nor
"for those onely, who either by my mouth, or by the publick fame
"have heard of you ; but for the rest, who either have not heard,
"or else having heard will not believe so great a change ; but when
"they themselves shall see the truth, they will not onely believe,
"but love and imitate. It is for their sakes therefore, that I desire
"you to honour these parts with your bodily presence : Let the Eyes
"of our flocks also behold the glory of Christ in so eminent
"a Couple, the great exemplars to both Sexes, to tread pride under
10 "their feet, and not to despaire of attaining to perfection. And in
his fifty ninth Epistle to *Paulinus*, when (according to the custome
of those holy times) hee had sent his Presbyter to him to be
instructed, *he cannot* (saith he) *profit more by my Doctrine, then he
can by your life.* Saint *Hierome* useth the same Engine to bring
down the high thoughts of *Julian* ; "Art thou (saith he) nobly
"descended ? So were *Paulinus* and *Therasia*, and far nobler in
"Christ. Art thou rich and honourable ? So were they : and from
"the height of honours and worldly riches became poor and
"inglorious, that they might gain Christ. Dearly did *Anastasius*,
20 who succeeded *Siricius* in the Sea of *Rome*, affect this holy
Bishop, as appears by his owne words in his sixteenth Epistle to
Delphinus the Bishop of *Burdeaux*.

But amidst all these triumphs of the Church of God, for the
conversion of so eminent a person, and the frequent gratulations
of learned men, exprest by their letters or personall visits, there
were none that raged with so much hatred and malice against him
as his own kindred, and former acquaintance. *A Prophet hath
no honour in his own Country, and those of his owne house will be
his Enemies.* There are no such persecutors of the Church, as
30 those that do it for selfe-ends, and their private advantage.
Sweetly doth he complain of these bitter, unnatural dealings in
his fifth Epistle to *Severus*. *Potiore mihi parente germanus es,
quam illi quos caro tantùm & sanguis mihi sociat*, &. "You
"are my Brother now by a greater Father, then those who are
"tyed to me by flesh and blood onely. For where is now my
"great affinity by blood ? Where are my old friends ? where is my
"former acquaintance ? I am become as a dream before them all,
"and as a stranger to my owne brothers, the Sons of my Mother.
"My kinsmen and my friends stand looking upon me afar off, and
40 "they passe by me like hasty floods, or the streames of a brook
"that will not be stay'd. They convey themselves away, and are

10 perfection] prefection *1654*

"ashamed of me, who displeased them by pleasing God. And in
"his first Epistle, I beseech you (saith he) If I shall have need
"(for now my servants, and those I made free-men, are become
"my despisers,) that you would take care to send the old Wine,
"which I beleive I have still at *Narbon*, hither unto me, and to
"pay for the carriage: Do not fear, dear brother, to make the
"poor your debtor, *&c.* The Noble Spirit is the bravest bearer of
indignities: and certainly extraction and a virtuous descent (let
popular flatterers preach what they will to the contrary,) is
attended with more Divinity, and a sweeter temper, then the 10
indiscrete Issue of the multitude. There is an eminent difference
betwixt flowers and weedes, though they spring from the same
mould. The Ape contending with the Lyonesse, told her, that
she was a very fair creature, but very barren: For you (said the
Ape) bring forth but one at a birth, and I bring six, or more;
'Tis true (replyed the Lionesse,) but thy six are six Apes, and my
one is a Lyon. The greatest part of men, which we commonly
terme the populacy, are a stiffe, uncivill generation, without any
seed of honour or goodnesse, and sensible of nothing but private
interest, & the base waies of acquiring it. What Virtue, or what 20
humanity can be expected from a *Raymond Cabanes*, a *Massinello*,
or some Son of a Butcher? They have one barbarous shift, which
Tigers and Beares would blush to commit: They will cut the
throats of their most generous and Virtuous Benefactours, to comply with times, and advantage themselves; Yea, they will rejoyce
to see them ruined, and like inhumane Salvages, insult over their
innocent and helplesse posterity. I could compare those fawning
Hypocrits, that waite not upon men, but upon their Fortunes, to
that smiths bitch in the *Apologues* of *Locmannus* the *Persian*,
which sleeping in the forge, could not be awaked with all the 30
noise of the hammers, the Anvile, and the Bellowes: but if the
smith would offer to stirre his teeth to eat, shee would start up
presently, and attend upon him with all officiousnesse. She would
share with him in the fruits of his labours; but would not watch
and look to the shop one minute while he laboured.

Paulinus had now first lost these false friends, but was loaded
for it with the love and commendations of true ones; And I know
not which offended him most, to be despised by the first, or
commended by the last. He had (like Saint *Paul*,) great heavinesse, and continuall sorrow of heart, to see that his brethren and 40
kinsmen according to the flesh, hated him because he loved

25 times] [the] times *Gu*

Christ: And on the other side, his humility would not suffer him
to beare the *labour of love,* I meane the generall applause and
sincere commendations conferred upon him by his Christian
friends. *Severus* in one of his Epistles written to him (after hee
had spent some lines in the commendation of his zeale and
constancie,) contrary to the custome of that plaine age, subscribed
Te multa dilectio ad himself, his Servant. To the first he replyed,
mendacii peccatum that *his excessive love had drawn him to the sin*
traxit. *of untruth*: And the last he desired him to
10 desist from, for this reason; *Cave ergo ne posthac,* &c. "Have
"a care hereafter (saith he) that you who are a Servant of Christ,
"called unto liberty, terme not your self the servant of a sinner,
"and of one that is not worthy to be called your fellow-servant.
"The virtue of humility will not excuse the vice of flattery. Thus
Gregorie the great, when Pope *Anastasius* had exceeded towards
him in his laudatory elocutions, blasted them all with this humble
reply; *Quod verò me os domini, quod lucernam,* &c. "Your
"calling me the mouth of the Lord, a shining light, and a strong
"helper, is nothing else but an augmentation of my iniquity; for
20 "when I deserve to be punished for my sins, then do I instead of
"punishment receive praise. *Severus,* in another of his Epistles to
Paulinus, earnestly intreated him to suffer his picture to be taken
by a limner, which he had sent to him for that purpose, that he
might have it to set up, together with the picture of Saint *Martin,*
before the sacred font in a fair Church which *Severus* was then in
building. This friendly motion *Paulinus* was very much offended
with, and would by no means consent unto, teling *Severus, that too*
much love had made him mad; And in his eighth Epistle, reasoning
with him about this request, *What kind of picture* (saith he) *would*
30 *you have from me, the picture of the earthly, or the Heavenly man?*
I know you love onely that incorruptible image, which the King of
Heaven doth love in you. I am ashamed to picture what I am, and I
dare not picture what I am not. But *Severus* resolving to force it
from him, would not be satisfied with any other returne; wheruppon
he sent it to him, with these following verses, the elegant expresse
of his unfeined humility. The first coppy relates to the *pictures,*
and the latter to the *Font.*

Abluitis quicunç animas & membra lavacris,
Cernite propositas ad bona facta vias, &c.

40 You that to wash your flesh and Soules draw near,
Ponder these two examples set you here.

12 not] nor *1654*

Gerat *Martin* shewes the holy life, and white;
Paulinus to repentance doth invite.
Martins pure, harmlesse life tooke Heaven by force,
Paulinus tooke it by teares and remorse.
Martin leads through victorious palms and flowers,
Paulinus leades you through the pooles and showres.
You that are sinners, on *Paulinus* look,
You that are Saints, great *Martin* is your book.
The first example bright and holy is,
The last, though sad and weeping, leads to blisse.   10

The verses relating to the *Font*, were these.

Hic reparandarum generator fons animarum
    Vivum viventi lumine flumen agit, &c.

Here the great well-spring of wash'd Soules, with beams
Of living light quickens the lively streams;
The Dove descends, and stirs them with her wings,
So weds these waters to the upper springs,
They strait conceive: A new birth doth proceede
From the bright streams by an immortall seed.
O the rare love of God! sinners wash'd here,   20
Come forth pure Saints, all justified and clear.
So blest in death and life, man dyes to sins,
And lives to God; Sin dies, and life begins
To be reviv'd: Old *Adam* falls away,
And the new lives, born for eternal sway.

Nor did the manners of holy *Paulinus* differ from his mind: all
his Garments, all the Utensils of his poor Cot, were so many
emblems and memento's of humility. Grace is an Elixir of a
contrary Nature to the Philosophers stone, it turn'd all the gold
and Silver vessells of this great Senatour into earthen dishes and 30
wooden spoons. Righteousnesse and honesty are alwaies poor.
In his first Epist. to *Severus*, he presents him with some of this
innocent furniture; *Misimus testimonialem divitiarum scutellam
buxeam*, &c. "I have sent you (saith he) a platter made of a box-
"tree, for a testimoniall of my riches; receive it as a pledge or
"earnest of Evangelicall poverty, and let it be an example to you,
"if as yet you will make use of any Silver platters. To this he
addes, that he was very desirous to be supplyed with some more
earthen dishes, which (saith he) *I do very much love*; and then
subscribes his reason, *quòd secundum Adam cognata nobis sint, &* 40
domini thesaurum in talibus vasis commissum habeamus; because they
are near kin to us by *Adam*, and because the treasure of the Lord
is committed to our care in such vessells. Certainly poverty (as

21 justified] justfied *1654*

man is now to be considered) is his best, and his true estate.
Riches, though they make themselves wings, yet do they not fly
to Heaven. The home or house of gold, is the heart of the
Earth, and mineralls are a fuel of hell-fire. Poverty was the
Inauguration of the first man, who was made naked, and all his
posterity are born so. *This onely have I found* (saith *Solomon*)
that God made man upright, but he hath sought out many inventions.
By Covetousnesse we loose our uprightnesse : Wee come here
light and easie, but we load our selves afterwards with unnecessary
10 burthens. *Perditio tua ex te*, these weights that we take up, sink
us down : Our temporall misery as well as the Eternal is from our
selves. The merriest creature that I can
see, is the * *Sparrow*. This makes me
think, that hee is not troubled with fore-
thoughts, which are the hands of covetousnesse. What man and beasts scatter
and leave behind them, is his provision :
his table is laid every where, and the first
bush he meets with, is his bed. Our
Saviour, who knew the nature and thoughts
of all created things, was pleased to send
us to school to the birds. They are
alwaies full of Musical livelinesse, and a
certain bright freedome, which descends
not so low as men and beasts. Spirits,
when they have businesse upon Earth,
must assume bodies. Clarity and purification is a kind of poverty : it is a state
that hath cast off dregs & burthens. Divine is that saying of
30 *Gr. Pisides.*

* *Paulinus calls Christ*
(mistically) a sparrow :
Hic est ille passer, qui
requirentibus se in viis hi-
lariter ostendit; nunc in
portis ht obvius, nunc in
platis occurrit, nunc in
muris vel turribus sublimis
convocat ad se amatores
suos, & invitat eos in alti-
tudines habitationum sua-
20 rum, ut impleat verbum
suum, & exaltatus omnia
ad se trahat. Quis dabit
nobis pennas columbæ
deargentatas, ut pennati
pervolemus ad bravîum
supernæ vocationis, se-
quentes istum passerem
solitarium, qui est unicus
dei filius, supervolitantem,
qui in altis habitat, & hu-
milia respicit ?

Τὸ πτωχὸν ἦθος οὐρανόδρομον φύσει.
Poor habits are naturally heaven-seekers.

But *Paulinus*, though he was poor, yet was he charitable, and
withall liberall. The widowes mite is more then the rich mens
abundance. In the four hundred and tenth year after *Christ,*
when the *Gothes* raged in *Italy*, and had sackt *Nola*, *Paulinus*
(amongst many others,) was taken prisoner by
them ; *And thus* (saith Saint *Augustine*) *as I*
afterwards learnt from him, did he then pray in his heart.
40 Domine, ne excrucier propter aurum & argentum; ubi enim

Lib. I. de Civitate
dei.

omnia mea sunt, tu scis. *O Lord suffer me not to be troubled with the losse of Gold & Silver, for thou knowest where all my riches are laid up.* His treasure was laid up in Heaven, where he commanded us to lay it, who foretold, that these calamities should come upon the World. And God (without doubt) had reguard unto his prayer, for the barbarous enemie leading all the rest into captivity, he onely was left behind. But amongst all these plunderings and outward afflictions, hee never failed in his daily almes to the poor, nor was the hand of his faithfull *Therasia* any way shortned. At last his store failing, and no more provision being left, then onely one loafe of bread; A poor man comming to the door for reliefe, *Paulinus* commands it should be given him. But *Therasia* (arguing with her selfe, that no begger could be poorer then *Paulinus* now was, and that it was as much charity to keepe it for him, as to give it to another,) conceal'd the loafe, and suffered the poor man to go without it. A day or two after, some men that were sent with relief to *Paulinus,* from his friends, arrive at *Nola,* and tell him that they had been there much sooner, had not one of the ships, which was loaden with corn, been cast away almost in the Harbour; the rest that were fraught with Wine and other Victualls, being come safe to shore. Whereupon *Paulinus* turning towards *Therasia,* put her in mind of her overmuch carefullnesse, with these words, *Understand now* Therasia, *that this great ship full laden with Corne, was cast away for that one loafe of bread which thou didst steale from the poore man.*

But passe we now to his *Episcopall* dignity. In his own Workes we have not one line that mentions this Ecclesiasticall honour, nor any other passage of his life, that might but seem to conduce to his own glory. They breath nothing but humility, nothing but self-deniall and dedignation. Wee must be guided then through this part of his life by other Authors, and such faithfull records as are come unto us, from the hands of learned and publick persons; who either upon the generall interest and concernments of the Church, or their own private merits, and not by reflection were acquainted with him. The first that offers himself to us, is *Uranius,* his own Presbyter, who in that short narration which he wrote of his life, sets him forth to posterity in this following Character; *Cum autem ad summum sacerdotij gradum,* &c. "When he was honoured (saith he) with the highest degree in "the Priesthood, he did not shew himself such a Bishop that "desired to be feared, but one that endeavoured to be beloved. "He was never so farre angry, as not in his anger to shew mercy.

"Nor could that man indeed be angry, for he regarded not
"calumnies, and he avoyded hatred. He never sate in Judge-
"ment, but mercy sate close by him. He was truly such a Bishop
"as laboured to get the love of all. For hee lived a Consolatiõ
"to all, and their great example to make sure their Salvation.
"Nor is this my voyce onely: even the barbarous Nations who
"knew my Lord *Paulinus* by report onely, will testifie as much.
"And worthily was hee beloved of all, who was a friend to all.
"For who was there cast down, and he did not lift him up? who
10 "ever called to him for help, and was not piously and comfortably
"answered? For he was pious, tender hearted, humble and
"courteous, hating none, despising none. He gave to all, he
"cherished all: he encouraged the fearfull, pacified the violent,
"those with his words, these with his example; Some he com-
"forted with his letters, and those that wanted, with his mony.
"He loved not any riches, nor any treasures, but those which
"Christ promised to his followers. Gold and Silver, and the
"other accommodations of life he approved of, if they were liberally
"given to the poor, not covetously hoorded up. Briefly, he had
20 "in him all goodnesse, for he loved Christ. Hee had Faith,
"Meeknesse, love towards his neighbours, a constant care of the
"poor, compassion upon the weak, and laboured for nothing in
"his life, but peace and charity. All his endeavours were to make
"men good, and to save their Soules. What place is there in the
"World, what solitude, what Seas which acknowledge not the
"good works of holy *Paulinus*? All men desired his acquaintance,
"and did extreamly long to have a sight of him. Who ever came
"to him without joy, or who went from him, but he desired to
"stay longer? those that could not see him in the body, desired
30 "to see him in his writings; for he was sweet and gentle in his
"Epistles, elegant and ravishing in his Poems. What more shall
"I say? The relations that may be given of him, would be scarse
"credible, but that his knowne integrity is above falshood.

Nola was at this time a very famous and splendid City, nothing
inferiour to the best *Emporiums* of *Italie*, and had withall a very
rich *Sea*; which questionlesse was a great occasion, that the piety
of this blessed Bishop was so renowned, and so familiarly spoken
of in the most remote parts of the World. So the just and
faithfull God exalteth those that humble themselves, and honours
40 those that honour him. He had beene faithfull in those things
that were his own, and was therefore intrusted with the treasures
of the Church. *Prosper* in his second book, *de vitâ Contemplativâ*,

and the ninth Chapter, tells us, how hee disposed of them ; *Sanctus Paulinus* (*ut ipsi meliùs nostis*) *ingentia prædia quæ fuerunt sua, vendita pauperibus erogavit : sed cum posteà factus esset Episcopus, non contempsit Ecclesiæ facultates, sed fidelissime dispensavit.* "Holy *Paulinus* (saith he) as you best know, sold all those "princely Possessions which were his own, and gave of them to "the poor : but when he was afterwards consecrated Bishop, he "neglected not the revenues of the Church, but was a most faith- "full Steward and dispenser of them. So faithfull, that when he lay upon his death bed, hee had not one piece left to relieve him- self, but was driven to lay out for some Cloathes which he had given to the poor, a small summe of mony, which God ordained to be sent to him for that very purpose a litle before the hour of his dissolution. So that living and dying, he kept to the Apostles rule, and *owed no man any thing but love* : Hee was a great lover of learned and holy men, and confesseth in one of his Epistles to *Alypius*, that his affection to Saint *Ambrose*, was the first inducement which he felt to incline him to Christianity. His dearest and most intimate friends were Saint *Augustine*, Saint *Ambrose*, Saint *Hierome*, Saint *Martin* the Bishop of *Tours*, *Delphinus* the Bishop of *Burdeaux*, and *Amandus* his Successour ; *Alypius* the Bishop of *Tagasta*, *Januarius* the Bishop of *Naples*, afterwards a Martyr, *Victricius* the *Rhotomagensis*, *Aper*, *Severus*, and *Nicetas* of *Dacia*. I may say of him as the Scripture saith of *Moses*, he was the meekest man upon the face of the Earth. He was not onely obedient and serviceable to these Fathers, and pillars of the Church, but to his own *Presbyters* and *Domesticks* : he judged himself the most unworthy, and the most unable of all his brethren. *Victor* the Monk, sent from *Severus* to see him (according to the custome of those times) washed his feete. This was a ceremony, which in that age of holinesse could not be refused. But *Victor* by this did not onely wash his feet, but his face also ; for he drew tears from him, because hee might not deny him the performance of that Evangelical service. *Servivit ergo mihi peccatori, & væ misero mihi quod passus sum ; he served me a sinner* (saith the holy Bishop) *and woe is to me because I suffered him.* But he staid not at tears, for as soone as *Victor* had done washing his feet, to requite his service, he fetched him clean water, and held the bason while he wash'd his hands. He was not like that insolent *Abbot* that did cast off his humility with his *Cowle*, and being asked by his brethren, *why he was then so proud, that was formerly such an humble Monk*, made answer ; *that in his*

Monachisme, when he went so low, and stooping, he was searching for the keyes of the Abbey; but now having found them, he did hold up his head to ease himself.

This true carriage of an Evangelist, made him both honourd and beloved; the *Church* rejoyced, and glorified God for him, and the *Court* admired him. Holynesse is a light that cannot be hidden: It is a candle set upon a hill: stars never shine more glorious, then when they are neare black Clouds. In the year of our Lord, four hundred and nineteen (a grievous *Schism* then
10 happening in the Church,) there was a convention of certain Bishops and Fathers at *Rome*, to quiet those groundlesse perturbations, and stop the breach. But *Honorius* the Emperour, judging by his skil in the temper of those Church-men, that no good would be done without the presence of *Paulinus*, who then lay sick at *Nola*, dispatched his Imperial letter to this holy Bishop, wherein he earnestly intreated him (if possible) to shake off his present indisposition, and to repaire in person to the Synod, lest that great blessing of peace, which he and the Church did earnestly hope and long for, might by his absence unfortunately miscarry.
20 This royall record (because it is a monument of no lesse sincerity then concernment, and discovers unto us much of the face of those times) I shall *verbatim* insert.

Sancto & venerabili Patri, *Paulino,* Episcopo *Nolensi.*

*Tantùm fuit apud nos certa sententia, nihil ab his sacerdotibus, qui ad Synodum convenerant, posse definiri, cum beatitudo tua de corporis inæqualitate causata, itineris non potuit injuriam sustinere, ut propter absentiam sancti viri, non quidem obtentura: Interim tamen vitia gratulantur, cùm prava & vetus ambitio, & cum
30 benedicto viro sanctææ vitæ diù velit habere certamen, ut contra hæc Apostolicæ institutionis bona, de præsumptis per vim parietibus existimet confidendum. O verè digna causa quam non nisi coronæ tuæ beata vita designat! Dilatum itaæ Judicium nuntiamus, ut divina præcepta ex venerationis tuæ ore promantur, qui ea secutus implesti; nec potest alius eorum præceptorum lator existere, quam qui dignus Apostolicis disciplinis est approbatus. Specialiter itaæ domine sancte, meritò venerabilis pater, Justus dei famulus, divinum opus, contempto labore, tributum hoc nobis visitationis tuæ (si ita dicendum est) munus indulge, ut postpositis omnibus, quantùm tem-*

perantia his & tranquillitas suffragantur, Synodo profuturus, sine intermissione etiam desideriis nostris, & benedictioni quam cupimus, te præstare digneris.

To the holy and reverend Father PAULINUS, *Bishop of* Nola.

"Such a firm opinion have we that nothing can be agreed and "concluded upon by the Bishops met in this Synod, (your Holi-"nesse by reason of your bodily indisposition being not able to "travel hither) that for your onely absence it is not like to con-"tinue: In the mean time offences triumph and rejoyce at it, and 10 "the old and wicked sinne of ambition, which of a long time "desires to contend even with your holynesse and upright life, "presumes now, and is confident that having forcibly taken the "wall from us, it will carry you also against the wholsomnesse of "Apostolicall institution. O! a cause truly worthy not to be "determined, but by your holy life, which is your Crown! we "therfore declare unto you, that we have suspended our judge-"ment for the present, that we may have the truth of these Divine "precepts pronounced by your reverend mouth, who have both "followed them, and fullfilled them: For none can be a fit arbiter 20 "of those rules, but he that hath approved himself worthy and "conformable to Apostolicall discipline. Wherefore, holy Sir, "worthily reverend Father, the faithfull Servant of God, and his "Divine work, we intreat you particularly, that slighting the "troubles of this Journey, you would favour us with this gift and "tribute (if I may so speak) of your presence: and laying aside "all other concernments (so far as your health and ease will per-"mit,) be in your owne person at this Synod, and vouchsafe to "lend your assistance to our desires, and that blessing which wee "earnestly long for. 30

Wee see by this letter in what account hee was with the Emperour, and that his integrity and holyness were not dissimulations and popular *Fables,* but experimentall truths so known and so believed; hee was a true Christian, and no Impostour. It was not the Custome, but the nature (if I may so say) of those Primitive times to love holy and peacefull men. But some *great ones* in this later age, did nothing else but countenance *Schismaticks* and *seditious raylers, the despisers of dignities,* that covered their *abominable villanies* with a pretence of *transcendent holinesse,* and a certain *Sanctimonious excellencie* above the Sons of men. This 40 *Vaile* (which then *cousend* weak eyes) is now fallen off their *faces,*

and most of their patrons have by an unthought of Method
received their rewards : The rest without doubt (though they shift
themselves into a thousand shapes) shall not escape him, *whose
anger is not yet turned away, but his hand is stretched out still.*
But returne we to *Paulinus* : Whose Charity and tendernesse
towards the poor, was both inimitable and incredible ; This iron
age wants faith as well as mercy : When he had given them all he
had, to the last that begged he gave himself. *Gregorie* the great,
in the third Book of his *Dialogues*, and the first Chapter, hath
10 recorded this memorable passage. I shall cut it short, and in as
few words, as conveniently may be, give you all that is material.
When the *Vandals* had miserably wasted *Campania*, and carried
many of the inhabitants into *Africk*, blessed *Paulinus* gave all
that he had both towards his own sustenance, and the reliefe of the
poor, amongst the prisoners and Captives. The Enemy being
departed, and his prey with him ; a poor Widow (whose onely
Son was (amongst the rest of the Natives) by a Son in law of the
King of the *Vandals* carried into Bondage,) comes to petition
Paulinus for so much Money as might serve to redeem him.
20 *Paulinus* told her that he had nothing then left, either in money
or other goods, but promised, if shee would accept of him, to go
with her into *Africk*, and to be exchanged for her Son. The
poore Widow taking this for a meere scoffe, turnes her back to be
gone. *Paulinus* followes after, and with much adoe made her
believe, that he meant it (as he did indeed) in earnest. Upon
this, they travell'd both into *Africk*, and having opportunity to
speake with the Kings Son in Law, the poor widow begged of him
first, to have her son restor'd unto her *Gratis* : but the youthfull
and haughty *Vandal* averse to all such requests, would hear her
30 no farther ; whereupon she presents him with *Paulinus*, and
petitioned to have her Son set at liberty, and the other to serve in
his stead. The Prince taken with the comely and reverend
countenance of *Paulinus*, asked him, what his occupation or trade
was ? *Paulinus* answered, that he never followed any trade, but
that he had good skill in dressing of Herbes and Flowers. Upon
this, the Prince delivered her Son to the Widow, who took him
home with her, and sent *Paulinus* to work into his Gardens.

The Prince delighting much in Flowers and Sallets, would very
frequently visit *Paulinus*, and took such delight in him, that he
40 forsook all his Court-associates to enjoy the company of his new
Gardiner. In one of these visits, *Paulinus* taking occasion to

10 as] as, *1654*

confer seriously with him, advised him to be very carefull of himselfe, and to consider speedily of some means to secure and settle
the Kingdome of the *Vandals* ᵃ in *Mauri-*
tania ; for (said he) the King your Father
in law will shortly dye. The Prince something troubled with the suddain newes,
without further delay acquaints the King
with it ; and tells him withall, that his
Gardiner (whose prediction this was)
excelled all other men both in wisedome
and learning. Whereupon the King
requested, that he might see him ; you
shall, replyed the Prince, for to morrow

*This was about the year
of our L.* 428. *about which
time the Vandals after their
excursions through* Polonia,
Italy, Franconia, *and* An-
dalusia *had setled in* Africk,
*where they continued quiet-
ly until the reigne of* Jus-
tinian, *but rebelling against
him, they were together* 10
with their King Gillimer
*totally overthrown by the
great Captaine* Belisarius
An. Christi 533.

when you are at dinner, I will give order that hee shall come in
person with the dishes of Sallate to the Table. This being agreed
upon, and accordingly performed, the old Tyrant upon the first sight
of *Paulinus* exceedingly trembled, and speaking to his Daughter,
who sate next to him, to call to her husband, he told him, that the
prediction of his Gardiner was very true ; for *yesternight* (said he)
I saw in a dream a great tribunal with judges sitting thereon, and 20
*amongst them this Gardiner, by whose judgement a scourge which had
been formerly put into my hands, was taken from me.* But learn of
him what his profession is, and what dignity he had conferred upon
him in his own Country, for I cannot believe him to be (as he
pretends) an inferiour or ordinary person.

As soon as dinner was ended, the Prince stole from the *presence*
into the Garden, and earnestly intreated *Paulinus* to tell him, who
he was ; I am (said he) your Gardiner, which you received in
exchange for the Widowes Son. I know that, replyed the Prince,
but I desire to know your profession in your own Country, and 30
not the servitude you have put your self in with me for the present ;
To this *Paulinus* answered, that he was by profession a *Bishop*,
and a servant of Jesus Christ the Son of the living God. At these
words the Prince was mightily troubled, and requested him to
depart againe into his own Country, assuring him, that before he
departed, he would give him any thing that he should please
demand. *Paulinus* replyed, that he would desire nothing, but to
have those Captives which were carried out of *Campania*, set at
liberty, and transported to their Native Country. To this the
Prince consented, and for *Paulinus* his sake, furnished them with 40
shipping and all other necessaries for their voyage, and sent them
home joyfull in the Company of their blessed and beloved Bishop.

2 (*note*) *which*] *which* 1654

Some few daies after, the old Tyrant (as God had foretold by his holy Servant) departed out of this World *into his owne place*; And so that scourge which God had put into his hand for the punishment of a great part of the Christian World, was taken away, and the instrument cast into the fire. Wherefore whoever thou beest, that readest this book, and art a sufferer thy selfe, or doest see and grieve for the calamities of the Church, *the oppression of the poor, & the violent perverting of judgement & justice in a province, do not thou marvel at the matter,* nor vex thy self; *for he that is higher then the highest, regardeth it, and there be higher then they. Envy not the glory of Sinners, for thou knowest not what will be their end;* but *submit thy self under the mighty hand of God,* expecting with patience the time of refreshing, and I do assure thee upon my Soul, thou shalt not be deceived.

Paulinus, with all his joyfull Captives, was now landed in *Campania,* where all the Inhabitants, as upon a solemne feast-day flocked together to welcome him, and to poure their joyes into his bosome; some received their Sonnes, some their brothers, and some their husbands: both the receivers and the received were beholding to *Paulinus.* They commended, honoured and admired him: He exhorted, incouraged and confirmed them. Mutuall Consolations are a double banquet, they are the Churches *Eulogiæ,* which we both give and take. What the *Campanians* most admired in *Paulinus,* was that which the Scripture commends in *Moses*: *youthfullnesse in old age.* He was now as earnest, as hearty, and as active for the glory of God, as in his most vigorous years. *His spiritual force was not abated, nor the Eye of his Soul any way dimmed.* Hee did not coole towards his *setting,* but grew more large, more bright, and more fervent. Bearing trees, when their fruit is ripe, bend their boughes, and offer themselves to the gatherers hands. He knew that his time of departure was at hand, and therefore *Moses*-like he made his *Doctrine to drop as the raine, and his speech distilled as the dew. Hee poured out his milk and his Wine, and made them drink abundantly.* To labour in the heat of the day, and to give over in the cool, is great indiscretion, the contention should be alwaies hottest towards the end of the race.

I am now come to my last *Paragraph,* which all this while I did reserve for his *Works of Piety.* And these indeede (if wee consider his unworldlinesse, and religious poverty) were very great and very sumptuous. He repaired and beautified the four old *Basilica's,* or Churches, dedicated to the Martyr *Felix,* and built the *fifth,* which

14 deceived.] deceived, *1654*

exceeded them all, both for beauty and largenesse. This he
dedicated to our Lord and Saviour *Jesus Christ.* It was adorned
with two stately Porches, the one opend towards the way of
Publick resort, the other was a private *Postern* ; and the path
leading to it, was through a pleasant *green field* set with *fruit-trees*
and other *shady wood,* fenced about with a very high and sumptuous
wall ; The entrance into this Court was through a fair Marble-
Gate, in whose Front were cut these following verses.

Cælestes intrate vias per amœna vireta, &c.

Through pleasant green fields enter you the way   10
To blisse ; and wel through shades and blossoms may
The walkes leade here, from whence directly lyes
The good mans path to sacred *Paradise.*

This Church was joyned to the other four, and an entrance made
from the one into the other, by high and spatious *Arches,* supported with pillars of Marble. Through these pillars (whose height
did almost reach to the roof,) as through a *traverse* was to be
seene, by those that came from the old Church into the new, the
picture of the Crosse, limned in most lively and glorious Colours,
and hung with Garlands of palms and flowers ; above it shined 20
a cleare and luminous skie, and on the Crosse, which was all
Purple, sate perching a flock of white Doves ; at the bottome of
this *Paisage* were written these verses.

Ardua floriferæ Crux, &c.

The painfull Crosse with flowers and Palms is crown'd,
Which prove, it springs ; though all in blood 'tis drown'd :
The Doves above it shew with one consent,
Heaven opens onely to the innocent.

In the Courts belonging to this Church, were very faire and
spatious walks, paved with stone, and covered over head against 30
the violence of weather. The outside was supported with Pillars,
and the Inner was divided into neat and cleanly Cells, opening
towards the Walks, where the people that came thither to celebrate
the *Vigils* of *Felix,* reposed themselves. Round about these Courts
were great *Cisterns,* and *Lavers* of severall kinds of Marble most
curiously polished, whose diverse formes and colours were very
delightfull, and much recreated the beholders. The Porches,
which were very large, and contained within them many private
Oratories, or places of prayer, were all richly pictured with sacred
Histories out of the *Pentateuch,* the book of *Joshuah, Judges* and 40
Ruth ; This Church is fully described in his twelfth Epistle to

Severus, and his ninth *Natalis,* when *Nicetas* came out of *Dacia*
to see him.

> *Ecce vidès quantus splendor velut æde renatâ*
> *Rideat, insculptum camerâ crispante lacunar*
> *In ligno mentitur ebur ; tectoque supernè*
> *Pendentes lychni spiris retinentur ahenis,*
> *Et medio in vacuo laxis vaga lumina nutant*
> *Funibus, undantes flammas levis aura fatigat,* &c.

> You see what splendour through the spatious Isle,
> As if the Church were glorified, doth smile.
> The Ivory-wrought beams seem to the sight
> Ingraven, while the carv'd roofe looks curl'd and bright.
> On brasse hoopes to the upmost vaults we tie
> The hovering Lamps, which nod and tremble by
> The yeelding Cords ; fresh Oyle doth still repair
> The waving flames, vex'd with the fleeting aire.

Having finished this Church, hee built another, not far from
Nola, in a litle Town called *Fundi,* where his possessions (which
he afterwards sold and gave to the poor,) were situate ; this also
he dedicated to our Lord *Jesus,* whom he used to call the *Saint of
Saints, and the Martyr of Martyrs.* In this Church in the great
Isle leading to the Altar, he caused to be put up another peece of
Limning, or sacred *Paisage,* which for beauty and excellencie
exceeded all the former. We have it most lively described and
explained in these following verses.

> *Sanctorum labor & merces sibi rite cohærent,*
> *Ardua Crux, pretiumque crucis sublime, corona,* &c.

> The paines of Saints, and Saints rewards are twins,
> The sad Crosse, and the Crowne which the Crosse wins.
> Here *Christ* the Prince both of the Cross and Crown
> Amongst fresh Groves and Lillies fully blown,
> Stands, a white Lamb bearing the purple Crosse,
> *White* shewes his purenesse, *Red* his bloods dear losse :
> To ease his sorrowes the Chast *Turtle* sings,
> And fans him swetting blood with her bright wings ;
> While from a shining Cloud the *Father* Eyes
> His Sons sad conflict with his Enemies,
> And on his blessed head lets gently down
> Eternal glory made into a Crown.
> About him stand two flocks of differing notes,
> One of white sheepe, and one of speckled goates,
> The first possesse his right hand, and the last
> Stand on his left : The spotted Goates are cast
> All into thick, deep shades, while from his right
> The white sheepe passe into a whiter light.

20 he dedicated] de dedicated *1654*   21 *Martyr*] *Marty 1654*

But in all these sacred buildings, our most pious and humble Bishop did not so much as dream of *Merit.* He thought (as blessed Mr. *Herbert* did) that they were good works, if sprinkled with the blood of *Christ*; otherwise hee thought them nothing. It will not be amisse, nor perhaps needlesse, to produce his own words in his own defense: *Nisi dominus ædificaverit domum, vano ædificantes labore sudabimus. Oremus ergo dominum, ut dum nos illi ædificamus domicilia quæ videntur, ille nobis intus ædificet illa quæ non videntur, domum videlicet illam non manufactam.* "Unlesse "the Lord build the house, wee labour in vaine to build it. Let us 10 "therefore (saith he) pray to the Lord, that while wee outwardly "build unto him these visible buildings, hee would build inwardly "in us those which are invisible, that is to say, the house not "made with hands. How can a servant merit by making use of his masters goods? All we do, and all we give are but his concessions and favours first given unto us. *Cum suis & hìc & ibi rebus locupletamur,* in this World, and in the World to come all our magnificence is but his munificence. But *Paulinus* was not onely outwardly pious, but inwardly also. He did so abound with private devotions, that all the time from his Baptism to his buriall, 20 may be truly called his *Prayer-time.* All that he did think, all that he did speak, and all that he did write, was pure devotion. Either publick or private prayers took up all his time. Our Saviour tells us, that *Gods Elects cry day and night unto him,* and Saint *Paul* adviseth us *to pray without* *Luk.* 18. *ceasing, and in every thing to give thanks, for this* (saith he) *is the will of God in Christ Iesus concerning you.* Holy *Paulinus* called Saint *Paul* his Master, having made himselfe his Disciple, hee would not neglect his commands: *If you continue in my word* (saith our Saviour) *then are you my Disciples indeed.* 30

To this I shall adde his Conformity and obedience to the Church, a blessing of no small consequence in all ages, especially in this age of *Schismes* and *Heresies.* Hee highly honoured the memory of the Saints of God, and was a most chearfull and devout observer of Sacred Festivals, or holy daies. His pious affection to these blessed seasons, together with the necessity and convenience of them, he hath most elegantly and learnedly demonstrated in his Poems.

——— *hos per longa morantes*
Tempora, dum tardi splendens rota vertitur anni 40
Sustineo intentis affecto pectore votis:
Quos cupio totis mihi prælucere diebus,

Vel quando veniunt ita compensare moras, ut
Æstivis possent spatiis producere lucem,
Aut illum pensare diem, qui sistere Jussis
Syderibus, longo lassavit lumine mundum,
Humanos duplicans dilatâ nocte labores.

   Ergo velut cælum stellis, & floribus arva
Temporibusque annos dominus, sic ipse diebus
Tempora distinxit festis, ut pigra diurnis
Ingenia obsequiis, saltem discrimine facto,
Post intervallum reduci sollemnia voto 10
Sancta libenter agant, residesque per annua mentes
Festa parent domino, quia jugiter intemeratos
Justitiæ servare piget: delinquere suetis,
Parcere peccato labor est: decurritur omni
Valle, per ascensum non est evadere cursu.

   Inde bonus dominus cunctos pietatis ut alis
Contegat, invalidis niti virtutis ad arcem
Congrua sanctorum dedit intervalla dierum,
Ut saltem officiis mediocribus ultima Christi
Vestimenta legant, & eos sacra fimbria sanet. 20
   Primus enim gradus est cælo pertexere cunctos
Continuâ bonitate dies, & tempore toto
Pascha sacrum Christi Cultu celebrare pudico.
Quod si mista seges tribulis mihi germinat, & cor
Incultum stimulat terreni spina laboris,
Vel festis domino studeam me offere diebus,
Ut vel parte mei tanquam confinia Vitæ,
Corpore ne toto trahar in Consortia mortis.

Englished thus.

Those sacred daies by tedious time delai'd 30
While the slow years bright line about is laid,
I patiently expect, though much distrest
By busie longing, and a love-sicke brest:
I wish, they may outshine all other daies,
Or when they come, so recompence delaies
As to outlast the Summer-hours bright length,
Or that fam'd day, when stopt by Divine strength,
The Sun did tyre the World with his long light,
Doubling mens labours, and adjourning night.
   As the bright Skye with stars, the fields with flowers, 40
The years with diff'ring seasons, months and houres
God hath distinguished and mark'd; so he
With sacred feasts did ease and beautifie
The working dayes: because that mixture may
Make men (loath to be holy ev'ry day,)

12 *jugiter Paulinus: Jupiter 1654*   19 *ultima*] *ultimæ 1654*

After long labours with a freer will
Adore their maker, and keepe mindfull still
Of holynesse, by keeping holy daies :
For otherwise they would dislike the wayes
Of piety as too severe.   To cast
Old customes quite off, and from sinne to fast
Is a great work.   To runne which way we will,
On plaines is easie, not so up a hill.
   Hence 'tis our good God (who would all men bring
Under the Covert of his saving wing,)   10
Appointed at set times his solemne feasts,
That by mean services, men might at least
Take hold of Christ as by the hemme, and steal
Help from his lowest skirts their Soules to heal.
   For the first step to Heaven, is to live well
All our life long, and each day to excel
In holynesse ; but since that tares are found
In the best Corn, and thistles will Confound
And prick my heart with vaine cares, I will strive
To weed them out on feast-daies, and so thrive   20
By handfuls, 'till I may full life obtaine,
And not be swallow'd of Eternall paine.

Two places upon Earth were most renowned with the memory
of our Saviour, *Bethlem* for his *birth*, and mount *Calvarie* for his
passion.   To extirpate all remembrance of his *Humanity* out of
these places, *Hadrian* the persecutor caused the Idol of *Jupiter* to
be set up, and worshiped in *Mount Calvarie* ; and in *Bethlem* he
built a *Mosquie* for that *Egyptian* block *Adonis*, which the Idolatrous *Jewes* called *Thamuz*.   Some men amongst us have done the
like : Two *Seasons* in the year were consecrated by the *Church* to   30
the memory of our *Saviour* : The *Feast* of his *Nativity* and
Circumcision, and the *Feast* of his *Passion* and *Resurrection*.   These
two they have utterly taken away : endeavouring (in my opinion)
to extinguish the *memory* of his *Incarnation* and *Passion*, and to
race his blessed name out of those *bright columnes of light*, which
the *Scripture* calls *daies*.   They will not allow him two daies in the
year, who made the dayes and the nights.   But it is much to be
feared, that he who hath appointed their daies here, will allow them
for it long nights.

   Holy *Paulinus* had now attained a good old age, the fore-   40
runners (as Master *Herbert* saith) were come, and the *Almond tree
did flourish* : hee was all white with years, and worshiped (like
Jacob) *leaning upon the top of his staffe*.   His virtuous and deare
Therasia had died (I believe) long before this time ; God having

ordained him to be hindmost, who was the stronger Vessell, and best able to bear her absence, and the unavoydable disconsolations of flesh and blood. And now (having for some time stood gazing after her,) he begins to follow, God visiting him with a strong paine in the side, which in a few daies did set him at liberty to overtake her, by breaking the prison.

Three daies before his dissolution, *Symmachus* and *Hyacinthinus,* two Bishops of his acquaintance came to visit him ; whereupon hee spoke to *Uranius* his Presbyter, that hee should prepare to attend
10 him in the administration of the Sacrament ; for (said he) I desire to receive it in the company of my brethren, which are now come to see mee. This sacred Solemnity was no sooner ended, but suddenly hee began to ask, *where his brothers were?* One that stood by, supposing that he had asked for the two Bishops, answered, *Here they be* : I know that, replyed *Paulinus,* but I aske

Januarius was for my brothers * *Januarius* and *Martinus, who*
Bishop of Naples, *were here with me just now, and promised to come*
and a Martyr ; and to me again. And having thus spoken, he
Martinus *was the* looked up towards Heaven, and with a voyce as
Bishop of Tours *in*
20 France. chearfull as his countenance, which seemed to shine and revive with joy, he sung out the one hundred and twentieth Psalme, *I lift up mine Eyes unto the hills from whence cometh my help. My help commeth from the Lord, who made Heaven and Earth.*

This being done *Posthumianus,* another Presbyter that was then present, told *Paulinus, that there were forty shillings unpaid for the Cloathes which he had given to the poor, before he fell sick.* To this *Paulinus* replyed with a smile, that he remembred it very well : *and Son* (said he) *take no thought for it, for beleive me, there*
30 *is one that will not be wanting to pay the debt of the poor.* The words were no sooner out of his mouth, but presently there comes in from the parts of *Lucania* (now called *Basilicata*) a Presbyter sent from the holy Bishop *Exuperantius* to visit *Paulinus* ; who brought him fifty shillings for a token from the Bishop. *Paulinus* receiving the money, blessed God, saying, *I thank thee O Lord, that hast not forsaken them that seek thee.* Of these fifty shillings he gave two with his owne hand to the Presbyter that brought them, and the rest he delivered to *Posthumianus* to pay for the Cloathes which were given to the poor.
40 The Evening now drawing on, hee remained quiet and well at

20 (*note*) France] France *1654*   27 *he fell*] *be fell 1654*   33 *Paulinus*]
Paul nus 1654

ease untill midnight : but the paine then increasing in his side, he was troubled with a great difficulty, and shortnesse of breathing, which held him till five in the morning. The day begining to break, he felt the usuall motions of holynesse awaking his Spirit, to which (though weak) he chearfully obeyed, and sitting up in his bed, celebrated *Mattins* himselfe. By this time all the *Deacons* and *Presbyters* of his diocesse were gathered together at the door, and came (like the *Sons* of the *Prophets*) to see the translation of their aged Father. After some short exhortations to holynesse and Christian courage, he lifted up his hands and blessed them, 10 mindfull (it seems) of our Saviours carriage at his ascension, whose peace he prayed might rest upon them.

Shortly after (the pain still encreasing and prevailing against him) hee became speechlesse, and so continued untill the Evening ; when suddenly sitting up (as if hee had been awaked out of his sleep) he perceived it to be the time of the *Lucernarium*, or Evening-Office, and lifting up his hands towards Heaven, he repeated with a low voyce, this verse out of the Psalmes, *Thy word is a Lantern unto my feet, and a light unto my paths.* About the fourth hour of the night, when all that were present sate diligently 20 watching about him ; his poor Cottage did suddenly shake with such a strong Earth-quake, that those who kneeled about his bed were something disordered with it, and fell all trembling to their prayers. The Guests of Eternal Glory were now entred under that narrow roof, where (after the abdication of his great worldly honours) he had lived so long in all holynesse and humility. For in that instant of time (saith *Uranius*) he was dissolved, the blessed Angels testifying that they were present to conduct his happy and glorious Soul into the joy of his Master. By the like signe did *Christ* signifie to his Church in *Hierusalem*, that he 30 heard their prayers when they were persecuted by the mercilesse *Jews*. *Gregory* the great, in the place before cited, makes expresse mention of this Earthquake. And thus we see after what manner the righteous are taken away, though no man will lay it to his heart.

Three daies (saith *Uranius*) before *John* the Bishop of *Naples* departed out of this life, he affirmed that he saw *Paulinus* all clothed with Angelicall brightnesse, which shined like the stars, holding in his hand a kind of Heavenly foode in form like a honey-combe, but white as the light, and speaking to him, *brother Iohn, what do you here? pray, that you may be dissolv'd, & come unto* 40 *us, where we have enough of this provision which you see in my hand.*

5 sitting] sittting *1654*

This pious Bishop did not long survive this vision, for the Sunday following, after he had ended his Sermon, and blessed the people (having the day before celebrated the Communion, and distributed to the poor,) he fell sicke and dyed in the Church.   So that I may say of him, *Episcopos Concionantes, & Concionatores stantes mori docuit*: Hee taught Bishops to dye preaching, and preachers to die standing.

Blessed *Paulinus* departed out of this life in the year of our Lord four hundred and thirty one, in the seaven and seaventieth year of his age, upon the tenth of the kalends of *Iuly*, which according to our account is the two and twentieth day of *Iune*. His body was carried from *Nola* to *Rome*, and decently interred in the Church of St. *Bartholomew*, neare the Apostles own Tombe: where they both lye expecting the second comming of our Lord and Saviour *JESUS CHRIST*; which of his great mercy I earnestly beseech him to hasten, and to appeare himselfe the onely faithfull Judge, and most just Determiner of *Right* and *Wrong*, of *Truth* and *Falshood*.

Gloria tibi mitissime Jesu!

St. *Paulinus* to his Wife *Therasia*.

Come my true Consort in my Joyes and Care!
Let this uncertaine and still wasting share
Of our fraile life be giv'n to God. You see
How the swift dayes drive hence incessantlie,
And the fraile, drooping World (though still thought gay,)
In secret, slow consumption weares away.
All that we have, passe from us: and once past
Returne no more; like clouds, they seeme to last,
And so delude loose, greedy mindes.   But where
Are now those trim deceits? to what darke sphere
Are all those false fires sunck, which once so shin'd
They captivated Soules, and rul'd mankind?
He that with fifty ploughes his lands did sow,
Will scarse be trusted for two Oxen now,
His rich, towd Coach known to each crowded street
Is sold, and he quite tir'd walkes on his feet.
Merchants that (like the Sun) their voyage made
From East to West, and by whole-sale did trade,

Title St.] Saint catchword 1654   5 (poem) gay LCGu: gry 1654

Are now turn'd Sculler-men, or sadly swett
In a poore fishers boat with line and nett.   20
Kingdomes and Cities to a period tend,
Earth nothing hath, but what must have an end :
Mankind by plagues, distempers, dearth and warre,
Tortures and prisons dye both neare and farre ;
Furie and hate rage in each living brest,
Princes with Princes, States with States contest ;
An Vniversall discord mads each land,
Peace is quite lost, the last times are at hand ;
But were these dayes from the last day secure,
So that the world might for more yeares endure,   30
Yet we (like hirelings) should our terme expect,
And on our day of death each day reflect.
For what (Therasia !) *doth it us availe*
That spatious streames shall flow and never faile,
That aged forrests live to tyre the Winds,
And flowers each spring returne and keepe their kinds ?
Those still remaine : but all our Fathers dyed,
And we our selves but for few dayes abide.
     This short time then was not giv'n us in vaine,
To whom tyme dyes, in which we dying gaine,   40
But that in time eternall life should be
Our care, and endlesse rest our industrie.
And yet, this Taske which the rebellious deeme
Too harsh, who god's mild lawes for chaines esteem
Suites with the meeke and harmelesse heart so right
That 'tis all ease, all comfort and delight.
" To love our God with all our strength and will ;
" To covet nothing ; to devise no ill
" Against our neighbours ; to procure or doe
" Nothing to others, which we would not to   50
" Our very selves ; not to revenge our wrong ;
" To be content with little ; not to long
" For wealth and greatnesse ; to despise or jeare
" No man, and if we be despised, to bear ;
" To feede the hungry ; to hold fast our Crown ;
" To take from others naught ; to give our owne ;
These are his precepts : and (alas !) in these
What is so hard, but faith can doe with ease ?
He that the holy Prophets doth beleeve,
                    35 *live LGu: hie 1654*

And on Gods words relies, words that still live 60
And cannot dye; that in his heart hath writ
His Saviour's death and tryumph, and doth yet
With constant care, admitting no neglect,
His second, dreadfull comming still expect:
To such a liver earthy things are dead,
With Heav'n alone, and hopes of heav'n hee's fed;
He is no Vassall unto worldly trash,
Nor that black knowledge, which pretends to wash,
But doth defile: A knowledge, by which Men
With studied care loose Paradise agen. 70
Commands and titles, the vaine worlds device,
With gold, the forward seed of sin and vice,
He never minds: his Ayme is farre more high,
And stoopes to nothing lower than the skie;
Nor griefe, nor pleasures breede him any pain,
He nothing feares to loose, would nothing gaine;
What ever hath not God, he doth detest:
He lives to Christ, is dead to all the rest.
This Holy one sent hither from above
A Virgin brought forth, shadow'd by the Dove; 80
His skin with stripes, with wicked hands his face,
And with foule spittle soyl'd and beaten was;
A Crown of thornes his blessed head did wound,
Nayles pierc'd his hands and feet, and he fast bound
Stuck to the painefull Crosse, where hang'd till dead
With a cold speare his hearts dear blood was shed.
All this for man, for bad, ungratefull Man
The true God suffer'd! not that sufferings can
Adde to his glory ought, who can receive
Accesse from nothing, whom none can bereave 90
Of his all-fullnesse: but the blest designe
Of his sad death was to save me from mine;
He dying bore my sins, and the third day
His early rising rais'd me from the clay.
To such great mercies what shall I preferre,
Or who from loving God shall me deterre?
Burne me alive, with curious, skilfull paine
Cut up and search each warme and breathing vaine:
When all is done, death brings a quick release,
And the poore mangled body sleepes in peace. 100
Hale me to prisons, shut me up in brasse:

My still free Soule from thence to God shall passe ;
Banish or bind me, I can be no where
A stranger, nor alone ; My God is there.
I feare not famine ; how can he be sed
To sterve, who feedes upon the living bread ?
And yet this courage springs not from my store,
Christ gave it me, who can give much, much more ;
I of my selfe can nothing dare or doe,
He bids me fight, and makes me conquer too : 110
If (like great Abr'ham,*) I should have command*
To leave my fathers house and native Land,
I would with joy to unknown regions run,
Bearing the Banner of his blessed Son.
On worldly goods I will have no designe,
But use my owne, as if mine were not mine ;
Wealth I'le not wonder at, nor greatnesse seeke,
But chuse (though laugh'd at,) to be poore & meeke.
In woe and wealth I'le keepe the same stay'd mind,
Griefe shall not breake me, nor joyes make me blind : 120
My dearest Jesus I'le still praise, and he
Shall with Songs of Deliverance compasse me.
    Then come my faithfull Consort ! joyne with me
In this good fight, and my true helper be ;
Cheare me when sad ; advise me when I stray ;
Let us be each the others guide and stay ;
Be your Lords Guardian *: give joynt ayde and due ;*
Helpe him when falne ; rise, when he helpeth you ;
That so we may not onely one flesh be,
But in one Spirit, and one Will agree. 130

FINIS.

OXFORD : HORACE HART M.A.
PRINTER TO THE UNIVERSITY